Quixotism

SUNY series in Latin American and
Iberian Thought and Culture

Jorge J. E. Gracia and
Rosemary Geisdorfer Feal, editors

Quixotism

The Imaginative Denial of Spain's Loss of Empire

Christopher Britt Arredondo

State University of New York Press

Published by
State University of New York Press, Albany

Printed in the United States of America

For information, address State University of New York Press,
90 State Street, Suite 700, Albany, NY 12207

Production by Michael Haggett
Marketing by Michael Campochiaro

Library of Congress Cataloging-in-Publication Data

Britt-Arredondo, Christopher, 1966–
Quixotism : the imaginative denial of Spain's loss of empire / Christopher Britt-Arredondo.
p. cm. — (SUNY series in Latin American and Iberian thought and culture)
Includes bibliographical references and index.
ISBN 0-7914-6255-2 (hardcover : alk. paper)
1. Spain—History—1868–1931. 2. Don Quixote (Fictitious character) 3. Literature and society—Spain. 4. Politics and literature—Spain. I. Title. II. Series.
DP243.B74 2004
946'.074—dc22

2004012238

10 9 8 7 6 5 4 3 2 1

Contents

Acknowledgments

I have written this book with two purposes in mind: so as to expose the intellectual roots of Spanish fascist culture; and in order to denounce the complicity of certain scholars with that culture. Accordingly, what I offer in these pages is a polemic on modern Spanish national identity. I argue against those Spanish intellectuals whose interpretations of Cervantes' *Quixote* helped shape a fascist ideology for modern Spain. I argue also against certain scholars whose erudite studies of these Spanish intellectuals have served, either by design or by inadvertent error, to propagate a fascist national identity for modern Spain. The alternative interpretation of the intellectual and literary history of modern Spain that I present in these pages is one that I hope will contribute to the modernization of a field of study that remains, to this day, unnecessarily constrained by the memory of its nationalist legacy.

Throughout this book, I have wanted to recognize the intellectual clout and scholarly authority of all those thinkers and literary critics whose ideas populate these pages. By carefully charting the similarities and contrasts of opinion among the intellectuals I identify as the main architects of Quixotist discourse, I have sought to present as coherent, nuanced and persuasive an argument as possible. I have been helped with this undertaking by a number of recent studies of the process of national identity formation in Spain. It is my hope that the authors of these recent histories of modern Spain will find my own work to be as insightful as I have found theirs to be.

I especially want to thank Eduardo Subirats for his abiding commitment to this project, which began to take shape many years ago during lively debates in his office at Princeton and which has continued to benefit from his keen and kind attention. Without his constant challenges, I might never have been motivated to articulate my thoughts in as reasoned a manner as I have here sought to do. I am also indebted to Arcadio Díaz-Quiñones, whose critical appraisal of my work in its earlier stages convinced me of the need to supplement my study of Quixotism in Spain with an analysis of the uses to which the figure of Don Quixote was put in twentieth-century Latin America. Paul

Fenn deserves very special acknowledgement. The excitement that he has brought to this book as a reader has helped me sustain my own commitment to it as its author. I would do a great injustice to the true history of this book were I to not also acknowledge the many insights that Nicholas G. Round and Susan Kirkpatrick shared with me after reading earlier drafts of the manuscript. Thanks to their generous comments, the arguments I put forth in this book are sharper than they otherwise would be.

I thank José Quiroga for helping me to rethink the order of my arguments and reconceive this project as a book. Inés Azar has likewise encouraged, supported and challenged me throughout the writing process. I thank Isabel Vergara for her helpful comments on my assessment of Miguel Antonio Caro's interpretation of the Quixote figure. Also, Masha Belenky and Leah Chang were of considerable help to me as I worked to polish the Introduction. I am grateful to Raquel Caputo for her help in preparing the index.

Throughout the writing process, I have had the opportunity to test my ideas in conversation with many people. In this respect, I particularly thank Arthur Denner, Jim Fernández, Alf Hiltebeitel, Eduardo Navadijos, and Margarita Serje. From SUNY Press, I thank Michael Rinella, Mike Haggett, and Marilyn Semerad; each, in his or her own way, has helped me weather more than one storm in the teacup that is a first book.

Finally, for their patience and loving support, I thank my wife, Marina Salcedo, and son, Adrian Britt. I dedicate this book to my parents, Maria Eugenia Arredondo and Robert McCammon Britt, from whom I first learned the value of a good argument.

INTRODUCTION

Monumentalizing Quixote

The twentieth century was Spain's first century without empire. For approximately four hundred years, from 1492 to 1898, Spain had been an empire: a sometimes waxing and sometimes waning empire, but an empire all the same. In the fateful summer of 1898, imperial Spain collapsed definitively, losing the remaining vestiges of its once extensive colonial empire either to independence, as was the case with Cuba, or to the United States, as was the case with Puerto Rico, the Philippines, and Guam. This collapse came about with remarkable speed. At sea in both the Pacific and the Caribbean, Spain's dilapidated, wooden warships proved to be no match for the superior firepower of the U.S. Navy's steel-hulled destroyers. In both theaters, Spain's fleets were lost, quite literally, in a matter of hours. On land, the imperial forces of Spain faired no better. Fifty thousand soldiers died from illness or malnutrition and another ten thousand perished in combat. Faced with these resounding defeats, in December of 1898, Spain signed the Treaty of Paris, confirming internationally that it had ceased to be an empire at precisely the time that other European nations and even some of their ex-colonies, such as the United States of America, were staking claims to empire in Africa, the Americas, and Asia.

For Cuban, Puerto Rican, and Filipino nationalists, the U.S.-abetted war for independence was, at best, an ambiguous success. Puerto Rico, Guam, and the Philippines became "protectorates" of the United States while Cuba, an independent nation-state, shared a similar economic fate. All these colonies and their peoples were, in a very real sense, caught between empires: to one side, there was the anachronistic Christianizing imperialism of Spain, to the other, the modern republican imperialism of the United States of

America. Having first been "liberated" as Christians by Spanish imperialists, the populations of Cuba, Puerto Rico, and the Philippines were once again "liberated" in 1898 as protected subjects of an emerging U.S. empire. In neither case were the men and women of these lands permitted to liberate themselves independently.

For those within the United States who were eager for empire, the war was a spectacular success, a "splendid little war" as it came to be known, that expanded their country's "rough-riding" economic and political imperialism into the Caribbean and the Pacific. There were, certainly, others within the United States who opposed this expansionist creed, protested against the extension of American sovereignty by methods of conquest, and perceived the emergence of U.S. imperialism as a betrayal of the republican principles and democratic institutions of the United States. The debate between imperialists and anti-imperialists in the United States was won, if not in words then certainly in deeds, by the imperialists. Witness, in this respect, the U.S. role in the formation of Panama in 1903, as well as the unrelenting slaughter of independence-minded Filipinos by U.S. troops during the early years of the twentieth century. To be sure, the events of 1898 marked the emergence of the United States as a formidable, new imperial power.

In Spain, by contrast, the events of 1898 were almost unanimously perceived as a calamity. 1898 came to be known there as the year of "The Disaster." In this sense, Spaniards did not view Spain's defeat in 1898 only as a political setback; they also read it as a sign of the Spanish nation's decadence. Among leading Spanish intellectuals of the time, such as Joaquín Costa, Angel Ganivet, Miguel de Unamuno, Ramiro de Maeztu, and Ortega y Gasset, the "Disaster of 1898" gave rise to a critique of those aspects of Spanish national life that could both explain their nation's decadence and offer hope for its regeneration. Being, as they were, writers, poets, and philosophers, these intellectuals preferred to present their critique metaphorically. By seizing on the imaginative and suggestive powers of literature, in their essays they represented the events of 1898 as an encounter between a Hispanic Don Quixote and his Anglo-Saxon nemesis, Robinson Crusoe. According to this depiction, the events of 1898 were, at heart, a conflict between the archaic spiritual, moral, and civilizing ideals of the Spanish empire and the progressive technological and economic ideals of an increasingly secularized Anglo-American empire.

The appeal of this metaphor was not limited to Spanish intellectuals. Throughout Hispanic America, the victory of the United States over Spain in 1898 was perceived as a threat to the region's sovereignty. Hispanic American thinkers such as the Uruguayan politician and essayist José Enrique Rodó and the Nicaraguan poet and journalist Rubén Darío associated the figure of Robinson Crusoe with the secular values of U.S. economic imperialism and exalted the figure of Don Quixote as representing the region's superior cultural and spiritual values. In defense of the sovereignty and independence of their countries, these Hispanic American intellectuals articulated their Quixote myths within the parameters of a republican discourse. The Quixote myth-makers of early twentieth-century Spain did not, however, do so. Instead, Costa, Ganivet, Unamuno, Maeztu, and Ortega developed a rich blend of Quixote myths that helped lay the cultural, ideological, and imaginative groundwork for Spanish National-Catholic fascism.

In 1975, after forty-five years of Franco's dictatorial rule in Spain, the Spanish nation was guided by the able hand of its monarch, King Juan Carlos I of Spain, through a relatively peaceful process of transition to democracy. By 1982, democratic Spain had become a member of the North Atlantic Treaty Organization. Then, in 1986, Spain became a full-fledged member of the European Economic Community. Finally, in 1992, with the quintecentenary of the so-called Discovery of the Americas, the World Fair in Seville, and the Olympics in Barcelona, Spain found itself with a historic chance to showcase its newfound modernity to the rest of the world.

Eager to erase the "black legend" of bloody conquest and brutal colonization that many non-Spanish historians (in particular Anglo-American historians) had tended to associate with the "Discovery," the government of Felipe Gonzalez sought, in 1992, to commemorate, neither conquest nor colonization, but the would-be scientific and foreward-looking "spirit of discovery" that had ostensibly led the Spanish nation to seek new lands in 1492. In keeping with this celebration of an always and already Enlightened and enlightening Spanish national culture, the government also used the World Fair of 1992 to showcase Spain's technological advances, scientific prowess, and postmodern design. Finally, with the Olympics of 1992, the government sought to portray to a global TV audience the welcoming image of a Spain which, although "Still Different," was also now truly cosmopolitan, completely European, and fashionably postmodern. Spain had become so modern by 1992 that the memory of its decadent backwardness of 1898 could now and forever fade away into oblivion. Six years later, in 1998, when Spaniards were faced with the unwelcomed task of commemorating the events of 1898, it was precisely this spirit of blissful oblivion that held sway over the nation's historical consciousness.

Commemorating 1898

By 1998, much of the Spanish-speaking world's attention was centered on the commemoration of 1898. In Cuba, it was a matter of celebrating one hundred years of independence. In Puerto Rico, it was rather a question of debating that nation's ambiguous relationship to Spain and to the United States. Elsewhere in Latin America, the commemoration of 1898 was seen as an opportunity to either protest or celebrate U.S. involvement in twentieth-century Latin American affairs. Surely, with so much being said about 1898 and so much being done to commemorate and better comprehend the significance of that emblematic date, there was reason to expect that, in 1998, Spaniards would finally take it upon themselves to reassess their own understanding of how Spain's final demise as an empire helped fashion the intellectual and political culture of early twentieth-century Spain. By and large, they failed to satisfy that expectation.

This was particularly true of those who, in addition to being Spanish, also happened to be Hispanists. In their official capacity as learned experts of all things Spanish, these Hispanists (some of them historians, others literary critics) were invited to participate in state-sponsored commemorative events in Spain. The hispanophilia that underscored these tributes led many of these Hispanists to argue that, 100 years after the imperial collapse of 1898, Spain had regained its "rightful place" as one of the cultural centers radiating the light of European civilization. Spain's peaceful transition from fascism to democracy, they alleged, helped restore the moral authority of the Spanish nation. As a result, by 1998, Spain could once again contemplate itself with pride in the mirror of its national-imperial memory and celebrate the role it now played in bolstering economic development and democratization among its ex-colonies in the Americas. "Once an empire . . . Always an empire!" Although unspoken, this was the essentializing slogan around which numerous Hispanists organized their commemoration of 1898 in the showy, postmodern Spain of 1998.

The tenor for this celebratory strategy was set by the neo-imperial cultural policies of President Aznar and the intellectuals invited to form with his government an official, organizing commission for the centenary commemoration of 1898. As early as April of 1997, in a speech delivered in Salamanca, Aznar described the triumphalist vision of 1898 that was to be propagated, extended and diffused throughout a seemingly endless year of conferences, exhibitions and reeditions of the most celebrated literary works of the period. 1898, Aznar proposed, had not only been a time of imperial-national crisis but also the beginning of a scientific, industrial, and cultural renaissance that, at long last, had culminated in the postmodern Spain of 1998. "In the course of one century," Aznar began his discourse, "from 1898 to 1998 . . . Spain has overcome the initial and inevitable frustration [the frustration, that is, of losing its empire] such that it can now face its present and future with optimism."[1] A bit further on, the President assured his public that "[we Spaniards] form, as it is only natural that we should, part of the politically, economically and scientifically advanced societies of Europe. We are today . . . that nation on the rise, hardworking and cultivated, European and American, of which the thinkers and poets of '98 dreamed."[2] With these choice words, Aznar turned the act of commemorating 1898 in 1998 into an opportunity to proclaim the modernizing triumph of a "New Spain": a Spain that, as Aznar put it, was "on the rise," was "hardworking and cultured," and was as "European" as it was "American."

This strategy of forgetful commemorating was not limited, in 1998, to the members of Aznar's organizing commission. Such tactful forgetting informed museum exhibitions as well as a good number of the putatively critical studies of turn-of-the-century Spain designed for mass consumption by Spain's university and private publishing houses.[3] Javier Figuero, author of one such study titled *La España del Desastre,* echoes the official stance when he writes that "in this year of 1898 . . . a new common sentiment of hope and modernity began, slowly but surely, to develop."[4] For his part, José Andrés Gallego, who is the author of a work deceptively titled *Un 98 diferente,* repeats the commemorative officialese by arguing for the ideological continuity between the Spain of 1898 and the Spain of 1998: "Today's politics," he affirms, "has the color of regeneration, which has been successively inherited generation upon generation by the majority of the governments of Spain that have been interested in improvement . . . whether their name was Costa or Maura, Canalejas or Primo de Rivera, Azaña or Franco, even Felipe Gonzalez or Aznar."[5] Illustrative of the ease with which this official strategy of forgetful commemorating took root among less academically inclined writers is Javier Leralta's tourist guidebook to Castile and the Spanish national literature of the so-called literary generation of '98, *Viajes y viajeros del 98.* Leralta suggests that the "essential" Spain discovered and described by the authors of the generation of '98 is still palpable today: "The generation of 1898," he explains, "discovered Castilla, the wide-open, gothic and quixotic Spain spread over the Castillian plains . . . A century has passed, one hundred years during which we have seen this land, this country, grow and we have also seen the same landscape and the same people, the same towns and the same mountains [that the members of the generation of 1898 saw] . . . Our fields remain impregnated with metaphors and forms of consciousness, above all forms of consciousness."[6] Not unlike his predecessors of 1898, in whose writings modern Spain was turned into the eternal land of Don Quixote and twentieth-century Spaniards into modern-day Quixotes, Leralta in 1998 travels through Spain, through Castile, through La Mancha in order to commune with the essential spirit of a still "wide-open, gothic and quixotic Spain."

It is important to note how closely this strategy of forgetful commemoration follows the rhetorical tactics that Unamuno, Ganivet, Azorín, Maeztu, Ortega, and others among their contemporaries used in an attempt to repudiate Spain's loss of empire and affirm the imperial essence of Spanish national identity. Faced, as they were, with the final crisis of Spanish imperialism in 1898, these thinkers did not only seek to make sense of modern Spain's decline from empire but to also offer their compatriots an imaginative program for national and imperial regeneration. They identified Spain's new role in the modern world with the idealistic mission undertaken by Don Quixote in Cervantes' famous seventeenth-century novel. Inspired by the example of Don Quixote's quest to recuperate the Golden Age of chivalry, they suggested that modern Spain also needed to revive its chivalric values and seek to recuperate its Golden Age. Only for these modern Spanish intellectuals, the chivalry of Spain's Golden Age had little if anything to do with the humanist values upheld by Cervantes' Don Quixote and a great deal more to do with the heroic, warring values that had led to the conquest and colonization of Spain's European, American, and Asian empire. What these thinkers had in mind, then, by promoting the iconographic association of the Spanish nation with the figure of Don Quixote, was the spiritual and cultural reconquest of Spain's empire. Their Quixotism was a formula for negating the historical, ephemeral reality of Spain's decline as an empire and affirming the essential, ever-lasting reality of the Spanish nation's imperial identity.

Of course, not all of the events and publications dedicated in 1998 to the commemoration of 1898 followed this Quixotist strategy of forgetfulness. In forums where the playing field was shared more equally by Latin Americanists and Peninsularists, the critique of empire of the one group helped to offset the nationalistic and neo-imperialistic apologetics of the other. This dichotomy of views was apparent in commemorative events that were cosponsored by the Spanish Ministry of Culture and sister organizations based in one or another of the ex-colonies that won their independence from Spain in 1898. One such forum was the 1998 April–June edition of *Casa de las Américas*, published out of Havana, Cuba. Here, together with María-Dolores Albiac Blanco's defense of the supposed liberalism of the writers of 1898, José-Carlos Mainer's assertion that the mission of the writers of the generation of '98 was to incorporate into Spanish letters an international and modernizing perspective or Miguel Rojas Mix's insistence on reading Ganivet's and Unamuno's obsession with Don Quixote as an expression of these thinker's antireligious laicism, one can entertain María Luisa Laviana Cuetos's uncompromising criticisms of how the commemoration of 1898 was being used, in 1998, to exalt the supposed civilizing influence of late-twentieth century, neo-imperialist economic investments in Cuba and other countries of Latin America.[7]

Indeed, throughout this year of commemorations, it was mostly Hispanists with a thorough knowledge of the national histories and literatures of Latin America and the Caribbean, such as the Cuban historian Manuel Moreno Fraginals or the Puerto Rican intellectual historian Arcadio Diaz-Quiñones, who proffered strictly rigorous critiques of Spanish imperialism.[8]

By and large, critiques that were carried out from these postcolonial perspectives did not however take into account the role that Spain's demise as an empire played in the narrative construction of an ambiguously modern Spanish national and imperial identity. Alternatively, critiques that were voiced from the perspective of exile did take this development into account, notably those of Spanish expatriates such as Juan Goytisolo, Eduardo Subirats, and Luis Fernández Cifuentes.[9] The alternative points of view that these interpreters of Spanish fin-de-siècle literature presented were, nevertheless, rather more the exception than the rule.

By organizing their commemorations of 1898 around a strategy of official forgetfulness, Hispanists were in fact doing nothing in 1998 that they had not already been doing throughout the twentieth century. As has been the tradition among Hispanists specializing in modern Spanish literature, they neglected to critically reassess their understanding of how Spain's loss of empire helped shape the intellectual and literary culture of early twentieth century Spain and generally limited themselves to rehashing the debates that have conventionally framed their field of study: Who are the members of the literary generation of '98? Should the literature produced by these writers be studied as a Spanish version of modernism? Or should it be viewed as constituting the Silver Age of Spanish national letters, second only to the literature of the Golden Age? Once again, in 1998, the fact that in the year of 1898 Spain lost the few remaining vestiges of its once extensive colonial empire, notably Cuba, Puerto Rico, and the Philippines, either to independence or to the United States, entered only nominally into discussions of the literary culture of turn-of-the-century Spain.

Over the years, the incessant discussion of the aesthetic "problems" attending the notion of the literary generation of '98 has served to minimize the decisive role that several of the authors typically associated with that generation—namely Unamuno, Ganivet, Azorín, and Maeztu—played in the narrative construction of a Spanish national modern heroic and imperial identity. What is more, the discourse on the generation of '98—a discourse that was put into circulation as early as 1913 by Azorín—is one of the principal narratives by means of which these thinkers sought to legitimize the heroic national identity that they imagined for their beloved Spain. Consequently, the real trouble surrounding the notion of the generation of '98 concerns neither who qualifies as a member nor, for that matter, the relation of this generation to the predominant aesthetic tastes of the time; rather, it revolves around how this concept allows for an uncritical perpetuation of the nationalist elitism and imperialist messianism inherent in the thought of the same writers it purports to understand.

Were it merely a question of recognizing the extent to which the discourse on the generation of '98 has helped disseminate the heroic and nationalist ideals propagated by Unamuno, Ganivet, Azorín, Maeztu, Ortega, and other Quixotists of modern Spain, Hispanists today might not need to trouble themselves with too radical a reform of their historical imagination and cultural memory. The fact remains, however, that beginning with the generation of '98, much of the literature produced in twentieth century Spain has been rigidly classified, catalogued and canonized into generations: the generation of 1914, the generation of 1927, the post–Civil War generation, and so on ad nauseum until the the so-called generation of the transition with which the century was brought to a cumbersome close. Although the identities of these later generations have not come to be regarded with the same reverence nor been the subject of as much fallacious debating as that of the generation of '98, their very legitimacy is made suspect by the fact that, as generations, they are made to "follow" the founding generation of Spain's first century without empire.

In providing a critical reconstruction and revision of both the literature associated with the generation of '98 and its reception among Hispanists, this book helps clear the ground for an alternative understanding of the literary and intellectual culture of early twentieth-century Spain. To the iconolatry that has informed most interpretations of Unamuno, Ganivet, Azorín, Maeztu, and Ortega over the past 100 years or so, *Quixotism* opposes an iconoclastic interpretation. Appropriately, this book focuses on how the Quixotism espoused by these thinkers helped to reorder modern Spanish notions of decadence and reconfigure modern Spanish national identity. It was precisely this Quixotism that helped lay the cultural groundwork of Spanish fascism. In time, it served even to justify the outbreak of the Spanish Civil War of 1936–1939. This jingoistic Quixotism is by no means a thing of the past. It lives on to this day. Only a few years ago, in 1998, it motivated the optimistic forgetfulness that marked official Spanish commemorations of 1898.

Institutionalizing the Generation of '98

Considering that *Quixotism* explores the impact of Spain's loss of empire not only on the development of twentieth-century Spanish literature but also on the reception of that literature, it is important to revisit the process by means of which the generation of '98 was conceived, disseminated, and institutionalized. Literary histories and manuals teach that the notion of the generation of '98 was originally conjured up by Azorín in a series of essays published between 1912 and 1915. What is rarely if ever mentioned, however, is that these essays form part of a much larger project designed to systematically reevaluate Spanish literature in light of the nation's perceived modern moral decadence and to recuperate Spain's traditional or "classical" values.

In one of his essays of 1913 titled "El amoralismo de los clásicos," Azorín explains that the modern Spanish nation is decadent to the extent to which it has become morally stagnant: "What do we mean when we speak of a moral man? A man who acts in accordance with the precepts . . . the customs, the institutions of the time and the country in which he lives. And an immoral man . . . is one who acts in contradiction to these laws, practices, institutions and customs."[10] Here, Azorín defines morality and immorality respectively as obedience to or rejection of societal norms. Neither, he argues, is the result of a creative act of will.

For Azorín, such moral decadence or stagnation of the will-to-create is characteristic of the modern age of democracy; an age for which, he claims, the creative spontaneity and genius of the nation's literary "classics"—among them Cervantes, Garcilaso, Fray Luís de Leon, Lope and Calderón—is incomprehensible, even censurable: "to us today—sentimental and democratic as we are—that spontaneity [of the classics] can seem to be immorality itself."[11] Modern cultural and political values, suggests Azorín, represent an obstacle to the proper recognition and appreciation of Spain's creative and spontaneous genius.

In order to regenerate the decadent nation, therefore, Azorín reasons that the Spanish masses must be given examples of amoral or supramoral thought, examples of a kind of thought that moves in a realm beyond the stagnant cultural forms of morality and immorality and that, consequently, might act as a foundation for a new "classical" culture. Accordingly, Azorín defines what he calls the amorality of the Spanish classics as a foundational, original act of heroism: "An amoral man is a man who is strong enough to position himself beyond good and evil and proceed according to his own will and instinct."[12] This is the Nietzschean standard by means of which Azorín would associate the Spanish classics—"our predecessors of the 16th and 17th centuries"—with the conquering spirit of Spanish imperial dominion.[13]

It is from the heroic height of this imperial-national origin that, argues Azorín, modern Spain has fallen and, from this "Golden Age" of literature that modern Spanish culture has strayed. Azorín finds evidence of this decline in much of the writing of late nineteenth- and early twentieth-century Spain. For instance, he views the literature produced by those who immediately preceded his generation of '98, such as the regenerationist essays of Joaquín Costa, as "immoral"; this is literature that, because it is critical of the political and economic realities of Restoration Spain, can be said to reject the codes of conduct and thought of the society.[14] Conversely, Azorín views the literature produced by writers who came immediately after his generation of '98, such as the work of Ortega y Gasset, as "moral"; this is literature that, because it is "logical" and "rigorous," can be said to obey the scientific spirit of the age.[15] In this way, Azorín relegates both the older and the younger among his contemporaries to the "modern" and stagnant cultural forms of what is immoral and moral.

Only the literature produced by him and the other members of his generation of '98 succeeds as "classical." This is the case, in Azorín's view, because theirs is a literature that transforms the quotidian sensations of modern Spain's decadence into vehicles of expression for eternal, essentialized, national truths. Spain, as revealed in this literature, is, for Azorín, forever Castile; forever the land of the self-sacrificing, spiritual conquistador Don Quixote; forever the cultural and linguistic heartland of the ascetic, mystical values needed to counter the hedonistic and secular tendencies of the modern world. This supramoral, heroic, and messianic Spain is also an ahistorical and mythological Spain; it is, in short, the Spain narrated into the popular, national imaginary of twentieth-century Spanish culture by the promoters of Quixotism.

It would be misleading, however, to claim that this view of the generation of '98 as representing a new national origin has gone unchallenged. Already in the 1920s the supposed members of Azorín's own generation of '98 began to distance themselves from that claim. Pío Baroja, for instance, rejected the generation of '98 as a false collectivity; Unamuno did so because the group lacked volitional cohesion; and Maeztu, because its putative cause, the "Disaster of 1898," was itself an invented origin.[16] But Azorín's would-be generational cohorts were not the only ones to voice their opposition to Azorín's heroic and foundational view of the generation of '98.[17]

Writing in 1923, Ortega, who had previously been dismissed by Azorín as a "moral" and therefore stagnant thinker, put forth his own, competing theory on generations. According to this theory, a generation cannot be represented by its literary elites because every generation is a mix of elites and masses, each generation is, as Ortega puts it: "a new integrated social body, with its select minority on the one side and its masses on the other."[18] Moreover, each generation has its own mission: "Each and every generation has been launched over the domain of existence with a specific vital trajectory."[19] This mission, Ortega is careful to explain, can only be realized when each generation's prophet-like elites impose their future-oriented will on the incredulous and indecisive masses. For Ortega, then, every generation marks, if not an origin, then certainly a new beginning, a new opportunity for the aristocratic organization of society and, ultimately, of the nation.

The simultaneously generational and national elitism central to Ortega's theory of generations is also at the core of much of the apologetic theorizing that, since the early 1930s, has surrounded the notion of the generation of '98.[20] The work of the literary historian Pedro Laín Entralgo is paradigmatic in this regard. In his celebrated book of 1945, *La generación del noventayocho*, Laín Entralgo regards the writers of that literary generation as ortegean elites who, characteristically, have a mission to complete. That mission is to recreate "a la española" the intellectual, political, social, and technological creations of the putatively heretical, modern world. Moreover, for Laín Entralgo, this founding spiritual mission is forever to be the mission of every patriotic Spaniard: "Whether they know it or not, the weight of the dream that was invented at the turn of the century by an egregious group of Spaniards will forever weigh upon the soul of every Spaniard."[21] Laín Entralgo marries Ortega's generational elitism to Azorín's generational "classicism" such that all generations, beginning with Azorín's, are shown to have the same nationalist mission. Thus, what began with Ortega as a criticism of Azorín's claim to singularity and originality becomes, under the weight of Laín Entralgo's interpretation, a continuum of modern Spanish nationalist peculiarity.

Since at least the late 1960s some Hispanists have sought to do battle with this monumental institutionalization of the literary generation of '98. In an essay of 1969, provocatively titled "La invención del 98," Ricardo Gullón argued against the use of a generational scheme in the study of twentieth-century Spanish literature because, according to him, such a scheme tends to pervert the appreciation of literary works as art.[22] For Gullón in 1969, culture was apparently not to be confused with the worlds of history, social criticism, and political philosophy, not even when the literature in question—the writing of Ganivet, Unamuno, Maeztu, Azorín and Ortega—plainly concerns itself with those same disciplines. Still, in deference to Gullón's New Critical approach to the notion of the generation of '98, Hispanists have, at least since the 1970s, been apt, when referring to the notion, to do so with guarded distance, rendering it as "the so-called generation of '98." What they have not done is heed Gullón's call to stop using the term altogether.

In 1990, for instance, Gullón's plea was taken up again, this time by the North-American Hispanist Inman Fox. In an engaging and at times polemical essay titled "Hacia una nueva historia literaria para España," Fox rightly points out the decidedly ideological and political content of Azorín's thoughts on the generation of '98.[23] This observation leads Fox to complain that Azorín's invention of that generation, coupled with its subsequent institutionalization, has sadly politicized and otherwise violated the Kantian autonomy of literature as a disinterested, aesthetic field of endeavor. Indeed, despite his having identified the possibility of reading Azorín's invention of the generation of '98 as a historical fiction that conforms to a political and nationalist agenda, Fox bureaucratically shies away from the challenge of debunking the monolithic status of the generation of '98 and asks us, instead, to accept Gullón's view of Spanish national culture as a protective enclosure and sacrosanct refuge, a place that is to remain free from all political or nationalist posturing.

On balance, Gullón and Fox are right to complain. But they seem somehow to have missed the point. The problem with using the notion of the generation of '98 to study the literature of turn-of-the-century Spain is not that it violates the autonomy of fiction, nor that it steers literary criticism away from the utopian analysis of literature, but that, in the form in which it has been handed down to the present, it reproduces the implicit assumptions concerning Spain's heroic and classical past that motivate the nationalist imperialism professed by Unamuno, Ganivet, Maeztu, Ortega and, certainly also, Azorín himself. *Quixotism* departs from this tradition and its underlying historical assumptions. The interpretations of Unamuno, Ganivet, Maeztu and Ortega developed throughout this book do not rely on the generation of '98, neither as an operational tool nor even, more simply, as a designation. The readings offered here are based in an entirely different critical category: Quixotism.

Setting Quixotism Apart from the "Quixotic"

For years now, the terms "quixote," "quixotic," and "quixotism" have been used in literary and extraliterary contexts to convey a sense of extravagant enthusiasm for unrealizable, impractical, and visionary ideals. In this respect, these three terms comprise something like a commonsense criticism of idealism. The colloquial connotations of the term *quixote,* for instance, are such that this name is disparagingly applied to anyone who is thought to be inspired by lofty ideals. Similarly, the failure to realize elevated ideals often evokes the quixotic image of an inept, foolish, and grotesque humanity. It is in this derogatory sense, also, that the term *quixotism* is used to refer to the exaggerated chivalric sentiment, self-righteousness and false pride that seem, inevitably, to characterize quixotic ideas and actions. In sum, *quixote, quixotic,* and *quixotism* are generally used to demonstrate just how proximate human greatness can be to the ridiculous.

For Spanish nationalist thinkers of the late nineteenth and early twentieth centuries such as Ganivet, Unamuno, Maeztu, and Ortega, however, the notion of the quixotic corresponds to a sense of chivalric enthusiasm and idealism that is anything but satiric. Ganivet, for instance, in his 1897 *Idearium español,* refers to Don Quixote as the "Spanish Ulysses"; similarly, Unamuno, in his 1905 *Vida de Don Quijote y Sancho,* envisions Don Quixote as the "Spanish Christ"; additionally, Ortega, in his 1914 *Meditaciones del Quijote,* views Don Quixote as representing "Spanish national melancholy"; finally, Maeztu, in his 1925 *Don Quijote, Don Juan y la Celestina,* conceives of Don Quixote as constituting one part of the "Holy Trinity" of Spanish national values. Rather than embrace a criticism of idealism, the Quixotism proposed by these thinkers extols obsessive devotion to utopian ideals as a solemn, dignified, and virtuous habit of mind. Quixotic behavior, for these Spanish intellectuals, is a sign of nobility. Fittingly, the Quixotism of Ganivet, Unamuno, Maeztu, and Ortega constitutes an attempt to recuperate, if not altogether reinvent, Don Quixote as a sometimes stoic and mystical, sometimes redemptive and messianic hero who embodies the leadership ideals that these intellectuals believed could regenerate post-1898 Spain.

This romanticized view of Don Quixote as a regenerating hero leads to two fundamental questions. How did modern Spain's Quixotists understand their nation's perceived decadence? Why did they choose the figure of Don Quixote to represent the nation's longed-for regeneration? The short answer to these questions is that, with the definitive and sudden collapse of the Spanish empire in 1898, these intellectuals found themselves at pains to explain the process of Spain's decline from empire. Rather than promote a critical understanding of the historical events that had led to Spain's demise as a world power, they set out to deny that their nation's loss of empire was irrevocable. Consequently, they did not view decadence only, or even primarily, as a process of political and economic decline, but as a moral sickness from which the Spanish nation could recuperate. Keeping in mind this desired reversal of national fate, they turned to the example of Don Quixote: the madman who, in defeat, recuperates his sanity. Moreover, in the ironic dualism that is written into Cervantes' *Quixote* as a narrative principle, they uncovered a model for both imagining and narrating the desired moral reversal and transformation of the Spanish nation. They produced conjectural national histories that presented the "true" history of the Spanish nation's decline from empire as "false." Against this background of "false historical reality" they affirmed their own "truer" versions of the nation's "essential history." According to these conjectural national histories, Don Quixote embodied the Spanish nation's essential heroic, empire-building characteristics. By extracting the figure of Don Quixote from its original discursive context and recontextualizing it within the framework of modern Spanish nationalist discourse, they transformed Don Quixote into a hero capable of the sort of ascetic self-discipline and self-sacrificing leadership that they believed would regenerate Spain and allow the nation to reclaim its cultural hegemony over the Hispanic world.

These two questions concerning the perceived decadence of turn-of-the-century Spain and its assumed need for heroic regeneration do, of course, require much more than just this abreviated answer. Although the story of these thinkers' regenerative Quixotism is true, to this day it remains largely untold. Thus the long answer to these questions is what this book aims to provide. Indeed, the argument that I set forth in the following chapters proposes that the Quixotism of Ganivet, Unamuno, Maeztu, and Ortega is indispensable to a proper understanding of the rise of a modern national identity in Spain; in particular, of the National-Catholicism that took hold of the nation after the collapse of the Second Republic in 1936.

Their Quixotism, in other words, helps explain the cultural climate out of which Spain's experience with fascism was born.

Scholars dedicated to the study of fin-de-siècle Spain have rarely used the term Quixotism. When they have, as does Paul Descouzis in his 1970 *Cervantes y la generación del 98,* they have done so exclusively as a literary category, relating it to a series of essays written on Cervantes' famous novel, between the years of Spanish colonial bankruptcy (1895–1898) and the Spanish Civil War (1936–1939). Among the early twentieth-century writers responsible for its inception, however, the term Quixotism denotes far more than a literary category. For Unamuno, Ganivet, Maeztu, and Ortega, Quixotism involves a confrontation with the crisis of Spanish imperial identity, it embraces a national revival, both in a literary and sociopolitical domain, and it comprises an elitist, heroic ideal thought to be capable of regenerating Spain's cultural empire-building strength.

In keeping with how these thinkers used the term, in this book Quixotism is also understood to comprise more than a literary category. Here, Quixotism is treated as a critical category. This is true in two senses. First of all, Quixotism provides for an analysis of the philosophical, historical, and political arguments that several prominent Spanish intellectuals sustained in their confrontation with the crisis of Spanish national and imperial identity at the turn of the century. In this regard, Quixotism denotes a nationalistic heroic idealism, even a neo-Christian messianism, which is of political relevance, not only to fin-de-siècle Spain, but also to the National-Catholic Spain of the Franco era. Second, Quixotism functions as a critical category in that it enables a revision and reconstruction of the writings of modern Spain's Quixotists. In this sense, Quixotism demonstrates that the nationalist literary revival of early twentieth-century Spain involved not only the creation of a modern national literary canon but also the construction of its own putatively critical schemes for self-analysis. Chief among these was, of course, the generation of '98.

To the extent to which these schemes still dominate the study of modern Spanish literature, Hispanism, today, can claim to be free neither from the nationalist prejudices of the Quixotists nor from the intellectual dullness, incompetency and deception that routinely accompany nationalist attitudes. This is particularly true of the generational scheme that gave rise to the notion of the generation of '98 and of those Hispanists who, to this day, insist on studying the diverse literatures of early twentieth-century Spain as if they constituted a monolith. The term Quixotism is used throughout this book both to name one of the principal literary developments of the turn of the century and provide for a critique of that process. In promoting this critical use of the term, however, I do not mean to make any universal theoretical claims for Quixotism as a category. Far be it from me to replace the monolithic generation of '98 with yet another colossus. The animating idea behind *Quixotism* is, rather, to free up the discursive playing field that defines modern peninsular studies today. I mean, in other words, to contribute to the modernization of a field of study which remains, to this day, constrained by the memory of its premodern, Quixotist legacy.

Quixotizing Restoration Spain

Despite its novelty, the Quixotism of Restoration Spain was by no means the first instance of an interpretation that sought to explain the symbolism of the *Quixote* and of its protagonists in terms of the ideology, aesthetics, and sensibility of the modern era. Instances of this loosely symbolic use of the figure of Don Quixote as an icon for modern Spanish national identity abound in criticisms of the *Quixote,* both within and outside of Spain, and date back to as early as the late seventeenth and early eighteenth centuries. In late seventeenth-century France, for instance, several thinkers interpreted the *Quixote* as a parody of Medieval Spanish civilization and its chivalric customs.[24] In Spain, this line of interpretation endured well into the latter half of the nineteenth century in the works of such thinkers as Campoamor and Azcárate.[25] For their part, English novelists of the eighteenth century such as Fielding and Sterne took the *Quixote* as a model for a realist aesthetic of modern tragicomedy. In Spain, this realist interpretation of the *Quixote* was further developed and nationalized by Galdós.[26] Finally, Russian and German romantics, in particular Turgenev and Heine, turned the figure of Don Quixote into a positive symbol of the traditional "Man of Faith," as against Sancho or the modern, skeptical "Man of Reason." This romantic interpretation flourished in Spain, toward the middle of the nineteenth century, under the influence of Nicolás Díaz de Benjumea's ocultism.

Benjumea's Romantic interpretation of the *Quixote,* as presented in his 1861 *La Estafeta de Urganda,* underscored the supposed timeless wisdom and universal appeal of Cervantes' celebrated novel: "Cervantes has been and is the idol of all nations, and as with the Spain of Charles and Phillip, I dare suggest that the sun does not set on his fame. The *Quixote* is a profane version of the Bible."[27] Although, as Anthony Close has noted, Benjumea turned Don Quixote into "an abstract epitome—Soul, Idealism, Faith, thirst for Justice—with Sancho as his symbolic antithesis," Benjumea's enthusiasm for Cervantes and the *Quixote* was not limited to a celebration of their abstract and universal appeal.[28] For Benjumea, the *Quixote* also held a particular, national appeal. That attraction was principally identified with the figure of Don Quixote, who Benjumea took to represent a new type of chivalry, which, once purged of its crudity and barbarism, would lead toward the modernization of nineteenth-century

Spanish society and mores.[29] In this way, Benjumea anticipated the themes to be developed later by the Quixotists of Restoration Spain.

Not unlike the allegorical interpretations set forth by the romantics, in their readings of the *Quixote* the Quixotists linked the figures of Don Quixote and Sancho to abstract ethical values; moreover, like the romantics, they too conflated the moral aspect of their interpretation with a powerful and creative critique of contemporary Spanish society. But the Quixotist critique, unlike that of the romantics, was specifically suited to the contemporary national issues and imperial crises of Restoration Spain.

Spanning the years 1874–1931, Restoration Spain was troubled by colonial wars, economic modernization, electoral fraud, the rise of organized class-consciousness, and the disintegrating pressure of separatist, micronationalist movements. This crisis-ridden, sociopolitical milieu engendered a heated and prolonged national debate concerning the causes of Spain's apparent decadence and the remedies deemed necessary to regenerate the failing modern nation. As developed by Ganivet, Unamuno, Maeztu, and Ortega, Quixotism came to play a central and defining role in the character and direction that this national debate was to follow.

In its least ambitious cast, the Quixotism of these thinkers sought to identify the figure of Don Quixote with the moral transformation and spiritual regeneration of the Spanish nation. This national variety of Quixotism proposed Don Quixote as an exemplary patriot who, by reason of his devotion to elevated moral ideals, could provide the Sanchos of Spain—the "resentful" and decadent masses of Ortega's "invertebrate Spain"—with a model for piety. As such, under the guise of a principally moral critique of decadence, Quixotism propounded an elitist solution to the nation's socioeconomic and political crises.

In addition to a program for national regeneration, Quixotism was a project for the spiritual and cultural conquest of a modern Hispanic empire. In this, its most ambitious configuration, Quixotism proposed Don Quixote as an icon for the defense of a Hispanic cultural empire with Castile as its center and the whole of the Iberian Peninsula as well as all of Latin America firmly in its grasp. Quixotism thus fashioned the defense of this cultural empire as a spiritual counterweight to the secular tendencies of the modern, Anglo-Saxon world. This perspective on Spanish imperial regeneration gained considerable appeal among Spaniards eager to blame the United States for Spain's loss of its colonies in the Caribbean and the Pacific: hence, the iconographic juxtaposition of the Spanish Don Quixote with the Anglo-Saxon Robinson Crusoe that figures predominantly in the Quixotist canon, from Ganivet's *Idearium español* to Unamuno's *Vida de Don Quijote y Sancho.*

This twofold program for modern national and imperial regeneration was marked by a profound sense of change in the Spanish nation's historical self-consciousness. Given that what remained of the Spanish empire had been so convincingly lost either to independence or to the United States, the nation could do little else but consider itself in the negative light of its own decline. No longer was it viable for Spanish patriots to narrate a history of Spain's continuous and unfettered rise to imperial glory. The only empirically faithful history that could now be narrated was that of the events that had led to Spain's decline from imperial glory: hardly an inspiring story for national regeneration. So, rather than narrate an honest, empirically sound and critically rigorous history, the Quixotists of Restoration Spain opted for a narrative of identity embedded in mythical time; they opted for the fictionalization of Spanish history, for its nationalization.[30]

As such, the Spanish language, the production of literature in that language and the distribution and consumption of this literature were of paramount importance to the Quixotists. Despite the contrasting cultural and linguistic differences among Spain's historical regions, the claim that Castilian (or Spanish) was to be acknowledged by all Spaniards as the language of the nation—a claim that was as old as Nebrija's 1492 defense of Castilian as the language of imperial Spain—can be found repeatedly throughout the Quixotist canon. This position was often fiercely defended even by those who, like the Basque Unamuno, were of a non-Castilian speaking region or background. Also in keeping with this posture, Quixotists like Azorín, Ganivet and Unamuno zealously defended the primacy of Spain's "Classical" Castilian literature—the so-called Golden Age of Spanish letters. Among these "Spanish" classics, they saluted Cervantes' *Quixote,* in particular, for the purity or "casticismo" of its Castilian and recognized it as a work that had contributed significantly to the richness of the "Spanish" idiom and indeed expressed the full spectrum of the nation's spiritualizing "philosophy."[31]

This Quixotist defense of Castilian as the Spanish national language, and the celebration of national literary classics attendant to it, was made all the more tenable by the significant growth in Restoration Spain of an intellectual print-culture. This growth translated into an increase, not only in printing presses, publishing houses, newspapers, magazines and literary societies, but also in a readership eager to consume this ever growing and varied literature.[32] Together, the writers whose thought was published in these new public venues and the growing reading class for whom and to whom they wrote, constituted an increasingly influential cross-section of Spaniards. In addition to the old ruling classes, this new and growing "reading class" consisted of a rising middle strata of commercial, industrial, and professional bourgeoisie.[33]

Strategically focused, as they were, on the presence and power of this rising middle class, the Quixotists sought to create their own domain of sovereignty within the sociopolitical reality of Restoration Spain. That domain was public discourse and, in particular, the published debate on Spanish national decadence and regeneration. Quixotism was, in this regard, finely attuned to Regenerationism, or what Sebastian Balfour has aptly characterized as "the revolt of the middle classes."[34] Yet Quixotism, in its attempt to vie for and consolidate the growing power of the middle classes, differs from Regenerationism in at least one fundamental aspect.

Regenerationism, which was a positivist-minded reform movement roughly contemporary with Quixotism, sought to remedy the perceived decadence of the Spanish nation almost exclusively by means of economic and political reforms; it sought, in short, to do political battle with the sociopolitical regime of the Restoration. The focus of the Regenerationist critique of decadence was on the material or "outer" domain of Restoration Spain's social institutions and practices and not on national identity per se. Quixotism, by contrast, did not seek primarily to do political battle with the regime but to declare sovereignty over Spain's national culture. The focus of its critique on decadence, as in the case of Unamuno's notion of a national "intrahistory" from which the modernizing nation had strayed, was with the nation's "inner" or spiritual domain.[35] The aims of Quixotism, therefore, were distinct from those of Regenerationism in that, rather than effect some measure of political and economic reform, Quixotism sought to encourage the spiritual and moral transformation of the decadent Spanish nation.

On the whole, Quixotism sought to preserve and deepen the nation's faith and trust in the essential marks of its cultural identity. Yet, it is not as though Quixotism left this cultural domain unchanged. Rather, it transformed the nation's cultural essence, providing for the regeneration of, not only the Spanish nation, but also an Hispanic cultural empire. In this regard, Quixotism, although not a form of political nationalism, did constitute a form of cultural nationalism. Indeed, insofar as modern Spanish national identity was first and foremost the product of a cultural nationalist movement, it was the Quixotists of Restoration Spain who originally imagined it into being.

Angel Ganivet, who viewed Spain's national decadence in terms of *abulia* or a pathological lack of will, interpreted Don Quixote on the basis of a classical, Herculean model of heroism whereby Don Quixote's penitent labors, stoicism, and ascetic discipline were to act as the foundation for a new, albeit traditional, cultural order. Unamuno, by contrast, equated decadence with the Spanish nation's abandonment of a traditional and mystical love of wisdom in favor of a modern cult of the utilitarian values of science, industry, and capital; consequently, he sanctified the figure of Don Quixote after the premodern Christian model of the sacrificial savior. Maeztu, who attributed decadence to the betrayal of the nation's original adherence to values of honor, reinvented Don Quixote as an idealizing lover whose noble spirit was to guide Spain toward the recuperation of its once extensive imperial power. Finally Ortega, for whom decadence was a mass phenomenon, depicted Don Quixote as a tragic figure who, having been pulled down from the ideal realm of tragic heroism by the lowly and sneering resentment of the masses, was to be vindicated as the symbol of Spain's victimized elites.

Each of these thinkers did interpret the decadence of modern Spain in subtly different ways, and each did assign a correspondingly dissimilar regenerative value to the figure of Don Quixote. These nuanced differences notwithstanding, the coincidence of opinion among these four intellectuals ran deep. Indeed, there was more at stake than a shared interest in using the figure of Don Quixote to give expression to regenerative national values. The subtly divergent views that these thinkers held in regard to decadence and regeneration cohered, to a great extent, because conceptually they shared two common denominators: a moral critique of decadence and a premodern concept of regenerating, empire-building heroism.

The moral critique identified decadence, first and foremost, with the resentment that Spain's modern masses, represented by Sancho Panza, had developed for the nation's Don Quixotes. This critique also perceived the masses's attempts at self-government as leading inevitably to a state of anarchy. As imagined and narrated by the Quixotists, this anarchy was the end result of the encounter, in 1898, between Don Quixote and Robinson Crusoe. It was then that Sancho had lost his faith in Don Quixote and tried to become ever more like Robinson. But, argued the Quixotists, the modernizing example of Robinson only served to alienate Sancho from his true nature and distract him from his true vocation as Don Quixote's squire. And so, this critique created the theoretical need for elitist regenerative solutions, for ways that Don Quixote might regain Sancho's faith.

The regenerating elitism that the Quixotists recommended for modern Spain was meant, in part, to defend the nation's cultural domain against the inroads of Robinson-like mass modernization and, in part, to clear the debris of Spain's recent political and imperial decline and forge a path for the Quixotist organization of the modern the nation. This putatively regenerating elitism was decidely antimodern, anti-Robinsonian. It was neither conceived as a novum organum capable of generating a new national life, nor was it conceived as the embodiment of what, according to Kant at least, should be the spirit of all enlightened, modernizing thought: *sapere aude*. Instead, the regenerating elitism theorized by modern Spain's Quixotists was based in an authoritarian national political tradition that offered examples of willing obedience to extrapersonal forms of guidance. The Quixotists modeled their regenerating heroism, in other words, after the premodern ascetic self-abnegation of Spanish mystics such as St. Theresa of Avila and St. Ignatius of Loyola and the also premodern crusading self-sacrifice of Christian conquistadors such as Hernán Cortés and Vasco Nuñez de Balboa.

Here, then, are the premodern regenerating values according to which the Quixotists idealized Don Quixote. As a wise mystic and spiritual conquistador, Don Quixote was to correct Sancho Panza's Robinson-inspired resentment of elitism and put an end to Sancho's anarchic attempts at modern self-government. By resorting to premodern elitism, the Quixotists reasoned that Spain could overcome its modern decadence and even save the rest of the modernizing world from the threat of spiritual decadence posed by the increasing dominion of Robinson Crusoe's utilitarian and materialistic values. Together, promised the Quixotists, Don Quixote and Sancho Panza would set out on a new "modern" adventure to reclaim their nation's lost glory, assert Spain's perennial spiritual lordship over the Hispanic world, and call attention to this spiritual empire as the one remaining place in the modern world where Robinsonian decadence could not and would not corrode the civilizing values bequeathed to the world by the Spanish empire.[36]

Commemorating the Quixote, Disseminating Quixotism

The celebration of Don Quixote as a premodern hero capable of regenerating a modernizing and decadent Spain was not limited to these thinkers alone. Nor was its dissemination due only to the persuasive force of the rhetoric with which modern Spain's principal Quixotists elaborated the discourse of Quixotism. As is often the case with the invented traditions and rituals of a nation, there was an element of historical chance involved in the success with which Quixotism was eventually circulated and made part of the modern Spanish national imaginary. Nineteen hundred and five marked the tercentenary of the publication of Cervantes' *Quixote*. Considering that this opportunity to commemorate the *Quixote* arose only six years after the imperial crisis of 1898, it is not surprising that many of those who did participate in the commemoration chose to frame their views on the *Quixote* within the immediate context of that crisis and the debate on Spanish national decadence that it served to intensify. The rise and eventual acceptance of Quixotist discourse as both a critique of decadence and a program for regeneration owed as much to the historic events of 1898 as it did to the coincidental commemorative events of 1905.

Typical of this commemoratively inspired Quixotism is Manuel de Sandoval's sonnet titled "A Don Quijote," which was published in 1905 in *La República de las Letras*. This unexceptional example clearly identifies a heroic and idealized Don Quixote with the regeneration and spiritual salvation of an ambiguously modern Spanish nation perceived to be in the throes of decadence:

To Don Quixote

> Break from the sepulcher that encloses you,
> illustrious Manchegan, the heavy stone,
> and may your generous madness
> astound and amaze the land once more.
> Already Rocinante, your warring stag,
> awaits faithfully at the edge of your grave;
> mount him, take up your powerful lance,
> and against all that is evil and unjust, fight.
> Without fear that they might humilliate you,
> vile and disgusting pigs that they are,
> sally forth, as before, at the break of day!
> Return to the countryside that remembers you,
> to see if a MADMAN can regenerate and save the nation
> destroyed by the SANE![37]

Sandoval's sonnet reads like a desperate prayer for national salvation. The narrative voice speaks in an apostrophic mode, invoking the warrior spirit of Spain's dead national hero, Don Quixote, in the hopes that the current condition of the Spanish nation, a nation destroyed by the political exercise of modern reason, might appeal to Don Quixote's high sense of justice and charitable service and urge him to return from the dead to roam the national countryside. Don Quixote, Sandoval's prayerlike sonnet suggests, is to regenerate the nation by means of his irrational generosity. The highly idealistic and selfless character of Don Quixote is thus made to stand as an example of the sort of leadership values required for regenerating the nation: values associated with the courage of a warrior as well as with the generous, sacrificial selflessness of a messianic figure.

These regenerative ideals and heroic values informed most of the major commemorative events that were staged in Madrid in an effort to highlight the relevance of Cervantes' *Quixote* to the post-1898 realities of Spain. Of these events, perhaps the most prestigious and certainly the most literary was the conference sponsored by the Sección de Literatura of the Ateneo de Madrid in May of 1905. Among the Ateneo's officers figured such prominent cernvantine scholars as Navarro y Ledesma (one of Cervantes' more celebrated biographers), Francisco A. de Icaza (whose studies of the reception of the *Quixote* in Latin America remain, to this day, an indispensable scholarly reference), and the young philosopher José Ortega y Gasset (who in 1914 would publish his first book-length project, *Meditaciones del Quixote,* dedicated to Cervantes' masterpiece). The conference at the Ateneo lasted ten days. It included, in addition to essays read by the likes of Azorín, Ramón

Perez de Ayala and Rafael Salillas, poems that had been composed for the ocassion and read by their author, the Nicaraguan modernist poet Rubén Darío, as well as a theatrical interpretation of the Maese Pedro episode of Part II of the *Quixote*. The responsibility to offer some closing remarks at the conference fell to Navarro y Ledesma who, after summarizing the contributions of all those who had participated, went on to formulate in paradigmatic terms what was to be, for years to come, the basic structure of Quixotist discourse.

Navarro y Ledesma begins his discussion by postulating the existence, among the members of the Spanish nation, of an undying "quixotic sentiment," which explains the nation's ability to survive even in the face of great adversity: "There exists among us, perhaps as never before, a quixotic sentiment that has survived the centuries and defeated our defeats."[38] A bit further on, he equates this Spanish national "quixotic sentiment" with the survivor's love of life and suggests, much in the same spirit as Sandoval's sonnet, that the Spanish nation seek its redemption via a resuscitated Don Quixote. "Our sentiment of love revives Don Quixote . . . Let us ask the Hidalgo to lift the stone off his sepulchur; but let us also be careful to not allow him to ascend to the heavens as did the other Redeemer."[39] Here, Navarro y Ledesma presents the nation's "quixotic sentiment" as nothing short of faith in redeeming heroism. Once Don Quixote has been revived and freed from his crypt, reasons Navarro y Ledesma, he will lead the Spanish nation in its quest for regeneration. As Navarro y Ledesma presents it, this process consists of two dialectically related moments. The first is critical, negative, a negation of negation itself. "Let us kill death," he preaches.[40] The second moment is reconstructive, affirmative, the creation of life itself: "Let us seize life from death."[41] In the terms of the Quixotism that thinkers such as Unamuno, Maeztu, Ganivet, and Ortega propounded, Ledesma y Navarro's two-step program for national regeneration would become a critique of decadence and, on the basis of that critique, an imaginative and narrative construction of a perpetual Spanish cultural empire.

Observing the Monument

While literature was the primary mode of expression and reception for Quixotism, Quixotism was not exclusively a literary, discursive phenomenon. Artists, architects, and politicians all joined in the mythmaking of a regenerated Quixotic Spain. In 1905 the Spanish government issued its first cultural stamp commemorating the tercentenary of *Don Quixote*'s publication.[42] Some twenty years later, in 1925, or two years after Primo de Rivera had come to dictatorial power, a spectacular monument to Cervantes, which had been in the planning stages since 1916, was finally erected in Madrid. This monument was intended as both a means to celebrating Cervantes' literary achievements and as a vehicle of expression for the post-1898, pan-nationalist longings of modern Spain for the cultural and spiritual reconquest of the Americas—an imperialist project which, as early as 1899, the editors of the Madrid based, regenerationist magazine *Vida Nueva* expressed in unequivocal terms: "The days of hatred are over and a new era of love should commence. The time has come for Spain to re-conquer America, or better still, the heart of America. We undertake the labors of peace; for without peace it would be futile to think of those markets for our industry and commerce."[43]

Madrid's Quixotist monument depicts Cervantes seated on a throne, flanked to either side by Don Quixote and Sancho. Beneath the three figures there is a fountain, which the architects of the monument describe as "the source of the Castilian language: on its basin will be carved the coat of arms of all the Castilian speaking nations."[44] After describing how the fountain's water is to flow over these coats of arms uniting the nations they represent, the authors of the project further explain that in this manner "the artists have wanted to express the historic fact of the invasion of the New World by our language. The relationship between the fountain and the monument is the following: because Cervantes represents the height of our literature and is the sovereign of the Castilian language, his works should be seen as the principal disseminators of the language."[45] Evidently, Don Quixote here becomes the symbol for the reconstruction of a Hispanic cultural order of which Spain is to remain the generative center. This monument to the so-called universal appeal of the figure of Don Quixote is made all the more significant by the fact that it stands, to this day, at the center of one of Madrid's principal downtown squares appropriately named "La Plaza de España"—or what in Quixotist terms might better be referred to as "La Plaza del Hispanismo."

After the fall of Primo de Rivera, the neo-imperial spirit animating this early twentieth-century monumentalization of Don Quixote was first kept alive by the fascist ideologues of the Falange. Of the twenty-six points that make up the Falange's so-called Programmatic Norms the second point sustains that: "Spain is a universal unity of destiny. Any conspiracy against that unity is repulsive"; the third point continues along similar lines, maintaining that: "We have an imperial will . . . Spain asserts its being the spiritual axis of the Hispanic world as a preeminent title in universal endeavors"; and the fifth point insists: "Spain will once again seek out its glory and riches by sea."[46] This programmatic discourse continues the recuperative imperialism articulated, some years before, by the Quixotists. Still, that the neo-imperial longings of the Quixotists was incorporated into the official discourse of fascist Spain should, probably, come as little surprise. After all, it was Franco himself who, as coauthor of the film "Raza," proposed the victory of the fascists in the Civil War as retribution for Spain's loss of empire in 1898.[47]

It is remarkable, nonetheless, that after Spain's transition to democracy these longings for empire should once again have found political leaders willing to publicly own up to them. Such is the case, most notably, with the leader of the Partido Popular, Jose María Aznar. In a book that he wrote in 1994 titled *La segunda transición*, Aznar affirmed that: "Spain is not only a Mediterranean country. Its Atlantic profile, which looks at America, has not been sufficiently highlighted in recent years so as to make its imprint on our foreign policy. We must recuperate it, because it would be a form of historical suicide to renounce or delay . . . the 'transatlantic destiny' of Spain."[48] Here, much like the ideologues of the Falange before him and the Quixotists before them, Aznar maintains that the essence of the Spanish nation is imperial.

This neo-imperialism, this neo-Quixotism, formed the basis of Aznar's official commemorative strategy of 1898. By toeing the line of Aznar's official strategy of commemorative forgetfulness, in 1998 too many Hispanists effectively neutralized their ability to speak critically. Not unlike the stone-cold silence that Don Quixote's statue emits from atop its pedestal in the center of Madrid's Plaza de España, the silence of such Hispanists is a monument to Quixotism. And not unlike the criticism that Spanish, Puerto Rican, and Cuban intellectuals such as Juan Goytisolo, Arcadio Diaz Quiñones, and Manuel Moreno Fraginals formulated in 1998 from the alternative perspectives of their exile and Spain's ex-colonies, in this book I venture to offer my interpretation of Quixotism as an intervention that might pierce the monumental silence.

I

The Birth of Quixotism

1

Quixotist Madness

By the time that Ganivet, Unamuno, Maeztu, and Ortega had begun to publicize their Quixotism and to play it against the reality of Spain's loss of empire, an ongoing debate concerning the perceived decadence of modern Spain had already been under way for nearly two decades. At issue in this national polemic was the relation of the putatively "liberal" state of the Restoration to Spanish national decadence. Did the new regime, with its studied policies of moderation, serve to hinder decadence or to further it? Those who defended the Restoration by arguing that it provided a political formula for national regeneration were, by and large, members of the ruling class who had a vested interest in the regime's continuance. To either side of these partisan moderates there were, however, those who believed that the new liberal regime was at fault for the nation's ongoing decline. What these critics of the Restoration could not agree upon though was whether the regime advanced decadence because it was too liberal or not liberal enough.

The profoundly conservative view held the Restoration accountable for the nation's continuing decadence by arguing that the democratic principles on which it was based served only to lead the nation astray from its traditional forms of political and moral life. According to this view, the Restoration was a final chapter in a long history of Spanish national decline that had begun with the enlightened despots of the Bourbon monarchy who, conservatives believed, had wrongly imported foreign models of modernizing reform and sought to impose these on the unsuspecting and steadfastly traditional Spanish nation. This process, argued the conservatives, was advanced still further under Napoleon and then again by the liberals who, ever since the Constitution of

1812, had made repeated attacks on the sovereign powers of the crown and the moral authority of the Catholic Church. Insofar as the regime of the Restoration was itself modeled after the constitutional monarchy of Great Britain, conservative critics saw it as a continuation of this liberal, Europeanizing trend. National regeneration, from this perspective, entailed turning back the clock in order to recuperate the nation's traditional identity and the values that had once led to its rise to empire. Spain, the conservatives believed, needed to cleanse itself of all those foreign ideals that had been forced on it by its Europeanizing leaders and, once again, affirm its essential, Catholic and monarchical hispanicity.

By contrast, the radically progressive view attributed the decline of the Spanish nation to its failure to modernize sufficiently and reconfigure the state in keeping with the liberal political ideals of the Enlightenment. The feudal character of traditional Spanish social and economic relations; the religious intolerance and inquisitorial zeal of Spanish Catholicism; the absolutist legacy of the Spanish monarchy; the corruption and incompetence of the political class; and the apathy of the Spanish masses: progressives viewed all of these as key aspects of Spain's renowned *atraso*. Insofar as the Restoration system did not break suitably with tradition, progressives held it to be responsible for the nation's stagnation. National regeneration, from this perspective, implied the Europeanization of Spain, which involved the adoption of ambitious programs for economic, political, and cultural reform modeled after the modernizing societies of Northern Europe.

At odds with these opposing extremes, Cánovas del Castillo (1828–1897), who was the principal architect of the Restoration's two-party political system, portrayed the new regime as a moderating corrective to modern Spain's ideological divide and to the political instability and social upheaval that this rift had generated throughout much of the nineteenth century.[1] In particular, Cánovas proposed the Restoration as a corrective to the chaotic and tumultuous events of the Sexenio Revolucionario of 1868–1874. To his credit, the political arrangement that Cánovas fashioned for Spain did usher in the longest period of relative political calm in modern Spanish history: in fact, the Constitution of 1876 was not officially replaced until the Second Republic was declared in 1931. The Restoration achieved this remarkable political stability, however, by divorcing itself from those it governed and, in effect, arrogating the nation's sovereignty.

Despite the chaos that surrounded the Republican revolution of 1868, this revolution had successfully established, for the first time in modern Spanish history, the sovereignty of the Spanish people in the political configuration of the state. With the Restoration, and the Constitution of 1876 in particular, Cánovas managed to undo all this, while paying lip service to the revolution's liberal doctrine of popular sovereignty. Indeed, Cánovas rejected voluntaristic, majoritarian conceptions of popular sovereignty such as Rousseau's general will and posited, instead, the existence of an enduring national will whose essential spirit was embodied in the institutions through which the nation had historically organized itself: the monarchy and the parliament.[2] Accordingly, Cánovas appealed to Spanish national history in an attempt to legitimize the Restoration and justify the fact that, under the Constitution of 1876, the monarchy and the parliament had been empowered as the nation's exclusive cosovereigns.

In addition to appropriating the nation's sovereignty and reinvesting it in the institutions of the state, Cánovas' design of the Restoration monarchy provided for the imposition, from above, of a political power-sharing formula that further excluded the majority of Spaniards from political life. This formula consisted of a negotiated agreement between the two dynastic parties, the Conservatives and the Liberals, to alternate in governing the nation. The two parties were to do this, and did in fact do so, to the exclusion of all other political affiliations. Although by 1900 Restoration Spain was theoretically one of the most democratic liberal states in the world—universal suffrage had been established by 1890, its constitution allowed for freedom of thought and belief, fundamental rights had all been proclaimed, and a respectable judicial system had been set in place—the reality, in practice, was quite another. Despite appearances to the contrary, Cánovas' system left practically nothing to popular decision. Elections were carefully managed from above by the Minister of the Interior and the local power bosses or caciques who oversaw the voting process to the advantage of the government's appointed candidates. Under the Restoration system devised by Cánovas, governance was essentially reduced to a matter of oligarchic dominion.

But while Cánovas and other political leaders whose power had been authorized by the Constitution of 1876 praised the regime for its reliability and stability, the Restoration was not able to silence or otherwise co-opt all of its detractors. To both sides of the political divide, there were those who voiced their opposition to the regime of the Restoration and attempted to envision, and in some instances enact, cultural and political alternatives. Chief among these were the Spanish Catholic integrists and their progressive rivals at the Institutción Libre de Enseñanza; the anarchosyndicalists of the Confederatión Nacional de Trabajo (CNT) and the unionized socialists of the Unión General de Trabajadores (UGT); the micronationalists of the Basque Countries and Catalonia; and the regenerationists. The Quixotism of Ganivet, Unamuno, Maeztu, and Ortega evolved alongside this complicated mix of cultural, economic, and political projects for social reform. It is, therefore, important to become familiar with these critics of the Restoration and to consider both what they have in common with the Quixotists and how they differ from them.

Fighting in the Classroom

Considering that Cánovas had appealed to the nation's past in an attempt to legitimize his scheme for the exclusive cosovereignty of the monarchy and the parliament, it is not surprising that the regime's critics took issue with his interpretation of Spanish national history. Located at the far right of the political spectrum, the Spanish Catholic integrists opposed the Restoration because the Constitution of 1876, while affirming Catholicism as the official state religion, also allowed for certain freedoms of thought and belief that the integrists perceived as a threat to both the nation's traditional religious identity and the monarchy's traditional defense of that identity.[3] Indeed, Spanish Catholic integrists maintained that the Spanish nation was, in essence, a creation of Christianity.[4] Theocratic in their politics, the integrists looked on the Restoration's liberal doctrines not only as a moral threat but as a political one too; they saw in the regime's toleration of freedom of thought and belief a force that threatened, eventually, to splinter the union of church and state and, ultimately, undermine the nation's historical, political, and religious integrity.

Although by rejecting the liberal doctrines on which the Restoration was founded the integrists did not pose a serious political threat to the regime, they did present it and its defenders with a significant ideological challenge. In particular, the integrists took issue with Cánovas' idea that Spanish national history somehow justified limiting the sovereign powers of the Catholic monarchy and forcing it to share those powers with a parliament that consisted, at least in part, of liberals. According to the integrists, the only Spanish national history worthy of that name was one that conceived of the Spanish nation as a community of obedient believers, with the absolute monarchy as its guide and protector. Freedom of thought and of belief, they maintained, cultivated dangerous critical habits of mind that would pervert the moral fiber and fragment the religious unity of the nation.

Exemplary of this position was Manuel Merry y Colón's proposal to purge "our History of the series of errors with which Protestantism, Philosophism, and Rationalism have tried to obscure our national glories, which, insofar as they have been great and many, have been eminently Catholic."[5] Significantly, Merry y Colón set out to do just this in a history textbook that was published in 1889. In effect, integrists like Merry y Colón sought to voice their opposition to the Restoration regime within the confines of a domain over which they, as members of the Jesuit and Dominican orders, did tend to have considerable power: the classroom.

As the dominant force in Spanish primary education, the Jesuits and Dominicans had access to the minds of the vast majority of the nation's children. What they did not have as much access to, however, were the minds of Spain's next generation of political elites, namely, its high school and university students. Accordingly, the integrists sought to achieve ideological control over the content of the national history that was taught in Restoration Spain's secondary schools. When in 1899 the neo-Catholic marqués de Pidal was named to the Ministry of Development, the Catholic integrists jumped at the opportunity to further their objectives via the very regime they opposed. To their delight, Pidal proposed a history curriculum that emphasized the classical and Christian roots of Spanish nationhood.[6] Shortly thereafter, the integrists stepped up their campaign and proposed that the state adopt a single textbook for national history. That book was to be approved by the members of the Higher Consultative Committee, who were themselves to be appointed by Pidal. By 1902, however, the Spanish Catholic integrists' campaign to ideologically dominate the instruction of national history at the secondary level had mostly been co-opted by the regime, where its objectives were left to flounder in the face of opposition from the more liberal of the two dynastic parties.[7]

The failure of the Spanish Catholic integrists to dominate national historical pedagogy at the secondary-school level did not, however, keep their views from being disseminated outside the classroom. Throughout the 1870s and 1880s, the integrist take on Spanish national history was championed by none other than the celebrated founder of "modern" Spanish philology and the author of, among other works, a monumental, three-volume, patriotic defense of the Spanish nation's essential Catholic cultural identity: Menéndez y Pelayo. Published between 1880 and 1882, Menéndez y Pelayo entitled his defense of Catholic Spain *La Historia de los heterodoxos españoles*. In this polemical study of Spanish national, literary, and intellectual history, Menéndez y Pelayo advances the idea that the Spanish nation's traditional commitment to Catholic orthodoxy is precisely what allowed it to modernize itself and civilize a good portion of Europe as well as the greater part of the Americas: "Spain, evangelizer of half the globe; Spain, hammer of heretics, light of Trent, sword of Rome, cradle of St. Ignatius . . . ; that is our greatness and our unity: we do not have any other."[8] Echoes of this jingoistic defense of Spanish Catholic national history would find their way into the Quixotist canon: first, during the 1890s, in Ganivet's celebration of Spanish Catholic mysticism and asceticism; then, during the 1910s, in Unamuno's interpretation of the Spanish nation's profoundly Catholic "tragic sense of life"; and finally, during the 1930s, in Maeztu's defense of the underlying Catholic unity of the Hispanic world.

The Spanish Catholic integrists were, however, by no means the only ideologues to vie for the minds of Restoration Spain's youth. Nor were they the only one's to exercise some degree of influence on the Quixotists of Restoration Spain. To the left of the political divide, there were the progressives who, not unlike their ultraconservative counterparts, also funneled their opposition to the Restoration regime through the educational system. Faced with the general inadequacies of the state-run school system and the expanding influence of the Spanish Catholic integrists, a group of university professors, most of them veterans of the republican politics of the Sexenio Revolucionario of 1868–1874, set out to establish an independent school. Founded in 1876 and headed by the educational reformer Francisco Giner de los Ríos (1839–1915), the Institución Libre de Enseñanza (ILE) was initially conceived as a free university, independent of all political or religious dogma.[9] It sought to instill in its students—at first at the university level, then at the secondary level, and later still at the elementary level—an appreciation for their own innate curiosity, intelligence and creativity.[10] By encouraging its students to think for themselves and by nurturing their self-confidence, the professors of the ILE aimed to develop the kind of engaged citizenry that could help the nation reform and become a full-fledged member of the European community of modern societies.

Although the ILE never enrolled more than 250 students a year, it was responsible for the formation of a new generation of thinkers who would emerge in the 1890s, achieving prominence among Spanish republican and socialist circles. Together, and in conjunction with other like-minded political allies, these graduates of the ILE constituted what was referred to at the time as the "extended Institución."[11] From 1881 on, this loose affiliation of the ILE's graduates and their political allies began to campaign for state-sponsored educational reforms during periods when the Liberal party was in power. As was the case with the Spanish Catholic integrists, much of their focus was on the content of the national history courses then being taught in Spain.

Chief among those who were associated with the "extended Institución" and seeking to construct a usable past for the Europeanization of Spain was Rafael Altamira (1866–1951). As against the traditional study of Spanish politics, warfare, and diplomacy, Altamira championed the study of the social, institutional, and cultural history of the Spanish nation. What Altamira sought was to narrate a national past that would not take the form of heroic mythology but rather that of a rationally ascertainable process of social evolution. To that end, between 1900 and 1911, Altamira published a four-volume manual titled *Historia de España y de la civilización española.* In it, he set out to debunk both the heroic myths associated with the rise of the Spanish empire as well as the antiheroic black legends associated with Spain's conquest and colonization of the Americas. The tone, throughout, was descriptive and factual. The facts, he believed, would speak for themselves, showing that, as a matter of documented and historical fact, Spain was capable of adapting to the realities of the modern world and overcoming its infamous backwardness.[12] The lesson to be learned from the development of

Spanish civilization, Altamira suggested, was that the Spanish nation could and should continue to Europeanize itself.

In addition to publishing his views on the progression and evolution of Spanish civilization, Altamira also promoted the expansion of the public school system, the modernization of the curriculum, and the transformation of both the content and methods of history teaching at all levels of instruction.[13] In 1900, a decree that was modeled after Altamira's pedagogical ideals was signed into law, thus creating the first formalized degree programs in history at selected Spanish universities. Due to a lack of qualified instructors and the preponderance of history professors who resisted modern historical methods, however, the reforms that Altamira had inspired and promoted could not but fail.[14] In the end, the attempts of the "extended Institución" to reform state-run schooling met with the same fate as had those of the Spanish Catholic integrists. By seeking to undo the balance of the Restoration's two-party, power-sharing formula, each canceled the other out and the ideologically moderate status quo prevailed.

The progressive and Europeanizing views on Spanish national history that Altamira and other members of the extended ILE put forward also found their way into the Quixotist canon. During the 1890s, at the start of his career, Unamuno argued against the decadent madness of Don Quixote—a madness that he associated with the Spanish Catholic integrist celebration of Spanish national and imperial unity and the idea that this unity had to be defended at all costs. In opposition to this imperialist madness, Unamuno affirmed the moderating sanity of Alonso el Bueno's humanism and reason. For his part Maeztu, during the first years of the 1900s, saw fit to argue for the inversion of the nation's traditional religious values, identifying Christian notions of virtue with decadence and the secular values of liberalism with regenerating vitality. Finally, during the 1920s and 1930s, Ortega challenged both the idea that Spanish national identity was essentially Catholic and that this Catholicism had led the nation to imperial glory by presenting an elitist program for regeneration that was based in the celebration of Germanic, as opposed to Latin, cultural and political vitality.

But if the power-sharing scheme of the Restoration's two dynastic parties managed to co-opt and mutually cancel out the opposing extremes of Spanish Catholic integrism and Europeanizing progressivism, within the discursive field of Quixotism, no such moderation or balance would, in the end, be struck. From Ganivet to Maeztu, and from Unamuno to Ortega, the Catholic integrist ideal of national and imperial unity would eventually take precedence over the progressive ideals of economic and political modernization. Reasons for this are admittedly complex and vary from Quixotist thinker to Quixotist thinker. Suffice to say, for now, that the preference of the Quixotists for national unity over the modernization of the state was a direct result of their understanding of decadence. For them, decadence was not as much an historical event or process as it was a moral state of being. Essentially ahistorical in their approach to Spanish national decadence, the Quixotists were concerned not only with the nation's past but also, and perhaps even more so, with its present.

FIGHTING IN THE STREETS

As can only be expected, the claims of the Restoration to embody the historical essence of the nation and institutionally represent its sovereignty were not contested only from within the classroom. Out on the streets of Spain's industrializing cities or out in the agricultural fields of the countryside, workers organized, confronted the industrial tycoons and landed gentry, and challenged the stability of the Restoration regime. They did so by producing a series of unprecedented general revolutionary strikes that were marked, if not by political success, then certainly by instances of extreme crowd violence that sent a debilitating shock wave through early twentieth-century Spanish society. Here then, were the "anarchic Sanchos" about whom Unamuno was apt to complain from 1905 onward and the "resentful, invertebrate masses" over whom Ortega agonized with paternalistic arrogance from as early as his 1914 *Meditaciones del Quijote*.

In order to understand the rise of organized class-consciousness among the working class in Spain, it should be noted that, during the Restoration, Spain's economy grew inconsistently and unevenly. At first, the economy developed steadily; industries, ranging from agriculture to mining and textiles, became more productive, and the middle classes began to save and invest their money. This period of steady economic growth (roughly 1875–1888) made for what has at times been portrayed as modern Spain's most pleasant belle époque. After the War of 1895–1898, however, the growth of the Spanish economy in previous years was dwarfed by its international debt. Then, during the Great War of 1914–1918, circumstances gave way to an economic boom of unexpected and sudden, rapacious growth. This economic expansion notwithstanding, it was during this same period that economists, politicians, and intellectuals alike came to the realization that there was no longer a single national economy in Spain but two: the industrializing economy of the northern coastal regions and the stagnant agricultural economy of the far larger and more populous interior and southern regions. Wealth abounded in Restoration Spain, but it was distributed unevenly and most inequitably. Despite its spurts of growth and timid industrialization, Spain's economy remained that of a relatively backward, semifeudal society, an "agricultural albatross," as one historian has aptly put it, with wealth concentrated in the hands of a wealthy few and the vast majority of working-class citizens left longing for a greater share in that wealth.[15]

The unequal and uneven development of the Spanish economy, its general failure to modernize, the disinterest of the ruling landed oligarchy in needed agricultural reforms, and the absence of a modern spirit of entrepreneurship: these were all factors in the rise of organized class-consciousness among the industrial and agricultural workers of Restoration Spain.[16] Indeed, if there was any single, unifying characteristic in the industrial workers' movements of early twentieth-century Spain, it was precisely the tendency of those workers to organize, to create a unified front and to syndicalize. This tendency to organize politically came in response to a growing awareness among workers that spontaneous and somewhat sporadic acts of protest and violence did less harm to the ruling class, which had all the financial and military resources at its disposal, than did organized and well-timed acts of protest based on the working class's numerical strength and potential to control the processes of production.[17]

Hence, the rise, in modern Spain, of a culture of general revolutionary strikes and the propagandistic use of sporadic acts of terrorist violence. Those chiefly responsible for these practices were the anarchosyndicalists, who caused the governments of Restoration Spain the most serious and consistent alarm—in fact, Cánovas del Castillo would be killed, in 1897, by an act of anarchist terrorism. By 1902, the anarchosyndicalists had staged their first general strike; in 1909, Barcelona lived through what came to be known as The Tragic Week, a week during which time the city fell into a state of utter chaos. By sending in troops, the government was able to pacify the city, but only after 150 people had died, another 400 had been wounded, and numerous convents, churches and small businesses had been destroyed.[18] By 1910, and largely in response to the events of 1909, a national confederation of anarchist syndicates was formed: the CNT.[19] In 1917, the leaders of the CNT, together with those of the Socialist UGT, declared a national general strike, which came to be known as the "Semana Cómica."[20] Again, in 1919, a strike by CNT workers at La Canadiense power plant effectively paralyzed the city of Barcelona and then escalated into another general strike. General strikes of this sort were called again in November and December of 1920; and yet another strike was called in 1923, on the very first day after Primo de Rivera assumed dictatorial powers. But because the anarchists of the CNT and the socialists of the UGT could not or would not cooperate, none of these strikes lasted more than a few days and their bid to impose industrial stoppage and establish a worker's utopia basically failed.[21]

The relative success of the workers' syndicates and unions inspired the formation of associations among other social groups and classes. The two most significant of these were a clandestine military syndicate called Las Juntas Militares de Defensa, which Ortega also associated with the resentment of the masses, and the republican-minded Asamblea de Parlamentarios.[22] These associations were nowhere as successful in achieving their goals, as were the anarchosyndicalists. Yet, their very existence indicates the extent to which there was no single social group or class, in Restoration Spain, that was immune to the social upheavals and economic divisions of the time. Insofar as the Quixotists shared a common class identity—they were all members of the bourgeoisie—they were no exception to this rule.

It is worth noting, in this light, that early in their careers, both Maeztu and Unamuno flirted with socialist ideology and revolutionary idealism. In both instances, it was a question of a fairly unorthodox adherence to socialist dogma. In the case of Maeztu, who in the 1890s made repeated calls for a proletarian-led revolution, his socialism was tempered by his embrace of Nietzschean individualistic vitalism.[23] In the case of Unamuno, a proud thinker who was perpetually bent on going it alone and forever impatient with any systematic program of thought that required the rigors of disciplined analysis, socialist ideology could not but prove a youthful intoxication and eventual source of frustration. More interested in the religious, spiritual and mythical aspects of Spanish national culture than in the material underpinnings of those realms of inquiry, shortly after 1894—the year in which he joined the Socialist Party—his thought turned away from the rationalization of economic and social phenomena and toward an intimate, agonic spiritualism.[24] For his part, Ortega flirted with republicanism, but his dislike of the monarchy did not necessarily translate into a liberal's love of democracy.[25] In the end, not unlike Ganivet who as early as the 1890s proposed a national dictatorship as the regenerating solution to "modern" Spain's social decadence and fragmentation, Maeztu, Unamuno, and Ortega would each, in his own way and in his own good time, embrace either dictatorship or oligarchy as the proper response to the challenge presented to Spanish national unity by the class warfare of early twentieth-century Spain. And yet, during the Restoration, it was not only class warfare that threatened to undermine Spanish national unity. That unity was also put into question by the emergence of micronationalist movements in the Basque Countries and Catalonia.

Fighting from the Periphery

In addition to generating organized forms of class consciousness among the working class, the sometimes steady, sometimes rapacious growth of the economy in Restoration Spain increased the size of the bourgeoisie. This was nowhere as evident as it was in the industrialized centers to the north: in particular, Catalonia and the Basque Countries. The growth in size, wealth, and power of the bourgeoisie led, in these industrialized pockets of Spain, to the rise of regional micronationalisms. These movements were characterized, in part, by opposition to the political, social, and economic status quo of the Restoration regime and, in part, by a sense of their own unique cultural identity, language and history, as distinguished from the Castilian-centered Spanish nation. These regional micronationalisms weakened the political structure of Restoration Spain by stressing local ties that challenged the all-pervading hold of the two dynastic parties on parliamentary life. As such, they put into question the very legitimacy of the parliament's claim to represent the Spanish nation's sovereignty.

Although Basque micronationalism did emerge during the years of the Restoration, at the time, it never went beyond a local irritant. The micronationalist movement in Catalonia, by contrast, posed a substantial, destabilizing threat to the regime of the Restoration. Its proponents had particularly intimate ties to that region's economy, often voicing economic grievances and firmly believing that Catalonia had special regional economic interests, which the central government in Madrid tended to ignore.

This movement emerged as an important political force in the 1890s. Through electoral victories in 1901, the movement was transformed into a political party, the Lliga Regionalista, whose basic resolutions were home rule for a Catalan-speaking state with offices reserved for native or nationalized Catalans. In 1913 the Lliga succeeded in creating the Mancomunidad which "united the pre-existing powers of the four [Catalan] provinces in a single body, restoring a geographical replica of the historic principality without any diminution of the sovereign powers of the Spanish nation."[26] The Mancomunidad dedicated much of its effort to reviving and protecting the Catalan language, the region's history, folklore, and cultural institutions. The Mancomunidad was not, however, an autonomous state and many Catalan nationalists on the left regarded its monarchism, its moderation and ambivalent nationalism as suspect. Thus, in 1922, a new, more radical Catalan party was formed, the Acció Catalá, which was made up mostly of younger Catalan nationalists who were prepared to commit themselves to terrorist acts in the name of Catalan separatism and nationhood.

In the summer of 1921, some twenty-three years after the so-called Disaster of 1898, Restoration Spain found itself in the throes of yet another colonial war, this time with the Moroccan guerrillas of the Rif. During the "Disaster at Annual," as it came to be known, thousands of Spanish soldiers were killed or wounded. Spanish prisoners taken by the guerrillas numbered in the thousands, a vast amount of military equipment was abandoned to the enemy, and General Férnandez Silvestre, the expedition's commanding officer, perished in ambush.[27] These events, coupled with the alarm inspired by the separatist violence of the younger Catalan nationalists, were to be the main culprits in the final collapse of parliamentary rule in Restoration Spain. Fearing the mobilization of the working classes, many of Catalonia's more moderate micronationalists, most of whom were among the well-to-do business class, heralded the military takeover in 1923 by Primo de Rivera.

On assuming dictatorial powers on September 13, 1923, Primo de Rivera proclaimed that his intention was to maintain control of the government only long enough to effect needed national reforms. Thus, not unlike the Restoration itself, his dictatorship was presented as a corrective measure necessary to restoring national order. However, the country's "national interests" invariably seemed to demand that Rivera prolong his stay in power, which he did for seven years.

Meanwhile, postwar Europe underwent a parliamentary crisis that saw the rise of comparable authoritarian regimes in several countries. Rivera's dictatorship, however, proved difficult to categorize. It still is. Because of his corporativist economic reforms, some historians have viewed him as a fascist who was inspired by Mussolini's Italy.[28] Others have viewed him as an enlightened despot.[29] Still others have depicted Rivera's dictatorship as "a regime of landowners, of order-loving people and small gentry which . . . follow[ed] a policy of pure conservatism, varied with flashes of paternalism."[30] From this latter perspective, Rivera's dictatorship was, in principle, a continuation of the regime of the Restoration, without the inconvenience of a parliamentary system. Indeed, the Constitution of 1876, not unlike the legal status of the King himself, was never abrogated by Primo de Rivera and his collaborators. It was merely suspended indefinitely for the sake of national unity.

With the rise of Primo de Rivera to dictatorial power, the Quixotists got, finally, what they and others in Spain had been calling for: a would-be regenerating dictatorship. Ganivet, who had died before the turn of the century, of course left no record of his opinion of Rivera's dictatorship. What he might have thought of it can be left only to conjecture. For his part, Unamuno, who in the early 1920s had fiercely critiqued the monarchy for its interventions in parliamentary life, became even more vehement in his criticisms of the Restoration after Primo de Rivera's golpe de estado. As a result, his tenure at the University of Salamanca was annulled; he was demoted from his Vice-Rectorship at the University; and, adding injury to insult, he was sent into exile. Ortega, on the other hand, sustained in the face of the dictatorship an ambiguous balance between shrouded criticism and silence that would mark also his position vis-à-vis the Franco regime. Finally, Maeztu, embraced the dictatorship wholeheartedly, becoming one of its most articulate defenders and its ambassador to Argentina. In order to understand the diversity of reactions that the Quixotists had to the Primo de Rivera dictatorship, the origin of the Quixotist notion of a regenerating dictatorship must be examined. That origin lies in the regenerationist movement of late nineteenth-century and early twentieth-century Spain.

FIGHTING WITHIN THE CENTER

Outside the industrialized pockets of the north, the members of the middle class in Restoration Spain were nowhere near as wealthy as their micronationalist counterparts in Catalonia. They did, however, also see in the regime's political scheme, not the source of the nation's regeneration, but rather a violation of its sovereignty. Finding themselves excluded from the political machinery of the two official dynastic parties, a group of largely middle-class intellectuals, professionals, and military officers came to dominate the extra-official discourse on decadence in Restoration Spain. Known as the regenerationists, they propounded a view of the Restoration that, not unlike the progressives of the ILE, attributed to this regime Spain's continued failure to fully modernize.

Despite the insistence with which the regime's privileged leaders portrayed life under the Restoration as a belle époque, the domestic troubles that recurrently frustrated Spain's political and economic modernization throughout the 1880s and 1890s—oligarchic corruption, uneven economic growth and class warfare, separatist regional nationalisms—led the regenerationists to write about Restoration Spain as if it were an ailing body politic and to present themselves as that body's most capable, sure-handed surgeons. In keeping with the prevailing positivism of their time, regenerationists such as the geologist and paleontologist Lucas Mallada (1841–1921), the political reformer, lawyer, and historian Joaquín Costa (1844–1911), the geographer, psychologist, and novelist Ricardo Macías Picavea (1847–1899), the ecclesiastic-turned-political philosopher Damián Isern (1852–1914), the editor and journalist Luís Morote (1862–1913) and the military General and essayist Ricardo Burguete y Lana (1871–1938) wrote comprehensive clinical analyses of the ailments they perceived to be troubling Spain. Their treatises were replete with diagnoses, prognoses and the therapeutic programs that they deemed necessary for regenerating Spain.

The development of regenerationism followed the course of an intellectually based reform movement that later transformed itself first, into a nationalist political reform party, second, into an attempt to reform Restoration Spain's political system from within, and third, into an outright justification for a national revolution from above. Despite its various transmutations, regenerationism never truly succeeded in its bid to reform the Restoration regime. It did, however, have a lasting influence on the intellectual culture of Restoration Spain, laying the ideological groundwork for Primo de Rivera's dictatorship and preparing the way for the Quixotists of Restoration Spain to do the same for Franco's fascist regime.

As an intellectual movement, regenerationism had its origins in the mixture of Krausism and positivism espoused by the professors of the ILE, most notably Francisco Giner de los Ríos. From Krausism, the regenerationists derived a post-Kantian idealism; from positivism, an investigative methodology of observation. The end result of this mix was an inductive metaphysics that appealed, for supporting evidence, to experimental science. This dual perspective led the regenerationists to view Spain both as a geopolitical entity and a metaphysical agent. Spain, for the regenerationists, thus constituted an organic whole. Accordingly, they perceived decadence as a threat to the overall vitality of the nation.

Prior to Spain's loss of empire in 1898, this organicist view of the nation and its decadence led the regenerationists to propose concrete educational, agrarian, and political reforms. A survey of the titles under which the regenerationists published their ideas for reform during the 1880s and early 1890s is illustrative in this respect.[31] After the final collapse of the Spanish empire—an event that the regenerationists framed as "The National Disaster" and "Disgrace" of Spain—the focus of the regenerationist critique of decadence shifted away from concrete problems of reform and toward a more general attempt at explaining the reasons behind Spain's imperial decline. Representative of this post-Disaster perspective are Picavea's 1899 *El problema nacional,* Isern's 1899 *Del desastre nacional y sus causas,* Morote's 1900 *La moral de la derrota* and Joaquín Costa's highly influential critique of the Restoration government *Oligarquía y caciquismo,* published in 1901. These and other similarly focused treatises on modern Spanish decadence were widely read and helped to convert the term "regeneration" into a catchword for national reform. In turn, this helped the regenerationists attain a level of visibility they had never before enjoyed.

Spain's loss of empire enabled the regenerationists to crystallize as a public intellectual movement and, thus, to begin exploring political avenues for their programs of reform. From as early as 1898, Joaquín Costa, who was one of the leading figures among the regenerationists, had been pushing for the formation of a national party capable of remedying the country's continued political and economic troubles. By establishing the Cámara Agrícola de Alto Aragón, first regionally and then nationally, he had sought to organize the small farmers and merchants who had fared so badly in Restoration Spain's slowly modernizing economy; but these efforts were met with mixed results. Eventually, Costa joined forces with two other men: Santiago Alba, an agrarianist, and Basilio Paraíso, the regenerationist leader of the Liga Nacional de Productores, an assembly representing small to medium-size business interests. Together, they founded the Unión Nacional. Although backed by considerable popular support, the Unión Nacional failed to consolidate its political base, because it could offer no coherent mandate or program of action for its middle-class constituents. The party was itself politically divided; hence, the activities of the Unión Nacional were largely limited to those of a lobby.[32]

On the whole, then, Costa's political brand of regenerationism was a failed attempt by a relatively small pack of middle-class intellectuals and businessmen to consolidate the interests of the "productive masses."[33]

For its part, the regenerationist government of Francisco Silvela, which was established shortly after the events of 1898, also failed in its effort to reform Spain's political and economic reality. Silvela's reform of the Restoration system was essentially an attempt to co-opt Costa's political regenerationism and, consequently, to regenerate the nation from within the two-party political system of the Restoration. In 1897, following the assassination of Cánovas by an anarchist, Silvela rose to power as President of the Conservative Party. He then served as Prime Minister from March 1899 to October 1900. His government introduced various electoral reforms designed to limit the power of the "caciques," or local political bosses, and passed a number of new laws intended to protect workers, especially women and children. Although there were plans in place for other more extensive reforms, especially in the agrarian sector, these were never realized. After the War of 1895–1898, the Spanish government was running a deficit; of the 750 million pesetas it generated each year, 400 million went to pay the public debt.[34] Consequently, Silvela's government was forced to raise taxes, a move that prompted widespread protests among the working class and even the rank and file of Costa's Unión Nacional. In reaction to this open resistance to his programs for national regeneration, Silvela became so profoundly frustrated that he resigned his office and permanently withdrew from political life.

Silvela's withdrawal from politics did not, however, spell the end of the "revolution from within" that had been instituted by his regenerationist government. His successor as the leader of the Conservative Party, Antonio Maura (1853–1925), would also pursue this strategy while in government. His tenure as Spain's would-be political regenerator—he was in office from 1907 to 1909—was marred, however, by the repeated revolutionary strikes and terrorist tactics that Spain's growing number of unionized socialists and anarchosyndicalists used in an effort to break down the restricted power-sharing formula of the Restoration regime. Tensions between the working class and Maura's autocratic regenerationist policies mounted when the government, facing the rebellion of local tribes in Spain's Moroccan possessions, called up the military reservists, many of whom were members of the working class. The result was Barcelona's "Semana Trágica." Following those troubled events, Maura was forced to resign from office.

Notwithstanding the failures of Silvela and Maura, there remained among Spain's ruling class, and especially among the military, those who were eager to see another regenerationist government established. They would have to wait for the authoritarian rule of Primo de Rivera (1923–1931) in order to see their wish come true. Even under Rivera's leadership, which included recurring attempts at regenerating the Spanish economy and modernizing the infrastructure of the country, the social, regional, and economic crises of Restoration Spain could not be dispatched. Consequently, regenerationism under Primo de Rivera ultimately failed as well, resulting in the final demise of the Restoration and, in 1931, the establishment of the Second Republic.[35]

These failures within the political domain of statecraft notwithstanding, regenerationism achieved considerable success within the cultural domain of nationalist discourse. This success can be explained, in large measure, by reason of the rhetorical force and appeal of the regenerationist critique of the Restoration. Regenerationism matched the simplicity of the two-party political system with an equally simple rhetoric of decadence and regeneration. In this regard, regenerationism was truly a product of the Restoration. Its most succinct, eloquent and influential spokesman was Costa, who, in his 1901 *Oligarquía y caciquismo,* provided a stinging critique of the Restoration's political, two-party, power-sharing formula and its relation to the nation's enduring decadence.

Fighting from Above

Costa's basic complaint, maintained throughout *Oligarquía y caciquismo,* was that under Canovas' power-sharing system the Spanish nation would never be able to enjoy sovereignty because all governance effectively remained in the hands of a corrupt oligarchy and the local political bosses who enforced the oligarchs' commands. Costa's critique of the Restoration regime thus focused, initially, on that regime's institutionalized cosovereigns: the monarchy and the parliament. He argued that all of nineteenth-century Spanish political history constituted a national struggle for sovereignty against the monarchy. In this sense, he mentioned the failures of both the 1812 Cortes of Cadiz and "La Gloriosa" of 1868 to fully achieve national sovereignty: "Liberty had been inscribed on paper, yes, but it was never incarnated."[36] With the constitution of 1876—or Cánovas' system—Costa maintained that the Spanish people's struggle for liberty had been set back even further and that the nation had been erroneously linked back to the crown as if the entire revolutionary struggle of the nineteenth century had never come to pass. The point of his analysis was to demonstrate how neither the monarchy nor the parliament of Restoration Spain were truly representative of the nation's sovereignty, because that sovereignty had actually been transferred into the hands of what Costa regarded as an "oligarchy without any base in public opinion and no power other than a purely material one."[37]

Costa defined this ruling oligarchy by stressing the idea that those in power in Restoration Spain were not a "natural aristocracy" but the degenerate form of such an elite, an oligarchy. A truly aristocratic government would have in mind the interests of the nation as a whole; by contrast, Costa sustained that the oligarchy in power in Restoration Spain was only interested in furthering its own self-interests. National sovereignty in Restoration Spain, alleged Costa, had been lost to the arbitrary authoritarianism of a corrupt aristocracy.

With regard to the two dynastic parties of the Cánovas's system, Costa was no less intense in his critique. He claimed, first of all, that there were no true parties in Spain, only the ruling oligarchy and the *caciques* who served its interests. With regard to the role and presence of *caciques* in modern Spanish political life, Costa linked them to the decline of the nation and to what he perceived as its modern decadence: "The nation continues to live without laws, without guarantees, without tribunal, subject to the same degrading dominance of that inorganic feudalism, which keeps Spain separated from Europe by the distance of an entire historical era."[38] As against the "natural" authority of intelligence and virtue, Restoration Spain was governed, according to Costa, on the basis of the brute force of the *caciques*.

Hence, reasoned Costa, the need to do away with the reigning oligarchy and the *caciquismo* attendant to it. The recuperation of the nation's sovereignty, he sustained, needed to take the form of "a revision of the revolutionary movement of 1868."[39] Notwithstanding the populism and republicanism inherent in Costa's call for a revision of the revolutionary movement of 1868, his reconstruction of that movement did not lead to the goal of reestablishing a liberal democracy in Spain. Instead, it led to the implantation of an aristocratic regime run by true moral and intellectual elites, and not the official elites of Cánovas' corrupt system. "Aristocracy, understood in its Aristotelian sense," asserted Costa, "would be legitimate in our country; what is more, one can feel the vital need for it."[40]

It is by means of remarks such as this, or the call that Costa makes for a regenerating iron surgeon capable of single-handedly curing the nation of its ailments, that Costa began to reveal a darker side to his regenerationism: "That surgical policy," affirmed Costa, "has to be entrusted to an iron surgeon, one who is capable of governing the nation's anatomy and will feel infinite compassion for it."[41] Here, Costa did not place the task of regenerating the nation's sovereignty in the hands of the Spanish masses; nor was it really placed in those of an able aristocracy. It was entrusted, rather, to a regenerating dictator (significantly, when in 1923 Primo de Rivera declared himself the dictator of Restoration Spain, he justified his golpe de estado, in part, by evoking Joaquín Costa's call for a curative iron surgeon).[42]

In this darker sense, Costa's regenerationism constituted an elitist program of dominance not unlike that of the Restoration system, under Cánovas, that it purported to critique. Costa cited, as a form of moral and intellectual corruption and official hypocrisy, the way in which Cánovas' unspoken, oligarchic elitism made a mockery of liberal democracy and the civil society attendant to it. Yet, in its place, he did not propose a culture of liberal values. He rather posited an honestly authoritarian social and political order under a sincere form of elitism that imparted transformative values from above. For Costa, dictatorial iron surgery was the only efficient way to eradicate the political corruption of the Restoration system and establish a true social, moral and cultural order that could then be handed down to the people.[43]

Fighting for Madness

From the death of Costa in 1911 and on into the 1930s, thinkers ranging from Azorín, Unamuno, Maeztu, and Ortega to the fascist Giménez Caballero acknowledged their intellectual debt to Costa and paid homage to the example of his elitist project for regenerating the nation.[44] Indeed, despite his failures as the political leader of the regenerationist national party Unión Nacional, Joaquín Costa did succeed in popularizing the idea of a regenerating national dictatorship. As interpreted and used by the Quixotists, Costa's elitist formula for national regeneration—or what Tierno Galván calls *costismo*—would lose much of its political underpinnings and acquire a more fanciful, literary quality.[45] They would replace Costa's curative and regenerating iron surgeon with their own spiritually regenerating Don Quixote. What is more, the Quixotists would not limit the scope of this doctrine of regenerating elitism to the modern Spanish nation alone. They would use it in an attempt to justify the spiritual reconquest and cultural recolonization by the Spanish nation of its ex-colonies.

Toward the end of his life, even Costa came under the influence of this Quixotist interpretation of his call for a regenerating national dictatorship. He abandoned the clinical rhetoric of regenerationism and its iron surgery and embraced, indeed endorsed, the fanciful neo-imperialist imagination of Quixotism: "in order to maintain the moral equilibrium of the infinite game of history, humanity needs to oppose the Anglo-Saxon race with a great and powerful Spanish race: the greatness and vastness of the Earth would not be matched by human greatness if, beside the British Sancho [Robinson Crusoe], the pure, luminous, and idealistic Spanish Quixote were not to rise up, filling the world with his acts of madness, affirming across the centuries the utopia of the Golden Age, and maintaining intact, down here on Earth, that spiritual knight-errantry that leads us to believe in something, feel passion for something, sacrifice ourselves for something and, by virtue of that passion, that faith and that sacrifice, assures us all that the world can yet be something more than a factory and a marketplace where everything is bought and sold."[46]

Here, Costa recuperates the figure of Don Quixote as an emblem for the ascetic and self-sacrificing discipline of a regenerating national morality. Moreover, he pits this imagined spiritual power of the Spanish nation against the evident economic force of the modernizing, technological, Anglo-Saxon world. Ideally, Costa's Don Quixote should sally forth and, by means of his enthusiastic idealism, spiritually and morally conquer Robinson Crusoe. At work in this idealized vision of Don Quixote's eventual victory over Robinson Crusoe is the same imaginative denial of Spain's loss of empire and neo-imperialist desire that motivates the Quixotism of Ganivet, Unamuno, Maeztu, and Ortega.

The regenerative ideal of a nation-defining and empire-building dictatorship was not all that the Quixotists shared with Costa. The visionary wealth of Joaquín Costa's critique of Restoration Spain's decadence also encouraged the Quixotists to adopt the regenerationists' organicist conception of the nation and, thus, to view decadence as a kind of disease. But unlike the regenerationists, who viewed the national organism in anatomical terms, the Quixotists understood the Spanish nation as an essentially metaphysical entity and its decadence, therefore, as a moral, spiritual malady.

The beginnings of this Quixotist construction of Spain as a metaphysical and moral agency can be found in the organicist rhetoric of regenerationist essays, such as Mallada's 1890 *Los males de la patria,* where Spain is portrayed as an indisoluble whole. "[The nation's troubles]," writes Mallada, "may very well stem from its geographic latitude . . . our long-standing record of civil discord is no doubt another influence, as is also . . . the poverty of our soil; but everyone is familiar already with our renowned laziness, our outrageous indolence, our tremendous apathy."[47] As Mallada here portrays Spanish decadence, it is not merely an external, corporeal phenomenon. Mallada's Spanish body politic also suffers from apathy, laziness, even indolence. At issue, for this representative regenerationist thinker, is Spain's national character, its inner and psychological lack of vitality, as much as its outer, political and economic ailments.

This holistic view of the nation, of its land and of its people that was fashioned in regenerationist essays such as Mallada's contributed substantially to the formation of the Quixotist "Myth of Castile." According to this myth, Castile—the land of Don Quixote, of monstrous windmills and of the valiant knight's beloved Dulcinea del Toboso—was viewed as the heartland of the Spanish nation and of the overseas empire that Spaniards, under the spiritual leadership of the Quixotists, were to conquer and colonize once again.

One famous, if not infamous, expression of this Castilian myth can be found in Unamuno's 1895 *En torno al casticismo,* where this quintessential Quixotist develops the notion of the Spanish nation's essential identity on the basis of a dialectical relationship between Castile and Spain: "whereas Castile formed the Spanish nation, the nation has increasingly hispanicized Castile."[48] Here, Unamuno affirms Castile's landscape as symbolic of Spain's national identity. Castile-Spain is, for Unamuno, "a uniform and monotonous landscape . . . over which the intense blue of the sky extends itself."[49] This idealized national landscape inspires a religious sense of humility: "this infinite countryside, in which man is humbled without losing himself and in which he feels a spiritual dryness comparable to that of the land, is, not so much a pantheistic landscape, but a monotheistic one."[50] Castilian monotheism, in turn, gives rise to "a vulgar, rudimentary realism and a dry, formulaic idealism that march together, associated, like Don Quixote and Sancho."[51] Unamuno's construction of an essential, eternal Spanish national identity is consequently linked to Castile, the Castilian language, Christian monotheism and the figure of Don Quixote.

Similarly, in *La ruta de Don Quijote,* published in 1905, Azorín confuses the landscape and people of modern Castile with the historical and moral, empire-building character of the conquistadors: "Is this not the birthplace of the great wills, strong, powerful, tremendous, but solitary and anarchic of the adventurers, navigators and conquistadors?"[52] Just as Unamuno's version of the Myth of Castile is dedicated to the construction of an essentially Castilian Spanish national identity that is to be equally imposed upon Spain's culturally diverse regions, so Azorín's formulation of the myth is intended as a genealogy for the conquering and civilizing spirit of a heroic nation of warriors. Together, they make for a national identity that is simultaneously religious and bellicose. Both this literary construction of Castile as the spiritual center of an "Hispanic" cultural empire and the enthusiastic recuperation of the figure of Don Quixote as an emblem for the heroic regeneration of the nation, are based on a fanciful vision of the nation that is akin to the idealism inherent in Mallada's and other regenerationists' views of Spain as an organic and willful whole.

By inserting the figure of Don Quixote into the clinical discourse fashioned by the regenerationists, the Quixotists managed to shift the focus of the debate on decadence from bodily illness to madness. In effect, the Quixotists transformed the rhetorically constructed surgical ward of the regenerationists into a madhouse. Only, from the outset, it was never exactly clear who the Quixotists believed to be mad and most in need of therapy: the leaders of Restoration Spain or their critics? And among these, who was maddest? The regenerationists, the Spanish Catholic integrists, the progressives of the ILE, the anarchosyndicalists, or the micronationalists? The gesture by means of which the Quixotists inserted Don Quixote into the ongoing debate on decadence and sought to unsettle its binary and factional oppositions was, clearly, not without irony. If any one figure from Spain's real or imagined past(s) qualified as the prototype of the nation's would-be saviors, it was Don Quixote.

In his *Quixote,* Cervantes presents his readers with an image of an overly zealous and credulous reader of chivalric romances—the hidalgo Alonso Quijano, who takes it on himself to single-handedly restore to the modernizing Spain of the early seventeenth century the aristocratic and chivalric values he believes it has lost. Meaning to regenerate Spain from its ensuing modern decadence, this enthusiastic reader decides to abandon his readerly life and instead "author" his own adventures as a knight-errant. After thus arrogating the author's authority, he renames himself Don Quixote and sets off on his quest to realize his imagined destiny as the chivalric regenerator of a morally declining and socially modernizing Spain. In the end, Don Quixote fails to accomplish this monumental task: he does not transform the changing Spain of his time with his acts of chivalry; the boorish Spain of the Sansón Carrascos defeats him.

Don Quixote's failure in the realm of practice is nevertheless rendered ambiguous by his success in the imaginative realm. Don Quixote repeatedly imagines his physical defeats as moral victories. Moreover, he convinces others to share in his imaginative version of events. Some, like the Priest and the Barber, do so in an attempt to bring him back to his senses. Others, like Don Quixote's squire Sancho Panza, do so hoping to further their own interests as well as those of Don Quixote. Still others, like Sansón Carrasco, do so out of a seeming desire for vengeance. Finally, there are those who partake of Don Quixote's imaginative version of reality in order mostly to amuse themselves. Such is the case, for instance, with the Duke and Duchess. They amuse themselves, however, at the expense of Don Quixote, humiliating him morally with their pretended respect for his chivalric enterprise and confining him physically in their castle. In effect, their putatively "playful" games frustrate Don Quixote's efforts to present himself as the noble regenerator of a modernizing and decadent Spain. In Cervantes' *Don Quixote,* it is not clear who are the real decadents, the real madmen and fools; everybody and nobody is at once revealed to be subject to—as well as the subject of—madness. Moreover, and perhaps more important still, it is never made clear in Cervantes' *Don Quixote* whether madness is a decadent force or a regenerative one.

A similar ambivalence is at work in how the Quixotists incorporated Don Quixote's contagious madness into the ongoing national debate on decadence. They used Don Quixote's madness as an image of the modern nation's decadence as well as of various potentially regenerative responses to it. In part, Unamuno, Ganivet, Maeztu, and Ortega used the figure of Don Quixote to suggest that Spain's decadence was not merely the result of some bodily ailment—a stagnant economy, for instance, or a corrupt political regime, but that it stemmed from a far more fundamental psychological and moral disorder. At issue, for Unamuno and Maeztu, for instance, was what they perceived as the modern Spanish nation's increasing dissociative tendencies, an abnormal propensity to fracture the cultural, religious, and moral foundation that had traditionally served to unite the nation. In this, Unamuno and Maeztu took up a position with regard to the Restoration that was not unlike that of the Spanish Catholic integrists. But it was also not unlike Don Quixote's position vis-à-vis the perceived decadence of his immediate, modernizing world. How, then, is one to interpret their position? Did they genuinely hold to the views of Spanish Catholic integrism, or did they, by associating that position with a form of quixotic madness, mean to ridicule the integrist position? It is only on the basis of a close reading of their Quixotist works—a task I undertake in parts II and III of this book—that one can arrive at a convincing answer to these mutable questions. My purpose here is more simply to point out the ambivalence and its potentially unsettling, paradoxical nature.

To that end, it should also be noted that the Quixotists used the figure of Don Quixote to suggest that the anarchosyndicalists and the regenerationists were foolish for attempting to reform the regime of the Restoration by engaging it in a windmill-like battle that had to be fought on the regime's own political terms. For Ganivet, Unamuno, and Maeztu, Spain's regeneration had much less to do with the practicalities of modern statecraft than with the recuperation of the national values that had, ostensibly, once made it great—linguistic and cultural unity, social and political hierarchy, and a militant, empire-building brand of Catholicism. In this, these Quixotists took up a position with regard to the anarchosyndicalists and regenerationists that was not unlike that of the Duke and Duchess vis-à-vis Don Quixote. Their battles against the regime of the Restoration became a source of amusement to the Quixotists.

Consider, in this vein, what Unamuno writes in his 1905 *Vida de don Quixote y Sancho:* "Our Sanchos of today," he declares, "are looking for what they call concrete solutions . . . Concrete solutions! Oh you practical Sanchos, you positivist Sanchos, you materialist Sanchos! When will you hear the silent music of the spiritual spheres? . . . Our country will have neither agriculture, nor industry nor commerce, nor will it contain any roads that lead to a worthwhile destination until we discover our Christianity, a quixotist Christianity."[53] It is sheer regenerationist folly, Unamuno suggests, to believe that without first undertaking to spiritually transform the modern Spanish nation, Spain will ever overcome its decadence. The problem with modern Spain, Unamuno contends, is not that it has yet to fully modernize its political and economic institutions—its lack of progress; it is, rather, that it has lost its way in the labyrinth that is modernity and embraced the promise of progress. "Perhaps disease itself is the essential condition of what we call progress," writes Unamuno in this regard, "and progress itself a disease."[54]

This amused and condescending attitude toward the masses and their hunger for progress could also become, for instance in the Quixotist works of

Ortega, an outright desire to castigate, discipline, and humiliate the masses. Thus Ortega, who consistently argued for the so-called "Europeanization" and modernization of the Spanish nation, could portray with singular contempt any attempt by the masses to govern themselves: "people who, by reason of the perversion of their ability to love, decide to hate every individual that is exemplary for the simple reason that he is superior to them, and who, despite their being vulgar and nothing better than a mass, believe that they can do without guidance and govern themselves in their thinking and in their politics, in their morality and in their tastes, will inevitably cause their own degeneration. To my mind, Spain is a lamentable example of just that perversion."[55] Clearly, for Ortega, the idea that the masses should even aspire to self-governance is sheer folly. They have only one role to play in the modernization and eventual Europeanization of Restoration Spain: they must abandon all attempts to govern themselves and to rule the nation, abandon all claims to sovereignty and to self-determination, and lovingly submit themselves to the guidance and direction of those who, like Ortega, purport to know what is best for them and Spain.

By thus portraying both the leaders of the Restoration and its critics as mad, the Quixotists, in effect, *Quixotized* the national debate on decadence and regeneration. In doing so, they not only reconfigured the terms of the debate but also came to dominate and redirect its focus. Whereas prior to their interventions the debate had centered largely on the issue of the modern nation's sovereignty and its relationship to the Restoration regime, after their initial interventions the focus shifted away from the political arena and toward that domain of Spanish life over which the Quixotists held considerable sway: literary culture.

The strength of their position in this realm was twofold. On the one hand, the Quixotists presented themselves as the nation's most capable exegetes of the *Quixote*. As such, they could claim, better than anyone else, to be able to make sense of the madness of Don Quixote. It was on the basis of this claim that both Maeztu, who in the 1890s took Cervantes' *Quixote* to be a decadent novel, and Unamuno, who during the same period portrayed Don Quixote as a decadent madman, presented themselves as the nation's most capable therapists. Following the events of 1898, however, the Quixotists abandoned this position. Rather than help the nation recover its sanity, they now sought to persuade the nation that its apparent madness, its decadence, was in fact what was most true, most beautiful, and most powerful about Spain. In other words, they stopped speaking about Don Quixote and actually began to interpret him, to act like him, be him. As such, they proposed to lead the modern Spanish nation, not toward the safety of political stability, nor toward the magnificence of modern progress, but toward the imagined recuperation of Spain's lost empire.

Perhaps it was sheer madness to imagine that, in the modern world, the Spanish nation could once again rise to some form of imperial glory, even if just within the cultural realm; but this was no less mad, alleged the Quixotists, than the desire of the ruling class to secure a lasting political stability at whatever the cost to the nation's sovereignty or the enthusiasm that progressives and regenerationists showed for modernizing reforms, even though these reforms would turn the nation into a mirror image of the very same modernized, democratic and technologically advanced people who had defeated Spain and stripped it of its few remaining colonies. Honor and pride, narcissism and jingoism: these are the self-gratifying, entrenched and defiant terms to which the Quixotists, in a fit of Quixotist madness, reduced their Quixotism.

By incorporating the figure of Don Quixote into the regenerationist critique of modern Spain's decadence and treating this figure as representative of Spain's eternal, spiritual and civilizing values, the Quixotists disseminated a discourse of regenerative madness. In part, this involved the delusional madness of imagining away modern Spain's loss of empire. It also involved the madness of justifying ascetic discipline and self-sacrificing punishment as spiritually purifying and regenerating acts. Finally, it involved the madness of preferring mass obedience of a national dictatorship to individual self-government in civil society. But it would, of course, be left to the fascist ideologues of Franco's regime to see to it that these delusional, ascetic, and self-denying forms of Quixotist madness took on the form of still another sort of madness altogether: the angry madness of violent national purification that sparked the Spanish Civil War of 1936–1939 and that then became the hallmark of political and intellectual culture in Spain under Franco.

2

Quixotist Imagination

In their bid to redefine the national debate on decadence, the Quixotists of Restoration Spain seized on the figure of Don Quixote; they drew attention to the protean nature of this figure's madness; and, treating that madness with studied ambiguity, they offered a unique interpretation of the nation's modern decadence and provided an imaginative program for its regeneration. By inserting madness into the debate on decadence, the Quixotists portrayed this debate as if it were in itself symptomatic of the nation's decadent divisiveness and essential lack of unity. They depicted the various factions that were involved in that debate—the Catholic integrists, the progressives, the anarchists, and the micronationalists—as distinct manifestations of the nation's decadent madness. In doing so, however, the Quixotists also highlighted the nation's potential unity in madness. Ganivet, Unamuno, Maeztu, and Ortega located the life of the modern Spanish nation between two forms of madness: on the one hand, the decadent madness of fragmenting chaos; on the other, the regenerating madness of a will to unifying form.

In effect, Quixotist literature seeks to cure the Spanish nation of its decadent madness while simultaneously affirming the nation's regenerating madness. It opposes, as a form of decadence, the impulse to remember all those events that led to the nation's decline from empire. Conversely, it asserts, as a form of regeneration, the impulse to forget those very same events and imagine an alternative history. Deeply concerned with the dynamics of remembering and forgetting, Quixotist literature is conjectural in spirit. It is, in part, a negation of historical experience and, in part, an affirmation of an essential, ahistorical being. As such, Quixotist literature narratively constructs the variously stoic, mystical, messianic, and tragic Don Quixote that Ganivet, Unamuno, Maeztu, and Ortega imagine into existence.

Insofar as this attempt to imaginatively fashion an ideal national history and identity is carried out in the face of a political, economic, and social reality that is perceived as decadent, the Quixotist literature of Restoration Spain belongs, above all, to the modern essayist tradition. As an *essai* or attempt, Quixotist literature is primarily driven by a haphazard, albeit powerfully creative and polemical, impetus toward imaginative experimentation. In line with Hobsbawm's notion of invented traditions for emerging nationalisms, Quixotist literature should be viewed not only as a means for imagining possible new forms of Spanish national identity, but also as a means for formalizing and ritualizing those same forms of identity.[1] As an essay on national cultural and spiritual transformation, Quixotist literature interprets and acts out an ideal synthesis of the modern Spanish nation's peculiar dialectic of remembering and forgetting.

By concentrating their interpretative efforts on an ideal national history, the Quixotists in effect sought to withdraw the nation from the modern world or, at the very least, to make it participate within that world as the elect instrument of a transcendental will. This ascetically motivated desire to withdraw the nation from the modern world is evident in the Quixotists's penchant for fictionalizing Spain's national history—a history that they model after the adventures narrated in the *Quixote*. For Ganivet, Unamuno, Maeztu, and Ortega, Cervantes' *Quixote* embodies a closed, fixed, and unchanging Spanish national history. In order for this preestablished textual history to be properly understood, however, the Quixotists reason that it must be interpreted. In this regard, Quixotist essays constitute a hermeneutic enterprise. Accordingly, the Quixotists present themselves in their essays as the Spanish nation's message-bringers. They do not, however, purport to analyze and assess the *Quixote* only or even primarily as literature, but to understand and reveal its hidden spiritual meanings. By thus interpreting the *Quixote* as an ideal and timeless totality, the Quixotists presume to uncover the Spanish nation's essential, eternal identity: its "true" history.

And yet, the Quixotist essays of Ganivet, Unamuno, Maeztu, and Ortega are interpretative in another sense as well. Insofar as these essays represent a strategy for intervening in the ongoing cultural and political debates of Restoartion Spain, there is a certain theatrical quality to them; they are, as one would say in Spanish, "interpretaciones de un papél," a sort of acting-out or staging of an assumed identity. Thus, from the works of Ganivet and Unamuno to those of Maezu and Ortega, the Quixotists of Restoration Spain portray themselves not only as the decadent nation's message-bearers but also as its regenerating Quixotes. In effect, they present themselves as a band of would-be Quixotes that is everywhere surrounded by an anonymous crowd of hostile, licentious, and anarchic Sanchos. By doing so, the Quixotists dramatize their moral critique of Spanish national decadence and its attending opposition between regenerating elites and decadent masses.

In the figure of Don Quixote, the Quixotists discover an example of how best to frame their promises of elitist national regeneration. Because Don Quixote is unhappy with the decadent Spain of his own time, he, who is either unwilling or unable to distinguish history from fiction, convinces himself that only by imitating the heroes of chivalric romances will he be able to bring about the regeneration of the society and recuperate its Golden Age. The Quixotists, thus, see in Don Quixote an exemplary will to adopt a life of ascetic discipline in order better to realize, in the future, the ideals of the past. In other words, the Quixotists appeal to the example of Don Quixote in order to argue that for the decadent Spanish nation of their own modern era to regenerate and recuperate its conquering and imperial ideal national identity, its members must first transform themselves spiritually by means of ascetic self-discipline. In this way, the Quixotist flight from the world and from history is meant to prepare the way for the nation's eventual participation in the modern world as that world's spiritual guide and redeemer.

The Quixotist Critique of Decadence

Based, as it is, in a negative historical consciousness, Quixotism denies the need for any examination of decadence in the historical context of the modern nation. It is precisely this otherworldly ascetic idealism that distinguishes the Quixotist critique of decadence from those that were put forth by Restoration Spain's Catholic integrists, progressives, micronationalists, and regenerationists. At the turn of the century, of course, Restoration Spain was not the only place where decadence was a heated topic of debate. Elsewhere in Europe, intellectuals theorized decadence and imagined possible means for regeneration. What distinguishes the Quixotist critique of decadence from these other aesthetic, sociological and genealogical critiques of decadence is its emphasis on otherworldly ascetic idealism.

In this regard, Quixotism is not a Spanish equivalent of French or British decadentism (Mallarmé, Wilde et al.). This is not to suggest, however, that Quixotism shares none of decadentism's aesthetic concerns. The Quixotist experimentation with literary form and style, as in Unamuno's invention of the so-called *nivola* or Ganivet's parody of colonial chronicles; the cultivation of the essay as a transformative genre, including the attempt to elevate the essay to a place of national literary importance; or the ambiguous affirmation and rejection of the vanguard by Quixotist thinkers such as Ortega: all attest to a concern, among the Quixotists of Restoration Spain, for the aesthetics of a modern, national Spanish identity. Yet, the Quixotists view the cultivation of decadentist and vanguard aestheticism as a sign of moral effeteness and exhaustion, even of hedonism, and not as an expression of the ascetic discipline required of those who would morally regenerate the modern Spanish nation. As the editors of *Vida Nueva* put it in 1898, aestheticism is to be considered a disease: "a form of leprosy that only stains the paper on which its name is inscribed."[2] Similarly, Ortega y Gasset, writing in 1911, sustains that: "Decadentism, the art of falling down, is fatal for those who, like ourselves, fear they have already fallen."[3]

Moreover, the Quixotists are not interested in presenting themselves as dandies who brandish their wayward literary and ethical mores in the face of a hostile, orthodox, bourgeois society; they rather prefer to present themselves as the leaders and task-masters of a spiritually wayward flock or nation: witness, as an anecdote, Unamuno's studied attire, which gave him the appearance of a Protestant minister. In the place of hedonism and the, to them, artificial cultivation of artistic sensibility, Quixotists cultivate spiritual and moral heroism. This is especially evident in the way that the Quixotists mythologize Spanish national history by using the Quixote figure to symbolize what they take to be the essentially ascetic and mystical character of the nation.

To clarify further, the Quixotist critique of modern decadence is similar, in some respects, to the sociological critique of modern decadence as developed by Simmel, Tönnies, Weber, or Spengler. Both types of critique point to modernity as a force encouraging social fragmentation; both see the exercise of abstract reasoning as responsible for the apparent loss of communal unity in modern, industrialized societies; both associate this loss with the competing interests of civil society; and both see in traditional, agrarian societies something akin to a Paradise Lost (Unamuno's celebration of the Spanish nation's traditionally agrarian way of life or Tönnies's *Gemeinschaft* are exemplary in this regard); and both types of critique decry the modern breakdown of traditional communal values.

These similarities notwithstanding, the Quixotist critique of modern decadence is not a sociological treatment of civilization and its discontents. Whereas a sociological critique would be based on the pretense of objective authority and present its theorization of decadence as inductively derived from the study of empirical phenomena, the Quixotist critique is based on the pretense of a charismatic or revelatory authority and presents its knowledge of decadence as deductively derived from the mysterious disclosure of a transcendental moral truth or will. Hence, it is worth considering, in turn: Unamuno's notion of "intrahistoria" as the eternally present source of an ideal national identity;[4] Ganivet's notion that Spain's ideal national identity has its source in a "mother force, something strong and indestructible, like a diamond" that is revealed by the mystery surrounding the Catholic dogma of the

Immaculate Conception;[5] Maeztu's invocation of a divinely revealed historical national mission as the ideal against which to measure decadence: "Those nations that have already attained universal value must feed off their own historical current. It is the path that God designates. Beyond it, there is nothing but error";[6] or Ortega's appeal to the inherent lack of an aristocratic social instinct according to his definition of Spanish decadence as a "radical perversion of social instinct."[7]

The Quixotist critique of decadence, as against a sociological theorization of the same, is primarily motivated by a moral conception of historical reality. Unamuno's critique of the modern European cult of science makes this readily ascertainable: "I should confess," writes Unmauno, "that the more I think about it, the more I realize just how profound my revulsion is for all the accepted guiding principles of modern Europe, for the scientific orthodoxy of today, for its methods, for its tendencies . . . Science . . . seeks the means to prolong, increase, facilitate, broaden, and make life more agreeable . . . [it seeks] happiness."[8] As opposed to this scientific ataraxia—this tranquil, self-certain, and involuntary contentment with the progress of life's little felicities—Unamuno posits the ecstasy of mystical wisdom, the voluntary discipline of ascetic negation and creative, passional love. "With the discovery of America and our becoming embroiled in the business of Europe, we found ourselves suddenly dragged along by the current of other nations. The powerful current of the Renaissance entered Spain, and it began to erase our medieval soul. And the Renaissance was just that: science . . . and life. And we came to think less about death, and our mystical wisdom began to dissipate."[9] Here, Unamuno is not seeking to understand science and the social transformations of the modern age in systemic, organizational terms; rather he is seeking to denounce secular happiness as a form of moral corruption, as a hiding place for bad conscience, self-hatred, and the failure to face death—or decadence—with courage. "True life," Unamuno insists in this regard, "is a preparation for death."[10] Still, in a typically Quixotist fashion, Unamuno does not limit himself to a critique of the morally corrupting tendencies of modern science. Instead, in the place of science, he posits the mystical tradition of wisdom and the ecstatic union with the eternal, universal, spiritual truth of death as a regenerative force: "The object of science is life, and the object of wisdom is death."[11]

Insofar as it is primarily moral, therefore, the Quixotist critique of modern decadence is closer to Nietzsche's genealogical critique of *ressentiment* or slave morality than it is to the sociological theories of Spengler, Tönnies, Weber, or Simmel. But Quixotists like Unamuno or Ortega are not, as some critics would have it, Nietzschean.[12] Contrary to Nietzsche's critique of decadence as the result of ascetic cultural practices, modern Spain's Quixotists celebrate the ascetic negation of worldly passions as precisely that which will permit an ecstatic union with the essential, ahistorical and transcendental truth. Moreover, it is in the service of this same ascetic ideal that the Quixotists of Restoration Spain attempt to justify modern Spanish decadence.

The ascetic notion of instinctual inhibition and, indeed, of death itself as a justification for life, is at the heart of the Quixotist defense of Spanish decadence. In this sense, Maeztu writes that "life consists in . . . being filled with anxiety over the contingency of no longer being."[13] This most ascetic of ascetic ideals—death—is also used as a way to profess faith in Spain's supposedly singular and ahistorical national destiny; that is, it is used to narratively construct an ideal modern national identity on the basis of a purified or erased historical consciousness. This death-filled, ascetic consciousness gives rise, in turn, to two utopian visions against which the Quixotists measure the perceived decadence of modern Spain.

The first of these utopias is external to the Spanish historical experience, yet contemporary with the perceived decadence of modern Spain. This modern utopia is primarily represented, in Quixotist literature, by the Anglo-Saxon world. Against this modern utopia, Restoration Spain is perceived as backward and guilty of negligence. Angel Ganivet's judgment, in *Idearium español,* of Spanish decadence as "abulia" or a pathological lack of creative will; J. Francos Rodríguez's critique of the modern Spanish nation as having been corrupted by "the begging that has become a general system of Spanish life";[14] Enrique Lluria's depiction of the Spanish nation as a "moribund nation"[15] where "the dead govern the living";[16] or Ricardo Burguete's vision of a vacillating and cerebral decadence as opposed to a virulent affirmation of the will's power to achieve desired ends as exemplified by "determined men"[17] are all examples of how the Quixotists tended to perceive the proverbial backwardness of Spain as a result of the modern Spanish nation's lack of moral fortitude.

The second utopian point of reference against which Quixotists typically measure modern Spanish decadence is the Spanish Empire of the sixteenth and seventeenth centuries. Maeztu, for instance, depicts the Spanish conquest of the Americas as "an evangelical mission" that created "the physical unity of the world" and "the moral unity of the human species."[18] In this regard, Quixotists conceive of Spain's imperial past as the worldly realization of a universal, Catholic empire, which has, nevertheless, been lost as a result of Spain's failure to modernize.

In contrast to this idealized past, the Quixotists perceive modern Spain as well as the whole of the modernized world as decadent. Maeztu, for instance, suggests that the spiritualizing imperialistic project of the Spanish must be revived in order to save, not only Spain, but the entire modern world from impending doom: "the entire world urgently needs . . . the resuscitation and expansion of that Spanish spirit that conceived of all men as brothers . . . As such, the labor of Spain, far from being in a state of ruin or having been reduced to dust, is . . . an interrupted symphony that awaits the musicians who will know how to continue it."[19]

The principal aim of the Quixotist critique of decadence is, thereby, to revive the spiritually civilizing cultural practices of the Spanish nation: to wit, cultural conquest and civilizing colonization. Indeed, by submitting the nation to a regime of ascetic and mystical exercises intended to punish and purify the national body and ultimately redeem the nation's spirituality, Ganivet, Unamuno, Maeztu, and Ortega set out to prove that the Spanish nation is still capable of remarkable, creative and foundational acts of will.

The Quixotist Promise of Regeneration

The Quixotist critique of modern Spanish national decadence is indissolubly linked to the promise for moral transformation and regeneration. Just as the Quixotist critique of decadence is organized around two utopian instances of generative life, so the Quixotist promise for moral and spiritual regeneration tends to comprehend both of these utopias—first, the United States and northern Europe and their modern, scientific, technological, and industrial prowess, against which modern Spain is viewed as backward; and second, the traditional Spain of past imperial glories, against which modern Spain is perceived as fallen. Quixotist regeneration promises modernization while also promising a renewal of Spain's past imperial greatness. As such, Quixotist promises of regeneration are characterized by a problematic and hesitant longing, which oscillates between the hope for a Europeanized or modernized Spain and the desire to Hispanicize, or spiritually reconquer Europe and the Americas.

The Quixotists entrust their project for modernization to the nation's spiritual elite. Not unlike the self-disciplined aristocracy of Plato's ideal Republic, the elite that the Quixotists posit is also deemed superior to the rest of society in its ascetic quality: a will toward self-sacrifice in the service of a communal ideal. Thus, the Quixotists promote the figure of Don Quixote as emblematic of the nation's spiritual elite and proffer the figure of Sancho Panza as symbolic of the adulation and submissiveness that correspond to this elite or what Ortega, unabashedly, calls "the best."

To take another example, Maeztu understands modernization to be a question of reorganizing every sector of the national economy, from mining and textiles to the institutions of print-capitalism, into centralized corporativist guilds.[20] These guilds, he explains, are to be hierarchized according to merit, which he defines loosely along the ascetic principle of proven service to an ideal.[21] In this way, he entrusts both his project for modernization and the preservation of the nation's cultural identity to the same spiritual and traditional moral authority.

The Quixotists, however, do not always consider modernization in this relatively positive light. Burguete's 1905 "La orientación de los fuertes de espíritu," exemplifies the ambiguity with which Spanish intellectuals, who'd come under the sway of Quixotist rhetoric, regarded modernization. In this essay, Burguete distinguishes between three types of men and nations—instinctual, intellectual and passionate—of which only the latter are to qualify for leadership in the modern world. With the dawning of the Modern Age, he argues, the Spanish nation ceased to be passionate and became morally hesitant and intellectually inclined: "If anything, it is the excess of cerebral activity that influences our vacillations. We do not require vacillating men; what we need are determined men."[22] Burguete exalts the passionate type—the Quixotes—as an example of the moral and spiritual character required for Spanish national regeneration. Thus, for Burguete, the Spanish nation is to be modernized, not by the intellectual, vacillating and hypothetical work of scientific experimentation, but by an exercise of sheer willpower and ardent self-confidence in the nation's spiritual and passional strength.

This ambiguity, which expresses both the Quixotist anxiety for assimilation to the modern world and the need to affirm the Spanish nation's unique spiritual identity, gives way, in Unamuno, to an outright negation of the need for modernization. That negation is combined with an impassioned defense of the nation's imagined spiritual superiority: "Let them invent!"—he writes with regard to the modernizing nations of North America and Europe—"Let them dedicate themselves to science, from which we will benefit; as for ourselves, we have our own labors."[23] As such, Unamuno presents the labor of modernization under the aspect of a remedial, physical project that is alien to the nation's true mission in the modern world. Indeed, rather than entrust the process of modernization to an authoritarian solution, Unamuno brushes it aside as an exclusively European project. Concern for modernization, Unamuno sustains, only distracts the nation's spiritual elite from the far more profound and spiritually creative labor of cultural empire-building. And so, Unamuno, by negating the nation's need for modernization, affirms the scientific, technological and industrial backwardness of Spain as proof of the nation's supreme spirituality.

Also at stake in this self-affirming celebration of Spain's perceived backwardness is the Quixotist longing for the paradise lost of Spain's civilizing, Christian empire. Azorín's conception of Spanish national Classicism; Ganivet's vision of a spiritual empire in the form of a pan-Hispanist cultural confederation; Unamuno's tragic Spain and the spiritual leadership of Latin America and Europe attendant to it; Maeztu's defense of the notion of Hispanism as a spiritual *patria* or fatherland for all peoples of so-called

Hispanic origin: these are all examples of that nostalgic longing for Spain's lost imperial paradise.

Quixotist promises for national regeneration vacillate between the seemingly intangible glories of the future and the distant glories of the past. The formula for this not-too-happy, uneasy, and problematic union is Spanish spiritual and passional leadership of the modernized world. Unamuno formulates it thus: "What, then, is the new mission of Don Quixote today in this world? To cry aloud, to cry aloud in the wasteland."[24] The basic task of Quixotism, thereby, becomes to confront the modern, secular world with a confession of faith and, in the process, to spiritually conquer it, leading it toward a brighter, Hispanic future: "because he is not a pessimist, and since he believes in life eternal, Don Quixote must fight, attacking modern, scientific, inquisitorial orthodoxy in order to bring about a new and impossible Medieval Age, dualistic, contradictory, passionate . . . The world must be as Don Quixote wants it to be."[25]

II

Decadence

3

Paralyzed Imperialism

Hispanists today remember Angel Ganivet mostly as a precursor to the literary generation of '98. This is the case not because they recognize in Ganivet an irresistible intellectual force that profoundly influenced the thought of those who supposedly came after him. Rather, Hispanists have relegated this native of Granada to the status of a forerunner because they deem his work to be, in one sense or another, incomplete, insufficient, even deficient as compared to that of Unamuno, Maeztu, or Ortega. No doubt, this assessment of Ganivet's literary and intellectual status vis-à-vis the full-fledged members of the generation of '98 stems from the fact that in 1898 Ganivet committed suicide, thus cutting short his intellectual and literary career.

Yet when Ganivet's views on modern Spanish national decadence and regeneration are read alongside those of the more renowned Quixotists of Restoration Spain—such as Unamuno, Maeztu, and Ortega—Ganivet's imagination in no way seems deficient as compared to theirs. Admittedly, his critique of decadence is a crude, unsophisticated prototype upon which these other thinkers would eventually improve. Like Unamuno, like Maeztu, and like Ortega, however, Ganivet was an accomplished Quixotist. What is more, his Quixotism is not prior to that of his contemporaries; he articulated his plans for a Quixotist regeneration of modern Spain in dialogue with other Quixotists, particularly Unamuno.[1] Therefore, my decision to here consider Ganivet before Unamuno, Maeztu, and Ortega is not without irony. In doing so, I mean to disuade others from reading Ganivet as an insufficient first and, to persuade them to read Ganivet—not as a recuperated member of the generation of '98—but as a Quixotist.

Of the various essays that Ganivet did produce during his relatively short career as a writer, his most widely acclaimed—and to this day most commonly studied—is his 1897 treatise on Spanish national decadence, *Idearium español.* At one point in this unruly, circuitous and sinuous essay, Ganivet pessimistically ascribes the origin of modern Spanish decadence to the nation's overly zealous impulse for adventure. "The origin of our decadence and current postration," he explains, "can be found in our excess of action, in our having undertaken enterprises that were enormously disproportionate to our power."[2] Elsewhere in the *Idearium* Ganivet adds to this a second judgment concerning the origin of Spanish national and imperial decadence: "Just when our nation was constituted, our spirit overflowed the banks of the river bed that had been assigned to it and spilled over into the rest of the world in search of vain and external glories; as a result, the nation has been converted into a barracks of reservists, a hospital of invalids, a flower bed of beggars."[3] With these two coincident assessments of the origin of Spanish national decadence, Ganivet depicts a Spanish nation that is impossibly split against itself. It is divided between two national histories. The first is the worldly history of Spain's rise to and decline from what Ganivet calls "vain and external glories." The second is the providential history of the nation's purported destiny: "the river bed that had been assigned to it." Accordingly, the task that Ganivet sets for himself in the *Idearium* is to imagine a national history that will at once be capable of recognizing this schism and overcoming it.

Ganivet is successful in his bid to do so insofar as he constructs the contrast between Spain's worldly and ideal histories in the terms of a tale of conversion. Thus conceived, the national history that Ganivet narrates in his *Idearium* reads like a recuperative quest for an essential, but lost identity. This tale, as I reconstruct and revise it here, has three parts. The first posits the essence and original historical expression of the nation's identity. The second narrates the nation's betrayal of that essential identity or its decadence. And the third narrates the nation's recuperation of that identity or the Quixotist promise of regeneration.

Ganivet's integrating national history begins with the proposition that the Spanish are a fiercly independent people. It is this spirit of independence, he explains, which drove the Spaniards—a creative, heroic, and virtuous Christian people—first, to reconquer the Iberian peninsula from the Moors and then, to discover and conquer the Americas. Yet, it is this same spirit of independence that also explains, for Ganivet, the Spanish nation's decline from imperial glory. That decline is expressly associated with the era of Spain's colonization of the Americas. The Spanish nation's innate spirit of independence, he argues, led Spain's colonial administrators to govern over their colonies in pursuit of their own, as opposed to the empire's, best interests. These administrative interests, he further sustains, were characteristically mercantile. Thus, Spain's colonial experience was marred by what Ganivet considers to be a perverted and vice-ridden, modern version of the nation's characteristic independence: the modern Spanish tendency toward "undisciplined individualism." The result, as evidenced for Ganivet throughout the nineteenth century, was the fragmentation of the colonial empire into smaller, ultimately undisciplined, independent states.

Consequently, Ganivet links the regeneration of the Spanish nation to the recuperation of the nation's lost imperial unity. In this regard, nation and empire are indissolubly mixed for Ganivet. Indeed, Ganivet understands the achievement of Spanish national and imperial regeneration to depend on the recuperation of the same creative and heroic virtues which once led Spain's fiercly independent, yet disciplined, heroes—El Cid and Cortés, among others—to conquer the national empire.

According to Ganivet, the mechanism for this moral and spiritual transformation is elitism: "the submission of large masses of men to a governing intelligence."[4] Ganivet's regenerating elite is characterized by its adherence to the ascetic ideal of self-discipline. It is by means of the example set by the elite as well as by means of the forceful imposition of this elite's ascetic idealism on the masses, that the nation will transform itself from a disorganized mass of undisciplined individualists to a faithful congregation of disciplined individuals. As such, Ganivet's regenerating national history describes the transformation of the nation from a decadent state of anarchy to a regenerating state of aristocracy.

Mystical Essence and Stoic Heroism

The *Idearium* opens with a passage that contemplates the modern and decadent nation's need and even spiritual longing for a disciplinary moral transformation: "Many times, reflecting on the passion with which the dogma of the Immaculate Conception has been defended and proclaimed in Spain, it has occurred to me to think that at the bottom of that dogma there must be a mystery which, by means of hidden paths, is connected to the mystery of our national soul; and that perhaps that dogma is the symbol—admirable symbol!—of our own life, a life in which, after a long and arduous maternal labor, we have reached old age with the spirit of a virgin; we are like a woman who, although she has always felt the irresistible pull of a vocation for monastic and ascetic life, was nevertheless forced into marriage and converted into a dutiful mother but who, at the end of her days, now discovers that her spirit was contrary to her labors and that, although she is surrounded by her children of flesh and blood, her soul is still alone, open like a mystical flower to the ideals of virginity."[5]

In this opening passage, Ganivet portrays modern Spain as a tired, old, mystical virgin who has forcibly been led to mother an empire of nations; she is a victim of historical circumstance, a dutiful, noble and self-sacrificing woman. The maternal labor of colonial administration has alienated her from the spiritual ideals of her true vocation as a virgin. This woman is saddened and deeply troubled by her own awareness of her failures and the disjuncture that this symbolizes in her life's history. She has failed to live up to her ideal of a monastic and spiritual life and, has failed miserably as well in her endeavor to successfully mother her children who, themselves being equally aware of her inadequacy as a parent, have revolted against her, abandoned her and chosen to fend for themselves in the modern, secular world she has unwittingly played a significant role in forming.

Yet, from her failures, this woman takes respite. Finally, she is alone. Her solitude, however marred by loneliness, grief or resentment, is also her one remaining opportunity to realize her true monastic, contemplative and spiritual vocation. Even in her old and battered state, she remains a mystical rose open to the ideals of virginity; that is, she still finds, within herself, the desire to negate the world, her lived experience, and start anew, cloistered in an interior garden. She is ready to do something other than bear and rear children, something other than acquire and administrate colonies.

Ganivet's next rhetorical move in the *Idearium* is designed to respond to this desperate and downtrodden woman's longing for a monastic life of spiritual discipline. He introduces the regenerating agency of a disciplined, virile will-to-power: the traditionally Spanish, Senecan stoic. Guided by his inner truth and strength, indifferent to the favorable or unfavorable turns of the old Spanish woman's tragic history, this stoic hero, because he has within himself "something that is strong and indestructible, like a diamond," is able, by maintianing himself "firm and erect" to offer guidance to the woman.[6] In this way, Ganivet attempts to persuade his readers that the Spanish nation can, not unlike a weary woman, be redeemed by the spiritual guidance and spiritual fortitude of an ascetically disciplined and disciplining stoic agency. By virtue of his ethical consistency and volitional force, this priestly figure is singularly qualified for the task of aiding this woman's longed-for spiritual transformation. Together, stoic priest and mystical virgin, are to generate a new beginning, an apocalyptic spiritual transformation of the nation.

Ganivet, assuming the tone of a stoic, regenerating priest, formulates the apocalyptic spiritual transformation of the nation as a creative act of self-abnegation: "When in the presence of the spiritual ruin of Spain, one must replace one's heart with a stone; one must be disposed to throw away a million Spaniards to the wolves, if we are not to all throw ourselves away to the pigs."[7] In order to regenerate, argues Ganivet, the Spanish nation must first deepen the schism that characterizes its decadence, separating the ill, who suffer from a pathological lack of will and self-discipline, from the healthy who, like the stoic hero, are capable of creating a desired future. The morally decadent elements of the Spanish nation must be annihilated: "they [the decadent] must all be mixed together, they must be fused together by an ardent fire from on high which, because it is destructive, creates; and, because it burns fiercely, purifies."[8] The healthy, revitalized survivors of this purifying fire from on high, must be urged to join together in the celebration of a new national life. Purified of the decadent instinct for insubordination, Ganivet's nation of heroic survivors is to regenerate and recuperate the historical nation's imperial glories by means of an ascetically disciplined independence.[9]

Anarchic Decadence

In keeping with the regenerationist theories in vogue at the time of his writing the *Idearium,* Ganivet derives the notion that the Spanish are a fiercely independent people from a theory concerning the influence of geography and topography on national character. Positivist in its general character, Ganivet's theory has no real scientific basis. It consists, by and large, of a series of assertions that are related to one another, if not by reason, than certainly by the rhetoric of organicist discourse.[10] This topographically predetermined independent spirit of the Spanish nation, argues Ganivet, has historical, political and cultural manifestations, all of which contribute to the nation's perceived modern decadence.

Modern Spanish national history, he exclaims at one point in the *Idearium,* is "an unending series of invasions and expulsions, a permanent war of independence."[11] As Ganivet sees it, the basic trouble with the Spanish nation's innate spirit of independence is that it constantly threatens to undermine national unity. Such was not, however, always the case. El Cid, the epic hero of the Christian peninsular Reconquista is celebrated by Ganivet as an independent "self-employed warrior"; yet, despite the apparent self-serving independence with which El Cid wages his war on the Moors—his spontaneous and natural impulse toward independence, Ganivet argues that he is responsible for uniting the Spanish nation under a single political and religious order.[12] Ganivet sustains that this premodern tradition is then carried on by, among others, Cortés in his conquest of Central America.[13] Ganivet views independence of this conquering type as a creative act inspired by an ideal spiritual goal. The generative nature of this conquering independence, however, undergoes a significant transformation with the rise of mercantile-driven imperialism. Accordingly, Ganivet sees the self-promoting independence of colonial administrators as serving no ideal of a moral or spiritual order: "those who serve for brief periods of time in the colonies in order to obtain riches and honors are not conquistadors; rather, conquistadors are those who conquer out of necessity, spontaneously, by reason of a natural impulse toward independence."[14]

In an article of 1898 titled "¡Ñaññññ!," Ganivet sums up his quarrel with modern mercantile imperialism as follows: "In order to civilize peoples, beliefs that cannot be believed and laws that cannot be obeyed are imposed on them; among so many foolish civilizers and mundane philanthropists, a true man never emerges who, without vain ideas, will look with loving eyes upon his stupified and abjected common man, and after seeing what is inside that man and what in him can truly be given spiritual life, will with force and even cruelty sink his fingers into that human clay and infuse it, by virtue of his nature and not by means of conventional ideas, with new life."[15] Here, Ganivet depicts mercantile imperialism not as an act of civilizing and philanthropic love but as a deceit and an act of vanity. Its aim is portrayed as the satisfaction of the colonizer's interests. By contrast, there is a truely philanthropic form of imperialism: spiritual conquest. For Ganivet, it is an art not unlike that of the potter's. However cruel, the art of the spiritual conquistador is aimed at spiritual transformation, it seeks to civilize, to mold, and breathe new life into a formless and indistinct mass of humanity. Whereas the spiritual conquistador treats men as ends in themselves, the mercantile colonizer treats men as means to an end—this twisted Kantian moral imperative is also a recurring theme in Unamuno's and Maeztu's critiques of Spanish national and imperial decadence as in Ortega's elitist sociological theories for regeneration.

Yet Ganivet's quarrel is not with mercantile reasoning alone; instead, his purpose in criticizing modern mercantile imperialism is to reevaluate Spain's history of discovery, conquest and colonization in light of this modern imperial form. It is in this respect, then, that Ganivet draws a distinction between the spontaneous work of conquest and the strategic work of colonization. For Ganivet, the conclusion to be drawn from this contrast is that the latter enslaves the national spirit to the material need of focusing on administrative concerns and distracts it from the ideally spiritual and foundational work of conquest: "Perhaps our nation would have been more fortunate if, reserving for itself the pure glory of its heroic exploits, it had left to other more practical nations the duty to populate the discovered and conquered lands as well as all the lowly tasks of colonization."[16] Ganivet presents the failures of Spain's experiment with colonization as a mark of the Spanish nation's essential spirituality. The fiercely independent and spontaneously creative Spanish nation, or so argues Ganivet, simply was not meant for the lowly, rationalized labor of public administration.

For Ganivet, the Spanish, by virtue of their independence and stoicism, are more adept at conquest and war—activities which, according to him, require great personal sacrifice in the name of some higher national or religious ideal—than they are at the administration of colonial booty. In this manner, Ganivet explains the decline of the Spanish empire from its supposed spiritual ideal as the result of the distracting forces of mercantilism—avarice, greed, and worldly power—or what amounts to much the same thing, a lack, among the modern Spanish people, of personal ascetic discipline. Hence, Ganivet reprimands the undisciplined independence of the Spanish in categorical terms: "to colonize does not mean to go into business, but to civilize nations and expand ideas."[17]

The undisciplined independence and self-serving individualism which, for Ganivet, explains the nation's loss of empire is also at the core of what he decribes as Restoration Spain's state of "perpetual civil war."[18] In an attempt to bring to light the political heritage of this social evil, Ganivet appeals, in the *Idearium,* to the medieval Spanish tradition of the "fuero" or local legal codes. Ganivet views this tradition as an adaptation of the law to suit the interests of specific, subnational groups. As such, he suggests, it is appropriate to the Spanish nation's innate spirit of insubordination. Indeed, Ganivet reasons that the ideal of each and every Spaniard is to have his own personalized *fuero* stating, as he puts it, that: "This Spaniard is authorized to do as he pleases."[19] Anarchy, as Ganivet conceives it, is the lack of willingness to subordinate individual interests to a supra-personal order; it is the most decadent expression of independence.

In this regard, Ganivet's quarrel with mercantile imperialism is also not limited to a critique of the spiritual depravity of much modern imperialism. It involves a critique of liberal political ideology as well, and of the emerging capitalist economic system attendant on it. Ganivet conducts his argument to that effect along primarily moral lines. He distinguishes between the pursuit of interests, on the one hand, and the pursuit of moral virtue, on the other. Politically, Ganivet is prone to confuse the competitive pursuit of interests—sanctioned by liberal ideology in the form of civil society and institutionalized by it in the form of parliamentary government—with a state of civil war. In this regard, he refers to civil society as "civilized war . . . profoundly egotistical and savage."[20] Moreover, he views capitalism as an economic system that is primarily driven by the pragmatic consideration of "strategy" rather than by a moral "sense of justice."[21] Liberalism, capitalism, and mercantile imperialism are devoid of the spiritual and civilizing ideals that Ganivet associates with the Spanish conquests of the Iberian Peninsula and the Americas. As against the decadent negotiation of competing interests, Ganivet posits the imposing virtues of the stoic, mystical and ascetically spiritual conquistadors of premodern Spain.

Ganivet's vision of modern Spanish national decadence does not end with these political perspectives, however. Ganivet also traces the decadent state of the arts in modern Spain to this same spirit of anarchy. According to Ganivet, the Spanish nation's traditional spirit of independence has produced masters—Cervantes, Calderón, Lope de Vega, Velázquez—but the insubordination of other artists makes the formation of schools and movements a near impossibility, resulting in the destruction and annihilation of the elevating work of the masters.[22] Unless the insubordinate spirit of the Spanish masses is disciplined, Ganivet prophecies, the nation will forever and always have "masterpieces created by the masters and a rapid degradation provoked by the audacity and lack of discipline of the aprentices."[23]

Underlying the decadent effects of the undisciplined independence of the Spanish people in political, social, and cultural endeavors is Ganivet's view of the Spanish as constituting a morally decadent nation. In this regard, Spanish national decadence is formulated by Ganivet as a sickly lack of will. The symptoms of this pathology are, according to Ganivet, first, a debilitated attention span and the inability to associate ideas and, second, a petrification of the understanding or a dogmatic adherence to established truths.[24] As compared to the spiritually transformative and creative labors of Spain's conquering heroes, the modern Spanish nation is little more than, as Ganivet would have it, a regenerationist "hospital of invalids."[25]

Aristocratic Regeneration

From the nation's troubles with colonization to the nation's social anarchy and moral vice, Ganivet treats the Spanish nation's spirit of independence as both the source of the nation's generation and the cause of its perceived fragmentation and decadence. Disciplined independence, on the other hand, is to be the origin of Spanish regeneration: "the undisciplined individualism that, today, debilitates us and keeps us from lifting our head will one day be an internal and creative individualism, and it will surely lead us to our grand, ideal triumph."[26] It is by reason of this "interior and creative individualism" that Ganivet will, in the end, appeal to philosophy and religion, and in particular, to stoicism and mysticism, in an attempt to provide examples of a disciplined independence.

Thus, Ganivet's vision of a regenerating Spain is intimately bound to the ascetic desire to forge a crystaline and purified subjectivity—an "inner" spiritual and cultural sanctum—on the basis of a radical negation of the everyday and worldly. The mystical virgin and the stoic warrior of the opening passages of the *Idearium* are, consequently, posited as ideal expressions of this ascetic formula for regeneration. These two "Spanish philosophies," mysticism and stoicism, hold special regenerative promise for Ganivet, in that they symbolize the nation's creative independence of mind and moral discipline.

The independence of mind that Ganivet attributes to both mysticism and stoicism results from the principle of negation inherent in each of these methods of arriving at a purified identity. Each is a formula for creating an empty, purified inner sanctum. Internalization, or the folding in of one's self onto oneself as would a mystical rose, means purification; it means the emptying out of the material world, its history and its failures from one's consciousness; it means forgetting and erasing history and the identity tied to it. It is on the basis of this tabula rasa that Ganivet will attempt to construct an ideal, mythological, essential national identity.

But the independence of mind that is required for the ascetic negation of the world is tempered, in Ganivet's version of mysticism and stoicism, by the discipline of an interpretive and mediating power. The goal of the mystic in mastering himself is ecstasy. The Spanish mystic's ecstatic relationship to God is traditionally mediated, however, by Church authority: either sanctioned or discredited by it.[27] Likewise, the stoic, whose goal in achieving self-mastery is ataraxia, must master his worldly passions with ethical impartiality. He must voluntarily submit his passions to the abstract stoic ideal of the impassive self. Mysticism and stoicism combine, thereby, to form Ganivet's virtuous national identity: a nation of ascetic voluntary servants united under a single religious order and responsive to a single, transcendental will-to-discipline.

This purified national identity is in line with Ganivet's ideal of Spain as a "Christian Greece" or spiritually artistic nation.[28] In this regard it is art, or rather the national genius which it represents, that is to be the basic instrument for spiritual regeneration. Keeping in mind Ganivet's views on conquest and colonization, it is clear that art is not merely an instrument for regeneration, but also a weapon in the nation's cultural arsenal for spiritual reconquest of the lost empire: "to colonize," Ganivet insists, "means to civilize nations and expand ideas."[29]

It is by means of artistic genius that the Spanish nation is to commune with and conquer other peoples, leading them into the profound and universal world of Spanish mystical truth and ascetic morality. But, in order for this ideal event to occur, the creative practice of art must be spiritually disciplined; the insubordinate imitators of the masters, who reduce the masters's spiritual genius to a lowly art of the masses, must be made subordinate to the national and spiritual ideal. Ganivet's formula for regenerating Spanish art and culture—the spiritual stamp with which the Spanish nation is to mark the subjects of its cultural empire—is the disciplined concentration of all energies within the ascetically defined boundaries and transcendental order of the spiritualized nation.

Similar to the spiritual virgin of the opening passage who would fold up into herself like a mystical rose, Ganivet would have the nation negate the outside world and, like Santa Teresa herself, live within the walls of that interior, crystaline palace until the nation were ready to share with the world the spiritual wealth of its internal adventures: "All the doors through which the

Spanish spirit escaped Spain only to be spread out toward the four points of the horizon must be shut with deadbolts, keys and padlocks . . . and on each of those doors . . . we will place a sign that reads . . . in imitation of Saint Agustine: Noli foras ire; in interiore Hispaniae habitat veritas."[30] Spain is to be the land of perpetual truth, a bastion of spirituality, the City of God.

Once Ganivet's isolated Spanish nation should come to feel itself spiritually refortified it will, he prophesies, embark on new spiritual adventures of conquest: "A nation, founder of numerous nationalities, after a long period of decadence, succeeds in reconstituting itself as a political force that is animated by new longings for expansion: What form should this second evolution take in order that it might connect to the first and not break the historical unity to which both the one and the other ought to be subordinate?"[31] His answer is that spiritual empire building can satisfy both the need for national historical continuity and the spiritual desire to expand. Thus he suggests: "The problem . . . that Spain must solve is without any clear and precise precedent in history . . . if by means of our intelligence we were to succeed in reconstituting the familial unity of all the Hispanic nations and infuse them with a cult to one set of ideals, our own ideals, we would complete a grand historical mission and we would give life to a grand, original creation, unknown, thus far, in the annals of politics; and in completing that mission . . . we would be working in our own interests, in the name of interests that are more transcendental than the conquest of a few pieces of land."[32] The recuperation of the lost empire is to be achieved by means of the imposition of a civilizing, cultural ideal.

That ideal is represented by Don Quixote, the Spanish national type that "incarnates the nation's true qualities . . . our Ulyses."[33] For Ganivet, Don Quixote is a paradigmatic example of a disciplined mystic and stoic who has negated historical circumstance, emptied himself of material concerns and stepped beyond the world of lived experience into an ideal moral order. He is the model for a regenerative "spiritual metamorphosis" whose "action is a never-ending creation"[34]

Yet, explains Ganivet, Don Quixote owes his spirituality, his having liberated himself from "material preoccupations," to the fact that he is not alone in his adventures and is able to "unload on his squire," Sancho, his every worldly concern.[35] Ganivet's regenerative Spain, thus, will conduct its future, modern conquests as a team of Sanchos led by an elite force of Don Quixotes. The point of these prophesied conquests is to spritually transform the anarchic modern world of mercantilism and capitalism and make of it an ethical community.

The modern world, as Ganivet depicts it iconographically, is dominated by "the Anglo-Saxon Ulyses, Robinson Crusoe."[36] For Ganivet, Robinson has "the talent to fight only with nature; he is capable of reconstructing a material civilization; . . . he aspires to power, to 'exterior' governance over other men; but his soul lacks expression and he does not know how to commune with other souls."[37] Robinson's world is lacking in any substantial spiritual or moral center. Robinson's knowledge is not ethical, but technological. He is the master of Nature and of Man in his physical, animalistic aspect. Yet, as a mercantilist and colonialist, he fails to bind men spiritually. That noble capacity for spiritual heroism, for binding men together culturally is unique, for Ganivet, to Don Quixote whose exemplary "natural aptitudes . . . for ideal creations" qualify him, and the Spanish nation which he represents, for the spiritual leadership of the decadent, modern world; "upon our rebirth, we will find brotherly nations who we will mark with the stamp of our spirit."[38]

Sancho's role in this spiritual conquest of the modern world is, then, to replace Robinson Crusoe as master of Nature: "Sancho Panza . . . could become Robinson; and Robinson, in the case of an emergency, would placate his air of superiority and become a squire to Don Quixote."[39] Sancho, prophesies Ganivet, will have the power of science and technology at his behest and with it the power to dominate Nature. But not in the same manner as Crusoe. Sancho's dominance of Nature will always be subordinate to a spiritual ideal represented by the idealism and regenerative virtues of his master Don Quixote. Sancho will always be subject to the spiritual community. By virtue of his subservience to Don Quixote, Sancho's mastery of nature will, unlike Robinson's, be ethical.[40] In this way, Ganivet brings the modern conflict between worldliness and otherworldliness to an ideal conclusion by giving primacy to ethical knowledge over technical knowledge.

But even here, in its ideally regenerated form, Ganivet's unified national identity is fragmented and highly problematic. There is a difference, nevertheless, between this ideal fragmentation and the fragmentation Ganivet associates with anarchic decadence. The fragmentation of decadence is reductive and multiple; it is massive and undisciplined individualism. The ideal split between Don Quixote and Sancho is not anarchic but elitist, which is precisely what Ganivet's Quixotism is; it is a mythical formula for national and imperial unity forged on the basis of spiritual elitism.

4

Perverted Catholicism

A towering figure in the cultural life of Restoration Spain, the essayist, novelist, and poet Miguel de Unamuno y Jugo (1864–1936) struggled, throughout his long career as a public intellectual, to come to grips with the Spanish nation's modern decadence. Taken as a whole, his thoughts on decadence give the impression of being contradictory, inconsistent, and unsettled. This is so not only in consideration of how his views on decadence changed over the years, but also in the sense that he expressed these views in a manner that was always and already paradoxical.

From the very start of his intellectual career, Unamuno defended the contradictory nature of his thought as the surest proof of its proximity to truth. In this regard, Unamuno writes, in the introduction to his 1895 *En torno al casticismo:* "Truth is generally sought in the golden mean . . . by excluding the extremes . . . but in this way one arrives only at a shadow of the truth, cold and nebulous. It is preferable, I believe, to follow a different method: the method of the alternative affirmation of contraries; it is preferable to make the force of the extremes stand out in the soul of the reader where the mean can come to life, which, itself, is the result of struggle."[1] The pseudodialectical cast of Unamuno's method, whereby contraries are alternatively affirmed in the manner of a thesis and antithesis, generates the expectation for an eventual overcoming of the extremes in a new synthesis. But Unamuno never actually provides his readers with the anticipated synthesis. Instead, he aims to present his readers with a struggle, and even to burden them with that struggle, in the hope that they will thus be made to share with him the "agony" of truth.[2] This agonistic "procedure of contradictions," as Unamuno calls it, makes for a rather appealing and polemical writing style;

to be sure, it is what makes reading Unamuno so exciting at times. But what this so-called method achieves in terms of style, it lacks completely in terms of conceptual rigor. In spite of his often acclaimed philosophical intensity—Hispanists have tended to liken Unamuno to existentialist thinkers such as Kierkegaard—Unamuno does not, in fact, construct anything like a careful philosophical argument on decadence.[3]

What Unamuno does provide in his writings on modern Spanish national decadence is an example of how to perform restlessly within the realm of a contestatory discourse. Despite the chronological shifts and conceptual uncertainties that characterize his take on decadence, this agonistic performance remains a constant in Unamuno's approach to decadence. It, alone, is what allows for his views on the subject to be treated as a discursive whole. By voicing his views on decadence from this place of in-betweeness, Unamuno consistently denounces the factional extremes that result, according to him, in the decadent fragmentation of the Spanish nation. He argues that, in order to regenerate, the nation will need to subordinate its extremes to a unifying ideal around which it might, subsequently, reconstitute itself in solidarity.

In 1895, before the so-called Disaster of 1898, Unamuno portrayed the debate concerning the perceived decadence of modern Spain as a symptom of the nation's dissociative tendencies. Framing that debate in polemical terms, he identified two opposing factions: those who, like the Catholic integrists, favored *casticismo* or the nation's traditional sense of its religious, political, and cultural purity and those who, like the progressives of the ILE and to a lesser degree the regenerationists, favored Europeanization. Unamuno declined to side with either extreme and instead argued for a regenerating, paradoxical affirmation of both: "We must Europeanize and soak ourselves in the nation," he writes in this regard in *En torno al casticismo*.[4] The emphasis here is on the first of the two contraries: Europeanization. In this sense, it is also worth noting that in his reference to the Spanish nation (or pueblo), Unamuno here means a people seen in its *intrahistoric* light; that is, a people conceived primarily in terms of what is least distinctive about them—their common humanity and culture—which, argues Unamuno, the Spanish share with other European peoples.

It is this Europeanizing position of Unamuno's that has, over the years, led many of his more determined liberal apologists to view him primarily as a liberal-cum-socialist thinker who, by focusing on the cultural links that tied Spain to Europe, was principally interested in placing Spanish national culture at the service of a liberal, modernizing republic.[5] While certainly this interpretation of Unamuno's approach to the subject of decadence corresponds to his pre-1898 writings, it can be sustained in the face of his post-1898 Quixotist writings only by means of some fairly questionable and willful acts of ignorance.

Shortly after the events of 1898, Unamuno began to retreat from his Europeanizing formula for national regeneration and to entertain the notion of a regenerating Hispanicization of Spain. In the prologue to a 1902 edition of *En torno al casticismo,* Unamuno writes: "These pages contain the seeds of my subsequent works . . . I wrote these pages before the disaster of Cuba and the Philippines, before the great encounter between Robinson and Don Quixote . . . Today, in order to prepare these essays for publication, I have reread what I wrote then and I have found certain affirmations and judgments that I do not wish to let stand without certain corrections."[6] Interestingly, what he proceeds to "correct" in the rest of the prologue is his not having sufficiently underscored, in the original 1895 version of the essays, the extent to which Spaniards are unfamiliar with their true history, their intrahistory, which he now views not as European but as Quixotist. Some fourteen years later, in 1916, when Unamuno was preparing still another edition of *En torno al casticismo* for publication, he once again mentions the "temptation" to introduce "substantive alterations" into the text. As he had done in 1902, though, he again resists the temptation to alter the essays and instead limits himself to making a few clarifications.[7] More likely than not, Unamuno's ability to resist that temptation in 1916 has to do with the fact that he had already elaborated an alternative Quixotist interpretation of Spain's perceived national decadence in his 1905 *Vida de Don Quixote y Sancho* and, to a still greater extent, in his 1913 *Del sentimiento trágico de la vida en los hombres y en los pueblos.*

It is in his work of 1913 that Unamuno emphatically separates himself from the "regenerationist Europeanizing" that he had espoused in 1895, labeling it as "blasphemous."[8] "That horrendous regenerationist literature . . . that provoked the loss of our American colonies . . . In that ridiculous literature . . . I exclaimed 'Death to Don Quixote!' and from that blasphemy, which was supposed to mean the exact opposite of what it said—such was the state that we were in those days—emerged my *Vida de Don Quijote y Sancho* and my cult of Quixotism as our national religion."[9] Whereas in *En torno al casticismo,* Unamuno had formulated decadence in terms of the factional tensions between the nation's Hispanicizing isolationists and its Europeanizing progressives, in *Del sentimiento trágico de la vida* he conceptualized it in terms of the ideological tensions between the traditionally Catholic faith of the Spanish nation and European rationalism. In other words, by 1913, for Unamuno regeneration was no longer a question of the Spanish nation's need to Europeanize itself and soak itself in its people's European *intrahistory;* to the contrary, it was now a struggle between irrational faith and reasonable doubt, a "tragic" affirmation of faith-in-doubt. In a word, regeneration had become, for Unamuno, a matter of affirming the Spanish nation's irrational spirituality, its Quixotism.

Unamuno affected this shift in criteria in order to pluck a moral victory from the perennial secular "backwardness" of his defeated nation. Accordingly, from 1913 onward, Unamuno would argue that Spain was not to be viewed as the only, or even as the most, decadent nation of Europe. The Spanish nation's decadence, he sustained, represented not just the nation's lack of modernization but its essentially tragic sense of life, spiritual vitality, and cultural superiority. To his credit, Unamuno thus discovered an ingenious purpose for Spain's modern national decadence: it was to serve as the source of Spanish spiritual regeneration and as the justification, ultimately, for Spain's spiritual reconquest of a cultural Hispanic empire.

Curiously enough, rather than link this shift in Unamuno's views on national decadence and regeneration to the events of 1898 and to how these events gave rise, in Unamuno, to a fervent and at times even jingoistic patriotism, Hispanists have tended to explain the shift otherwise. Unable to reconcile Unamuno's Quixotism with his supposed liberalism, some Hispanists have gone to great pains to downplay the significance of his Quixotism. One strategy, described by Blanco Aguinaga, has been to propose an evolutionary scheme, whereby Unamuno's career as a thinker is said to progress from a youthful concern for Spain and its historical circumstances to a more mature concern for the universality of the personal.[10] Another strategy has been to regard the turning point in Unamuno's career as a thinker not at all as a process but as the result of a sudden crisis. Martin Nozick's invocation of a "spiritual crisis" is paradigmatic in this regard: "In 1897," writes Nozick, "a spiritual crisis marked the definite turning point in Unamuno's life and determined the sui generis religious orientation of his subsequent work."[11] The common denominator linking these strategies is the portrayal of Unamuno's post-1898 writings as being predominantly philosophical and religious and not particularly concerned with the modern Spanish nation's decadence and regeneration. In this sense, Hispanists have too often pointed to Unamuno's *Tragic Sense of Life,* highlighting the existentialist and intimate nature of the inquiry into faith that Unamuno undertakes there. A simple rereading of the book's entire title, however, suggests the extent to which this interpretation is at odds even with the most superficial understanding of that work: the full title reads, in English, *The Tragic Sense of Life: In Men and in Nations.*[12]

Hence, a far more satisfactory interpretative strategy is to take Unamuno seriously when, in his 1902 prologue to *En torno al casticismo* and at the very moment of his supposed "turning," he explains that: "These pages contain the seeds of my subsequent works."[13] Considering that the greater part of his output as a writer belongs to the post-1898 period, it only seems right to seek the roots of his Quixotism in those earlier writings and not, as has been the tendency, to want to distinguish the "young," "socialist," and "liberal" Unamuno from the "mature," "introspective," and "illiberal" Unamuno. There is only one Unamuno: the agonistic Quixotist.

The extent to which Unamuno was always and already this agonistic Quixotist is further born out by the trajectory that his personal life was to follow after the publication of his 1913 *Del sentimiento trágico de la vida*. During Primo de Rivera's dictatorship, Unamuno, who was opposed to the military regime's authoritarianism, was banished to the island of Fuerteventura. When he was finally given amnesty, he chose not to return home. Instead, he fled to the French Basque Countries where he lived for years in self-imposed exile. It was only when Primo de Rivera fell from power that Unamuno agreed to return home, where he was received as the champion of Spanish republicanism. However, when in 1936, Franco and his fascist legions revolted against the Second Republic and sparked Spain's bloodiest Civil War, Unamuno did not denounce these events. Instead, he embraced the fascist attack on the Republic, believing that it promised to bring an end to modern Spain's anarchy. Moreover, he welcomed the Civil War, seeing in it a necessary means to cleansing the nation. Then, in October of 1936, when Unamuno came face to face with those whose nationalist cause he had embraced, he retracted his support for the fascists and reaffirmed his previous republicanism. The fascists placed him under house arrest and two months later, on December 31 of 1936, he unexpectedly died. Contradictory, paradoxical, at once penetrating and indecisive in his thinking, Miguel de Unamuno—who had often defended the "agony" of arguing and living by means of what he called the "alternative affirmation of contraries"—represents as few other thinkers of his time do the tense intellectual, cultural, and political life of Spain as it began its first century without empire.

THE VANITY OF "CASTICISMO" AND THE ENVY OF "EUROPEIZACIÓN"

Unamuno dedicates a considerable portion of the opening passages of his *En torno al casticismo* to reconstructing the ongoing debate in Restoration Spain concerning the origins of the nation's modern decadence. He does so with an eye to intervening in that debate and shifting its focus toward the moral examination of what he calls the nation's *intrahistory*. Unamuno presents his distinction between history and *intrahistory* by means of an analogy that recurs throughout *En torno al casticismo:* the economy, politics and warfare of history are to the turbulent surface of the ocean as the moral character and national essence of *intrahistory* are to the calm depths of the ocean's floor. According to this analogy, the spectacle of history's waves crashing about on the surface of the sea does not explain the origin of modern Spanish national decadence; it merely describes particular manifestations of decadence. For Unamuno, the makers and shakers of history are decadents; all of them, "great anarchists."[14] The origins of modern Spain's decadence and the keys to the nation's regeneration must instead be sought, reasons Unamuno, at the deeper level of the nation's intrahistory, the unrevealed bedrock of the nation's vices and virtues.

As Unamuno reconstructs it, the debate in Restoration Spain concerning decadence bears the signs of the modern nation's decadent dissociative tendencies. To one side of this debate, Unamuno identifies the *casticistas*—the would-be defenders of Spain's national and cultural patrimony—who view all modern, foreign ideas as inherently pernicious. "Complaints are raised daily in Spain because foreign culture is invading us, dragging us along or drowning out our purity, and it is slowly but surely bringing an end, or so say the complainers, to our national personality."[15] On the other side of the debate, Unamuno identifies the *europeizantes:* "systematic haters of purity and of what is ours" who "with total confidence, hyperbolically reveal their desires . . . exclaiming: 'Let them conquer us!'"[16] Unamuno sides with neither of these two camps completely. Instead, he proffers an ambiguous definition of *casticismo,* which, he anticipates, will prove capable of subsuming both sides of the debate. His idea is that, in order to regenerate the modern Spanish nation it will prove necessary to "Europeanize and soak ourselves in the nation . . . believing that we shall not lose our personality in the process."[17]

The first step that Unamuno takes in an attempt to fuse the two sides of the debate is to demonstrate how, in spite of their differences, the *casticistas* and their rivals, the *europeizantes,* can be made subordinate to the same, albeit ambiguous, moral standard: "Those who would have us seal our borders and those who long for us to be conquered ignore the true reality of things, the eternal and profound reality of things, permitting themselves to be dragged along by that spirit of anarchism that is at the center of our soul."[18] By arguing that both the *casticistas* and the *europeizantes* are anarchists, Unamuno seeks, not just to relegate them and their views to the superficial level of historical analysis, but also to establish an intimate relation between the two as sinners.

The sins that Unamuno associates with the two sides of the debate are vanity (the *casticista* desire to individuate) and envy (the *europeizante* desire to acquire the individuating qualities of another). As concerns the vanity inherent in the *casticistas* and this sin's relationship to modern Spanish national decadence, Unamuno writes: "individual vanity is so stupid that it will drive some people, eager as they are to appear original and to distinguish themselves, to claim that they are proud of their own ignorance; likewise, there are nations that take pride in their defects . . . We Spaniards fall . . . into this sin."[19] When affirmed with blind patriotism, argues Unamuno, *casticismo* blinds the Spanish nation to its evident insufficiencies as compared to other, more modernized European nations. As concerns the envy of the *europeizantes* and this sin's relationship to modern Spanish decadence, Unamuno has less to say in

En torno al casticismo. However, in an article of 1909 titled "La envidia Hispánica," Unamuno does elaborate on this subject as follows: "Envy! This, this is the terrible plague of our [Hispanic] societies; this is the intimate gangrene of the Spanish soul . . . It is envy, it is the blood of Cain more than anything else, that has made us so unhappy, insubordinate and bellicose."[20] Here, Unamuno portrays the envy with which Spain's and Hispanic America's *europeizantes* regard the more modernized nations of Western Europe and North America as the motive force of Hispanic decadence. Envy, suggests Unamuno, led the *europeizantes* to abandon the cultural and spiritual values that had traditionally held the Hispanic world together.

It is in a novel of 1917, titled *Abel Sánchez,* that Unamuno reveals the full significance of these two vices with regard to modern Spanish national and imperial decadence. In *Abel Sanchez,* Unamuno focuses equally on envy and vanity, extending the guilt of the envious to include that of the vain and vice versa. Unamuno's point is that Abel, the vain individual, incites the envy of Cain, the envious individual; at the same time, Cain's envy stimulates Abel's vanity. According to this dialectical reasoning, Cain and Abel need each other in order to grasp the meaning and value of their respective lives. Abel requires Cain's envy, because it is only by means of that envy that his own vanity can be recognized for what it is: the arrogance of the more fortunate. Likewise, Cain needs Abel to be vain, for it is by means of Abel's vanity that Cain's envy is given significance, the significance of a rebellion against the seemingly unjust and arbitrary will of fortune. Considered in this light, envy and vanity are two sides of the same coin; they are two parts of a larger whole.[21]

Although in *En torno al casticismo* Unamuno does not explicitly work out the full implications of this vicious and decadent dialectic, he does posit it implicitly. It is under the rubric of the double vice of envy-vanity that in *En torno al casticismo* Unamuno forces the vainglorious *casticistas* and the envious *europeizantes* to associate as a complete, although seemingly self-contradictory, nation. Neither the *casticistas* nor the *europeizantes* hold the key to modern Spain's regeneration. They are both decadent. What is more, because their vices motivate and justify one another, their quarrel actually serves, according to Unamuno, to further exacerbate modern Spanish national decadence. Appropriately, it is at this juncture in his reconstruction of the debate between *casticistas* and *europeizantes* that Unamuno first intervenes in their debate, claiming to know how best to quiet them and, subsequently, regenerate Spain.

According to Unamuno, the Spanish nation will regenerate only when it recognizes its *intrahistoric* essence. It is by means of *intrahistorical,* mystical meditation that such regenerating revelation is to occur. To that end, Unamuno posits the guiding presence of the *vidente* or clairvoyant prophet, a national philosopher—Unamuno himself—who, because he is capable of elevating his consciousness into the mystical realm of "the light" is also capable of becoming "conscious . . . of that which remains unconscious in the nation."[22] Moreover, argues Unamuno, the *vidente* must take on this mediating role in order to "better guide" the nation.[23]

As one of modern Spain's would-be regenerating *videntes,* Unamuno assigns to himself the function of national confessor and priestly leader of the national, patriotic congregation.[24] In this regard, Unamuno formulates the study of the *intrahistorical,* subconscious realm of the nation as a confessional discipline: "So long as history is not a confession and an examination of conscience . . . there can be no salvation for us . . . It is by means of the examination of their historical conscience that nations penetrate their intrahistory and truly find themselves."[25] Unamuno as *vidente,* means to guide his national congregation through the spiritual exercises of a "regenerating penitence" and thus help it to become more aware of its supposed sins; he aspires to aid the nation in acquiring an ostensibly modern and critical self-consciousness of itself.[26]

The Intrahistory of *Casticismo*

The conjectural, Spanish national *intrahistory* that Unamuno narrates reveals *casticismo* to be, at once, the most virulent expression of the nation's decadent tendency toward anarchy and the original formula by means of which the Spanish nation sought to control, govern and limit its dissociative tendencies. In other words, Unamuno considers *casticismo* to be the peculiarly Spanish way of putting into practice the universal law of solidarity and subordination on which, he claims, all human societies are ultimately based.[27] Modern Spain will regenerate itself, argues Unamuno, only when it reaffirms the self-governing aspect of its traditional *casticismo.*

Unamuno discovers the most primitive Spanish expression of this law of solidarity and subordination among the Christian warriors of the Reconquest, who constituted, according to him, a loosely defined confederation of warrior communities. As Unamuno imagines them, these communities were forged "under the pressure of invaders," as a necessary act of self-defense and a means to defending the "essence" of the Christian way of life.[28] All members of these proto-national communities of Christian warriors carried within themselves what Unamuno refers to as an individuating and intimate anarchism, a desire to single-handedly defend their way of life from the threat of the Moors. In order for these individuating anarchists to band together and live in solidarity as warriors, they required an external force that could counter their intimate anarchism and unite them. In the practical realm, this unifying force was the *caudillo* to whom the warriors would promise their loyalty; in the ideal realm, it was the Catholic faith.[29] As such, political absolutism and religious order represent, for Unamuno, the Spanish nation's *intrahistoric* "norm and dike of anarchy."[30] According to Unamuno's *intrahistory* therefore, *casticismo* arose among Spain's proto-national communities of Christian warriors as a "method for gaining access to heaven."[31]

This method, by means of which Unamuno's proto-Spaniards sought to guarantee their entrance into heaven, became ever more sophisticated as Spain's Christian communities continued to fight and expand their control from the frontlines of Castile to Andalusia. According to Unamuno, the Christian communities of Spain were able to give the highest political expression to their *casticismo* when they completed the Reconquest and turned their energy toward the conquest and colonization of the Spanish empire: "following the spirit of conquest . . . the idea of a unifying conquest, of the Catholicization of the world . . . Castile . . . expulsed the Moors . . . and nailed the Castillian cross in Granada; soon after, they discovered the New World . . . and then came to pass all that with which my readers are already familiar."[32] In this cursory manner, Unamuno manages to narrate a conjectural national history which, despite having its roots in an individuating act of self-defense, nevertheless culminates in the effort to incorporate the entire world under its, now, universalizing ideal of unification or conquest: a Hispanic and Catholic defense of humanity.

The militant Catholicism of Unamuno's proto-national communities was not limited, however, to warfare. Spanish national *casticismo* also engendered its own philosophy: Spanish mysticism. For Unamuno, this national philosophy was at its height a formula for, as he puts it: "grounding individuality on the renunciation of individuality."[33] The Spanish mystic, as Unamuno understands him, is a spiritual warrior; he is an ascetically disciplined, voluntary servant who masters his anarchistic "individuating differences" in order to recuperate the full significance of his common bond with the rest of God's creation. As such, he is an example of how best to sacrifice personality to the *intrahistoric* quality of the nation's essential, life-affirming and defensive identity: an identity which, as Unamuno suggests, the Spanish nation shares with all other nations that arose as an expression of their own desire and need to defend their "pure" way of life from the "impurities" of those who would annihilate or otherwise dominate them.

But not everyone can be a mystic, claims Unamuno. The ability to enter into a state of ecstasy, to see the light of the transcendental will that unifies the universe, is reserved for a select few: the *videntes*. Thus, if the Spanish nation is to comprehend its own *intrahistorical*, eternal and essential character it is neither enough for the *vidente* to narrate a mythical tale of the nation's "defensive" and "life-affirming" rise to empire, nor is it enough for him to exhort his compatriots to submit to the ascetic practices of the Spanish mystics and thus hope, in vain, to achieve ecstasy. The nation also requires other, more easily ascertained images of its *intrahistoric* identity. Such images, claims Unamuno, can be found in the nation's literary masterpieces, particularly those belonging to Spain's "Golden Age of literature."[34] The trouble here, explains Unamuno, is that the literature of Spain's Golden Age coincides with the point at which the nation began its decline into decadence: "Our classical national literature began to bud when the process of decadence had already begun."[35] Spain's classic, pure national literature is also filled with the seeds of Spain's modern decadence. Consequently, as a *vidente,* Unamuno's task as interpreter of this literature must center on how the nation's classics, and especially Cervantes' *Quixote,* reveal the decadent aspect of Spanish *casticismo.*

In his 1895 *En torno al casticismo,* Unamuno views Don Quixote as a Christian warrior whose spirit of solidarity with the downtrodden is nevertheless undermined by his failure to recognize the authority of Spain's caudillo—the Catholic Monarch; he sees him also as a mystic whose ascetic discipline is meant to unite him, not with God, but with his beloved Dulcinea; finally, Unamuno sees in Don Quixote a mad and vainglorious reader who envies the fame of the knights-errant who went before him. Like the modern, decadent Spain that Don Quixote purports to combat, Don Quixote is an individuating anarchist through and through. Consequently, for Unamuno in *En torno al casticismo,* it is not the figure of Don Quixote, but that of Alonso Quijano el Bueno, that represents the Spanish nation's true, regenerating *intrahistoric* identity. In this regard, Unamuno values the "sane humanism" of Alonso Quijano over the "mad vanity" of Don Quixote. "This Alonso Quijano, who by reason of his virtues and despite his insanity deserved the title of The Good, is the eternal and permanent grounding of the heroes of [Spain]."[36] The vain and madly anarchistic Don Quixote is little more than an historical phantom whose imagined rise and fall from fame and glory Unamuno views as inconsequential with respect to the more profound, silent, and tranquil kindness of the *intrahistoric* Alonso Quijano. Thus, in the *Quixote,* Unamuno identifies the shortcomings and pitfalls to which Spanish national *casticismo* invariably yielded. The nation's *casticismo,* of which Don Quixote is an extreme and grotesque expression, led to the nation's isolation from the rest of the civilized world and to the perception, among the other nation's of that world, of the Spanish as a vain, envious, and anarchic nation.

In order to regenerate, Spain must shed its Quixote-like vanity and envy and awake from its madness. The means to accomplishing this is, Unamuno contends, to open up the nation to the revitalizing influences of other European cultures and, in the process, trust that the nation will recuperate an awareness and appreciation of the human origins that it has in common with those other cultures. Faith in this common origin, sustains Unamuno, requires that modern Spain's decadent, warring factions sacrifice their individuating and historically bound identities to the deeper, *intrahistoric* truth of Spain's defensive and universalizing spirit. By emphasizing the warring character of the relationship between these two modern Spanish communities, Unamuno—the *vidente* and would-be spiritual taskmaster of the nation—attempts to subsume their differences within the larger, unifying spirit of a potentially regenerative and modern warring community. The modern Spanish nation, preaches Unamuno, split within itself and split off from the rest of Europe, is by virtue of these very conflicts, a nation that contains, unbeknownst to itself, the prerequisites for its own moral and spiritual regeneration.

Redemptive Agony

In the arguments that he sets forth in his 1913 *Del sentimiento trágico de la vida,* Unamuno no longer considers Europe to be an appropriate model for Spanish national regeneration. Instead, he develops the view that there are two distinct, although interrelated, types of decadence at hand in early twentieth-century Europe. One is primarily Spanish and linked to the collapse of otherworldly religiousness—a process that Unamuno calls "de-Catholicization."[37] The other is primarily European and linked to the collapse of rational-scientific optimism—a process that Unamuno calls "progress."[38] Consequently, Unamuno contends that contemporary Europe, and with it Spain, is a ruined world built on the collapsed forms of two distinct belief systems: Catholicism and Rationalism.

These two worldviews are defined by Unamuno in terms of their ability to explain death and justify the suffering implicit in a life that is to end in the total annihilation of identity.[39] "When faced with the terrible mystery of mortality, man adopts different attitudes and seeks by various means to console himself for having been born."[40] Catholicism and Rationalism are, for Unamuno, man's two most basic attempts at comforting himself in the face of death and the suffering occasioned by the conscious awareness of its anticipation.[41]

Catholicism, contends Unamuno, explains and justifies the suffering that is caused by the conscious anticipation of death by promising eternal life. "The discovery of death is what reveals God to us, and the death of the perfect man, of the Christ, was the supreme revelation of death, of the man who was not supposed to die but did die."[42] Unamuno's point is that the Church, by means of its "dogma . . . of the resurrection and immortality of Christ," guarantees the resurrection and immortality of each and every supplicant that believes in the sacrificial character of Jesus Christ's death.[43] Catholicism promises to make the death of every individual seem, like that of the Christ, to be unjust. By means of Jesus Christ's suffering on the cross, man is given an opportunity to enter into solidarity with a transcendental order. Man's suffering, not unlike that of Jesus Christ, is thus justified by the promise of eternal communion with God. As such, Unamuno posits the mystical experience of this union, or ecstasis, as the essence of Catholicism.

Despite its essential power to console man, Catholicism, in its historical and institutional manifestations, nevertheless fails to satisfy man completely: "The Catholic solution to our problem," writes Unamuno, "to our only vital problem, the problem of immortality and the eternal salvation of the individual soul, satisfies the will and, therefore also, life; but . . . it does not satisfy reason."[44] Rationalism doubts the truth, even the verisimilitude, of the basic tenets of Catholic faith. Hence, for Unamuno, Catholicism is pitted, historically, against Rationalism.

Not unlike his treatment, in *En torno al casticismo,* of Castile's prototypical warring communities, Unamuno depicts Catholicism's historical struggle with Rationalism in terms of a vital defense of life: Catholicism "affirms what is vital, and in order to affirm itself it creates its enemy, rationalism, an entire dogmatic construction, and the Church defends that dogma against rationalism, against Protestantism and against modernism. It defends life."[45] Catholicism wages this defensive war against the skepticism of Rationalism by appealing to the authorities of "the tradition and the revelation of the word of God."[46] Yet, because "faith does not feel completely secure with the consent of the many, nor with tradition, nor under authority" it must seek out "the support of its enemy reason" and attempt to rationalize itself, thus satisfying the exigencies of reason.[47]

It is by virtue of this attempt to rationalize its central, vitalistic dogma—the dogma of the resurrection and immortality of individual human identities—that, argues Unamuno, Catholicism gives rise to its own decadence. The rationalization of Catholic beliefs leads inevitably to an abstruse, institutionalized system of beliefs: "in this way, Catholic dogma became a system of contradictions, more or less harmonized . . . that does not satisfy reason. And reason makes its own demands, as imperious as those of life."[48] In attempting to satisfy Rationalism by way of the application of theological reasoning, Catholicism weakens its vital power to console men for their suffering: "theology . . . is nothing more than dis-empowered Christianity."[49]

Unamuno identifies Rationalism as the source of the decline of Catholicism and, ultimately, as the origin of one aspect of contemporary European decadence: "the Renaissance, the Reformation and the Revolution have contributed to the de-essentialization, that is, the de-Catholicization of Europe, replacing the ideal of an eternal and transcendental life with the ideal of progress, of reason, of science."[50] Rationalism is at the heart of the collapse of Europe's, and Spain's, otherworldly religiousness: "The famous maladie du siècle . . . is nothing other than the loss of faith in the immortality of the soul and the human finality of the Universe."[51]

The ideal with which Rationalism seeks to replace the Catholic promise of eternal union with God is, as Unamuno conceives it, the enlightened notion of progress. Rationalism, in other words, seeks to console men for their suffering by promising the eventual worldly redemption of all mankind; by promising, as Kant does, the logical inevitability of perpetual peace. Yet, from the outset, Unamuno questions the notion of progress, and more in particular, its capacity to replace the Catholic sense of life with another sense that also satisfies man's innate "hunger for immortality."[52] Accordingly, Unamuno argues that progress is an antivital notion.[53] Progress, contends Unamuno, is an illness because it reduces life and consciousness "primarily to the service of the instinct of self-preservation" as opposed to elevating it by having it serve the "instinct of perpetuation."[54]

The world that Rationalism creates—a world devoid of a divine telos and, consequently, devoid of the human integrity and solidarity guaranteed by that telos, turns out to be one in which death and the suffering attendant on it are, ultimately, without any meaningful, transcendental justification. Suffering is no longer viewed as a means to fortifying human solidarity or even as a means to entering into communion with God, but as something to be avoided as an obstacle in the way of "the joie de vivre."[55] Consequently, Rationalism fails to aid men in their moral evolution.

Taken in this light, the decadence of modern Europe, as of modern Spain, is double. Modern man is, for Unamuno, stuck between these two collapsed forms. His suffering is without justification, without an explanation, without a sense of purpose. This "abyss," as Unamuno calls it, is the foundation on which modern man is to forge a "tragic sense of life." This tragic sense is, moreover, modern man's only source for giving meaning to his suffering: "Neither . . . can the vital longing for human immortality find a rational confirmation, nor is reason capable of giving us an incentive and consolation in life that would have us treat life as an end in itself. And yet here, at the bottom of the abyss, volitional desperation comes face to face with rational scepticism and they embrace like brothers. And it is from this embrace, a tragic embrace . . . that a wellspring of life, of a serious and terrible life, will flow."[56] As such, Unamuno places his hope for a regeneration of both modern Spain and the whole of Western civilization—in the face of the collapse of both otherworldly religiousness and rationalistic-scientific optimism—in the recuperation of a tragic sense of life.

This regenerating tragic view cannot, however, be sustained in the absence of tragic myth; hence, Unamuno's devotion to the search for a new and compelling form of tragic myth in the modern world. To that end, Unamuno justifies the terror and horror of suffering in a godless, modern world in terms of an otherworldly, divine and religious illusion: that is, the "tragedy of Christ, the divine tragedy."[57] This divine tragedy has, for Unamuno, its human and imaginative counterpart in "the human, intra-human tragedy . . . of Don Quixote," that is, in the national *intrahistory* of modern Spain's putatively sacrificial decline from empire.[58] Thus conceived, Unamuno's notion of the "tragic" is more in tune with the Catholic notion of agony,[59] or the idea that suffering is a means to redemption and communion with God, than it is with certain other post-Hegelian tragic or existentialist critiques of decadence with which Unamuno's tragic sense has often been associated.[60]

As exemplified by Nietzsche's 1866 *The Birth of Tragedy*, the post-Hegelian reading of the modern "tragic sense of life" relies, for purposes of regenerating the modern world, not on a religious but on an aesthetic transformation of life. In Nietzsche, tragedy is to fulfill the singular task of artistically transforming the "terror and horror of existence" into a "splendid illusion" by covering over the existential angst of modern man with a dissonant "veil of beauty."[61] Therefore this suffering is "justified," for Nietzsche, in aesthetic terms. This "metaphysical intention of art to transfigure" life, which Nietzsche (at least in 1866) discovers in Wagner's work, is not present in Unamuno's conception of the tragic sense of life.[62]

For Unamuno, life is not to be justified by means of an aesthetic transformation, but by means of spiritual labor, by the struggle of each man to bear his own cross: "to imitate Christ means for each man to take up his own cross . . . just as Christ took his up."[63] Moreover, insofar as Unamuno's Quixotism, which in *Del sentimiento trágico de la vida* he characterizes as "Spanish Catholic religiosity—quixotic religiosity," is but a human version of the divine tragedy of Jesus Christ, it is not, properly speaking, a specifically aesthetic formula for the regenerative transformation of the modern world, but a moral and religious one.[64] Finally, Unamuno's search for a new and compelling form of tragic myth does not lead him to posit anything that is, in fact, new or modern as potentially regenerative; instead, it leads him to seek to recuperate a medieval, Christian sense of the tragic.

The angst of the modern European man is to be overcome, according to Unamuno, by the recuperation of this so-called tragic or essentially Catholic sense of life. The Spanish nation, a nation of spiritual warriors for whom ascetic self-abnegation and mysticism are a national philosophy,[65] is singularly imbued with this regenerating tragic sense of life: "What I call the tragic sense of life in men and in nations is . . . our tragic sense of life, that of Spaniards and the Spanish nation."[66] Conversely, Unamuno considers that the other European nations, particularly the French, the Germans, and the British lack this tragic sense.[67] As far as Unamuno is concerned, it is left to the essentially Catholic Spanish nation to recuperate this tragic sense of life and, by so doing, first regenerate itself and then the whole of modern Western civilization.

In an attempt to reverse the decadent rationalization of the Spanish nation's vitality, Unamuno seeks to re-essentialize the Catholic character of

Spanish national identity. The key to this essentializing recuperation of the nation's *casticismo* is the conquest of death: not of decadence, but of death per se. By abstracting Spain's modern decadence from its historical context and placing it within the theoretical, metaphysical and religious context of death, Unamuno seeks not only to discover a sense of purpose behind Spain's modern decadence, but also to affirm that perceived decadence as the proof of his nation's (re)new(ed) messianic role in the modern world.[68]

Spain, reasons Unamuno, is best qualified to act as the spiritual regenerating force in Europe because its national tragedy, its rise and fall from Christian empire, is an intrahuman version of the divine tragedy. "The tragedy of Christ, the divine tragedy, is the tragedy of the cross. Pilate, the sceptic . . . wanted, by means of satire, to turn it into a comedy and he conceived that farcical idea of . . . 'Behold the man!' But the people, more human than he, the people that desire tragedy, shouted in response: 'Crucify him! Crucify him!' And the other tragedy, the human tragedy . . . is the tragedy of Don Quixote."[69] Unamuno presents the suffering of Jesus Christ on the cross and the suffering of a Quixotist Spain in the modern world as two events with a similar redemptive quality. Both suffer the ridicule of their contemporaries. Pontius Pilate ridiculed Jesus because he claimed to be king. Likewise, modern Europe has ridiculed Spain because it has claimed to represent God's will on Earth and attempted to counter the "progress" of the Reformation and the Enlightenment with the "faith" of the Inquisition. According to Unamuno, the ridicule that both suffer serves to increase the value of their suffering and, with it, the redemptive or tragic character of their self-sacrifice.

To suffer like the Christ is to bear one's cross. This, for Unamuno, means that agony is attainable by everyone or, at least, anyone who, like him and his Quixotist Spain, would labor spiritually. Thus for Unamuno in *Del sentimiento trágico de la vida,* suffering takes on the aura of the regenerator's ultimate *oficio* or calling in life. Suffering is what links the *vidente* to eternity; it is what makes his communion with the divine possible; and as Unamuno would have it, it is, finally, what permits all men to enter into community with one another. In this way, Unamuno imagines that modern Spain and Europe are to be re-essentialized, re-Catholicized. In this way too, Unamuno envisions a "tragic" Spanish nation which, in defense of its "tragic sense of life," might finally set about the life-affirming task of obeying its "instinct for perpetuation" and reconquer its lost historical glory and cultural imperium.

5

Diminished Value

The polemicist, essayist, and diplomat Ramiro de Maeztu y Whitney (1874–1936) was to fascist Spain what the poet and playwright Federico García Lorca was to republican Spain: a martyr. On July 30, 1936, with Spain in the throes of its civil war, Maeztu—who had spent the previous five years writing for the fascist journal *Acción Española*—was taken prisoner by a small band of republican militiamen and incarcerated in Madrid's Model Prison for Women. Shortly after midnight, on October 29, 1936, or the third anniversary of the founding of the Falange, Maeztu was executed. This Spanish nationalist thinker, for whom Hispanic cultural and spiritual unity had come to represent the ideal of a regenerated Spanish nation and empire, died at the hands of his own countrymen, a casualty of civil war and the split national identity of modern Spain.

Born in the Spanish Basque countries to a Cuban father and an English mother, Maeztu's polemical writings had not always appealed to Spain's *casticistas.* In 1891, at the young age of seventeen, Maeztu had left Spain for Cuba, where he worked at his father's sugar plantation and regularly read the works of Galdós, Ibsen, Schopenhauer, Marx, and Kropotkin to workers in a nearby tobacco company. On his return to Spain in 1894, Maeztu began his long career as an essayist and intellectual agitator. By 1897, he had managed to insinuate his way into the heart of intellectual life in Madrid, working closely with Azorín and Baroja. When, in 1898, Cuba won its independence from Spain, Maeztu's allegiances were torn. In part, he viewed Spain's final imperial collapse as did the regenerationists—that is, as a "National Disaster" that revealed modern Spain's decadence. In part, he sympathized with Cuban independence and saw in the superior technological and economic force of the

United States an example by means of which the Spanish nation might also enter into its own Gilded Age. Maeztu voiced these ambivalent views most thoroughly in his 1899 *Hacia otra España.*

In 1905, Maeztu left his native Spain for London, the capital of his mother's homeland. He spent the following fifteen years there working as a journalist and, eventually, as a war correspondent for Spanish and Latin American newspapers. During his tenure as a war correspondent, he visited frontlines in France, Italy, and Belgium and, in 1918, he accompanied the occupying Allied forces into Germany. It is to this period that belongs his most serious attempt at producing a political-philosophical treatise on decadence and regeneration: his 1918 *Authority, Liberty and Function in the Light of the War,* where he opposes the decadent notion of democratic liberty to the regenerating notion of syndicalist functionality.

In 1919, Maeztu returned to Madrid and began to disseminate among his Spanish compatriots his recently formulated ideas concerning modern European decadence.[1] Unlike Unamuno, who was adamantly opposed to the dictatorship of Primo de Rivera, Maeztu became one of the principal defenders of that military regime's authoritarian approach to Spanish national regeneration. He was rewarded for his support by being named Spain's Ambassador to Argentina: a position that he was to hold between 1928 and 1930. On his return to Spain from Argentina, he began to publish, in Acción Española, excerpts from a neo-imperialist apology that he had begun drafting while overseas: *Defensa de la Hispanidad.* It is in this text that the initial ambivalence that Maeztu expressed in *Hacia otra España* concerning Spain's loss of empire gives way completely to the antihumanist views he espoused in *Authority, Liberty and Function* and is replaced, ultimately, by an impassioned defense of Spain's would-be universalizing, civilizing, and spiritualizing mission in the modern world.

The Power of Gilded Individuality

Refashioning Ganivet's notion of "abulia," in his 1899 *Hacia otra España* Maeztu envisions modern Spanish national decadence as a state of progressive moral paralysis. "Paralysis," writes Maeztu in this regard, "there is no other way to define the continual deadening of our collective national life . . . Paralysis . . . explains the country's frightening indifference to public affairs . . . Intellectual paralysis . . . Moral paralysis . . . Paralysis of the imagination . . . Spain prefers its paralytic wheelchair, in which it is pulled backward and pushed forward by blind events, to the severe labor of recreating its will and forging its own path."[2] The modern Spanish nation, as Maeztu here describes it in regenerationist terms, is a paralytic body that has been overwhelmed by its inability to act and been defeated by its own helpless inactivity.

In keeping with Ganivet's idea that *abulia* is the result of the Spanish nation's past imperial and colonial enterprises, and in keeping also with Unamuno's idea that the nation's traditional sense of its *casticismo* explains its imperial rise and fall, Maeztu attributes the paralysis of the modern Spanish nation to the traditional values that governed the nation's life in the past. Life in "Old Spain," as Maeztu calls it, was characterized by the values of military honor, religious piety, and social harmony.[3] If between 1895 and 1898 Restoration Spain went to war with Cuba, Puerto Rico, the Philippines, and the United States, argues Maeztu, it was because the leaders of the Spanish nation felt compelled to reaffirm these traditional values. The modern Spanish nation's decadent paralysis led, in the end, to Spain's imperial collapse.

The origins of this decadent paralysis of the national will are tied to what Maeztu perceives as the nation's undying belief in a traditional notion of justice as harmony.[4] This tradition, he argues, is based in the classical view of the physical world as stagnant; it is grounded, in other words, in the failure of the human senses to perceive the world as it truly is, that is, a confused mass of atoms in perpetual motion.[5] As Maeztu understands it, the perpetual movement of atoms carries with it certain moral implications: "Things are not in harmony . . . every minute devours the previous, every life is the result of infinite deaths, and if a fundamental law could be inferred from this supreme brutality it would be the law of assassination!"[6] Reality, Maeztu argues, is harsh, and only an ethical system that is as equally severe as that reality can serve as a guide for right conduct in human affairs. Right conduct, in this sense, becomes predatory behavior where the lives of the fittest are sustained by the necessary deaths of their weaker victims of prey.

If, as Maeztu suggests, life is sustained by death, then any attempt at establishing harmony as the goal of social and political justice will necessarily meet with frustration.[7] Experience teaches, according to Maeztu, that justice is an impossible, utopian ideal. At best, he argues, "What is usually identified as justice for the weak is, and always will be, charity—I would say abdication—of the strong."[8] Justice, in the traditional sense, is, for Maeztu, nothing more than a formula for the decadent renunciation of power by the strong in favor of the weak. It is, in short, a formula for decadence.

Decadence, reasons Maeztu, sets in whenever a nation insists on expending its energy, its will power, in an attempt to realize the impossibility of a harmonious social order. Nations, he argues, are comprised of an instinctual, vitalistic aspect and a phantasmagoric, historical aspect. He refers to the vitalistic in Unamunoian terms as the "instinct of mutual association and defense" and to the historical as "entities of reason, bookish phantoms."[9] The vitalistic is connected to the defense of life; the historical, to the defense of the memory of a past life. Hence, for Maeztu, decadence results whenever a nation's vitalistic instinct is governed by its historical memory rather than by the severe, competitive, facts of immediate reality. And this, as Maeztu understands it, is precisely what happened with Spain and the War of 1895–1898.

In one of the several essays of *Hacia otra España* that Maeztu dedicates specifically to interpreting the war, "El sí a la muerte," he links the defense of "historical Spain" to the eventual defeat and decadent paralysis of "modern Spain." "Spain had to say 'yes' to the war," he postulates, "because our raison d'être has always been to fight and we weren't about to go against our nature at such a supreme hour."[10] Maeztu demonstrates how, during the war, the leaders of Restoration Spain elevated the defense of Spain's "historical" identity—"the expansive History of conquest of our nation"—to the level of a heroic, transcendental and absolute identity. This defense, reasons Maeztu, led to Spain's loss of its colonies and to the death of the Spanish nation's imperial identity. But Maeztu does not exactly criticize the leaders of Restoration Spain for having insisted on such a decadent defense of the Old Spain. Instead, he affirms the need of this Old Spain to die with honor and thus avoid destroying the nation's imperial legacy: "I want our fall to be a beautiful fall; if we have not known how to say 'yes' to life, I want us to know how to say 'yes' to death, converting death into something that is glorious, and worthy of Spain."[11] To do otherwise, he argues, would be tantamount to allowing the nation to die with the "repugnant agony of a condemned man who, . . . because he betrays the legend of his courage, . . . dishonors the prestige of death."[12] As such, Maeztu seeks to transform Spain's modern defeat into a moral victory.

In another essay of *Hacia otra España,* titled "El sí a la vida," Maeztu posits the pain and agony of defeat, indeed the imagined prestige of death itself, as a form of historical purification and an event that makes the idea of regeneration, or rather, the idea of a modernizing spiritual and moral resurrection, seem plausible: "after the pain," he writes, "one needs a far more tenacious and intense heroism to say 'yes' to life than to say 'yes' to death."[13] Here, Maeztu turns his back on any honorable defense of Spain's "historical" identity and, instead, posits the vital defense of its future destiny as a task requiring an even greater heroic effort. Thus, after a violent purge, after the death of the Old Spain, a New Spain is to emerge.

Maeztu entrusts the spiritual and moral transformation of the nation to an elite force of entrepreneurial and economically competitive individuals—"powerful and tenacious men, of unbreakable will," he calls them—for whom money has a "reverential" or spiritual value: "Morality is always found at the root of economic life. The economy is spirit. Money is spirit."[14] Maeztu posits the entrepreneurial spirit of these willful and capable men as a means to modernizing both the economy of Restoration Spain and the cultural value of Spain's national life.[15]

Maeztu's celebration of the regenerating power of economic self-interest is not, however, without qualification. Although he does embrace economic individualism as a legitimate, regenerating practice, he does not embrace the social and political theories that, since the Enlightenment, have been associated with it. Indeed, the competitive individualism of Maeztu's national utopia is devoid of either a social contract or a natural right theory that might universalize the right to competition of all members of the national community. Instead, he reserves the practice of regenerating competition to his competitive, supramoral elites who, by stimulating economic regeneration, will spiritually transform the decadent nation and claim their noble right to preside over it. "Let us sing to gold," he concludes, "*vile* gold will transform the yellow and dry countenance of our land into a youthful visage: *vile* gold will build the other Spain!"[16]

WISDOM AND THE GUILD

Even though, in his 1899 *Hacia otra España,* Maeztu does reject the search for justice as constituting a morally corrupting utopian ideal—"the notion of justice only intoxicates intelligence," he does admit to having always wanted to discover justice.[17] Indeed, he claims that this utopian search for harmonious community had, at one point, been the most basic concern motivating his thought, but that he abandoned it once he had realized that: "life is neither just nor unjust . . . it is . . . movement."[18] By 1916 and the publication of *Authority, Liberty and Function,* Maeztu rescinds his previous attacks on the notion of justice; and, with renewed anxiety, he takes up his old search for a harmonious community.

The experience of the Great War of 1914–1918 convinces Maeztu of the urgent need to seek out a formula for international harmony by means of which the modern world might be spared the repetition of the horrors of another world war.[19] As he understands them, the many horrors of the Great War all share a common origin; they stem from the misapplication of the same vitalistic values that he had affirmed as regenerative in *Hacia otra España.*

Thus, in *Authority, Liberty and Function,* Maeztu no longer regards the indefinite expansion of individual power as a regenerative force; rather, he views it as a chaotic, undisciplined, and decadent impulse toward individuation that violates the civilized ideal and "objective" value of human solidarity. Accordingly, Maeztu links the origins of the Great War, as of all wars, to the experience of decadence: "International conflicts arise chiefly because the course of history, with the growth of some countries and the decay of others, alters the status quo."[20] He explains this shift in the status of nations, as the failure, in cultural terms, to increase and perpetuate human solidarity.[21] Maeztu discovers the most extreme example of this tendency to affirm self-interests at the expense of solidarity at neither the economic nor the social level, but at the politicoethical level of the modern nation-state. This is particularly so of the German nation-state, which argues Maeztu is based in a fundamental confusion between would-be universal, objective values and subjective values. Echoing Anglo-Allied perceptions of the so-called Prussian state, Maeztu censors the German nation-state because, to his mind, it seeks to legitimize as a transcendental moral truth whatever it judges to be in its best interest.

Accordingly, Maeztu advances the thesis, in *Authority, Liberty and Function*, that the "civilized" modern world is in the throes of a crisis caused by the prevalence of decadent ethicopolitical values and, therefore, in desperate need of radical moral transformation. This position leads him to formulate a critique of the decadent "subjective values" on which modern nation-states base both their claims to moral agency and their right to pursue their own interests. In line with this critique, Maeztu posits the idea of a just society as one based, not in the will-to-power of the most fit and competitive, but in the "functional" and "objective" values of human solidarity. As such, Maeztu views the Great War as indicative of the need for "an authoritarian political instrument" capable of containing the "revolutionary aggression" characteristic of a modern world organized about the "subjective" principles of the nation-state.[22]

Concretely, what Maeztu proposes is a recuperation of the "objective" and "functional" values of the medieval guild-system or what he calls the "syndicalist ideal": "Trade Unions," ventures Maeztu, "do not seem . . . to be merely associations for the defense of working-class interests, but institutions of order and discipline. By their growth alone they have revealed . . . the possibility of a social order without the need of a sole power. If only the methods of the Trade Unions be extended to all classes in social life, organized with respect to their functions . . . then the need for a unitarian State will automatically disappear."[23] As international institutions of order and discipline and not as class-conscious, revolutionary organizations, then, Maeztu would have his guilds function as a corrective to the unrestrained pursuit of decadent self-interest that has, according to him, led to the War of 1914–1918.

The failure to increase and perpetuate human solidarity is largely explained, for Maeztu, by the "heretical" philosophical heritage of the modern world. Maeztu considers that the "subjective values" espoused by the modern political, ethical and metaphysical discourses of the Renaissance and the Enlightenment, which affirm the moral agency of man as a transcendental end in himself, fail to restrain or otherwise limit man's innate "tendency to grow at the expense of others."[24] Despite this "modern" focus of Maeztu's critique on European moral decadence, that critique is ultimately tied to a premodern notion of original sin: "For the causes of sin"—that is, the causes of modern decadence, writes Maeztu—"are two, and two only: lust and pride."[25] Out of lust, he argues, individuals, associations of individuals and even entire nations have, in the modern age, turned to the pursuit of happiness and luxury. They have become hedonistic.[26] Or again, out of a sense of pride, they have turned to the pursuit of power as an end in itself. They have become tyrannical.[27] By pursuing happiness and power as ends in themselves, therefore, the individuals, social associations and nation-states of the modern world have tended to transgress the "necessary" and "just" limits of human solidarity. They have fallen into an ethicopolitical state of decadence and sin.[28]

Consequently, if the modern world is to achieve some semblance of communal harmony, modern man must prove capable of mastering himself and his sinful nature; he must overcome the temptations of hedonism and tyranny. As Maeztu understands it, the problem with an ethicopolitical system based in "subjective values" is not only that under its sway modern men have failed to delimit their animalistic proclivities but also that they have actually been encouraged to exercise them with liberty.[29] The subjective principles of the modern age have thus encouraged men to "grant to their personality" an "excessive value"; that is, to legitimize themselves as hedonists and tyrants, as "sinner[s]."[30]

Maeztu considers that the Great War of 1914–1918 is a just punishment that has been dealt to the modern world following its "transgression of human solidarity."[31] In this regard, Maeztu posits the experience of the Great War as a morally transforming social and historical event: "War . . . creates the spirit of solidarity necessary for affecting . . . the transformation of . . . society."[32] Moreover, as a punishment for sin, war is also a necessary, recuperative discipline that can impose order on the lives of men: "war is a lesson in solidarity"; it is "a lesson in discipline."[33] And so it is that not unlike Unamuno in *En torno al casticismo*, Maeztu celebrates war as precisely that which gives rise to human solidarity. Because it requires of all members of a society that they set aside their personal interests and differences in order to defend themselves from a common enemy, war is the origin of an "ethically harmonious" and justly disciplined society.[34]

For Maeztu, the medieval guild system represents a peacetime equivalent to this wartime ideal of solidarity and discipline. The medieval "guild spirit," as Maeztu calls it, although mostly lost to modern man, can, he promises, "rise again."[35] Medieval guilds, for Maeztu, were "inspired by a spirit of 'balance of power' among their own members."[36] The basis for the internal constitution of these guilds was the complimentarity of "the two rules of Limitation and Hierarchy."[37]

The guild principle of limitation, Maeztu reasons, recognizes the common humanity of "the humblest of men" and "the most competent of masters," submitting the measure of their value, their personal earnings, power and wealth, to the notion of solidarity.[38] Conversely, the guild principle of hierarchy divides and subdivides the members of the guilds according to the excellence with which they serve the aims and goals of the guild; hence, the organization of guild membership into apprentices, craftsmen, and masters. By virtue of the self-sacrificing demands that they place on each individual, the guilds offer their members the chance for redemption and recuperation within human solidarity; and they also offer a controlled means for individuation and self-realization.

When viewed in such terms, Maeztu's guild system can be seen as a theoretical effort to justify anti-individualism and authoritarianism as a means for establishing a common sense of humanity. The modern model for this anti-individualist and hierarchically organized community is, for Maeztu, the national military: "Great . . . armies exemplify in themselves the spirit and the rules of the Guilds . . . the members of a Guild are associated in one thing, in a function . . . from [which] . . . they receive, like the army from the national defense, their discipline, their dignity, and their internal rules of compulsory work, limitation of pay, and hierarchy of functions."[39] Viewed in this light, Maeztu's guild utopia is reminiscent of the disciplined brotherhood in arms that Unamuno celebrates as the "warring community": "Every army," writes Maeztu, "is a guild in which, in the hour of danger, the whole nation incorporates itself."[40]

Inherent to the inhibiting and hierarchical principles of Maeztu's guild utopia, therefore, is the affirmation of an ascetic basis for "just" leadership and "just" public administration: "Given any scale of values"—writes Maeztu in this regard—"those men or associations of men are functionaries who devote themselves to maintaining or increasing values. To those functionaries are due the powers, rights, dignities, and pay corresponding to their function. The men or associations of men who do not devote themselves to preserving or increasing values are not functionaries; and therefore, they ought not to have any rights at all. And those who destroy existing values are criminals who deserve punishment."[41] Only those who have demonstrated their submission and service to the values of the guilds—the so-called functionaries—are capable, reasons Maeztu, of making any legitimate claim to "rights."

Accordingly, Maeztu posits the conscious awareness of man's innate sinful nature and the need to limit and govern it as the key to attaining self-mastery: "The Christian Church may offer to all Westerners the model of associations."[42] This is the case, maintains Maeztu, because the Church provides the "powerless" and "isolated individual" with a model for redemption and the recuperation of his place within human solidarity.[43] The Church, for Maeztu, "is an association founded on a thing, Christianity . . . [its] end . . . is not the association, but those things which [it] proposes to itself": the Christian ideal of universal, hierarchical and egalitarian spiritual unity.[44] The Church, then, like the military, is an exemplary association in that it provides a model for the organization of men around the primacy of things, of so-called "objective values"; in this case, the value of "Grace." Also, like the military, the Church unites men spiritually in the "functional labor" of attending to the maintenance and increase of human solidarity. In sum, Maeztu's guild utopia is modeled after the example of a Catholic crusade: the sword and the cross, united into a singularly spirited symbol for redemption.

Indeed, it is with the religious zeal of a spiritual conquistador that Maeztu calls for the sacrifice of all "subjective" personality to the "objective" spirit of solidarity implicit in his formulation of a guild utopia. In this sense, Maeztu—like Ganivet and Unamuno—assigns a central and exemplary function to sacrificial heroism. The function of the hero is, for Maeztu, to "stimulate the nations . . . and thinkers to adjust, as far as possible . . . to the mystery of life and reality: Death and Resurrection."[45] The hero is to do this by setting an example, that is, by committing the ultimate act of ascetic discipline and offering himself, symbolically, over to death: "Personality must be sacrificed."[46] Only by following this sacrificial and heroic example on a massive scale, suggests Maeztu, will the European nations—among them Spain—rise from out of their modern state of moral and spiritual decadence.

Ultimately, for Maeztu, the success of this regenerating sacrifice of personality is made to depend on men's faith in the objective values served by the guild system: "This act of faith"—affirms Maeztu—"is a kind of suicide, but it is a death followed immediately by resurrection. What we lose as personalities we reconquer, multiplied, as functionaries."[47] In the end, by the act of denying his subjectivity, passions, and worldliness, the individual is reborn in the splendor of a mystical awakening, depicted here as a reconquest of human solidarity. "The doctrine of Death and Resurrection"—concludes Maeztu—"opens also the way for the submission of man to higher things."[48] As in *Hacia otra España,* Maeztu's regenerated modern man has said "yes" to death in order to say "yes" still more definitively to life, only that this new life is that of a voluntary servant.

Love and Empire

If in *Authority, Liberty and Function* Maeztu's sacrificial heroism can be taken to pertain to any European nation, in *Defensa de la Hispanidad* it is claimed as a cultural and national patrimony exclusive to the nations of the so-called Hispanic world. It is in this work of 1934 that Maeztu names his redemptive and self-sacrificing hero the "Hispanic Gentleman."[49] The regeneration of Spain, of Latin America, and indeed, of the entire world is thus made to depend on the exemplary spiritual and cultural ideals of the Hispanic world's nobility.

Fifteen years after the Great War, Maeztu looked about and found no country, no nation, no culture to envy or to otherwise admire: "For the first time in two centuries, the Hispanic nations find that they can no longer venerate those great foreign countries . . . as they did when they thought or it appeared that they thought for all the nations of the world . . . Germany . . . France . . . The United States."[50] Moreover, when Maeztu wrote *Defensa de la Hispanidad,* the world economy was in the throes of a great depression. Nation's, states and industries the world over were crippled by debt, unemployment, and a growing sense of political instability. "The nations that we have held up as examples currently find themselves in such a critical and difficult situation that they can no longer point the other nations of the world toward prosperity . . . Onto what foreign nation can we now turn our gaze and not see signs of failure?"[51] "The gods," concludes Maeztu, "have departed."[52] These absent gods are, according to Maeztu, principally two: Liberalism and Communism. Both are forms of what Maeztu, repeating the thesis that he develops in *Authority, Liberty and Function* concerning subjective values, now calls "modern humanism."

The basic postulate of Liberalism, or what Maeztu calls "the humanism of pride," is that "if each man obeys only his own commands, he will develop his faculties to the fullest of possibilities."[53] Universal progress on an individual basis is, then, the basic promise inherent in this type of "modern humanism." This doctrine, which Maeztu admits to having been "universal in its origins," has nevertheless failed to live up to its universal, humanistic postulates: "the individualist banner . . . has wound up being the motto of those nations that believe themselves to be superior."[54] In this way Liberalism, rather than fulfilling its promise for universal progress actually encourages decadence: the pride of the few at war with the resentment of the many. Solidarity, or what for Maeztu ought to be the aim of "progress," is consequently forfeited to the pursuit of passion.

According to Maeztu, the basic postulate of Communism, or what he refers to as "materialist humanism," is that it is possible, on the basis of the supposed "essential equality of bodies," to create "a society in which social differences are inexorably suppressed . . . and in which all men work for everyone and each man receives his ration from the community."[55] According to Maeztu, by negating the individuating aspect of human labor, which aims to attain the recognition and esteem of one's fellow citizens, and by treating labor as though it were meant only to satisfy men's bodily needs, Communism fails to spiritually enliven human life. "The reason for the failure of communism is obvious, economics is neither an animal nor a physiological activity, but a spiritual one."[56] Labor, for Maeztu, in order for it to be at all spiritual and a means to redemption, must be carried out in accordance with the precepts of the ascetic and mystical voluntary servitude of a guild functionary. Thus, Communism, or "materialist humanism," is doomed to fail and has entered a state of decadence because its postulate of universal human equality is based in a spiritually decadent negation of "the equality of souls."

Having thus demonstrated to his satisfaction the death of these two modern gods—Liberalism and Communism—Maeztu posits, in their stead, the god of the Hispanic community of nations: "Spanish humanism." The basic postulate of this Spanish humanism, he explains, is that "there is no sinner who cannot be redeemed; nor is there any just man who is not at the edge of the abyss."[57] Thus, while recognizing that there are personal, social, and national differences that necessarily exist among men, Maeztu simultaneously affirms their essential spiritual equality in relation to his Spanish humanism. All men, regardless of their standing in life, are sinners and, therefore, in need of salvation. For Maeztu, only the Spanish and, by extension, the various other Hispanic nations contain within themselves the faith to save both themselves and others.[58]

In an attempt to prove his point, Maeztu constructs a suitable national-imperial history of Spain. He associates the period of greatest generative value enjoyed by the doctrine of Spanish humanism with the formation of the Spanish Empire in the sixteenth and seventeenth centuries. He cites the Christian Iberian peninsula, the discovery, conquest and colonization of the Americas and Spain's interminable wars against the "heretics" of the Reformation as proof of the Spanish nation's unshakable faith in the teachings of the Roman Catholic Church.[59] What is more, Maeztu views these events as the origin of universal, world history: "Those Spaniards . . . created the physical unity of the world . . . they constituted the moral unity of the human genus. By summoning the possibility of salvation and placing it before all men . . . they made Universal History possible, which prior to our sixteenth century had not been but a plurality of unconnected histories."[60] In short, he portrays the Spanish nation as having a unique, transcendentally sanctioned historical mission: "our destiny in the future is the same as it was in the past: to attract the different races to our territories and mold them in the crucible of our universal spirit."[61]

It is Maeztu's "Hispanic Gentlemen" who are to achieve this messianic, historical mission in the modern world. By organizing themselves, their nations and the world according to the precepts of Hispanicism, the modern values of liberty, equality, and fraternity are to be replaced by the Hispanic values of service, hierarchy and brotherhood. These are, of course, the values of Maeztu's syndicalist ideal, whereby the whole of humanity is to be organized in accordance with the disciplinary and ascetic heroism of sacrificial self-mastery.

The one figure that most thoroughly exemplifies this ideal is, for Maeztu, as for Ganivet and Unamuno before him, the figure of Don Quixote. "Don Quixote is love . . . he is the finale of the national epic of the sixteenth century, the disenchantment that follows overexertion and excessive idealism, but he is also the initiation of a new mandate: 'Don't be a Quixote!' This new command is at times prudent, at times it is the killer of enthusiasm . . . By means of which I mean to suggest that . . . the *Quixote* has yet to be recreated."[62] The story of the *Quixote,* which Maeztu here posits as a spiritualized version of Spanish and Hispanic national history, is to be rewritten following the "path set forth by God."[63] The spirit of Don Quixote is destined to erase modern history as well as to continue on its own course, making possible the perpetuation of Spain's so-called universalizing "national epic."

6

Resentful Masses

The affirmation of a charismatic and regenerative elite as against the perceived maliciousness and decadence of the modern masses is a constant, central, and organizing theme in the work of the Spanish philosopher and essayist José Ortega y Gasset (1883–1955). In an essay he published in 1902, at the age of nineteen, Ortega, whose father was one of the most influential newspaper editors of Restoration Spain, virtuously affirms: "When men of delicate criteria come to form part of the public, they lose their beautiful qualities. Thus, a multitude of one-hundred individuals who make up a community is inferior to the sum of those one-hundred intellectualities taken separately."[1] A few years later, in an essay of 1906, a still young Ortega asserts: "Within the republic, it is the man of letters who must awaken the minds of those who remain unaware; he must disturb the drowsiness of popular consciousness with sharp words and images of the nation."[2] In 1914, by which time he was teaching philosophy at the university in Madrid, he reformulates his elitism in terms of a patriotic mission: "It is necessary to aspire to introduce political action into the habits of the Spanish masses. How could this possibly be achieved without the existence of an enthusiastic minority, which, of its own accord, might operate on them with tenacity, with energy, with efficiency? There is no sense in pushing Spain toward appreciable improvements while the worker in the city, the laborer in the fields, the middle-class in the towns and in the capitals have not learned . . . to desire a clear, concrete and serious future."[3] With the publication of *España invertebrada* in 1922, elitism becomes the centerpiece of Ortega's sociological theorizing: "Herein lies the elemental creative mechanism of all societies: the exemplarity of the few articulates itself in the docility of the many. The result is that their example spreads and those who are inferior perfect themselves by adopting the sense of those who are superior."[4] Finally, in his 1931 *La rebellión de las masas,* a book that was to gain international acclaim for Ortega, he asserts once again: "by reason of its very essence, and whether one likes it or not, human society *is* always aristocratic; indeed, a society is a society only to the extent to which it is aristocratic, and it stops being one insofar as it stops being aristocratic."[5]

As this brief survey of citations illustrates, elitism is the prism through which Ortega consistently contemplates modern Spanish decadence and regeneration. As he understands it, decadence is a moral and political perversion. Decadence occurs, for Ortega, whenever a nation or civilization deviates from the aristocratic norms of a properly organized society and, instead of following the superior and guiding will of its intellectual and moral elite, chooses to follow the unruly and licentious will of its masses. In short, Ortega conceives decadence as an absence: specifically, it is the absence in national moral and political life of an active and ruling intellectual elite. Conversely, Ortega considers that regeneration becomes possible whenever a nation's masses acknowledge their inability to govern themselves productively and admit to needing the able leadership that only the elites can provide. In turn, this recognition serves as the basis from which the elite might impose its regenerating and civilizing will on the masses.

Given that Ortega was trained as a philosopher in Berlin, Leipzig, and Marburg, Hispanists have ordinarily sought to inscribe his elitist perception of decadence and regeneration within one or another modern European school of philosophy.[6] Thus, there is Ortega the existentialist, for whom decadence is said to be a question of the limits that the world of things-and-its imposes on personality; there is also Ortega the phenomenologist, for whom decadence is thought to be a question of the historically bracketed experience of elite consciousness; and then there is Ortega the vitalist, for whom decadence is supposed to be a question of the alienation that instrumental reason generates; finally, there is Ortega the Spanish liberal and defender of enlightenment ideals—the Ortega who, Hispanists are only too pleased to point out, opposed Primo de Rivera's military dictatorship, was elected as a representative to the constituent assembly of the Second Republic, and went into voluntary exile during Franco's regime: for this Ortega decadence is said to be a question of mob rule. Despite the range and diversity of these approaches to Ortega's elitism, the Hispanists who have proffered these views do have at least this much in common: they underscore the putatively cosmopolitan, European and modern profile of Ortega's theory of the elites.

But if there is any modern philosophical tradition to which Ortega's elitist theorizing truly belongs, it is the convention of political philosophy that has been built on the heroic myth of dominance. In an early modern thinker such as Hobbes, for instance, this myth serves to explain the contractual origin of the state and to justify the state's legal authority; similarly, in a high modern thinker such as Hegel, it functions as a paradigm for the dialectical progress of history toward its logical end in the state; finally, in a late modern thinker such as Nietzsche, it operates as a frame for a genealogical critique of the moral structure of modernity. In Ortega, this myth of dominance acts plainly as a justification for the moral superiority of a select group of regenerating master-elites who, by imposing their will on the masses, bring to an end the decadent rule of the masses, nationalizing them, civilizing them, and ultimately, enslaving them. To be sure, Ortega's elitism is centered on a premodern aristocratic and ascetic moral tradition that has much less in common with Hobbes, Hegel, or Nietzsche than with the Jesuits who were the schoolmasters of Ortega throughout his childhood. His theory, in short, could not be more *casticista.*

Ortega's elitism is best understood when it is regarded within the specifically national context from out of which it was born. Scrutinized in this light, the traditionally Spanish, premodern character of that elitism comes into full view. The principal motivating force behind his elitism is not, as many of Ortega's more enthusiastic apologists have tended to sustain, the so-called Europeanization of Spain.[7] Rather, Ortega's elitism is meant to provide for the moral transformation of the decadent Spanish masses such that they might eventually rise to a new imperial glory. It is in precisely these neo-imperialist terms that Ortega concludes his 1922 *España invertebrada:* "I conclude, therefore, this study of Spain's present with three simple observations: First. A nation lives by means of that which gave it life: aspiration . . . Second. Those grand enterprises cannot, today, consist of anything less than a gigantic, dynamic reform of the interior life of Spain oriented toward an international destiny: the spiritual unity of the Spanish-speaking nations . . . Third. A cult of select men."[8]

Not unlike Joaquín Costa's "iron surgeon," Ganivet's "disciplined individuals," Unamuno's "clairvoyants," and Maeztu's "Hispanic Gentlemen," Ortega's "select men" are defined by their capacity for ascetic self-discipline, their spirit of sacrifice, and their exclusive access to a metaphysical realm of transcendental truths. Commensurate with this archaic and messianic view of a regenerating elite, Ortega's theory of the masses serves, basically, to trivialize the masses. He constructs Spain's modern masses as an antiheroic negation of heroism and, in so doing, he intuitively ignores the historical, sociological, and philosophical definitions that could otherwise permit him to approach the masses analytically.

Belittling the Masses

According to Ortega, the Spanish masses resent the Spanish elites. It is in his 1914 *Meditaciones del Quijote* that Ortega first develops this view of the morality that motivates the masses as a particularly negative or negating morality. In this, his first book, Ortega presents the resentment of the masses as a sign of the demoralization of the Spanish nation. He presents it, in brief, as slave morality: "resentment is an emanation of the consciousness of inferiority," he explains with categorical certainty.[9] Or again: "Our plebian interior hates few things more than it does ambition. And the hero, clearly enough, begins by being ambitious . . . The instinct of inertia and conservation [of the masses] cannot tolerate ambition and so [they] seek revenge."[10] This, then, is the basic moral significance and ultimate social aim of the resentment of the masses: it is an emanation of the desire of the masses to humiliate heroism, originality, and individuality; its purpose is none other than to ridicule the elites and undermine their presumed superiority.

This demoralizing and criminal effect of slave morality on the nation is taken up again by Ortega in his essay of 1917 "Democracia morbosa." Here, Ortega, the supposed defender of Spanish republicanism, argues that democracy as a political doctrine only "appears to be something optimal."[11] Among its honorable achievements he includes "the leveling out of privileges, and not so much of rights."[12] However, Ortega warns: "the era during which democracy was a salutary sentiment and an ascendant impulse has come to pass. What today goes by the name of democracy is in fact a degeneration of hearts."[13] This degeneration carries with it certain political and social dangers: "an exasperated and unlimited democracy, democracy in religion or in art, democracy in thought and in gestures, democracy of the heart and in customs is the most dangerous illness from which a society can suffer."[14] Together, these dangers threaten to impose slave morality on all aspects of national life. They amount to what Ortega calls "plebeianism . . . the most insufferable of tyrants . . . [that] tyrannizes Spain today."[15] Accordingly, for Ortega, the demotic spirit that animates modern Spanish national life represents a hazard for the nation's elite. Cultural democracy, argues Ortega, assures the tyrannical and oppressive imposition on the nation's elite of the lowly and vulgar will of the masses.

The ultimate consequence of this resentful "aristophobia or hatred of those who are superior" is what in his essay of 1922, *España invertebrada*, Ortega refers to as an invertebrate nation and society, a society lacking its "nervous ganglion and cerebral center."[16] Ortega explains the state of the invertebrate society as follows: "[W]hen, in a nation, the masses refuse to be the masses—that is, refuse to follow the commanding minority—, the nation decomposes, the society becomes fragmented, social chaos and historical invertebration set in."[17] The loss of national unity and purpose is the basic consequence of the decadent and aimless morality of the masses.

The state of being invertebrate is, in Ortega's language, also commensurate with what he calls the rebellion of the masses. Ortega explains that when an aristocracy loses its "qualities of excellence" and becomes "inefficient and corrupt," that is, when an aristocracy becomes indistinguishable from the masses, the masses are in their right to overthrow the aristocracy—not in order to claim their own right to self-government, but to substitute it with another, more virtuous one.[18] In this regard, the rebellion of the masses is a potential source of societal regeneration. Ortega further explains, however, that the rebellion of the masses, because it is based in resentment, also tends toward decadence. This is the case, he reasons, since the masses "confusing things, generalize the objections inspired by that specific [decadent] aristocracy and . . . tend to eliminate any and all aristocratic purpose."[19] In such cases, the masses come to believe that "social existence is possible without a minority of excellence"—they become what Ortega considers to be "democratic"—but, as Ortega maintains, since this is "positively impossible" the society or nation "continues accelerating along its trajectory of decadence."[20]

That the rebellious Spanish masses have always presumed to usurp the mission of the elites and to rule over society by themselves is the central perversion, the basic lack of moral discipline, from which the Spanish nation has suffered historically; it is, as Ortega puts it, the nation's most "radical perversion of social instinct."[21] This perversion, he argues, is precisely what led the modern Spanish nation to lose its empire. Despite his assessment of the Spanish colonization of the Americas as "Spain's only true and substantively great accomplishment" Ortega also considers that this event was, at best, ambiguous: "In the Spanish [colonization of the Americas], it is 'the people' who directly and without any conscious purpose, leaders, or deliberate tactics engenders other nations. Herein lie the origins of both the greatness and the misery of our colonizing enterprise. Our 'people' did everything that needed doing: they populated, they cultivated, they sang, they cried and they loved. But they could not give to the nations that they engendered what they did not possess: a superior sense of discipline, a vivacious culture, a progressive civilization."[22] What the Spanish nation did offer to its colonies was, according to Ortega, the lack of discipline, the despondency, and the staid habits of mind of the Spanish masses. The example of resentment and hatred that this decadent nation offered its colonies perverted those same colonies, encouraging them to rebel and eventually seek their own independence. In this way, Ortega blames the resentment of the masses for Spain's loss of empire.

Indeed, according to Ortega, the Spanish nation has always lacked the leadership and guidance that only elites can offer. It has always been a nation without heroes. Consequently, the national history that Ortega narrates—particularly in *España invertebrada*—also lacks heroes; it is a negative narration marked by and organized about the absence of foundational protagonists: "the entire history of Spain," explains Ortega in this regard, "has been the history of decadence."[23] This absence of heroes, moreover, translates into the decadent protagonism of the masses: "in Spain, the 'people' have done everything, and what the 'people' have failed to do has remained undone."[24] Spanish national history, or at least its better half, has yet to be written because it has yet to be lived, demonstrated and recognized: that, in any case, is Ortega's regenerative assumption and premise. "If Spain has never been healthy—we have already seen that in its greatest hour it was not in a state of health—, it makes little sense to say that it has declined."[25] By thus denying heroic and everlasting value to the empire that the Spanish masses conquered, colonized, and eventually lost, Ortega sets the stage for affirming the present—the crisis-ridden milieu of Restoration Spain—as a new beginning from which a future-oriented and aristocratically disciplined Spanish nation might emerge and, at long last, stake a claim to ever-lasting imperial nobility.

Worshiping the Elites

For Ortega, the story of modern Spanish national decadence and regeneration narrates a moral problem; in particular, this is the problem of how to bring about the desired regenerating transformation of modern Spain. As one solution to this problem, Ortega examines the Spanish nation's moral transformation in pedagogical terms.[26] Under this guise, Ortega's regenerative moral transformation of the nation takes on the form of an altruistic endeavor. It is by means of the power of example, or what Ortega also calls "moral suggestion," that Ortega's moral pedagogues are to persuade the masses of the nation's need for moral transformation.[27] Yet, Ortega's faith in the pedagogic regeneration of the nation runs only so deep. It is not enough for the intellectual elite to encourage the moral transformation of the masses; Ortega's elite must also obligate the masses to transform themselves by means of what he calls "material imposition."[28] In other words, the elite must also force the masses to their knees, humiliate them, and thus "encourage" them to, as Ortega puts it, "repent."[29] For Ortega, the moral problem of regeneration is a question of both convincing and obligating, of educating the masses through example and of humiliating them by means of force. Consequently, Ortega's history of modern Spanish decadence presents a complicated mesh of two competing and, at times, counterpurposive rhetorical strategies: a strategy of altruism and a strategy of humiliation.

Ortega's strategy of pedagogical altruism is based in a notion of the elites as self-generating. In *España invertebrada* and its sequel, *La rebelión de las masas*, Ortega refers to a self-evident principle of selection as concerns his ascetically disciplined and altruistic elites. Their origins, he sustains, can be discovered in a mysterious, heroic moment of spontaneous self-generation. The elites, explains Ortega in this regard, "are individuals or groups of individuals who are specially qualified."[30] Ortega's "select man" is especially qualified in the sense that he has selected to separate himself from the masses "for special reasons, relatively individual."[31] He selects himself by demanding more of himself, and of life, than do the average stock of men. Ortega clarifies, in this respect, that "the select man is not the flippant man who believes himself to be superior to others, rather he is the man who demands more of himself, even though he may never come to realize, in his own person, the superior demands he places on himself."[32] By this, Ortega means that his "select man" seeks to overcome and perfect himself. It is in this sense that his values are ascetic, or what Ortega refers to as vital: he freely and willingly submits himself to a life of discipline designed to further the purposes of life as an ideal.

Ortega's mass-man, by contrast, does not require such discipline of himself: "The masses consist of all those who do not value themselves . . . for special reasons; instead, they feel 'just like everyone else' and, nevertheless, are not made anxious by this; they feel happy about their being identical to everyone else."[33] The mass-man finds security and comfort in numbers and in the death of individuality that is cultural tradition.[34] In this regard, "the mass-man is the man whose life lacks projects and is adrift."[35] His life is measured, always and already elapsed, a thing of the past, aimless and lacking in a future-oriented intention.

The altruistic and selfless intentionality of the elites can change all of this for the mass-man, and infuse his life with a new sense of direction and purpose. As is the case with Maeztu's functionaries and his "Caballeros de la Hispanidad," the example that Ortega's elites provide is, ultimately, one of voluntary servitude. "Contrary to what is commonly believed, it is the creature of selection, and not the masses, who lives in essential servitude. His life lacks all meaning unless it consists of service to something transcendental. For this reason, he does not experience his need to serve as oppression. When, by chance, this need is missing in his life, he feels disquieted and invents new, more difficult, more demanding norms that press him into service. This is life as discipline—the noble life."[36] When society is ruled by these ascetic and aristocratic spirits, the result is a society of voluntary servants, a nation of elites and masses that have freely given up their personal quest to attain a certain level of comfort and security in exchange for the purposeful goals of national unity and the historical mission that is tied to that unity. This is the ideal of a vertebrate society and in particular of a vertebrate Spain: a nation capable of achieving the dreamed of spiritual reconquest of itself, the Americas and Europe.

This image of altruistic example and exalted voluntary servitude is tempered, however, by a different view of the regenerating elites vis-à-vis the decadent masses and their ostensibly just right to rule over these masses. Ortega presents this alternative view of the regenerating mission of the elites when he defines their just rulership, not only in terms of an edifying exemplarity, but also in terms of an exchange of commands and obedience. In order to fully appreciate Ortega's conception of just rulership it is therefore necessary to consider his definition of three terms that are key to his theory of governance: command, obedience, and example.

First: to command. Ortega explains that "to command . . . is not simply a matter of persuading or obligating, but an exquisite mixture of the two."[37] To command is to encourage a specific action by means of both an enlightened appeal to reason, what Ortega calls "persuasion," and a humiliating appeal to the passions, what Ortega calls "obligation." Second: to obey. Ortega clarifies that obedience presupposes "docility" on the part of the person who obeys.[38] By docility, Ortega means voluntary servitude, a willingness to be ruled. Obedience, therefore, is the enactment or demonstration of the obedient person's willingness to be ruled. Third: to be exemplary. Ortega defines exemplarity in contrast to imitation. "When we imitate we act . . . outside of our authentic personality, we create for ourselves an exterior mask. Conversely, when we assimilate ourselves to the exemplary man . . . our entire person becomes polarized and oriented toward his way of being; we become disposed to truly reform our essence according to the quality that we admire in him."[39] Whereas imitation inspires only superficial reform, exemplarity inspires authentic, essential reform. Ortega sums up his argument concerning just rulership as commanding obedience through example in the following manner: "One obeys a command, and one is docile in respect to an example; the right to command is an out growth of exemplarity."[40] According to this argument, the elite rule justly when, in addition to leading the masses by example, they command obedience.

Hence, to rule by example alone, as Ortega's supposedly altruistic elites do in his imagined nation of regenerated voluntary servants, is not to rule justly at all. In order to rule justly and be fully justified in their governance over the masses, Ortega's elites must also exercise the power of command. They must demand obedience in addition to encouraging it through example. In view of this complex definition of just rulership, Ortega's happy notion of the nation as a unity of voluntary servants takes on the aspect of a not-too-happy unity of involuntary servants.

Ortega's second strategy for elitist regeneration of elitism thus turns on the humiliation of the involuntary servant. Unlike its altruistic counterpart, which presents the origin of elitism in terms of a hermetic system of self-selection, this strategy of humiliation presents the origin of elitism in terms of a dialectic of dominance or, to be more precise, a war. In this sense, the origin of Ortega's regenerating elite is located in the consciousness of the Other, of the masses, and not—as he would lead his readers to believe—in the elite's intuition of its own superiority. Ortega's "select men" do not merely select themselves; their superiority requires the recognition of the masses; it emanates, in short, from the masses' recognition of their own inferiority.

This is made abundantly clear by Ortega's use of the term recognition. In *España invertebrada* Ortega claims that the "maximum condition" for the nation's moral transformation and regeneration is: "The recognition that the mission of the masses is none other than to follow those who are best, and not aspire to supplant them."[41] Ortega's faith in the ability of the masses to willingly recognize their inferiority, however, is superficial at best. Referring to the inability of the masses to rule themselves and the nation successfully, Ortega writes: "In the end, their failure illuminates their minds, like a discovery, they begin to suspect that things are somewhat more complicated than they had supposed . . . When the collective sensibility of the masses reaches this state of ripeness, new historical eras tend to begin. Pain and failure create in the masses a new attitude of sincere humility, which makes them turn their backs on all those anti-aristocratic illusions and theories. Resentment of the eminent minority ceases."[42] Here, Ortega first presents the enlightenment of the masses—"failure illuminates their minds"—in terms of a discovery. Only a few sentences later, he shifts codes and what was previously a discovery, a pedagogical experience, turns into pain, an experience of bodily discipline and humiliation. Ortega thus bases the so-called recognition of the masses in pain—the pain of failure, a failure which Ortega, as a self-selecting member of Spain's would-be regenerating elite, is only too pleased to imagine, narrate and point out.

Indeed, Ortega's refashioning of enlightenment as pain suggests that humiliation, rather more so than pedagogy, is the principal strategy by means of which the elite is to realize its regenerating will. In *España invertebrada,* Ortega's seeming optimism concerning the spontaneous enlightenment of the masses is tempered by the suspicion that the Spanish masses, despite the crisis of the times, have not yet reached that state of "spontaneous repentance," which is the prerequisite for regeneration.[43] Indeed, by shifting codes and turning discovery into humiliation, Ortega surreptitiously replaces the notion of recognition with the idea of repentance. Repentance, more so than recognition, is a state of humility as it connotes sorrow and self-reproach, the willingness to do penitence.

The point of Ortega's regenerating project of moral transformation would seem to be, in the end, to lead the masses to a state of humility. The masses do not need to be "encouraged" only in order to recognize the superiority of the elites; they must also be "encouraged" in order to repent for their hatred of the elites. The way to do this, simply, is to humiliate the masses: "the illness [of the masses] consists precisely in their refusal to be influenced, in their being ill-disposed to the humble task of listening. The harder one tries to indoctrinate them, the more they hermetically seal their ears and violently trample their would-be instructor."[44] In order to cure the masses of this decadent illness, asserts Ortega, they must be made to feel pain.

Ortega's elites are capable of inflicting such regenerating pain because, as Ortega would have it, they alone are the inheritors of the vitality and asceticism of the sportsman. As such, Ortega characterizes his elites as participating in what he calls the sportsman's culture of "spontaneous effort."[45] In an essay of 1927, titled "El origen deportivo del estado," Ortega declares that war is the original sport and that the warrior is the original sportsman. Such is the case, reasons Ortega, because warriors satisfy the aristocratic dictum that: "To be the emperor of oneself is the first condition for governing others."[46] For Ortega, not unlike Unamuno and Maeztu, warriors represent an edifying example of self-discipline: "War raises leaders and requires discipline," he explains, "and unity in leadership and discipline . . . foment spiritual unity, a common preoccupation for all the great problems."[47] Consequently, it is the warrior who is both the original, creative agent of history and the first to select himself and impose his superiority on others. He and the wars he chooses are the creative, vital origin of the distinction between master and slave. Thus, for Ortega just as for Unamuno and Maeztu, the military serves as an example of an ascetic discipline by means of which a regenerative elite should be forged.

Likewise, in *España invertebrada,* Ortega upholds the argument that the vital "ethic of the warrior" is morally superior to the cultural "ethic of industry" of the slavelike modern masses; this is the case because the warring ethic of the elites is governed by "enthusiasm," whereas the industrial ethic of the masses is governed by "utility."[48] Here, Ortega echoes Unamuno's arguments against the modern and decadent "cult of science." Ortega writes: "The industrial spirit is governed by a cautious desire to avoid all risk, whereas the spirit of the warrior springs from an inspired appetite for danger."[49] The masses are cowards; their morality, reasons Ortega, is ultimately defined in terms of fear. A sustained fear of death is, then, the definitive source of the resentment that Ortega's masses feel for his fearless elites. By contrast, the power of the elites over the masses is based in their enthusiasm for the dangers of war. Considering that the ultimate danger of war is death itself, and second to death the humiliation of defeat and enslavement, the enthusiasm that Ortega's warring elites feel for the dangers of war is also marked by the ambition to wield the power of death over life.

Ortega reveals his enthusiasm for the generative qualities of war in his attempt to theorize a bellicose interpretation of history. He develops this bellicose interpretation of history in opposition to economic and utilitarian interpretations of history. According to Ortega, his bellicose theory of history has in common with the economic interpretation of history—particularly its Marxian form—the premise that: "historical reality is conflict, and what fights in history, more than men, are his instruments."[50] According to Ortega's theory, then: "life in each epoch would be defined, not in terms of the instruments of production, but rather, the other way around, in terms of the instruments of destruction. Social power is distributed in each epoch according to the quality and quantity of the means of destruction that each man possesses."[51] Here, the right to rule is defined in terms of the ability to destroy. Ortega's argument is that death—or rather the threat of death—is the ultimate measure and source of power. Seen from this perspective, to govern means to command obedience on the basis of, not only fear, but also death. The vanquished and humiliated literally owe their lives to their victors. Their lives are, in this sense, a gift that is granted in place of death, although with specific conditions attendant to it: limited freedoms and, as Ortega would have it, the enforced labor of nation building and spiritual neo-imperialism. The lives of the vanquished become, in this regard, a debt that they have incurred respecting the victors, and their labor becomes the only means for repaying that debt. They become slaves in the total sense of the word: they are property, a thing without life, a means of production.

Whereas Ortega's altruistic and pedagogical strategy presents a relatively free society where the masses might, in time, be persuaded to "select" and perfect themselves after the image of their morally superior elites; his strategy of humiliation leaves very little, if any, room for the masses to overcome the limiting conditions of their resentment. In the former case, Ortega imagines the regenerated nation as a unity of voluntary servants. In the latter case, he imagines the regenerated nation as a unity of involuntary servants. In either case, the regenerated nation that Ortega imagines and narrates into being consists of servants. This confusion of voluntary and involuntary servitude in Ortega's elitist theory for Spanish national regeneration suggests that Ortega presents the scenario of voluntary servitude primarily as a blind behind which he hides the, as he would likely put it, "authentic" sense of his elitism: the humiliation of the masses as well as, ultimately, the discrediting of any tendency toward demotic cultural principles. This duplicity is pivotal to Ortega's reading of Cervantes' *Don Quixote* as a metahistorical tragicomedy of Spanish national history and is crucial, as well, to the sociological theory of the novel that he constructs on the basis of that reading.

III

Quixotism

7

Don Quixote as Spiritual Conquistador

Conceiving modern Spanish national decadence as *abulia* or a pathological lack of will, in his *Idearium español* Ganivet advocates a regenerating "restoration of spiritual life" modeled after the emblematic "metamorphosis" of the Spanish "national type," Don Quixote.[1] He further develops this theme of a Quixotist spiritual transformation of modern Spain in his novel of 1895 *La conquista del reino de Maya* as well as in its sequel of 1898 *Los trabajos del infatigable creador Pío Cid.* In the spirit of Cervantes' parody of chivalric romances in the *Quixote,* Ganivet's two novels parody the chronicles of conquest and colonization of Spain's early colonial era.[2] As such, they relate the story of how a late nineteenth-century Spanish conquistador, Pío Cid, after modernizing a savage African kingdom, undergoes a spiritual transformation that leads him to view his modernization of that kingdom as a spiritually corrupting act. In turn, Pío Cid's critical self-awareness gives rise to what Ganivet would have his readers take as a model for the recuperation, by the modern Spanish nation, of its traditional, heroic, conquering identity. These two novels deserve to be studied in detail, therefore, because it is in them that Ganivet demonstrates how the Quixotist denial of Spain's loss of empire may lead to modern Spanish cultural and spiritual imperialism.

Underlying the transformative motif of these Quixotist novels is Ganivet's conviction that the decadence of the modern world can be explained by a lack of hero worship. The modern world, as Ganivet understands it, is not, however, a world devoid of heroes. For Ganivet, every age has its heroes, and the modern age is no exception: "Ever since the world became the world," he writes in *Los trabajos,* "there have been men who have influenced the spirit of other men."[3] These men of influence are, as Ganivet would have it, the rulers and heroes of the world. The trouble with the modern age, however, is that its heroes are often misunderstood and undervalued by the masses. For this reason, in order for the modern world to be saved from its decadence, its regenerating heroes must be willing to work in secrecy and have their labors go largely unappreciated. "The heroes of the future will triumph secretly, invisibly dominating the spirit and provoking an ideal world in each individual spirit."[4] Pío Cid, the protagonist of Ganivet's two Quixotist novels, is precisely this kind of modern hero who, by means of his self-sacrifice, can help the modern world overcome its decadent aversion to hero-worship.

Although he is a modern hero, Ganivet models Pío Cid, in part, after various classical heroic prototypes—Hercules, Jesus, el Cid, and Cortés, and in part, after a modern heroic prototype—Don Quixote.[5] While Pío Cid does incorporate these traditional heroic paradigms, his heroism is not limited to them; instead, because it is also modern, also Quixotist, it incorporates and overcomes them. According to Ganivet, his Quixotist hero must overcome these classical types because the traditional modes of heroism associated with them are inadequate to the needs of the modern age. Ganivet sees them, invariably, as antiquated and obsolete forms of heroism.

In *Los trabajos,* for instance, Ganivet has Pío Cid speak of the need, in Spain, for "a new Hercules . . . who might turn the nation inside out and upside down."[6] Yet, Pío Cid qualifies this assessment, placing doubt in the ability of the classical Hercules to regenerate the decadent modern Spanish nation: "I believe that . . . if Hercules were to be resuscitated he would want to have nothing to do with us . . . Here, he would have to clean the stables twelve times . . . and it seems to me that this kind of labor is more befitting of a garbageman than a semi-divine hero."[7] Thus, while suggesting the need for a new Hercules, Pío Cid expresses concern as to this classical hero's ability to redeem the exceedingly decadent modern Spanish nation. For Pío Cid, indeed for Ganivet, Spanish society has "evolved" and "progressed" beyond the redemptive capacities of the classical Hercules; it has become "modern" or decadent and, in consequence of this, the role in it of the classical hero has diminished.

Insofar as Ganivet's Quixotist hero, Pío Cid, is unlike Hercules and more like the garbageman that Hercules could never become, he represents a diminished form of classical heroism. In this regard, Ganivet conceives of modern heroism negatively. As a late nineteenth-century thinker who is deeply concerned with heroism, Ganivet is not alone in this negative assessment. As Michael K. Goldberg notes, for Carlyle also "the heroic form contracts with time, and evolving social conditions make it increasingly difficult for the heroic spirit to manifest itself."[8] Miguel Olmedo Moreno, who has studied the influence of Carlyle's descending scale of heroism in Ganivet, explains the relation between these two thinkers' negative views on modern heroism this way: "The fundamental characteristic that Carlyle assigns to the modern age—lack of faith in the virtue of individual effort—is precisely what makes the new age inadmissible for Ganivet and explains his revulsion for it."[9] Thus, Ganivet uses his Quixotist hero in order to criticize the modern age's lack of faith in "great individuals." To that end, in *Conquista,* he treats his "modern" hero and those who worship him with extreme irony, pointing out the diminished form of Pío Cid's heroism and the also diminished forms of worship that his would-be heroic deeds inspire among his followers.

Also like Carlyle, however, Ganivet conceives of modern heroism positively. In *Los trabajos,* Pío Cid overcomes the lack of faith that the modern world has in him, in part, because like Carlyle's "poet" he is an intellectual, a man of letters who conceptualizes and creates values. He triumphs also, however, because, like Carlyle's "king," his will-to-power permits him to impose his imaginative designs on other men. In this positive sense, Ganivet's Quixotist hero coincides with the modern heroism of Joaquín Costa's regenerative iron surgeon who, by virtue of his informing intelligence and will-to-power, is able to prescribe and, if need be, enforce a suitable cure for the nation's modern state of decadence. He is a modern philosopher-king or, as Ganivet would have it, a dictator: "The kind of government that suits us naturally is a strong and hard government, just like our temperament; to us, democratic philanthropy is tantamount to a degeneration of our character. Considering that each one of us is the king of his own house . . . we like for our king or ruler . . . to be a true ruler"[10]—and elsewhere he adds—"in order for us to behave justly, we need a dictator and a battery at every intersection."[11] Pío Cid proves, in the end, to be this regenerative ruler or dictator because he, not unlike the Don Quixote of Ganivet's *Idearium,* undergoes an ascetic spiritual transformation that permits him to overcome the diminished forms of his modern heroism and inspire a truly regenerating form of hero worship.

When it is considered in terms of literary modes, this spiritual transformation represents an inversion of the descending movement of modern heroism; it represents the recuperation of traditional heroic forms. In this sense, the story of Pío Cid's life and (projected) death moves from the low-mimetic realm of the picaresque to the high-mimetic realm of epic. In *Conquista,* which narrates the exploits of Pío Cid as conqueror and colonizer of the distant and unknown African kingdom of Maya, Ganivet presents the negative image of a decadent modern hero who, because he introduces certain progressive reforms into the traditional society of Maya, invariably ends by leading his kingdom toward a state of decadence. This image of Pío Cid as a low-mimetic, picaresque hero is, however, tempered by the novel's romanticizing final chapter, where Pío Cid's labors of conquest, as opposed to his labors of colonization, are celebrated as a spiritual creation. It is here that Pío Cid undergoes a regenerative, spiritual transformation; sheds his modern, progressive skin; and emerges as a true Quixotist hero who is capable of incorporating and thereby recuperating the nation's lost sense for heroism. Finally, in *Los trabajos,* which relates this hero's spiritual labors on his return to Spain, Ganivet presents the image of a civilizing modern hero who, by reason of sacrificing his life to the nation, is able to further its glory.

By itself, Ganivet's satirical foray into the realm of the novel—or what Lukács calls "the epic of an age in which . . . the immanence of meaning in life has become a problem, yet which still thinks in terms of totality"—is also a quest for an appropriately modern, totalizing, epic form of heroism capable of acting as the spiritual center of an imagined national community.[12] This quest leads Ganivet, in *La conquista,* to censure Pío Cid's cynical and modern rejection of traditional forms of heroism—divinity, prophecy, poetry, and priestliness—and, in *Los trabajos,* after Pío Cid has had his dream of spiritual transformation, to consider Pío Cid as a Quixotist who has improved on the same forms of obsolete heroism that he had previously rejected.

Pío Cid as Public Administrator

The central and organizing theme behind *La conquista* is that the modern notion of progress is actually a form of spiritual and moral decadence. Ganivet's contention is that the modern industrial, capitalist and empire-building nations of Europe have used the notion of progress as a ruse to justify the violence of colonization; and that they have done this both to themselves and to their colonized subjects by wrongly defining progress as a philanthropic and civilizing act. In an attempt to demonstrate this thesis, Ganivet has the novel's progressive protagonist, Pío Cid, felicitously discover, effortlessly conquer and haphazardly colonize the savage African Kingdom of Maya, only to leave behind, on his return to Spain, an ambiguous legacy of progressive social reforms that have gone awry.

Traditional societal bonds and communal values give way, in Ganivet's novel, to the aggressive and self-interested rationality of the civilized merchant. Pío Cid's public administration of the Kingdom of Maya achieves many of its more spectacular triumphs and social transformations by systematically opting for the individual as against the tribal collectivity, market transactions and money-thought as against human ties and blood, class consciousness as against tribal hierarchy, and "Gesellschaft" as against "Gemeinschaft." But Pío Cid's reforms systematically fail to provide for, and adequately replace, those social bonds and ties of authority that had been taken for granted in earlier Mayan society. Indeed, his reforms set out to and succeed in weakening those ties. The result is a society that is ambiguously split, fractured, and nervously modern. It is, to borrow from Spengler, an image of "Civilization" in its conclusive form: the conflict between money and blood, or decadence and vital regeneration.[13]

As with Spengler's celebration of the redemptive power of blood ties over and above that of money, Ganivet pits a regenerative will-to-power against the abstract reasoning that is preeminent in the capitalist world. The formal, rational, and abstract value of capital is, in this way, linked to the absence, in Pío Cid's modern Mayan society, of any ethical and spiritual nucleus capable of integrating and sustaining that society as a cohesive whole. As a modernizing colonizer who is primarily concerned with the public administration of his kingdom, Pío Cid fails to spiritually transform his colonized subjects. He fails to live up to Ganivet's notion of the modern Quixotist hero as a philosopher-king who, rather than colonize and publicly administer to his subjects, conquers them, eternally and spiritually.

Ganivet's critique of Pío Cid's failure to live up to this Quixotist paradigm for modern heroism is not, however, limited to this conceptual argument opposing the spiritual and ethical values of conquest to the secular interests of colonization. It also obeys a narrative strategy built on the (albeit ambiguous) parody of traditional mythological, religious, and literary models of heroism. Pío Cid's inability to conquer his subjects spiritually serves to demonstrate his heroic deficiencies, namely, his failure, as a "progressive" public administrator to incorporate these traditional, high-mimetic forms of heroism.

The first step Ganivet takes in this satirical direction is evident in the name he gives to his protagonist: Pío Cid. The name recalls that of the warrior hero of Spain's epic poem "Cantar del Mio Cid." But unlike the epic figure of el Cid, Ganivet's hero has an additional name denoting religious piety: Pío. In the opening chapters of *La conquista,* in which his protagonist discovers and conquers the Kingdom of Maya, Ganivet anxiously mocks both the epic and the pious aspects of Pío Cid's character.

Toward the beginning of the novel, Pío Cid mounts on top of a hippopotamus he has found near a riverbank. This animal is fortuitously equipped with a bridle and saddlebags. As Pío Cid sets off on his adventure of conquest, he allows the beast to weave its own course down the river, much the same as Don Quixote allows his old nag, Rocinante, to wander forth at the start of his first sally. Not surprisingly, Pío Cid characterizes himself at this point as "the most original knight-errant that the world has ever seen."[14] The allusion to the Spanish novels of chivalry, and particularly to Cervantes' parody of them in the figure of Don Quixote is not merely obvious, but also singularly suited to Ganivet's ironic strategy. By drastically contrasting Pío Cid with Don Quixote, and the bloated hippo with the skeletal Rocinante, Ganivet deflates the heroic and warring aspect of his hero and places him instead in the low-mimetic circumstance of the picaresque and grotesque.

Ganivet does not use this image to parody the warring aspect of his protagonist's name and character alone but also to call into question the supposed piety of Pío Cid's philanthropic pursuits. Elsewhere in the novel, Pío

Cid, still astride his hippopotamus, arrives at a Mayan village where he is enthusiastically greeted by its inhabitants. The Mayans call him Igana Iguru or "man from on high." In effect, the Mayans confuse Pío Cid for the white deity prophesied by their traditional lore. Rather than correct this error of identity and perception, Pío Cid takes advantage of his new, semidivine and prophetic position—and the power it affords him—and "civilizes" the savage Mayans. Thus, Ganivet's incorporation, in the person of Pío Cid, of the traditional heroic forms of the hero as divinity and as prophet is demonstrated to be based in a willful and cynical deception that is not without historical precedent. Indeed, it constitutes a parody of the Spanish conquest of the Americas.

The literary-historical model for this deceptive ruse is, undoubtedly, Bernal Diaz' chronicle *Conquista de la Nueva España,* which relates, among other things, how the Aztecs confused Cortés and his followers for a superior race of white gods. By suggesting this parallel between Pío Cid's conquest of the African kingdom of Maya (a name which itself resonates with Meso-American connotations) and Cortés' conquest of the Aztec empire, Ganivet would seem to imply that Pío Cid's pious and civilizing philanthropy is, not unlike Cortes' assumption of a semidivine status among the Aztecs, to a large extent a subterfuge for the commercial exploitation of the land and its people. Rather than a noble and pious warrior, Ganivet depicts Pío Cid as a modernizing merchant of progress, cynically disposed to deceive others as to the dark truth behind his colonizing impulse.

The principal thrust of Ganivet's satiric treatment of Pío Cid in *La conquista* is, however, directed toward an unfavorable comparison between this would-be "modernizing" hero and Don Quixote. Whereas Don Quixote struggles, by means of his adventures and penitent labors, to restore a rapidly changing Spanish society to its traditional feudal cohesion, Pío Cid attempts to do quite the opposite; he seeks to undermine the moral cohesion of a similarly traditional society.[15] Accordingly, Ganivet's satirical treatment of Pío Cid, who is forever at the mercy of the narrative's derisive rebukes, is intended to expose the dangers implicit in the supposedly philanthropic process of a civilizing modernization of traditional forms of communal life.

It is by means of such irony that Ganivet ultimately reveals Pío Cid to be a cynical misanthrope: "Contrary to what some pessimists believe"—predicates Pío Cid—"it is more difficult to govern animals than men, because animals do not submit themselves to anything but force or reason, which they interpret instinctively. Men, by contrast, are satisfied with a few cheerful and innocent lies, which even a man of mediocre intelligence can invent . . . In order for nations to be governed, there is no need for statesmen, or legislators, or soldiers but for poets, actors, musicians and priests."[16] Here, Pío Cid speaks with bitter cynicism concerning the traditionally heroic role of poets and priests. Insofar as poets articulate transcendental principles, they proffer an aesthetic justification of life. For their part, priests articulate redemptive, spiritual principles, and thus hold out an ascetic justification of life. Pío Cid depicts both principles as little more than the creation of "cheerful lies," a task for which even ordinary men are, to his mind, perfectly suited. The cynicism with which Pío Cid regards divinity and prophecy, poetry, and priestliness, demonstrates the extent to which, as a progressive colonizer, he both fails to incorporate these traditional forms of heroism and negates their value.

This extreme cynicism is the basis of Pío Cid's last and perhaps greatest reform: a government monopoly on alcohol, the justification for which is Pío Cid's observation that the prosperity of European nations seems to depend on the reduction of their people to the level of stupefied, drunken animals.[17] The consequences of this monopoly fit the theoretical description of a sociological state of decadence: a cash economy is established; a division of labor emerges that necessitates merchants; the law of supply and demand takes hold; and commerce, industry, and technology flourish together with the spiritless work, mindless materialism, and sensual stupefaction of modern metropolitan life. While the alienated denizens of the kingdom drink themselves silly, economic and political power are corporately centralized in the form of capital. It is by virtue of Pío Cid's capacity for mercantile reasoning, then, that the Mayan economy flourishes; and that the Mayan's traditional ties of "blood" are replaced by "money-thought" and market transactions. In effect, the shift from "Gemeinschaft" to "Gesellschaft" is finalized with this revolution in economic progress, the essential condition for which, according to Pío Cid, is: "the submission of large masses of men to a governing intelligence."[18] Such a "governing intelligence" is not, as Pío Cid amply makes clear, an aristocratic, disciplined intelligence but merely a mediocre one. The "great individual" to whom Pío Cid would have the masses submit is, in this regard, no different than the masses themselves. He is, as Ganivet would have it, a lowly and decadent dictator who, if need be, could even become the garbageman the classical Hercules could never become.

This negative image of Pío Cid as an incompetent and cynical public administrator whose reforms undermine traditional Mayan society and unwittingly bring to light the predominant barbarity of modern civilization is tempered, in the last chapter of *La conquista,* by an utterly different, positive version of Pío Cid's conquest and colonialization of the Kingdom of Maya. When combined, these two competing perspectives on the value and significance of Pío Cid's conquest produce a Janus-faced ambivalence that is similar to the ideal split between modern Spain's Don Quixotes and Sancho Panzas that Ganivet invokes, in his *Idearium español,* in an attempt to construct a spiritually unified and regenerating Spanish national-imperial culture.

The Spiritual Transformation of Pío Cid

Throughout most of *La conquista,* Pío Cid is negatively compared to Don Quixote. In this novel's final chapter, titled "Sueño de Pío Cid," Pío Cid is positively compared to both Don Quixote and Hernán Cortés. In fact, he is presented as a new type of conquistador: a Quixotist. The latent, satirical critique of colonialism underlying the main body of the novel gives way, in this final revelatory dream-chapter, to a celebratory discourse regarding Pío Cid's conquest, not only of his African kingdom, but also, by extension, of Hernán Cortés'—which is to say Spain's—conquest of the Americas.

The mouthpiece for this laudatory discourse is, appropriately enough, the ghost of Hernán Cortés, who appears to Pío Cid in his dream. According to Cortés, the Spanish conquest of the Americas took away Spain's "blood and life" in exchange for "the smoke of glory": "Of what value can one, two or four centuries of real domination be when, in the end, everything vanishes and those who had once been the most powerful and noble end up being humbled and slandered? Perhaps our nation would have been more fortunate if, reserving for itself the pure glory of its heroic exploits, it had left to other more practical nations the duty to populate the discovered and conquered lands as well as all the lowly tasks of colonization."[19] Here Cortés argues that, since the noble, warring spirit of the conquistador is not fit for the lowly, slavish work of public administration, it should instead dedicate itself to the spontaneous, creative acts of discovery and conquest.

Standing in direct opposition to this ideal concept of the warring Spanish spirit is the mercantile reasoning and administrative practicality of the decadent, modern, capitalist spirit of colonization. Yet, the infamy of Pío Cid's public administration of the Kingdom of Maya is pardonable, from Cortés' point of view, given the generally selfless nature of his conquest. For Hernán Cortés, Pío Cid's conquest is exemplary because it serves no practical purpose, yet does everything to further the spiritual glory of the Spanish nation without providing anything for the Spanish state. "The most grandiose enterprises are those in which money does not intervene, in which the costs are exclusively of the mind and the heart."[20] Pío Cid's modern conquest is consequently depicted as obeying what, in the *Idearium,* Ganivet calls "the genius of idea" as opposed to the more classical and epic "genius of action."

Meaning to define a modern heroism capable of overcoming the decadence of the modern, progressive age, Ganivet turns to the past for examples of conceptual genius and contemplative spirituality. Hernán Cortés, himself, is one such example. He is, for Ganivet, the quintessentially spontaneous, Spanish warrior who fought only for glory and not for material riches. The other example Ganivet presents through his mouthpiece Cortés, is that of Cervantes who, according to Cortés, wrote "his *Quixote* in order to indicate to us the heights that we can reach when we flee from the coarse and vulgar aspirations that are opposed to our nature and separate us from our congenital austerity."[21] Both these examples are intended, as Pío Cid correctly deduces, to inspire the modern Spanish nation to spiritually climb to the same ideal heights as those reached by Cervantes and Cortés, "immortal heroes . . . who were as likely to have written an epic with a pen as with a sword."[22] The final example, according to Cortés, is Pío Cid himself, which is to say Ganivet's epic novel *La conquista:* "of which our poor nation is in dire need."[23] Consequently, Pío Cid and the story of his conquest of the Kingdom of Maya take on a recuperative, heroic significance. Pío Cid is now placed in the same league with a virtuous warrior, Hernán Cortés, and a virtuous man of letters, Cervantes.

As both Quixotist hero and man of creative ideas, explains Cortés, Pío Cid was able, spiritually, to conquer the people of Maya: "The Mayans were as happy as beasts; you have made them miserable, like men. This is the truth. The savage, who lives in direct contact with nature, loves the simple life and rejects all effort that is not of immediate use."[24] The savage is depicted, here, as a slave to necessity. His blissful happiness is the result of ignorance, to which he is a slave. By conquering the savage Mayans, Pío Cid liberates them. To that end, Cortés' argument proceeds: "Civilized man detests that natural life [of the savage], and finds his good fortune in the painful effort that his own emancipation demands of him."[25] According to this reasoning, civilized man frees himself from necessity by struggling to conquer and dominate nature. It is his labor that liberates and redeems him. Whereby, Cortés concludes: "To conquer, to colonize, to civilize are, then, a matter of generating [in the savage] a love for the labors that will dignify him, make him a man and remove him from that state of ignorant bliss in which he would otherwise live eternally."[26] The consequence of this vitalistic moral reasoning is that Pío Cid's conquest of the Mayans may now be celebrated as a spontaneous work of genius that instills the Mayans with civilized man's love for independence. Pío Cid has enlightened his subjects.

In this regard, the civilization created by Pío Cid is depicted, not as promoting decadence, but rather as rewarding effort and liberating labor: a spiritual utopia. And so it is that Cortés celebrates the figure of Pío Cid as that of a Quixotist warrior of the spirit whose ingenious ideas have dominated and spiritualized the Mayans. Pío Cid, reasons Cortés, has bestowed on his subjects a certain hunger for self-realization that they had been previously lacking as savages.

Moreover, Pío Cid's civilizing spirituality has bestowed on the Mayans what Cortés claims are: "the means necessary for them to destroy themselves and thus joyously rise to the highest peaks of civilization."[27] Cortés views these instruments of destruction as a positive, revelatory sign, which serves the purpose of announcing the coming of a nobler human ideal. "Men are made dignified by death far more so than by their excessive love of life and cowardly desire to die in bed . . . Life is sweet; but how much sweeter it becomes when we sacrifice it to an ideal by means of which we may elevate ourselves."[28] Cortés would have Pío Cid sacrifice his life and those of other "modern" men for this higher human ideal. He envisions Pío Cid at the head of a horde of barbarian Mayan soldiers who destroy the civilized cities and nations of Europe in the hope that, from the ruins of this catastrophic event, a nobler way of life will take root and blossom.[29] In this way, death and destruction are posited as purifying events that are conducive to the spiritual transformation of the modern world.

The view presented here is that of an imperial, utopian future in which the destruction of modern imperfections and the annihilation of incompetence lead to a superior, masterful society. This idea is reiterated by Cortés in his final evaluation of Pío Cid's colonial experience in Africa: "What we call civilization today may very well be the barbaric precursor of another, more perfect civilization; just as in Maya the apparent civilization of today is merely an announcement of a magnificent future."[30] The regeneration of European civilization is to be forged by a new race of Euro-African barbarians: the noble, dominant African offspring of Pío Cid. What looks like barbarity to the colonizing Europe of the turn of the century, Ganivet suggests, may very well serve as the foundation for a more perfect European civilization. When one considers how, at the turn of the century in Spain, the term *African* was sometimes used as a synonym for *backward* (as in the statement "Africa begins at the Pyrenees"), the full implications of Ganivet's proposal for regeneration can be appreciated. A Spain that affirms its "African" difference, suggests Ganivet, may find ways to assert hegemony in a decadently modern Europe.

This new race of noble barbarians, descendents of African and Spanish warriors, is to give to the Spanish nation a new identity, a new glory, and a new justification for imperial hegemony. In this regard, Pío Cid's fictive journey into the heart of Africa is an analogue for Ganivet's historical journey into Spain's colonial past. Both go in quest of heroism. Pío Cid's progressive public administration of the Kingdom of Maya constitutes an attempt to generate civilization by means of material salvation. Clearly, this colonial model constitutes an antiheroic version of the spiritual heroes Ganivet claims to discover in the conquering experience of Spain's past. As a consequence, if modern Spain is to regenerate itself, here can be seen the need for the construction of a truly regenerative and heroic redeemer, of a modern hero capable of recuperating and incorporating those lost forms of traditional, conquering heroism. Hence, Pío Cid's transformation from public administrator to spiritual master. Hence, too, the symbolic identification of Pío Cid with Cervantes, the "man of letters," and with Hernán Cortés, the "king."

Pío Cid as Spiritual Conquistador

Just as in his 1896 *Idearium* where he portrays decadent Spain as an old, an exhausted woman who, having always desired to lead the contemplative life of a mystical virgin, is nevertheless forced into the arduous labors of maternity, so too, in his 1897 novel *Los trabajos del infatigable creador Pío Cid,* Ganivet presents the redemption of a fallen woman by a noble and ascetically disciplined man as a leitmotif for the national regeneration of modern Spain. To that end, in *Los trabajos,* the spiritually transformed Pío Cid remarks, with regard to one of the various fallen women whom he attempts to redeem, that: "At times I think that who is at my bedside is not a poor servant girl but Spain, all of Spain."[31] Elsewhere, in a sermon he titles "Ecce Homo," Pío Cid summarizes his philosophy concerning Spanish national regeneration.[32] "It is not easy to find a real man . . . a man's quality manifests itself not only in his words, but in his actions too, in his total understanding of life. We have here an ordinary event, which can serve to test this idea: What man has never found a fallen woman? This common discovery inspires several thoughts by which means each man measures his humanity. Most men do not think about anything except how to take advantage of the woman's misfortune in order to satisfy their sensual desires . . . In other men, who are more intelligent, sensual desire is dominated by curiosity . . . Truly, the more noble of the two are those who take pity on the fallen woman, love her, and through their love, regenerate and revive her."[33]

In *Los trabajos,* Ganivet portrays his Quixotist hero as being able to redeem and spiritually transform the nation—the fallen woman—by virtue of his piety and love. Love, explains Pío Cid to another of his feminine spiritual conquests, is "the human ideal . . . a generous condition: that of never thinking to use others as means to our own ends."[34] Thus conceived, the Spanish nation—the fallen, decadent woman—is to be regenerated by a generous act of patriotic love, by a "marvelous invention" that is capable of recuperating for the nation its innate drive toward a monastic life of pious spirituality.[35]

Yet, as Pío Cid explains to his friends in his sermon "Ecce Homo," this creative act of patriotism is not limited to the "human ideal" of love itself: "Those who look with love upon the destitute are more human than those who study them without loving them. But it is possible to do more for that fallen woman than redeem her through love: it is possible to rise still higher . . . More can be done . . . but I cannot divulge what this is because, if I were to declare it . . . I would reveal the primitive and timeless law of creation."[36] In and of itself, love is not sufficient to the task of regenerating the nation. In order for the nation to be redeemed, a more primitive and perennial kind of heroism must be created.

The title of Ganivet's novel suggests that Pío Cid, the "indefatigable creator," is just the sort of hero to whom the nation should turn. Yet, Pío Cid, to the initial disappointment and great consternation of his friends, does not explain how such a creation is to be generated. Instead, he shrouds the source of his own creative capacity in mystery and silence and, at least to his disciple-like friends, takes on the aura of a man of "rare wisdom," a prophet.[37]

Silence, according to Pío Cid, is among the more salient aspects of heroism: "Great mystics are formed in solitude," he explains to his friends, "and great philosophers in silence."[38] Taken in this light, Pío Cid, much like the Don Quixote of Ganivet's *Idearium,* can be seen as a philosopher and a thinker who shows a talent for "ideal creations."[39] Such spiritually transforming creations, explains Pío Cid, are born in silence: "Shadows are the proper place for creation; but if the creation is noble and spiritual, in due course it seeks out light."[40] Here, Pío Cid asserts silence, the essence of prophecy, as the origin of all great creations. Moreover, by keeping the source of his own creative wisdom locked within the crypt of prophetic silence, Pío Cid affirms his own heroic wisdom.

Elsewhere, however, in speaking with several of his feminine spiritual conquests, Pío Cid does divulge, in an unsystematic fashion, the secrets of his creative genius. On one such occasion, he links the creative aspect of silence to death itself, to death as the ultimate form of silence: "Death is fecund and creates life . . . if a man were to carry death deep within his spirit, and thus find himself obliged to labor, he would be a portentous creator. No longer needing to entertain thoughts of life, which are always small and miserable, he would create with thoughts of death, which are broader and nobler."[41] Here, before a gathering of fallen women, Pío Cid reveals the dark secret contained within his prophetic silence: that the power of death, and not the amorphous, abstract and shadowy silence of his sermon, is the ultimate source of all great creations. Thus, would Pío Cid recuperate, incorporate, and transform the traditional heroic value, not only of the prophet, but also of the poet: the untiring creator who justifies life on the basis of an aesthetic transformation of death.

Finally, in speaking to yet another of his redeemed fallen women, Pío Cid points out that the creative forces of silence and death are, in fact, divine powers: "Divinity has two principle attributes: creation and destruction."[42] As a silent prophet and creative poet, then, Pío Cid enjoys a direct and intimate link to the divine, the infinite and the eternal. He is an "indefatigable creator," a hero with godlike qualities: "One could sense in him a profound contempt for his common man . . . which was the expression of a mysterious power, similar to that which the pagan gods made manifest in their relations with their creations: a mixture of energy and neglect, of kindness and perversion, of seriousness and ridicule."[43]

Certainly, the silence that he keeps in the company of his disciple-like friends with regard to the mysterious "law of creation" is one instance of this divinely inspired mixture of respectful charity and deceiving perversion. Pío

Cid justifies this silence by cloaking it in the form of a prophecy: "I postpone the revelation until after my death . . . which soon will be upon me . . . I will leave it for you in a tragedy that I have written . . . the invariable tragedy of life."[44] This "invariable tragedy" of life is nothing other than death: "The only testament that an honorable man should leave behind . . . is . . . the example of his life."[45] So it is that by prophesying his own death as a revelatory and tragic event, Pío Cid affirms the exemplary and heroic quality of his life.

In the end, the ultimate act of patriotic love that is to regenerate the modern nation is this exemplary death: a sacrificial and heroic death which is intended to give rise to a tragic, poetically transformative form of "modern" hero worship. By virtue of the example it sets and the worship it inspires, this beautiful death is the one truly lasting creation that the Quixotist hero can bestow on his nation; for it is by means of the worship that his death inspires that the hero is able, finally, to conquer death. Through worship, his life is made eternal, because it is remembered and held up as an example; and it is made infinite, omnipotent, and all encompassing because, to the extent to which it is emulated, it is repeated over and over again. Through worship, the nation internalizes its hero, spiritualizes him. Thus, by conquering death the Quixotist hero of Ganivet's two novels—*La conquista del reino de Maya* and *Los trabajos del infatigable creador Pío Cid*—is able to offer himself for the spiritual transformation of his worshiping, faithful nation. It is in this regard that, for Ganivet, the figure of Don Quixote represents the promise of a regenerating "spiritual metamorphosis."

Confronted, as he was, with the historical demise of Spanish imperialism, Angel Ganivet generated an ambivalent national-imperialist discourse designed to repudiate the implications of Spain's loss of empire and, on the basis of that negation, affirm an essential, ahistorical Spanish national-imperial identity. By associating the figure of Don Quixote with the Spanish nation's conquering and spiritualizing heroism, Ganivet sought to confront the crisis of Spanish imperial identity and to regenerate Spain by means of a nationalistic, messianic idealism.

8

Don Quixote as Messiah

Nothing better dramatizes the development of Unamuno's thought concerning modern Spanish national decadence and regeneration than his shifting attitudes toward the symbolic meanings of Don Quixote. In his 1898 essay "Muera Don Quijote," for instance, Unamuno maintains that the decadent modern Spanish nation must abandon the Quixote-like madness of empire building and embrace a regenerating, sober, level-headedness: "We must forget our previous life of adventure and how we went about the world imposing on others what we believed was best for them and how we went in search of a deceptive empire . . . instead, the mission of our nation must be to Christianize itself . . . the hidalgo Alonso el Bueno can bring about a peaceful justice, without the blast of arms and without seeking to secure a place in ill-fated history . . . Death to Don Quixote and may Alonso el Bueno be reborn!"[1] Here, as in his 1895 *En torno al casticismo*, Unamuno takes Don Quixote's madness to represent the nation's clinging desire to revive its imperial identity by means of war.[2] Unamuno argues that it is precisely this madness that must be extinguished if the Spanish nation is to regenerate itself and become a "spiritual," "civilized," "European" nation concerned with the "peaceful justice" of life's *intrahistoric* day-to-day labors. By 1905, with the occasion to both commemorate the publication of Cervantes' *Quixote* and ponder the implications of the "Disaster of 1898," Unamuno recanted his call for the death of Don Quixote. Now, in the face of Spain's loss of empire, he praised the impassioned Don Quixote, as opposed to the repentant Alonso Quijano el Bueno, as the quintessential symbol of the Spanish nation's mission to "spiritualize" the modern world and replenish it with a "tragic" sense of heroism.[3]

This turn toward a spiritualizing Quixotism is most elaborately accomplished in Unamuno's 1905 philosophical-theological exegesis of the *Quixote, Vida de Don Quijote y Sancho,* where he compares Don Quixote's life of regenerating spirituality to that of Jesus. This interpretation of Cervantes' *Quixote* and the deification of the figure of Don Quixote attendant to it find their theoretical justification in an essay of that same year titled "Sobre la lectura e interpretación del 'Quijote.'" It is here that Unamuno denounces the "spiritual laziness," "moral cowardice," and "philosophical lack of ability" with which the "Masoretic school of cervantists" has, according to Unamuno, typically read and interpreted the *Quixote:* "The sad decadence of our national spirit is nowhere made as evident as in what happens with the *Quixote* in Spain."[4] Unamuno objects to the erudition of the cervantists, in other words, because he perceives in it a distinct failure to tease out the essential and, as he would have it, *intrahistorical* significance of the *Quixote,* a book that Unamuno now refers to as "the national Bible of Spain's patriotic religion."[5]

At the heart of this decadent spiritual laziness is the figure of Cervantes himself, whom Unamuno considers to be "a typical case of an author who is stupendously inferior to his work, his *Quixote*" and who, after writing the *Quixote,* "once again becomes the poor wandering writer that he had always been, prey to all the literary preoccupations of his time."[6] Unamuno completes the picture of Cervantes as a "temporary genius" by claiming that he was little more than a temporary mediator of the nation's essence: "Cervantes was nothing more than a mere instrument by means of which sixteenth-century Spain gave birth to Don Quixote."[7] Moreover, Unamuno sustains that "if Cervantes were to return to life, he would be a cervantist and not a quixotist."[8] This is the case, he argues, because Cervantes never truly understood the spiritualizing and transformative value of his hero, Don Quixote: "If one reads the *Quixote* attentively, one can observe easily enough that good old Cervantes could not match the Manchegan hidalgo's robust faith."[9] Consequently, Unamuno contends that Cervantes' authorial intent, in writing the *Quixote* is irrelevant with regard to "what the rest of us choose to see in it."[10]

Unamuno uses this deflated image of Cervantes as a man of inferior genius not only in an attempt to separate his own Quixotist interpretation of the *Quixote* from that of the cervantists, but also to help achieve a desired degree of autonomy for the figure of Don Quixote in relation to Cervantes' book.[11] "Ever since the *Quixote* first appeared in print and was made available to anyone who might pick it up and read it, the *Quixote* stopped belonging to Cervantes and became the property of all those who do read it and do feel it. Cervantes took Don Quixote from the nation's soul and from the soul of all mankind, and in his immortal book, he gave Don Quixote back to his nation and to all mankind. And ever since then, Don Quixote and Sancho have lived in the souls of the readers of Cervantes' book and even in the souls of those who have never read it."[12]

In this way, Unamuno is able to dispense with Cervantes' authority as author of the *Quixote* and elevate that book to near sacred status. "What has been done with the Sacred Scriptures of Christianity, why should this not be done with the *Quixote?*"[13] In order for this regenerating, allegorical reading to be at all possible, Unamuno reasons, Cervantes and the cervantists must be separated from the text: "Everything depends on separating Cervantes from the *Quixote* and making sure that the plague of cervantophiles or cervantists is replaced by a sacred legion of quixotists. We lack quixotism as much as we have an overabundance of cervantism."[14]

Just as in his 1895 *En torno al casticismo,* where Unamuno cites the need for a clairvoyant *vidente* who might glean and interpret the nation's intrahistoric identity, so too in this essay of 1905, Unamuno calls for a Quixotist who, by reason of his properly "mystical" interpretation of the *Quixote,* might reveal to the nation the spiritual significance and regenerative promise of its "national Bible." That exegete is, of course, Unamuno himself. Appropriately, Unamuno as Quixotist seeks to justify his philosophical rendering of Cervantes' *Quixote* as a labor of regenerating patriotism that is opposed to the decadent and stifling spirit of cervantine criticism in Spain.

When viewed in this light, Unamuno's Quixotism takes on the semblance of a "Mystical Reformation," a turning away from traditional cervantist "dogma" toward a much more personalized, interior, ascetic experience of enthusiastic faith: "There are those who read the *Quixote* out of a sense of obligation or because they have been motivated by what others have to say about it. But they read it without any damned enthusiasm whatsoever."[15] It is thus in an attempt to recuperate a tragic and regenerating heroism for modern Spain that Unamuno elaborates this mystical reading of the *Quixote* in his 1905 *Vida de Don Quijote y Sancho:* a reading which, in his 1923 "San Quijote de la Mancha," he reaffirms as "a campaign for the canonization of Don Quixote and for his becoming Saint Quixote"[16] and which, in his 1932 "En un lugar de la mancha," is given its definitive, religious and patriotic formulation: "From out of our national literature—and history is nothing more and nothing less than literature—a mythology arises, and from this mythology arises a religion . . . May Dulcinea, the one from Toboso, give us refuge and the truth . . . the truth of idealism."[17]

The Drama of Don Quixote's Regenerating Agony

Unamuno's 1905 *Vida de Don Quijote y Sancho* presents a drama of Spanish national history that can be likened to that of the Christian religion. In this regard, Unamuno's Quixotist drama unfolds in a modern world characterized by the fall of the Spanish empire and, indeed, of the Spanish people who, in their decadence, have chosen to ignore their historical "mission," that of pursuing the transcendental conquest of a spiritual empire.[18] There are three acts to Unamuno's Quixotist drama. The first act is the coming into history of Spain's national character, which is "incarnated" in the figure of Don Quixote. This first act has three parts: (1) the foundation of a Quixotist church through the gathering of disciples: Sancho and the creed of Dulcinea's eternal glory; (2) the redemption of mankind by way of Don Quixote's sacrificial death on the cross, that is, his return to "sanity"—where sanity can be taken to mean the constant "cross" or agonizing fight between reason and faith; and (3) Don Quixote's death, which is followed by his resurrection and ascension into "heaven"—where heaven can be taken to mean the status of a hero worthy of worship and remembrance in a fallen world that is otherwise devoid of heroism. The second act of Unamuno's Quixotist drama is that of the evangelization of Spain, and the world; and here it is Unamuno himself, as *vidente,* who acts as prophet and first priest of Quixotism. The third and final act is the second coming of Don Quixote and the final Day of Judgment that follows.

Act One: The Life, Faith, and Passion of Don Quixote

The key to the foundation of Unamuno's Quixotist church is the celebration of Don Quixote's apparent ability to "engender . . . lasting spiritual offspring," that is, to gather disciples and create a community of believers.[19] In this regard, the Don Quixote of Unamuno's *Vida de Don Quijote y Sancho* is, above all, a figure of exemplary faith: "Admirable Gentleman of Faith," Unamuno calls him.[20] As such, Unamuno places Don Quixote in direct opposition to the sceptical figures of the modern world as here symbolized by Alonso Quijano's niece, Antonia; by the erudite graduate of the University of Salamanca, Sanson Carrasco; by the priest and the barber and, to a lesser extent, by Don Quixote's squire, Sancho Panza. These skeptics all suffer from a decadent form of bad conscience, which Unamuno characterizes as "cowardice in the face of eternal problems . . . spiritual laziness."[21]

Not unlike the "modernized savages" that Ganivet's Pío Cid conquers, these "moderns," as Unamuno calls them, fail to recognize the need for idealistic heroes. Nor do they comprehend that modern Spanish national decadence is not a material and practical concern, but rather a moral and spiritual one.[22] As against their positivist understanding of modern Spanish decadence, their regenerationism, Unamuno depicts decadence as a strictly moral malady: "all our troubles stem from moral cowardice, the lack of initiative that each of us has for affirming his own truth, his own faith, and for defending it."[23] In this sense, he argues against "all those stupid graduates, priests and barbers of today" by proclaiming that, in order to regenerate itself, the Spanish nation does not require "practical solutions" but the faith and spiritual wisdom that Don Quixote's quest for eternal fame and glory exemplifies.[24]

At its basest and most profane level, however, Don Quixote's quest is driven by vanity. Unamuno nevertheless excuses this vanity, this fundamentally "sinful" desire for personal glory, by claiming that Don Quixote shares this vice with other heroes and saints: "Heroes and saints have always sought out glory, temporal or eternal, worldly or celestial."[25] Indeed, Unamuno portrays Don Quixote's search for fame as ultimately motivated by a religious and ascetic, saintly sentiment, which is characterized by his love for Dulcinea: "Don Quixote loved Dulcinea with undying love, without demanding that she love him in return; he gave himself completely and entirely to her."[26] Indeed, for Unamuno, Don Quixote's love for Dulcinea evolves from the worldly love of one man for one woman into the love of a mystical saint for all of God's creation. "Aldonza [i.e., Dulcinea] is the source of wisdom . . . She is the Virgin Mother . . . She is the incarnation of the eternal and infinite Consciousness of the Universe."[27]

The universal and specifically Christian character of this love for humanity is further exemplified, Unamuno avows, by Don Quixote's "baptism" and purification at the hands of an innkeeper in whose inn he "spiritually" transforms two fallen women: "Don Quixote turns two ladies of the night into maidens—Oh the power of his redeeming madness!—they were the first to serve him with selfless kindness . . . Remember Mary of Magdalene."[28] In this passage Unamuno emphasizes the nexus linking the life of Don Quixote to that of Christ—of whom Don Quixote is, for Unamuno, "always . . . a faithful disciple."[29] Moreover, like the "great quixotist" Ganivet, Unamuno here turns to the theme of the spiritual transformation of a fallen woman by a pious, moral leader in order to substantiate the good intentions underlying Don Quixote's regenerative powers of conquest.[30] Just as Spain's purportedly well-intentioned conquistadors had once sought to spiritualize the indigenous peoples of the Americas, so too Don Quixote is seeking to administer to the spiritual needs of these fallen women—and not to satisfy any base cravings of his own. Don Quixote is a spiritual redeemer and a savior, who is convinced that he is the "minister of God on Earth and the arm by means of which His justice is served."[31]

His attempts at exercising justice on Earth, at making the "realm of God . . . descend to Earth," however, do not always succeed.[32] Indeed, in some cases, such as when he frees the servant, Andrés, from his master's whip, Don Quixote's "good intentions" as "the minister of God" can lead to a greater injustice: in this case, a still more brutal whipping of the same servant he had set out to protect and redeem.[33] In this regard, reasons Unamuno, Don Quixote's failures become a transgression of God's will; they are examples of his vain and sinful nature: "perhaps, unfortunate Gentleman . . . it is your belief that you are the minister of God and that yours is the arm by means of which his justice is to be done . . . that is your greatest sin."[34] Don Quixote's disgrace, this falling away from God's grace, is also, insists Unamuno, the source of the Spanish nation's decadence: "Your nation also, arrogant Gentleman, believed itself to be God's minister on Earth . . . and it paid dearly for its conceit and it continues to pay dearly. It believed itself to have been chosen by God and this made it swell with pride."[35] This Quixotist faith in being God's chosen minister and nation, however, is not only the source of Don Quixote's and the nation's decadence, it is also, affirms Unamuno, the source for their regeneration. Their vanity is a "noble sin" and it is at the root of both Don Quixote's and the nation's heroic deeds.[36]

Indeed, despite his condemnation of this Quixotist arrogance, Unamuno seeks to excuse its shortcomings by arguing that it is, nevertheless, indicative of Don Quixote's and the Spanish nation's ardent belief and faith in the will of God. The moral value of an act is not, argues Unamuno, to be sought in its consequences, but rather in its intention, its motive: "convince yourself that everything that you do, irregardless of whether it seems good or bad to you, is done as God's minister on Earth. In this way, your actions will, in the end, all become good."[37] In short, the injustices arising from Don Quixote's and the Spanish nation's attempts to impose the will of God are seen by Unamuno as indicative of a noble, undying and profound faith in the will of God: "damage that has been inflicted with saintly intention is worth more than any benefit gained by means of perverse intentions."[38] Quixotism, as Unamuno constructs it, is a battle of love where violent acts of conquest and colonization become heroic and, as such, deserve being celebrated as generous and well-intentioned deeds.

The adventure in which Don Quixote confronts a group of merchants from Toledo and requires that they confess to the beauty of Dulcinea, despite their never having seen her, is, for Unamuno, "one of the most quixotist adventures of Don Quixote . . . one of the adventures that most lifts the hearts of those who are redeemed by his madness."[39] Accordingly, Unamuno compares this adventure to the Spanish nation's "adventure" of spiritual conquest in the Americas; the Spanish nation, explains Unamuno, "went off, with a firebrand in its right hand and Christ in its left hand, to force peoples in remote places to confess faith in a credo about which they knew nothing."[40] Consequently, Unamuno celebrates this act of imposing one's will, this drive to convert others to the nation's creed, to gather disciples and to found an empire as a glorifying act of faith.[41]

In this adventure, however, Don Quixote fails to impose his faith, a failure that is dramatized, for Unamuno, by the fact that he suffers a terrible fall.

Still, Unamuno solemnizes this fall: "Your triumph was always a question of desire and not results," he explains, directing himself to Don Quixote, "you, incomparable Gentleman, beat up and almost fallen apart, nevertheless consider yourself fortunate, viewing what has happened to you [your fall from Rocinante] as a 'misfortune befitting a knight-errant,' and by maintaining this perspective, you overcome your defeat, transforming it into victory."[42] Indeed, as Unamuno points out, "nothing is impossible for those who are faithful," not even the transformation of a physical defeat into a moral victory: "he who understands that his suffering is momentary has overcome it already by so understanding it."[43]

Such is, then, the perspective that Unamuno maintains, some seven years after Spain's defeat by the United States, in the face of Spain's imperial collapse. The faithful perspective to which Don Quixote holds true throughout his misadventure with the Toledan Merchants, is not unlike that which Unamuno recommends to his compatriots following Spain's imperial misadventure of 1898: by denying the implications of the fall, Unamuno reasons that both Don Quixote and Spain can transform their physical defeat into a moral victory.

Among the skeptics of the modern world, Unamuno recognizes that these examples of Quixotist imagination inspire laughter and ridicule rather than faith. Just as Don Quixote fails to inspire faith among the merchants, he fails also to inspire it in his niece as well as in a score of other skeptics; among them, the Duke and Duchess, the Priest, the Barber, and above all, Sansón Carrasco whose role in Don Quixote's life is to deceive, cheat, and ultimately defeat him in physical, hand-to-hand combat in Barcelona, or what Unamuno calls Don Quixote's Jerusalem.[44] At the hands of these skeptical and envious enemies "who cannot put up with heroic madness," Don Quixote is made to lead the life of a jester and a fool, as opposed to that of a celebrated and adored hero, as should be his due.[45] Marred, as they are, by "the madness of bad passions, resentment, pride and envy" these skeptics seek to envelop Don Quixote in a world of deceit and to make a mockery of him.[46] In this sense, suggests Unamuno, the mockery that Don Quixote suffers at their hands is not unlike that which the Spanish empire was made to "suffer" at the hands of England in the late eighteenth and early nineteenth centuries, when the British repeatedly bombarded, invaded, and occupied several of Spain's more strategic ports along the Atlantic coastline of the Americas or, still more to the point, the mockery that the United States made of Spain's naval and military forces in 1898. "Already we find the hero, insofar as he is a hero, being treated as a toy and the object of laughter . . . His most beautiful and spontaneous adventures are over; from here on . . . they will be . . . constructed for him by malicious men . . . Now the world recognizes and accepts him . . . but, only in order to ridicule him."[47]

According to Unamuno, this mockery ultimately marks Don Quixote, and the Quixotist Spanish nation, with the sign of nobility. It is precisely in this sense that Unamuno directs himself to his Quixotist nation, writing: "Your most bitter passion begins: the passion of ridicule. Yet, it is by reason of this ridicule that your adventures gain in profound seriousness what they have lost in rashness . . . You become somewhat de-quixotized, but you do so by quixotizing those who mock and ridicule you."[48] This view of the nation's "passion" by mockery is at the core of what in 1913 Unamuno would refer to as the Spanish nation's regenerative "tragic sense of life." And it was precisely this "tragic sense," Unamuno would argue, that qualified the technologically backward but morally superior Spanish nation for spiritual leadership and cultural imperialism in the decadent modern world.

The skeptic who is most profoundly and completely Quixotized and transformed by the "tragedy" of Don Quixote's passional, agonizing mockery is his squire, Sancho Panza, of whom Unamuno writes: "his entire life consisted of his slowly giving himself over to the power of a quixotist and quixotizing faith."[49] The spiritual transformation of Sancho follows the pattern of an ascetic renunciation of the material world with its attendant spiritual purification and the ultimate achievement of a state of elevated spirituality. Don Quixote first "seduces" Sancho into following him by promising Sancho an island, a kingdom of his own. In this regard, the adventures of Sancho, not unlike those of Don Quixote, take their origins in base desires and cravings. Whereas Don Quixote first sets out from La Mancha in search of fame, Sancho does so in search of material wealth and power; and it is this greed that first motivates Sancho to follow and serve his master, Don Quixote. Still, Don Quixote's example of faith and passional humility "drag Sancho along, transforming his greed into ambition and his thirst for gold into a thirst for glory."[50]

For Unamuno, this means that Sancho, like Don Quixote, is capable of Quixotist heroism: "there is more quixotism when a sane man follows a madman than when a madman follows his own madness. Faith is contagious, and Don Quixote's faith is so robust and arduous that it fills those who love him . . . by flowing over, it grows and by disseminating itself, its force augments."[51] In this regard, Unamuno suggests, Sancho's Quixotist faith is stronger than Don Quixote's. He notes, for instance, how, after Don Quixote's defeat in Barcelona and his return home to La Mancha—during which trip he is made to bear the "cross" of his mockery, defeat, and forced return to "sanity"—it is Sancho who complains about his master's loss of faith in glory. To Unamuno, this becomes even more evident when, on his death bed, Don Quixote renounces his heroic deeds and Sancho chastises him for his apparent weakness: "Wake up! Wake up and stop telling lies!"[52]

Unamuno represents Don Quixote's death as sacrificial and regenerating. "'Behold the son of God,' they said mocking Christ Our Lord; 'behold the madman,' they say about you, my lord Don Quixote. [. . .] Your death was more heroic than your life, because when you reached your death you performed the greatest act of self-abnegation, you renounced your glory, you renounced your work. Your death was an exalted sacrifice. At the height of your passion, weighed down with ridicule, you renounced . . . your works."[53] According to Unamuno, Don Quixote sacrifices his claim to glory in order that Sancho might be made to suffer alone, as Don Quixote once did, the passional burden of mockery: "Poor Sancho, you are alone now with your faith, with the faith that your lord gave to you! . . . Don Quixote lost his faith and died; you [Sancho] found it and live on; he had to die disenchanted so that you might live in a state of life-enhancing enchantment."[54] Don Quixote's sacrificial death engenders a still greater and more expansive faith among his disciples: the nation's belief in the Quixotist "life-enhancing enchantment": the belief that, by negating the implications of Spain's loss of empire, an eternal, spiritual empire may yet be won.

Consequently, Unamuno affirms that it is by virtue of its capacity to inspire Sancho's faith that Don Quixote's sacrificial death—like the nation's decline into decadence—can be seen as "the coronation of the life of Don Quixote . . . Don Quixote's death revealed the mystery of his quixotist life."[55] This mystery, according to Unamuno, is that life miraculously springs from death, when death involves self-sacrifice. Unamuno's Don Quixote can be assured of glory only by renouncing his search for fame; and it is only in this way, too, that he can be assured of Sancho's spiritual confirmation. By reason of Sancho's adoring faith in Don Quixote, Don Quixote is elevated, following his death, to the status of a divine hero who is resurrected from the dead and ascends into glory.[56]

Don Quixote's death, resurrection, and ascension are, in this manner, made to parallel those of Christ. They constitute a messianic formula for the regeneration of life. The Christian death that Unamuno elaborates for Don Quixote is ultimately meant as a justification and consolation for modern Spain's decline, defeat, and loss of empire: "Look . . . look upon the Spanish nation and see if it won't be cured of its madness to then only die. Over there, in the Americas, they finally defeated you Don Quixote, you returned home beaten and battered. Did you return home in order to cure yourself of your madness? Who knows! . . . Perhaps you came back to die. Perhaps to die, if it weren't for the fact that Sancho remains . . . Because Sancho, Gentleman, is the treasure house of your faith."[57] Indeed, by presenting Don Quixote's death as sacrificial, and Spain's loss of empire as a patriotic and divinely sanctioned act of sacrifice, Unamuno seeks to do more than simply console his nation; he seeks to regenerate it's faith in itself, its love for itself and for its so-called "mission" in the world: "Look, Lord"—writes Unamuno in addressing himself to God—"You founded this nation, the nation of your servants Don Quixote and Sancho, on the basis of faith in personal immortality; look, Lord, this faith is our reason for living and it is our destiny among nations to make certain that this truth of our hearts enlightens minds against the shadows of logic and reason and consoles the hearts of those who are condemned to the dream that is life."[58] In this way, Unamuno encourages the Spanish nation to take up the heroic, missionary labor of serving as God's faithful minister in a modern world otherwise dominated by the brute forces of Reason: the philosophical reason of the Enlightenment; the scientific reason of technology and industry; the economic reason of capital; the political reason of liberalism. By affirming its philosophical, scientific, economic, and political backwardness and seeing in this backwardness the proof of its spiritual superiority, Unamuno suggests that the Spanish nation will be able to provide the modern world with a regenerating cultural alternative to that world's progressive moral and spiritual decadence.

ACT TWO: THE QUIXOTIST EVANGELIZATION OF THE WORLD

Dating from his 1905 *Vida de Don Quijote y Sancho* to his 1933 *San Manuel Bueno, mártir,* the greater part of Unamuno's work represents an attempt to evangelize the world and to impose on it the creed of Quixotism. To this end, in January of 1928, Unamuno writes: "The sacred hour, during which we must expose the contents of our hearts to the light of the sun, is upon us, and may those who judge meanly be forever reduced to meanness—above all, myself. Yes, me, the spiteful one, the madman, the ambitious one, the energumen, me! I, who have made what is most intimate about our national soul, its eternal essence, its divine over-reason-for-being, the very juice of its quixotist Christianity, known to the nations that speak Latin, Anglo-Saxon, Germanic and Slavic languages . . . to all of civilized humanity. Imperialism . . . yes, but the imperialism of the spirit, of conscience and of justice."[59] For Unamuno, this spiritualizing and neo-imperialist Quixotism represents, as he phrases it in *Del sentimiento trágico de la vida,* "the role that is reserved to Don Quixote in the modern European tragicomedy."[60]

Unamuno insists that the only formula for Spanish national regeneration and the parallel conquest of this spiritual empire is to be discovered in the nation's Bible: "The fruits of our heroism were condensed in a work of ridicule; in a work of ridicule, the passing greatness of our Spain was made eternal; in a work of ridicule, our Spanish philosophy is encoded and summarized, the only true and profoundly true philosophy; in a work of ridicule, the soul of our nation, incarnated in the form of a man, penetrated the abyss of the mystery of life. And that work of ridicule is the saddest story that has ever been written; the saddest, yes, but also the most capable of consoling those who know how to savor, in the tears shed through laughter, our redemption from the miserable wisdom to which the slavery of life today condemns us."[61] Together, Unamuno's interpretation of the *Quixote* and the Quixotist Don Quixote that emerges from out of that interpretation are to regenerate the nation's faith in itself as well as the world's faith in the spirituality of the Spanish nation. According to Unamuno, Quixotism serves as a mythical formula for the Spanish nation to: "overcome defeat, transforming it into victory."[62]

Act Three: The Second Coming of Don Quixote

Central to Unamuno's task of Quixotist evangelization is the labor of prophecy. Appropriately enough, in his *Vida de Don Quijote y Sancho*, Unamuno prophesizes the second coming of Don Quixote. Like that of the Christ, Don Quixote's second coming is to carry with it the apocalyptic force of a final day of judgment, whereby the meek are to inherit the Earth. Thus, for Unamuno, it is only by way of Don Quixote's second coming to Earth in glory that Sancho will prove able to inherit a utopian, spiritualized order: "Don Quixote . . . will return when Sancho, who today lives overwhelmed by memories, feels the blood that he gathered together during his squirely wanderings begin to boil, and mounts . . . Rocinante, and dressed in the arms of his lord, takes his lance in hand and throws himself into acting like Don Quixote. His lord will then return and reincarnate himself in him. Take courage, heroic Sancho, and revive the faith that your lord first lit in you."[63] In a similar vein, Unamuno argues "it is Sancho who will establish quixotism forever in the world of men."[64] In this manner, Unamuno imagines Sancho in ultimate victory over the Sansón Carrascos and Antonia Quijanas, under whose skeptical modern leadership "all heroism has been smothered."[65]

As such, Unamuno's Quixotism provides for a critique of the political system of Restoration Spain: a government under whose leadership Spain lost the few remaining remnants of its empire to a nation that had once been little more than a colony itself, the United States of America. In a telling passage of his *Vida de Don Quijote y Sancho*, where he compares the regenerationist governments of the Restoration regime with the puppet show that Master Peter puts on in Cervantes' *Don Quixote*, Unamuno condemns the Spanish nation's would-be regenerating politicians: "Death to the scheming people of the theater! We must do away completely with all theaters, with all the sanctioned fictions . . . There is a puppet show in the capital of my and Don Quixote's country where the story of Melissendra's liberation, or Spain's regeneration or the revolution from above, is being presented. And there, in the Parliament, Master Peter pulls the strings that move all the puppets made of paste. A mad knight-errant should step into the midst of that farce, and refusing to listen to all the complaining voices, behead and destroy all those who gesticulate, and destroy, once and for all, Master Peter's property."[66] In one fell swoop, Unamuno would have a modern-day Quixote do away with the head of the restored monarch (Master Peter) and the political class (the figurines) that obey his meddlesome commands.

Unamuno, however, does not limit himself to fanciful, poetic analogies such as these. Rather, he argues emphatically: "in order to establish the kingdom of . . . sincerity, of truth, and of love . . . there must be war . . . we need . . . a civil war."[67] Quixotism, for Unamuno, constitutes a crusade, a divinely sanctioned war through which the resurrected spirit of the Spanish nation's savior, Don Quixote, is to bring about a reign of "sincerity," "truth," and "love." Just as Jesus Christ "said that He had not come to bring peace, but war," so too, according to Unamuno, Don Quixote is to come again in glory to foment civil war, a purifying death on a massive scale meant to rid the nation of its moral "impurities" and its parliamentary "moral cowardice."[68]

It is in this same context, then, that Unamuno's Quixotist utopia can be said to consist of spiritualizing masters and spiritualized servants. As regards the spiritualizing masters, these are to act as the nation's elite regenerators: "We have no choice but to speak to those who are simple, and to speak to them without even attempting to lower ourselves to their level; we must speak to them in a more elevated tone, certain that, even though they do not understand, they do understand us."[69] As regards the spiritualized servants, these masses are to "understand," literally stand beneath, adore, and obey their masters: "your ambition, Sancho, should be to look for Don Quixote: the ambition of those who were born to be governed should be to find someone who will govern them well."[70] For Unamuno, Don Quixote is the ideal leader for Sancho because his example can serve to inspire him to abandon the "false" and "modern" hope of self-government and to replace that misguided hope with a regenerating faith in Don Quixote. In this sense, Unamuno concludes, the Quixotist conquest of the nation becomes, and should be considered as, an ideal union of the nation's spiritualizing elite and its spiritualized masses: "When your faithful Sancho, noble Gentleman, mounts Rocinante . . . you will be resuscitated in him, and then your dream will become reality. Dulcinea will embrace you both, and pulling you with her arms to her breast, she will make the two of you one."[71]

This victorious embrace, linking a unified nation of elites and faithful masses to a divine order, is given a specifically Christian face in Unamuno's 1922 essay "La Bienaventuranza de Don Quijote." Here, Unamuno's Don Quixote, after having ascended into Heaven, is depicted in an agonizing embrace with the Christ: "Don Quixote rested his head on his shoulder . . . the shoulder of Christ and began to cry. He cried, he cried, he cried. His tears . . . became mixed with those of the Redeemer himself . . . And while the Gentleman cried, thinking on his public life . . . he heard . . . these words: 'Blessed are the madmen because they will become fed up with reason!' And the Gentleman felt himself in eternal glory."[72] Here, Unamuno's Quixotist Don Quixote—the agonizing, "tragic" and Catholic Spanish nation of his 1913 *Del sentimiento trágico de la vida*—is seen to be in perfect communion with an also agonizing Jesus Christ, whose final words to Don Quixote—'Blessed are the madmen because they will become fed up with reason!'—act both as divine justification for the nation's decadence and as prophecy of its future regeneration through the unifying violence of a civil war.

9

Don Quixote as Lover

On the face of it, Maeztu's Quixotism seems rather unlike the Quixotism espoused by Ganivet and Unamuno. Contrary to Ganivet's celebration of the *Quixote* as the Spanish nation's regenerating epic and in opposition to Unamuno's interpretation of the *Quixote* as the regenerating Bible of modern Spain, Maeztu viewed Cervantes' novel as a "decadent book" that was, for the most part, ill-suited to the needs of the still decadent modern nation.[1] Moreover, whereas Ganivet and Unamuno saw Don Quixote as a regenerating spiritual conquistador and a tragic, messianic hero, Maeztu took him to be an "impotent idealist" who, because of his impotence, could not alone provide the nation with an example of regenerating heroism.[2] These differences are not, however, as fundamental as one might assume. In point of fact, Maeztu's Quixotism is centered on an ascetic ideal that serves, much as it does in Ganivet and Unamuno, to critique the nation's decadence and to offer a promise of regenerating imperial reconquest.[3]

In Ganivet, stoic discipline leads to the celebration of a regenerating dictatorship based in modern heroic values. In Unamuno, ascetic idealism leads to the veneration of civil war as a spiritually purifying and nationally regenerating crusade. Similarly, in Maeztu, ascetic idealism serves to justify the military discipline and religious asceticism of a nationally regenerative and empire-building dictatorship. In the end, ascetic idealism leads, in Maeztu, to the National-Catholic ideology of Spanish fascism.

As such, Maeztu provides the clearest example of an intimate link between the Quixotism of Restoration Spain and Spanish fascism. When viewed in this light, his thoughts on both the *Quixote* and the figure of Don Quixote are an important point of reference, without which it would be difficult, if not altogether impossible, to fully appreciate the impact that Quixotism has had on modern Spanish national life. Indeed, there exist substantial elements of Maeztu's fascistic Quixotism in the thought of the other major Quixotists of Restoration Spain. Although neither Ganivet nor Unamuno was a fascist—Ganivet died years before the emergence of the Falange and Unamuno embraced the fascist cause only ambiguously—Ganivet did, like Maeztu, celebrate dictatorship; and Unamuno did, also like Maeztu, assert the nation-building value of military discipline and the spiritually edifying value of the nation's "tragic" faith. Moreover, for each of these three thinkers, Quixotism ultimately became a way to imaginatively deny the Spanish nation's loss of empire and to affirm Spanish national cultural imperialism.

But just as these similarities must not be overlooked, they also should not be overstated. This is particularly so as regards the nature of the imperial reconquest that each of these thinkers envisioned in his Quixotist essays. For Ganivet, that reconquest was always and already a desideratum; it was the imaginative realization of a desire for national regeneration. In the case of Unamuno, the reconquest of an eternal spiritual empire was, in part, a purely spiritual matter. In this respect, it concerned the struggle of the skeptical and reasoning modern individual to maintian his faith in the immortality of his premodern soul. It was a question, in other words, of existential angst. Still, the eternal empire that Unamuno envisioned was not only spiritual and philosophical; it was also national. In this regard, Unamuno envisioned the reconquest of empire as a reassertion of Spanish cultural hegemony in Europe and the Americas. Maeztu, by contrast, envisioned reconquest as neither a regenerating fiction nor as a moral victory, but as a realizable political and historical mission. In sum, Ganivet imagined a fictional reconquest; Unamuno, a primarily cultural reconquest; and Maeztu, a political reconquest.

As the only one among the major Quixotists of Restoration Spain who was an outright fascist, Ramiro de Maeztu formulated an interpretation of both the *Quixote* and Don Quixote that underscored how, by reason of its ascetic idealism, Quixotism could help lay the conceptual, ideological, and imaginary groundwork for Spanish National-Catholicism. Thus, it is because his Quixotism provides this nexus, directly linking the Quixotism of Restoration Spain to the ideology of fascist Spain, that it deserves careful consideration.

Maeztu's Don Quixote: From Impotent Lover to Ascetic Idealist

Maeztu's Quixotism evolved along the same lines that marked his career as a thinker. At first, he professed a vitalistic anti-Quixotism. He rejected the *Quixote* forthright, interpreting it as a decadent and melancholic work. Accordingly, during this first phase, he also rejected Don Quixote as the impotent counterpart to the vitalistic heroes he wrote about in his 1899 *Hacia otra España*. By the 1910s, however, Maeztu began to profess a Quixotism that was based in the so-called objective values of the guild-syndicalism that he outlined in his 1918 *Authority, Liberty and Function*. In this sense, he now read the *Quixote* as a tragedy that could bring about a national catharsis, and saw Don Quixote's love as an "objective" value that could inspire national regeneration. Finally, in his 1926 *Don Quijote, Don Juan y la Celestina,* Maeztu interpreted the *Quixote* as one of three enduring "Spanish national myths" and conceived of Don Quixote's love as a "cosmic" and all-embracing, civilizing love that could serve as the basis and justification for modern Spanish imperialism. This final phase coincides, in other words, with Maeztu's fascistic period.

From as early as 1901, or just three years after the events of 1898, Maeztu used the *Quixote* to comment on the Spanish nation's perceived decadence and need for regeneration. He spoke of Cervantes' novel as a depiction of the modern Spanish nation's decadence.[4] Maeztu's views to this effect were first formulated in his 1901 "El libro de los viejos" in which he explains: "Decadence begins . . . whenever we desire what cannot become reality, whenever we have to declare ourselves defeated in the face of an impossible dream . . . And if I am not mistaken in making this judgment, can there be any better example of a decadent book than the *Quixote?*"[5] Here, Maeztu views the *Quixote* as emblematic of the Spanish nation's descent into a state of decadence which, just as in his 1899 *Hacia otra España,* he conceives as the paralysis of the nation's will: "the *Quixote* . . . is the most polished mirror and most inspired apology of decadence, of a nation's exhaustion."[6]

In support of his thesis concerning the *Quixote* as a decadent narrative, Maeztu appeals to the historical context in which it was written. He refers, first, to Cervantes' life, explaining that "Cervantes was tired when he wrote the *Quixote;* he longed for rest; he dreamed of it; and it is in this need for rest that we should look for the intimate meaning of his work."[7] Next, Maeztu draws a parallel between Cervantes' state of weariness while he worked on the *Quixote* and Spain's exhaustion during the same period.[8] As such, Maeztu views the *Quixote* as a literary expression of the nation's historical decline and its melancholic response to that decline. Indeed, in 1901, Maeztu did not see in the *Quixote* anything that might recommend it to those who, like himself, claimed to be focused on regenerating the nation. Likewise, during these early years of Spain's first century without empire, Maeztu found nothing in the figure of Don Quixote that might recommend it as a model for regenerating heroism. Instead, he saw in Don Quixote a vain, impotent, old man whose limited power was disproportionate to his desire: "Don Quixote awoke from his insanity in order to die from melancholy."[9] For Maeztu in 1901, Don Quixote represented, in other words, a spirit of melancholic defeatism.

By the late 1910s, Maeztu began to see the relationship between the Spanish nation's need for regeneration and the *Quixote* in a rather more positive light. He now read Cervantes' novel as a tragedy that could offer the nation a much-needed sense of catharsis. With regard to the *Quixote*'s cathartic qualities, Maeztu writes, in his *Authority, Liberty and Function* of 1916: "Great novels are purifying in the same sense that Aristotle spoke of the catharsis of Greek tragedy. The hero of novels is not the hero described by the poet, but every one of his readers . . . Great novels are purifying because they free the soul from the delusion of individual happiness."[10] In this sense, Maeztu goes on to argue that the *Quixote* provides a unique form of cathartic purification that inspires the reader to pursue an idealistic and spiritual, as opposed to a hedonistic, and secular, form of happiness: "Don Quixote does not find happiness in his attempt to redeem the world, but melancholy and disillusion. His generous lance is broken on the hard skin of human egoism; and, at the moment of dying, Don Quixote turns his eyes to heaven; the Happy Isles are certainly not to be found in this world."[11] Here, Maeztu argues that as a "great novel" the *Quixote* is capable of purifying the nation—and, indeed, all of its readers the world over, because it inspires its readers to "rise a little above [them] selves . . . [their] own joys and sufferings" and to adopt an "objective," ideal love in place of the "foolishness of happiness."[12] Therefore, Maeztu concludes: "when Don Quixote dies, Quixotism remains in the air, a cultural value that we have to serve."[13] From out of the *Quixote*'s decadent melancholy arises the regenerative force of Don Quixote's Quixotist idealism.

Writing in 1926 about the events of 1898, Maeztu explains the reasons for this shift in his perspective regarding the regenerative value of both the *Quixote* and the figure of Don Quixote. His explanation is revealing and thus bears extended quotation: "When, in 1898, Spain lost the few remaining vestiges of its colonial empire in the Americas and the Far East, the figure of Joaquín Costa arose, exhorting us to: 'Place a double lock on the sepulcher of the Cid so that he will never mount his horse again.' Don Miguel de Unamuno . . . also formulated his sentence: 'Robinson has defeated Don Quixote' . . . If in 1895 we had given a degree of autonomy to Cuba and the Philippines, or if we had known how to inspire love or admiration, or even simply fear, perhaps we would have been able to retain our colonies. But the first thing that occurred to our independent thinkers was to attribute the war to a quixotic, imprudent and unjustified adventure . . . They beseeched us Spaniards to never be either Cids or Quixotes again, and it did not take long for those of us who, during those hours of humiliation and defeat, felt the need to rebuild the nation, to 'regenerate' it . . . to understand that this would not come about unless the regenerators adopted, at the very least, a bit of the forceful spirit of the Cid and the generous idealism of Don Quixote."[14]

Here, Maeztu explains how the negative views of Don Quixote that he and other thinkers, in particular Unamuno, expressed shortly after the war, eventually gave way to an altogether different, positive view of Don Quixote. This Quixotist view, as Maeztu explains it, arose out of the need to provide the decadent nation with a vision of its own regeneration. Thus, what had seemed to be quixotic vanity, impotence, and foolery during the war, became, once the war was over, the generous, self-sacrificing, and spiritually regenerative idealism of a newly Quixotized Don Quixote. In the end, the decadent melancholy that Maeztu had read into the *Quixote* in 1901 did not keep him, in the 1910s and 1920s, from seeing in the figure of Don Quixote the representation of a regenerating madness, or "generous idealism," that held forth the promise for modern Spanish national and imperial regeneration. Despite his downfall, Don Quixote could provide an example of heroic, regenerating "cosmic love," just the kind of love that, according to Maeztu, could serve as the impetus for conquest and the foundation for civilizing empire.

These retrospective comments of Maeztu's belong to an essay of 1926 titled "Don Quixote o el amor," which is one of the three essays included in his *Don Quijote, Don Juan y la Celestina*. In this work, Maeztu does not limit himself either to recalling his previous position vis-à-vis the *Quixote* and Don Quixote or to explaining why his views changed; he also expands on his views, suggesting that Quixotism is to play an important role in the modern Spanish nation's regeneration and reconquest of empire.[15] As such, his essays of 1926 represent Maeztu's definitive stance as a Quixotist.[16] By 1926, Maeztu had moved beyond vitalism and guild-syndicalism and become increasingly intimate with the Primo de Rivera dictatorship. In fact, Maeztu published his *Don Quijote, Don Juan y la Celestina* only two years before leaving Spain for Argentina, where he would serve as the dictatorship's Ambassador from 1928 to 1930. In this work of literary commentary, Maeztu anticipated several of the themes that he would develop still further in his 1934 *Defensa de la Hispanidad*. This book, which he began to write while in Argentina, would ultimately prove to be his most unmitigated defense of a regenerating modern Spanish imperialism. Indeed, the fascistic "Hispanic Gentleman" that figures in this book of 1934 as the modern world's regenerating hero finds his precursor in the Don Quixote that Maeztu formulated in his 1926 *Don Quijote, Don Juan y la Celestina*.

It is in this book of 1926 that Maeztu discusses the regenerative power of what he considers to be the Spanish nation's three most enduring "literary myths:" Cervantes' 1605 *Quixote,* Tirso de Molina's 1630 *El burlador de Sevilla,* and Rojas's 1499 *Celestina.*[17] Under the exegetical pressure that Maeztu brings to bear on these Spanish classics, a thematically unified trilogy of regenerating Spanish national values arises. It is precisely these values—love, power, and wisdom—that explain, according to Maeztu, the Spanish nation's initial rise to empire. Moreover, he argues that by embracing these values once again, the modern Spanish nation will be able to both regenerate itself and restore the spiritual unity of the Hispanic world.

For Maeztu, the "national myth" of Don Quixote represents the ideal of love; that of Don Juan, the ideal of power; and that of Celestina, the ideal of wisdom. Maeztu's aim, throughout *Don Quijote, Don Juan y la Celestina,* is to demonstrate that, for purposes of national regeneration, none of these three ideals is sufficient unto itself. In order to regenerate, the nation must affirm all three of these ideals, in unison. Thus conceived, Maeztu's Quixotist trilogy takes on the quality of what Ricardo Landeira has called "a medieval Christian image . . . a reflection of the Holy Trinity recorded by Dante Alighieri, 'Fecerni la divina Potestade / la somma Sapienza / e il primo Amore.'"[18] Indeed, by appealing to the image of the Holy Trinity, Maeztu aims to surround his Quixotism with an aura of divine mystery; as in Dante's epic of Christianity, this is the mystery of salvation. Except that for Maeztu, the notion of salvation proves, in the end, to rely not on the ability of the Spanish nation to rise to the heavens but, to the status of an everlasting imperial power.

Don Quixote's Cosmic Love

In "Don Quijote o el amor," Maeztu espouses the need to read Cervantes' great work with an eye toward simplicity: "What is in the *Quixote?* Let us not seek esoteric interpretations; let us read it with humility and simplicity."[19] Maeztu's "simple" reading renders a reconstruction of the *Quixote*'s plot which, not unlike Unamuno's reworking of the *Quixote* in his *Vida de Don Quijote y Sancho,* emphasizes Don Quixote's spiritual mission: that he become a minister of God's will and the means by which "His justice is done on Earth."[20] The *Quixote,* explains Maeztu, "is not only about . . . romances of chivalry, it is also about the ideal of knight-errantry, the impulse that pushes noble spirits to undertake grand enterprises and to do so with no consideration for the dangers involved and without ever stopping to calculate their own strength."[21] It is because he is willing to sacrifice himself with reckless abandon to his ideals that Don Quixote comes to represent, for Maeztu, the ideal of love: "Don Quixote is the prototype of love, in its most elevated form of cosmic love . . . Every great lover will forever propose that the Good be realized on Earth and will always attempt to resuscitate, during an Iron Age, the ideals of the Golden Age."[22] The recognition of this idealism and of "Don Quixote's supreme kindness . . . which is hidden behind his madness, his creativity, his valor and adventures" is, then, what Maeztu has in mind when he speaks of a "simple," "human," and "sympathetic" reading of the *Quixote.*[23] Indeed, his reading is romantic, in the sense that Anthony Close suggests it might be.[24]

Accordingly, Maeztu romanticizes Don Quixote's downfall by treating it as a melancholy and dispirited renunciation of his "noble" impulse toward heroism.[25] Don Quixote, Maeztu maintains, is "too old for his labors. He desires, but he cannot perform. This is, unmistakably, decadence."[26] Yet, not unlike Unamuno, who views Don Quixote's life in moral terms, Maeztu judges this melancholy ethically. He suggests that Don Quixote's decadence—and, ipso facto, that of the Spanish nation—is sinful, because Don Quixote fails to combine his love for divine justice with the strength and wisdom necessary to execute God's will on Earth: "Without power, love cannot move a thing, and in order to measure our own strength accurately we must see things as they are. Truth is an unavoidable responsibility. To confuse windmills for giants is not merely a hallucination, but a sin."[27] In this manner, Maeztu does more then simply romanticize Don Quixote as an incurable and melancholic lover, he treats Don Quixote's downfall as that of a spiritual castaway who, because he has sinned, has also fallen from God's grace.

In order to recuperate that state of grace and once again act as the agent of divine justice on Earth, the Spanish nation must, reasons Maeztu, make Don Quixote's "impotent" love virile once again. Maeztu discovers reasons to believe that this is possible in the *Quixote* itself: "although the *Quixote* is a decadent book," he writes in this regard, "it is still a healthy book . . . because the best thing that a man can do when he is tired is rest."[28] By convincing its readers that, in times of weariness, it is best to rest and regain one's strength, the *Quixote* holds forth the promise of a regenerating future. "We understand today that, for their own good, the Spaniards of Cervantes' time had to be disenchanted. We should point out, however, that what our nation needs now is not to become disenchanted or disillusioned, but, to the contrary, to once again feel an ideal."[29] Considering that the Spanish nation's imperial decline had begun during Cervantes' lifetime, Maeztu reasons that the nation has, by 1926, had enough time to rest and regain its strength. Thus it now becomes possible for the Spanish nation to look beyond the melancholy that informs the *Quixote,* and find in this "national myth" an example of the idealism by means of which the nation might recuperate its historical initiative.

"Among individuals, decadence is a sign of death. Among nations, this need not be the case. Instead, it can signal a new situation, a period of rest during which the nation loses its historical initiative but, in exchange for suffering a temporary decline in its status, creates a new ideal and generates the energy for maintaining that ideal. When nations . . . give themselves over to an ideal, this unity of affection multiplies their energy."[30] When nations reconstitute themselves by means of their love for an ideal, reasons Maeztu, they become strong enough to resist even death. The forces of "cosmic love," suggests Maeztu, will ultimately win out over those of decadence.

As one of Maeztu's three greatest "hispanic literary myths," the tale of Don Quixote affords the Spanish nation an opportunity to attend to its need for regeneration. On the one hand, the melancholy that Maeztu uncovers in the *Quixote* gives rise to a purifying catharsis; on the other, the "cosmic love" that Don Quixote represents inspires a concomitant desire for the power and the wisdom that are needed to make this ideal a reality: the Quixotist ideal of a universal and civilizing Hispanic empire. In this manner, Maeztu's "simple" reading of the *Quixote* provides the Spanish nation with an also "simple" choice: melancholic defeatism or regenerating love. As a Quixotist, Maeztu does not choose the decadent melancholy of the *Quixote*. He rather argues that, following the catharsis that is brought on by that melancholy, the only responsible choice is that of the regenerating and empire-building love of Don Quixote. The key to making sure that this all-embracing "cosmic love" actually serves as the basis for the creation of an Hispanic spiritual and political empire is, according to Maeztu, to be found in the values represented in the Spanish nation's two other enduring literary myths: that of Don Juan and that of Celestina.

Don Juan or the Rashness of Carnal Power

As a means to regenerating the historical and conquering initiative of the Spanish nation, Maeztu, in "Don Juan o el poder," posits the example of the Hispanic Don Juan and his virulent, overhuman will-to-power.[31] This Hispanic Don Juan, as opposed to the "Don Juan of the nations of the North, and even of Italy, who is a love-stricken Don Juan," is "the Trickster . . . of Tirso and . . . Zorrilla."[32] Whereas the Romantic Don Juan of the North—a Europeanized perversion of the Spanish Don Juan—is "a brave soul full of love, who wanders throughout the world vainly seeking an ideal woman," the Don Juan of the Spanish nation is "first and foremost a brute force, instinctive, petulant, but tireless, triumphant and devastating" and he does not believe in love.[33] Indeed, Maeztu's Spanish Don Juan is the prototype of "the man of passion who has no ideals," he is "the incarnation of caprice" and represents the Spanish nation's heroic and historical initiative to "impose our will on other men."[34]

In the face of the Romanticized Don Juan of the North, it is precisely this image of a Don Juan who lacks ideals and who represents the possibility of a life without ideals that Maeztu, in *Don Quijote, Don Juan y la Celestina,* sets out to recuperate for the Spanish nation. Maeztu's vindication of this virulent Don Juan—Tirso de Molina's trickster—does not preclude, however, the possibility of a Quixotist Don Juan who, like the romantic Don Juan of Zorrilla, discovers the existence of a divine order of justice or love. Maeztu's redemption of the Hispanic Don Juan thus comprehends both the violent energy of the faithless trickster of Tirso de Molina—the conquistador—and the spiritual values of the converted trickster of Zorrilla—what in his 1934 *Defensa de la Hispanidad* Maeztu would formulate as the "Hispanic Gentleman."

As in his 1899 *Hacia otra España,* where Maeztu calls for a regenerative inversion of values which might give way to a new elite of powerful personalities, in "Don Juan o el poder" Maeztu celebrates the example of personal freedom that is contained in the myth of Tirso de Molina's Don Juan: "Don Juan is freedom . . . irresponsibility, infinite energy . . . For those who are up to their necks in water, simply dreaming of such freedom is paradise."[35] It is in this liberating sense that Maeztu claims that: "Don Juan is power, and power is good."[36] It is perhaps only by means of the free reign of its national will-to-power, reasons Maeztu, that the decadent Spanish nation will be able to regenerate itself: "We are overwhelmed by problems that make us crazy because they have no solution. And then the alternative of absolute caprice appears before us . . . because . . . we do not know, in times when our ideals are in crisis, how to put life to any better use, the example of Don Juan becomes our temptation."[37] Thus, reasons Maeztu, does the figure of Don Juan—and the temptation to freely exercise the nation's will-to-power that he represents—hold some promise for national regeneration. Spain, Maeztu suggests, must render positive and reintegrate the conquering will-to-power of its empire-building conquistadors.

In order for it to be regenerative, however, this Spanish national will-to-power must not be exercised only "freely" but also "responsibly," and in service of a Quixotist ideal of love: "conserving one's energy is an elemental responsibility; using one's energy in order to strengthen the hold that love and truth have on men is a superior responsibility."[38] Consequently, in the process of considering the myth of Don Juan as a model for Spanish regeneration, Maeztu prefers the romanticized Don Juan of Zorrilla, who does discover the mercy of God and love, to the Don Juan of Tirso de Molina, who discovers neither God's mercy nor love. In Zorrilla's version of the myth of Don Juan, according to Maeztu: "Don Juan discovers . . . the possibility of a universe in which men and institutions cooperate in service of God, in which individuals find a happiness that is superior to the sort that they can achieve when they consider themselves as ends in themselves."[39] So it is that, for the decadent Spanish nation of Maeztu's time, the example of Zorrilla's Don Juan carries the promise of an ecstatic union with the divine will: a recuperation of the Spanish nation's "historical honor" and imperial legitimacy. Considering that Zorrilla's Don Juan does find faith, Maeztu is able to argue in his behalf—and that of the Spanish nation—that when exercised faithfully in the service of God's will, power is ultimately justifiable.

In its two Hispanic literary forms, that of Tirso de Molina and that of Zorrilla, the "Hispanic myth of Don Juan" presents the decadent Spanish nation with a moral choice: "We must choose between the intuition that tells us that Don Juan is evil because his life is an offense to the spirit of social service, of purity, of truth, of loyalty; and the impulse that drives us toward donjuanism, those passions that impel each of us like open mouths hungering for prey."[40] This choice, as Maeztu understands it, is between "absolute responsibility" and "absolute caprice." "If we choose responsibility," Maeztu promises, "history will back us up."[41] Consequently, the decadent Spanish nation of Maeztu's time can only regain its historical initiative and honor by choosing to act in conformity with the dictates of divine love in the same way that Zorrilla's Don Juan does: "knowing that we march in agreement with the stars, our arm will be infused with the same might that Don Juan receives from acting in accordance with his instinct."[42] To act otherwise would be tantamount to choosing the modern folly of happiness, as a result of which the nation would have to abandon its Quixotist ideal of imposing on the world an all-encompassing, universal, Catholic love.

Still, the act of placing the disciplined use of power in the service of the ideal of love cannot, by itself, make legitimate and real Maeztu's Quixotist ideal. Power, and the will-to-power of the Spanish nation, must also be constrained and purified of all caprice. The nation's power, in short, must be used wisely "in order to strengthen the hold that wisdom and love have on men."[43] Maeztu discovers a model for this purification of power in the myth of Celestina, whose understanding of the human world, Maeztu sustains, qualifies her as a saint and a sage. Thus, in order to fulfill his Quixotist promise for national regeneration, the love-inspiring but old and impotent Don Quixote of Maeztu's "Don Quijote o el amor" must possess not only the power of Don Juan but also the wisdom of Celestina.

Celestina or the Inadequacy of Hedonistic Wisdom

Just as already proved to be the case with Don Quixote's impotent love and Don Juan's whimsical and potentially tyrannical power, Celestina's mediating wisdom is misdirected, but not irretrievably so. In "La Celestina o el saber" Maeztu presents the figure of Celestina as a shrewd and discerning minister of pleasure: "the Saint of hedonism," Maeztu calls her.[44] In Maeztu's view, Celestina is to be commended for her "wisdom," that is, for the psychological acumen and the practical efficiency with which she succeeds in procuring the diverse pleasures so passionately sought by her patrons. Yet, insofar as her wisdom contains no transcendental ideal, and only serves to promote some loosely defined, utilitarian principle of happiness or pleasure, Maeztu sees her as capable of succeeding only in a pessimistic world. Thus, in order to reclaim Celestina as an appropriate model for purposes of promoting national regeneration, Maeztu suggests placing her wisdom in the service of the Quixotist ideal of a universalizing, Catholic love. Celestina, like Don Juan, must be Christianized, fully and successfully converted.

Celestina is a hedonist, according to Maeztu, in the sense that "for Celestina there is no greater good, which is to say, there is no greater God than pleasure. She dedicates herself to delivering it."[45] In this regard, the figure of Celestina represents also the threat of anarchism; in particular, she represents the anarchism of ideals that Maeztu, in his 1916 *Authority, Liberty and Function,* associates with the modern age of subjective values. However, because she is, in fact, perspicacious, capable, and practical in her service of hedonistic values, Celestina also represents the ideal of utilitarian wisdom. "Rather than 'the science of evil for the sake of evil,' Celestina represents science, period, without qualifications . . . her entire repertoire of symbols and hypotheses is motivated by one desire alone: to exploit the universe."[46] Celestina represents "utilitarian wisdom," therefore, in that as a witch she can dominate and manipulate nature, especially human nature.[47]

In part, Celestina's wisdom leads to the hazards of pleasure or to what Maeztu calls "passionate love." "Passionate love is a misfortune, because such an exalted sentiment as is love was not given to us so we might content ourselves with the particular, nor can passionate love satisfy a durable, cosmic, divine essence with the fleeting form of a lover."[48] This "tragic" lesson or "misfortune" is, according to Maeztu, the crux of the moral lesson contained in Rojas's *Celestina.* "From the same source of voluptuousness arises the bitterness of wasting one's life in the pursuit of pleasures."[49] By limiting the scope of love to the particular, argues Maeztu, passional love constitutes a transgression of the divinely sanctioned, societal "law of solidarity," because it tends to isolate individual men and women from the rest of humanity; it is a selfish and self-consuming love. Celestina's wisdom is, thus, pernicious insofar as it inspires, and seeks to justify, a hedonistic, self-serving, and anarchistic form of individualism. It is in this regard, then, that Maeztu writes: "Celestina represents the individual against society; the pleasure of the moment against the responsibility that the future imposes."[50]

Although Celestina is certainly crafty and wise in the way of the world, her hedonist morality leads, ultimately, to social and national decadence, to a lack of solidarity. Indeed, it is for this very reason that Celestina as well as her accomplices and patrons all meet with a violent death: their lust and greed inevitably lead to their downfall.[51] Maeztu, however, views this downfall as both tragic and potentially cathartic: "The spectacle of their disastrous end offers the purification that the soul of Man reaches in tragedy, because moral pain, not unlike physical pain, points out to us certain things that could place us in danger and which we should avoid."[52] Even decadence, which invariably results from the application of Celestina's craft and wisdom, contains within itself the prospect for regeneration.

Worldly wisdom does not necessarily lead to decadence, reasons Maeztu. Such wisdom can also lead to regeneration, as long as it is placed in the service of what Maeztu calls "theological virtues," which he here defines as "honor . . . faith in goodness, hope in the triumph of goodness and a burning charity when doing good."[53] This faith of the honorable, this affirmative faith of the courageous, is precisely what is lacking in the figure of Celestina.[54] Thus, reasons Maeztu, Celestina must crucify herself, her individuality, in order to be reborn in the image of the Quixotist nation. Her reward is to be the ecstatic love of the mystics; a privileged knowledge of the divine will; the justification to act in the world as the minister of divine justice; and the wisdom with which to place Don Juan's power in the service of Don Quixote's love.

No matter how deeply it has fallen into decadence, the Spanish nation has, and will always have, in its three representative literary myths of Don Quixote, Don Juan, and La Celestina, what Maeztu considers to be the formula for a society worthy of individual sacrifice: a harmonious society based in the objective values of love, power, and wisdom. What is more, according to Maeztu, this Quixotist trinity of regenerating values also contains a promise for recuperating and fulfilling the Spanish nation's messianic mission in the world. It contains the mystery of the nation's and the world's salvation. It promises the revitalization of Don Quixote such that someday—and someday soon is Maeztu's promise—the pessimists and the skeptics of the world might again turn toward Don Quixote, both to marvel at his creativity and renewed energy, and to rejoice at his renewed self-sacrifice in the name of universal love. Only then, imagines Maeztu, will Don Quixote's detractors universally proclaim: Don Quixote desires, and Don Quixote knows how to realize his desires.

10

Don Quixote as Master

Eager to step out beyond the professionally delimited spheres of "academics, journalism or politics" and into the increasingly dynamic domain of modern Spain's nascent cultural nationalism, in 1914 Ortega published his first book-length collection of essays.[1] Significantly, he titled this collection *Meditaciones del Quijote*.[2] Originally, Ortega had meant for the three essays that comprise this book to serve as the introduction to a literary history of the Spanish nation.[3] Ortega, however, evidently anxious to compete in the growing market for Quixotist formulae of national regeneration, abandoned the comprehensive ambitions of that initial historical project and settled, instead, for what he describes in the introduction to his book as a mere "attempt to produce a study of quixotism."[4]

To that end, Ortega seeks to distinguish the brand of Quixotism that he develops in his study from that of Restoration Spain's other Quixotists. "My quixotism," he affirms in this regard, "has nothing to do with the merchandise advertised in the market with that name . . . Generally, what passes for 'quixotism' is the quixotism of the character. These essays, by contrast, investigate the quixotism of the book."[5] Ortega denounces what he here calls the "quixotism of the character" because he sees in it a propensity to distort and misinterpret the significance, for modern Spain, of the *Quixote:* "considering Don Quixote in isolation has led to some truly grotesque errors," he claims.[6] "Some thinkers," affirms Ortega, "propose that we cease being Quixotes."[7] Although he names no names, he is in this instance referring to Costa, Unamuno, and Maeztu who, in the years immediately following the events of 1898, held to some fairly negative views of Don Quixote. Then, in a veiled reference to Unamuno's eventual "tragic" view of Don Quixote, Ortega adds: "other thinkers, according to the more recent fashion, invite us to an absurd existence, full of congested attitudes."[8] The distortions of this so-called quixotism of the character, reasons Ortega, result from a failure to consider the figure of Don Quixote within the context of what Ortega calls Don Quixote's "Spanish circumstance"; that is, the "quixotism of the character" fails to adequately juxtapose the elitist and tragic spirit of Don Quixote to the resentful and comic spirit of his squire, Sancho; it fails, in short, to properly situate the story of Don Quixote's life of adventures within the uniquely Spanish experience of modern decadence. Conversely, Ortega argues that his own rendering of the *Quixote* as a tragicomedy, or what he refers to also as "the Quixotism of the book," corrects these interpretative errors. He claims that his Quixotism alone exposes the true mechanism of Spanish national decadence—the comic resentment of Spain's Sanchos—by means of which Spain's tragedy-prone Don Quixote's have been, and continue to be, demoralized. Thus, reasons Ortega, it is to "the quixotism of the book" that the Spanish nation must turn for examples of regenerating heroism.

By redefining the scope of his study of the Spanish nation's literary history to the immediacy of the Quixotism of Restoration Spain, Ortega did not, however, abandon his initial goal of tracing the development of the Spanish nation's modern identity through a series of different literary genres. Subsequently, one of the basic postulates of the *Meditaciones* is that every historical epoch represents a specific type of man and that, moreover, each type of man possesses a specific genre, a genre of choice.[9] As such, Ortega divides Spanish national history into three vaguely defined moments for each of which he posits a genre: the epic for the nation's would-be glorious past, the novel for its present decadence and the essay for its future regeneration.

"The theme of epic," reasons Ortega, "is the past as such . . . [epic] flees from every present . . . it is not . . . remembrance; rather, it is an ideal past."[10] In this respect, Ortega maintains that the nation's epic literature embraces a vision of the world that is mythological and cosmological; it represents a past world in which, as he puts it: "adventure is allowed."[11] Thus, for Ortega, insofar as the history of the Spanish nation is focused on the past, it is invariably characterized by an idealizing drive for adventure; it is always "literature of the imagination."[12] In this sense, to narrate history means to imagine the past as an adventure. It is precisely such an adventure that Ortega sets out to narrate for the Spanish nation in his *Meditaciones:* only, the historical adventure that he imagines for Spain's past has a "negative" outcome. It is a misadventure—precisely the misadventure that he would purport to analyze more fully in his next book, *España invertebrada*.

The outcomes of this negative past, argues Ortega in the *Meditaciones,* are to be found in the decadent present. To the present, he sustains, belongs the novel. Yet, in the novel, the nation's negative historical adventure is not narrated; nor is it imagined. Instead, argues Ortega, it is simply posited as reality. It is described. Thus for Ortega the novel, and the *Quixote* is no exception to this "rule," presumes to "imitate" the world. The realist vision is born, argues Ortega, from a mimetic impulse: "The source of realism is found in a certain impulse that drives man to imitate."[13] Yet this impulse to imitate or mime, Ortega suggests, is ultimately comic: "He who imitates, does so in order to make fun of what he imitates."[14] Just as there is a drive toward adventure in epic, Ortega concludes that there is a tendency toward mockery in the novel. Specifically, what the novel ridicules is the epic will-to-adventure. It is this modern contempt for and resistance to epic adventure that Ortega sets out to correct. In this respect, Ortega's "quixotism of the book" is motivated by a desire that is akin to that which inspires the would-be "quixotism of the character" developed by Ganivet, Unamuno, and Maeztu. These Quixotists were also determined to encourage the modern Spanish nation to overcome its decadent aversion to heroes and hero worship.

Finally, for Ortega, there is the promise of the future. In particular, what the future promises is an opportunity for successful adventure; it offers an opportunity for negating the nation's negative history. This is the case, reasons Ortega, because the future, like the past, is not immediate. It requires the mediation of imagination; indeed, like the past, the future must be imagined. Hence the essay, which for Ortega represents a means to imagining the future. "[In my *Meditaciones*] I merely offer modi res considerandi, possible new ways of looking at things."[15] The future must be imagined as new. In order to be adequately imagined, the future requires neither the imaginative mediation of an historian nor the contemptuous mimicry of a novelist; rather, it calls for the prophetic foresight of an essayist. Ultimately, it is by means of such prophecy that, in his *Meditaciones del Quijote,* Ortega attempts to construct or "essay" a new, heroic, and Quixotist national identity for Spain.

Decadence in Retrospect

In the *Meditaciones,* Ortega conceives modern Spain's decadence as a manifestation of what he calls the "general reactionary constitution of our spirit."[16] The modern Spanish nation's relationship to its reality—to modernity, argues Ortega, is unoriginal, mediated, and built on the sepulchers of its "epic" ancestors: the founders of Spain's empire. The trouble with this retrospective relation to the realities of the present, claims Ortega, is that the so-called epic heroes of Spain's national-imperial past were decadent.[17] Their achievements were nothing more than the antiheroic excesses of the masses. Consequently, by insisting on the need to look at modernity through the eyes of its "epic" ancestors, the modern Spanish nation unwittingly perpetuates the decadence of its ancestors and thus seals its fate in decadence. "Land of our ancestors!"—exclaims Ortega—"not ours, not the free property of contemporary Spaniards. Those who passed before us continue to govern us; they form an oligarchy of death, which oppresses us."[18] Enslaved by the weight of its past, the modern Spanish nation is not free to determine its own future, realize its own destiny, and govern itself.

For this reason, Ortega makes an impassioned call for the nation to break with its tradition: "Traditional reality in Spain has consisted, precisely, in the annihilation of the possibility that is Spain . . . No, we cannot follow tradition; to the contrary, we must go against tradition, overcome tradition. It behooves us to save the primary substance of the race, the Hispanic module, from the rubble of tradition."[19] In urging his putatively "reactionary" modern nation to break free from its traditions however, Ortega does not espouse a modernizing project for enlightenment.[20] This is the case because what Ortega understands by the so-called reactionary spirit of the modern nation is that it is an extension of the resentment of the masses: "Our actions," writes Ortega in this regard, "are nothing more than reactions."[21] What is amiss in modern Spain's relationship to modernity, reasons Ortega, is heroic, noble, activity.[22]

Consequently, in order to regenerate the nation, Ortega proposes the narration of a new national history in which the true heroism of the Spanish nation's elites might finally be affirmed. As Ortega conceives it, this new and genuinely heroic national history is to take the dialectical form of a critical negation of the masses' resentful negation of heroism: "the death of that which is dead is life," offers Ortega axiomatically.[23] In this regard, Ortega's alternative national history develops into a future-oriented inversion of the "epic" national history that narrates the rise and fall of the Spanish empire: "those who love Spanish possibilities must sing the legend of the history of Spain in reverse, in order to arrive at those half-dozen places where the poor cordial viscera of our race beats with purity and intensity."[24] This inversion of the nation's national-imperial history sets the stage for a prodigious history, which will serve to guide the nation toward the fulfillment of its ideal historical trajectory.[25]

It is in this sense, therefore, that Ortega presents his *Meditaciones* as a spiritualizing act of "love" through which he seeks to "convert" and ultimately "save" the nation.[26] "These essays are," writes Ortega, "essays of intellectual love . . . they are 'salvations.' What is sought in these essays is the following: given a fact—a man [the Spanish masses] . . . an error [the resentment of these masses], an affliction [national decadence]—to guide it along the shortest path to its fullest meaning . . . This is love—love for the perfection of the thing loved."[27] Hence, Ortega's Quixotist collection of "salvations," a patriotic work of inspired and inspiring "love" for the nation, is intended to transform the nation's decadent masses by instilling in them an adulatory "reverence for the moral ideal," which is to be revealed to them by the nation's elite, that is, by Ortega himself, the patriotic "lover" of Spain.[28]

In writing of the need to "save" the nation by means of "love," Ortega's lexicon coincides with that of the other Quixotists of Restoration Spain. One of the key terms that Ortega shares with his fellow Quixotists is salvation. In his *Idearium* and in Los *trabajos del infatigable creador Pío Cid,* Ganivet compares Spain to a fallen woman who is to be saved by the stoic and self-sacrificing heroism of his Quixotist hero. In a similar vein, in his *Vida de Don Quijote y Sancho,* Unamuno envisions the Spanish nation's salvation by means of his Quixotist hero's messianic death. Finally Maeztu, who would publish his *Don Quijote, Don Juan y la Celestina* twelve years after Ortega published his *Meditaciones,* also envisions the salvation of modern Spain by virtue of his Quixotist hero's cosmic, universal, Catholic love. Significantly, when Ortega first presents the term *salvation,* he places it in quotation marks, thus signaling to his readers that he seeks to separate himself from the Christian overtones that the term acquires in the Quixotist essays of these other writers. To that end, he subsequently defines salvation in philosophical terms, as a desire for perfection. Notwithstanding the secular meaning that he initially assigns to the term, Ortega does take advantage of its religious connotations elsewhere in the *Meditaciones* where he conflates the nation with a semireligious congregation, depicts the figure of Don Quixote as a tragic representation of the nation's embattled elites, and interprets the *Quixote* as a symbolic allegory of what he refers to as the universal sense of life.

There is yet another key term shared by Ortega and the other Quixotists of Restoration Spain that should not go unmentioned. It is love. In Ganivet, love is associated with the ascetic and self-sacrificing practices of Spanish stoicism and mysticism; in Unamuno, in addition to mysticism, love is associated with a tragic faith in the eternal existence of the Spanish nation's cultural value; and in Maeztu, love is combined with power and wisdom to give form to a trinity of regenerating national and imperial values. Love, as Ortega would have it, "is a divine architect that came to the world . . . in order that everything in the universe might live together."[29] Not unlike the role of love in Ganivet, Unamuno, or Maeztu, the purpose of Ortega's "divine" love is to unite the nation along the ideological, imaginary lines of an ideal national identity.[30] In this sense, Ortega explains that his essays are motivated by a desire to inspire others to love: "In these essays I would like to propose to my readers . . . that they expulse from their minds every hateful habit and that they strongly aspire to see love, once again, administering the universe."[31] In other words, Ortega presents his *Meditaciones* as an invitation that he, as a representative of the nation's elite, extends to the nation's rancorous masses. His *Meditaciones* are intended, then, as an example of the regenerating love that is to govern over the nation in its adventurous quest for a New Age of heroism.

The success of this aspiring project for Spanish national regeneration, suggests Ortega, shall ultimately depend on the willingness of the masses to remove all hatred from their hearts and, consequently, to comply with the heroic ideals set forth by Ortega's new national history. However, should the masses prove unwilling to comply "voluntarily" with the regenerating wishes of the elites, Ortega reasons that the elites should then force the masses into involuntary compliance: "Love is combative," Ortega ventures, "this struggle with an enemy who one comprehends is true tolerance."[32] Tolerance, comprehension, contemplation: these are the supposed manifestations of the "love" that Ortega claims is behind his proposed "reform, correction and enhancement of the ethical ideal."[33] But Ortega's idea that love is combative demonstrates the extent to which the spiritual and moral transformation of the nation's masses is not to come about only by means of the elite's "tolerance" of the masses' resentment. The will-to-love of the elites can also be imposed. If in the decadent past Spain's resentful masses dominated its compassionate elites, in the regenerating future the elites will dominate the masses. Such is the promise contained in Ortega's inversion of the modern nation's "reactionary" and retrospective regard for the present.

The Tragicomic Novelty of Modernity

It is in Cervantes' *Quixote* that Ortega discovers a model for this elitist "love" that is capable of letting the Spanish nation recover its perennially lost heroism. In particular, what Ortega discovers in the *Quixote* is a model for what he calls "patriotic criticism."[34] In this sense, Ortega reads the *Quixote* as exemplary of the dialectical method on which the nation's new ideal history should be grounded. That is, he interprets the *Quixote* according to his own regenerative axiom of "the death of what is dead is life." He sees in the *Quixote* a life-affirming, elitist negation of the masses' resentful and spiteful contradiction of heroism.

With this regenerating negation in mind, Ortega theoretically reconstructs Cervantes' *Quixote* as a "tragicomedy," in which the tragic figure of Don Quijote first is pulled down from the ideal realm of tragic heroism by the lowly and comic resentment of Sancho and then is vindicated as the symbol of Spain's victimized elites. Thereby, Ortega applauds the *Quixote* because, as a tragicomedy, it tells the disheartening tale of Spain's "negative" national history and exposes "the psychological mechanics of Spanish reactionism."[35]

More than just a literary theory, Ortega's construction of the novel as a tragicomic genre is a theory on decadence and regeneration. Indeed, insofar as Ortega's theory of the novel is historically informed, that is, insofar as he identifies the novel with the modern age, it is also a theory that speculates on the tragicomic and decadent character of modernity.[36] In this respect, Ortega's "quixotism of the book" resonates with Unamuno's characterization, in his 1913 *Del sentimiento trágico de la vida,* of the role that Don Quixote must play in the modern world as being "tragicomic." And much like Unamuno, who ties his Quixotism to a critique on Spanish national decadence, Ortega puts forward his Quixotist theory of the novel as a tentative demonstration or "proof" of his critique of decadence. In his *Meditaciones,* this critique is based on the distinction between two basic types or "castes" of men: "the meditative and the sensual."[37]

This elitist distinction between meditative masters and sensual slaves is the central and organizing principle behind Ortega's theory of the novel.[38] Don Quixote, in Ortega's theory, corresponds to the high-mimetic realm of tragedy. Sancho, by contrast, belongs to the low-mimetic realm of comedy. Whereas tragedy, for Ortega, is an expression of the world of volition, of the subjective world of the self, comedy is an expression of the objective world of circumstance. Thus, because it contains these two realms, the novel encloses, according to Ortega, the dynamic tensions of tragicomedy.

In its most elemental form, Ortega understands tragedy to be an interpretation, or acting out, of human effort; it is a representation of man in his capacity as a desiring and willful subject: "the tragic subject . . . is tragic . . . only insofar as it desires. Volition . . . is the theme of tragedy."[39] Consequently, from the outset, Ortega seeks to dispel the "common" notion that tragedy deals, not with human effort, but with the failure of that effort: "Let us abandon . . . all those theories that, because they base tragedy in I know not what fatality, lead us to believe that it is defeat, the death of the hero, that gives such heroes their tragic quality."[40] For Ortega, the notion of a "tragic quality" is intimately bound up with the suffering of the protagonist or, as he puts it, "his affliction."[41] In this regard, the theme of tragedy in Ortega is not unlike that of tragedy in Unamuno: the redemptive suffering of a so-called proto-agonist.

According to Ortega, this affliction and agony can be viewed from two distinct perspectives: that of the protagonist himself; and that of the "common" man whom Ortega depicts as "crude." From the vantage point of the protagonist, the tragic quality of tragedy is an emanation of his own will: "it is essential to the hero that he desire his tragic destiny."[42] The protagonist wills the suffering attendant to his destiny because, for him, that suffering is not without meaning. The protagonist understands that it is precisely his agony, his personal sacrifice in the name of his most cherished ideal, which justifies and gives meaning to his life. By contrast, when viewed from the vantage point of those who are "crude," the protagonist's suffering is devoid of meaning; it seems absurd or, as Ortega puts it: "a bit improbable . . . those who are crude very justly think that bad things happen to the hero because he is obstinate in his pursuit of this or that goal. If he were to simply abandon that goal, everything would come to a happy ending."[43] The masses, in other words, view the tragic quality of tragedy in terms of some putative "tragic flaw" in the character of the protagonist. The protagonist is deemed irrational, obstinate, and impractical; and his suffering is seen as unnecessary. According to Ortega's mass man, all that the tragic hero has to do in order to put an end to his troubles is abandon his ideal. In doing so, he would then be able to lead a life of calm or, as Ortega stingingly puts it, "settle down and have lots of children."[44]

However, as Ortega conceives him, the tragic protagonist cannot stop willing, wishing and desiring to reform the world. To do so, in fact, would be tantamount to embracing nihilism. This is the case, for Ortega, because the hero, by definition, is pure will: "it is a fact that there are certain men who refuse to reconcile themselves with reality. Such men aspire to change the course of things: they refuse to repeat the gestures that custom, tradition, and . . . biological instincts impose on them. We call these men heroes . . . When the hero desires, it is neither his ancestors who desire nor contemporary mores that desire. He himself desires. And this desire to be who he is, is heroism."[45] Not unlike the tragic heroism imagined by Unamuno for the modern Spanish nation, according to which it is best for the nation to be ridiculed for its traditional, premodern faith than to give in to that ridicule and abandon its traditional cultural identity, Ortega's tragic hero prefers to suffer in the name of some willed ideal, in the name of his own intuited originality.

Indeed, it is precisely this heroic willingness to suffer and sacrifice himself in the name of a higher ideal that Ortega celebrates in the figure of Don Quixote. As a "tragic" hero, Ortega's Don Quixote is "a man who wants to reform reality."[46] Consequently, Don Quixote is made "tragic"—that is, representative of man in his capacity as a purely desiring and willful subject—not by virtue of any fatalistic flaw in his character, but by virtue of the unreality, of the ideal, in the service of which he suffers. Don Quixote suffers "tragically" in order that, by means of his very suffering, the actual world in which he lives might be transformed into a mythological and ideal world.

Don Quixote, however, does not only suffer as a tragic hero. Significantly, he also suffers as the hero of a tragicomedy. This is the case, because Don Quixote's impulse toward tragedy is carried out in an otherwise comic world. Whereas Don Quixote wills to see giants, castles, or armies, the real world only offers windmills, inns and herds of sheep. This world of realism or "circumstance," as Ortega is prone to call it, is represented, first and foremost, by Sancho. The role of Sancho, his "comic mission" in the *Quixote,* is, according to Ortega, to negate Don Quixote's idealism: "Cervantes pits Sancho against every adventure in order to make adventure impossible."[47] For Ortega, Sancho acts as an expression of the slavish "reactionary spirit" of the nation. He represents that "fatal" mechanism by means of which Don Quixote's idealizing and morally edifying will is forever frustrated, humiliated and, finally, annihilated. Sancho, submits Ortega, is incapable of "tolerating" Don Quixote's idealizing will because, for him to do so would threaten his "instinct of inertia and conservation"; Sancho, therefore, seeks revenge: "He retaliates . . . He opposes [Don Quixote] with realism and involves him in a comedy."[48] Sancho is the embodiment of resentment, the embodiment of what leads Don Quixote toward his tragicomic destiny: death.

As a tragicomic hero, then, Ortega's Don Quixote must suffer twofold. First, in order not to lose himself, he must suffer tragically; second, because he is continually exposed to the ridicule with which his "crude" squire, Sancho, regards the tragic quality of his suffering, he must also suffer comically. Consequently, for Ortega, the ability of Don Quixote to remain within the realm of tragedy and affirm himself as a hero, as a man of will, is made to depend on how well he can force Sancho to recognize his suffering, not as an absurdity, but as a vitally significant and life-affirming event. That is, in order to realize himself and to "save" himself from the nihilism of nonrecognition, Don Quixote must also "save" Sancho from his own, lowly reactionary spirit; Don Quixote must make profound, meditative and subjective that which, in its natural state of reaction, is only superficial, sensual, and objective.[49] He must conquer Sancho's "hate" and, in its place, inspire a properly edifying form of "love" or adulation. This heroic conquest and spiritual transformation of Sancho is, then, the regenerating role that Ortega assigns to Don Quixote in Cervantes' *Quixote*. As it turns out, however, the potentially regenerating Don Quixote that Ortega narrates into existence sadly fails in his attempts to gain Sancho's love. He fails to win the recognition and adulation of Sancho. Consequently, as the doubly agonizing hero of a tragicomedy, Don Quixote is destined to suffer both tragically and comically.

It is in this tragicomic sense, then, that for Ortega the *Quixote* is the quintessential realist novel. Don Quixote demonstrates the heroic will to rise above reality and to change it after the image of an ideal; Sancho demonstrates an element of spiteful resistance to that vital, idealizing will. This resentful spirit of resistance to change wins out, ultimately, not only in the *Quixote,* but also, according to Ortega, in all novels. This is why Ortega defines the novel as "the violent fall of the tragic body, defeated by the force of inertia, by reality."[50] For Ortega, the theme of the modern novel is decadence. However critically, it always tells the tale of a decline; it tells the story, like Ganivet's *Conquista del reino de Maya,* of the impossibility of heroism in the modern world.

Cervantes' *Quixote,* suggests Ortega, constitutes the most dynamic expression ever, of the novel. Don Quixote's fall from the heights of tragedy into the vortex of comedy is, as Ortega puts it, violent. From the time of Cervantes to that of Zola, however, Ortega considers that, as a literary form, the novel has lost its violent tragicomic tension and become little more than another, variously resentful or spiteful, cultural appendage of the modern age:

"If contemporary novels reveal with less clarity their comic mechanism, it is because the ideals that these novels attack are barely distinguishable from the reality that combats them . . . the ideal *falls* from the slightest of heights . . . the novel of the nineteenth century . . . contains the least possible amount of poetic dynamism."[51] The novel's loss of tragicomic tension in the nineteenth century can be understood, or so Ortega would have it, as yet another indication of the decadent influence that the masses have had on the aesthetics of the modern age.[52]

Ultimately, however, Ortega celebrates the loss of the novel's tragicomic tension as indicative of the end of the modern age and the beginning of a New Age: "The novel of the nineteenth century will soon be illegible," prophesies Ortega.[53] That the modern age is in the throes of its last painfully implacable days is evident, for Ortega, given that in modern Spain "men are not the subject of their actions; instead, they are moved by the environment in which they live . . . The environment is the only protagonist."[54] The modern Spanish nation, like the modern novel, is characterized, then, by purely comic, resentful circumstances. The "reactionary spirit" of the Spanish nation, which was also evident in the Spain of Cervantes' time, has, by Ortega's time, managed to do away with all individuality, all creativity, and all idealism. In order for the Spanish nation to "save" itself from this modern nihilism, reasons Ortega, it must reclaim the heroic and tragic self posited by Cervantes' *Quixote*.

In this "tragic" sense, Ortega's theory of the novel, his so-called quixotism of the book, is very much alike the so-called quixotism of the character that Ortega associates with the other Quixotists of Restoration Spain. Not unlike Ganivet, Unamuno, and Maeztu, Ortega posits the figure of Don Quixote as an icon for the redemption and salvation of the modern Spanish nation. Thus, Ortega affirms: "Don Quixote is the sad parody of a more divine and serene Christ: he is the gothic Christ, pestered by modern anxieties; a ridiculous Christ of our own neighborhood, created by an afflicted imagination that lost its innocence and volition and has gone in search of other new ones. Whenever there is a gathering of a few Spaniards who have been sensitized by the misery of their past, the squalor of their present and the austere hostility of their future, Don Quixote descends upon them . . . and like a spiritual thread, nationalizes them, placing beyond their personal sorrows a communal ethnic affliction."[55] Indeed, Ortega's Quixotism, for all its pretended emphasis on Cervantes' style, posits a Don Quixote that is substantively no different than the agonizing and redemptive Don Quixote narrated into existence by Ganivet, Unamuno, and Maeztu.

Like the other major Quixotists of Restoration Spain, Ortega celebrates the figure of Don Quixote as an agonizing spirit who, by reason of his suffering and melancholy, unites and nationalizes the Spanish nation. Indeed, the gathering of "sensitized" and Quixotized Spaniards that Ortega imagines is not unlike the gathering of a congregation. Ortega's tragic Don Quixote, like that of Unamuno, organizes this Spanish national congregation around an "inner" or spiritual domain that is so infused by intense and pathetic suffering that the personal frustrations and anxieties of the nation's individuals are entirely subsumed and united by it. Thus nationalized, these "sensitized" men take on the quality of the nation's true believers: its patriots. And so it is that Ortega's quest for the recuperation of a regenerating heroism, leads him, ultimately, to posit a tragic Don Quixote who symbolizes the Spanish nation's suffering in the face of its comic circumstance, its historical failure. In this manner, Ortega is able to unite the nation around the fallen, victimized and tragic figure of Don Quixote, who is, nevertheless, an heroic spirit in need of respite, in need of a New World and a New Age where his ideals may finally come to fruition.

The Prophetic New Age of Quixotism

As Ortega understands it, this New Age, which will eliminate the resentment and decadence of the masses, is to be known as the age of Quixotism. Ortega proposes: "Oh! If we only knew . . . what Cervantes' style consists of . . . we would have nothing more to accomplish . . . a poetic style includes a philosophy, a moral, a science and a politics. If some day someone were to discover for us the profile of the style of Cervantes, we could extend its lines to our other collective problems and awaken to a new life. In that case, if there is in fact courage and spirit among us, we would be able . . . to fashion the new Spanish essay."[56] Thus conceived, Ortega's proposed New Age of Quixotism is to be the age of a postmodern Spanish national regeneration.

Yet, Ortega explains, there remains a problem with modeling the New Age of Quixotism after Cervantes' *Quixote*. That problem lies in the elusive, regenerative significance of the novel: "There is no other book that has the same power to symbolize the universal sense of life, and yet, there is also no other book in which we will find fewer indications, fewer hints, of how to interpret it properly."[57] His own cautious remonstrations notwithstanding, Ortega, of course, assures his readers that, insofar as he is a true "lover" of both the nation and the *Quixote,* he is up to the challenge of revealing the secrets locked in Cervantes' style and interpreting the *Quixote* correctly. He assures his readers, in other words, that the interpretative essays or "salvations" that he has prepared for his *Meditaciones* do, in fact, provide a proper example of "patriotic criticism."

It is in this same regenerating spirit that Ortega volunteers his Quixotist theory of the novel, together with the heroically suffering figure of Don Quixote that emerges from that theory, as a twofold corrective to the nation's "collective problems." Inasmuch as it exposes resentment to be at the source of the nation's moral decadence and negative historical identity, Ortega's theory of the novel can be said to provide the elite with an ingenious "proof" of the need to formulate a critique of the nation's decadence. Likewise, to the extent that his tragicomic suffering serves to spiritualize and nationalize the more "sensitized" members of the national community, Ortega's Quixote can be said to provide the elite with an example of the ascetic discipline and idealism that shall be required of the nation's future-oriented Quixotists.

In the end, Ortega presents his theory of the modern novel as an example of the "patriotic criticism" which he claims to have uncovered in the *Quixote*. Underlying that criticism—be it his own or that of Cervantes—is what Ortega, not unlike Maeztu, calls Quixotist "love."[58] It is in this compassionate and charitable sense that Ortega defines criticism as a "zealous effort to empower the selected work."[59] Hence, the ultimate "work" that Ortega seeks to criticize or "love" in his *Meditaciones* is not the *Quixote* per se but rather the moral decadence of the masses, which the *Quixote* exposes. In the final analysis, therefore, Ortega's Quixotist theory on the novel is a means for justifying the putatively regenerating negation and subjugation of the masses.

It is in this manner that the "patriotic criticism" of Ortega's Quixotist theory on the novel, coupled with the self-sacrificing suffering of his agonizing Quixotist elite, are to open the way for the eventual reform or "salvation" of the Spanish nation. In other words, only by negating the negation inherent in the nation's antiheroic national history and cultural tradition can the nation be transformed and "saved." The new history that Ortega proposes, and the new heroic national identity attendant to it, is to be imagined and narrated into existence by the essay. This is true, first, in the sense that the nation is, in and of itself, an essay: "each race is, definitively, an essay on a new way of living, on a new sensibility."[60] And it is true, second, in the sense that, by reason of Ortega's definition of it, the essay focuses on the future. According to Ortega, the essay forms that genre of literature that produces: "possible new ways of looking at things."[61]

Underlying this imaginative and meditative practice of the essayist is what Ortega calls conceptualization. For Ortega, the concept is: "an organ or apparatus *for* the possession of things."[62] "Only a vision that is arrived at by means of the concept," he adds in this regard, "is a complete vision."[63] Thus, the ultimate aim of Ortega's essays is to posit a cultural elite that is capable of possessing the world conceptually. Indeed, it is in the spirit of this same meditative, conceptual "love" that Ortega writes: "I am myself and my circumstance; and if I do not save it, I do not save myself."[64] In order to "save" himself as a member of the nation's elite, Ortega must save his nation also; and this, he must do, by conceptualizing the nation as a totality, by "loving" the nation's masses and thus possessing and, if need be, controlling them.

In this regard, Ortega presents the essays or "salvations" that make up his first book as an invitation that he extends to the other members of the nation's elite, and in particular to its other Quixotists. Ortega would have his fellow Quixotists join him in the effort to "save" the nation by "saving" the elite. With his essays, Ortega informs his readers that he intends to "awake within brotherly souls other brotherly thoughts, even when these souls belong to rival brothers."[65] He means, in other words, to reach out within the elite to his "brothers," even when, like Unamuno, they are conceived and presented as his "rivals." When it is viewed in this light, the distinction that Ortega draws in the opening passages of his book between the "quixotism of the character" and his own putative "quixotism of the book" is little more than an attempt, by Ortega, to enter into "loving combat" with those who he understands to be, like himself, members of the nation's regenerating elite. Together, suggests Ortega, he and the other Quixotists of Restoration Spain will create a new cultural order: the Quixotist. "The only specifically cultural action is creation," affirms Ortega; he then adds, "Culture only has value as an instrument or arm for new conquests."[66] So it is that, by way of his Quixotist *Meditaciones del Quijote,* Ortega posits the creative, conquering and combative "love" of an elite-based Quixotism as the ultimate means to "save" the nation from the supposed hatred and decadent resentment of the modern masses.

CONCLUSION

Spanish National Quixotism

Written between the years of Spanish colonial bankruptcy (1895–1898) and the Spanish Civil War (1936–1939), the Quixotist essays of Ganivet, Unamuno, Maeztu, and Ortega played a decisive role in the configuration of a heroic modern Spanish national identity. As the Quixotists pictured it, the nation's heroic identity harkened back to the "Golden Age" of Spain's foundation as an imperial nation. Idealized, fixed, and ageless, the heroism that the Quixotists fashioned for modern Spain was characterized, at heart, by premodern forms of heroic virtue: the stoic discipline of Spain's Christian crusaders; the self-negating religious fervor of Spain's mystics; and the civilizing righteousness of Spain's empire-building conquistadors. By means of their Quixotist essays, Ganivet, Unamuno, Maeztu, and Ortega attempted to convince their compatriots that, if only they would once again embrace these premodern forms of heroism, the Spanish nation could prevail over its modern decadence and reconquer its lost empire.

In doing so, the Quixotists countered the reality of Restoration Spain's national and imperial decline with their own version of a regenerating, mythological truth. Indeed, much like Cervantes' Don Quixote, who repeatedly attempts to convince Sancho that windmills are giants, inns are castles, and whores are damsels, the Quixotists of Restoration Spain attempted to convince their readers that progress was a disease, that military defeat was a moral victory, and that the loss of political empire was, in point of fact, the discovery of an everlasting cultural empire. In this manner, the Quixotists acknowledged the realities that troubled Restoration Spain, but disregarded their "outer" political, economic, and social significance. By turning away from the "outer" and toward the "inner," spiritual and cultural domain of Spanish national life, the Quixotists prepared the way for an imaginative reversal of the nation's decline from imperial glory.

It was within the parameters of this interior cultural space that the Quixotists claimed to discover so-called classical expressions of the nation's enduring, essential identity. Moreover, they claimed that, by interpreting these timeless works of art in terms of the nation's perceived modern decadence, they could create a new spiritually and culturally transformative discourse for national regeneration. From among the various classical national myths on which the Quixotists focused their attention—the anonymous epic poem *Canto del Mío Cid,* Rojas's *Celestina,* Tirso de Molina's *El burlador de Sevilla,* and Cervantes' *Quixote*—it was the *Quixote* that ultimately won out.

In part, the preference that the Quixotists of Restoration Spain showed for the *Quixote* can be explained by the romanticizing interpretation that Cervantes' famous novel had already received at the hands of Benjumea during the latter half of the nineteenth century. Much like the Quixotists would do, Benjumea had idealized Don Quixote, celebrating him as a man of faith; he had opposed this faithful Don Quixote to a skeptical Sancho; and he had asserted the universal appeal of the *Quixote*. But unlike Benjumea, the Quixotists of Restoration Spain would further suggest that it was precisely because of its universal appeal that the *Quixote* could serve as the basis for asserting an everlasting Spanish cultural imperium.

The Quixotists also chose the *Quixote* because in 1905, or a mere seven years after the events of 1898, Hispanists throughout the world celebrated the tercentenary of the publication of the *Quixote*. It was during that year, at the Ateneo de Madrid, that Navarro y Ledesma formulated his views concerning the Spanish nation's "quixotic sentiment" and proposed a two-step program for the regenerating quixotization of modern Spain. In keeping with the spirit of Navarro y Ledesma's views on the *Quixote,* the Quixotists of Restoration Spain would turn this two-step program into an elaborate moral critique of decadence and creative program for regeneration.

Yet, for the Quixotists, the ultimate appeal of the *Quixote,* and what made it so compelling a novel to work with, was undoubtedly the reversible dualism that is written into it as a narrative principle. Cervantes used this reversible dualism for ironic purposes; with it, he parodied several of the narrative forms that were in vogue during the late sixteenth and early seventeenth centuries in Spain—namely romances of chivalry, pastoral, and picaresque—and created a truly novel narrative form: the modern novel as such. The Quixotists used this reversible dualism in order to achieve extraliterary ends. By elevating the *Quixote* to the status of the nation's regenerating Bible and by reinterpreting the figure of Don Quixote as an ascetic idealist, the Quixotists imagined the moral reversal and spiritual transformation that they desired for modern Spain.

What emerged from their varied interpretations of both the *Quixote* and the figure of Don Quixote was a fully Quixotized Spanish nation. Newly organized around the regenerating example of Don Quixote's ascetic idealism, the Quixotized nation that Ganivet, Unamuno, Maeztu, and Ortega imagined was deemed capable of reversing the fate that Spain had suffered in the "outer" domain of politics and of reclaiming its "inner" cultural hegemony over the entire Hispanic world. Once an empire, always an empire! Such was the claim that the Quixotists made in a bid to encourage both the nation's Quixote-like elites and its Sancho-like masses to identify with the image of an always and already heroic and imperial Spain.

By and large, the Quixotists succeeded in convincing their compatriots to accept this romanticized image of a regenerating imperial Spain. No doubt, their ability to do so was helped by the place of considerable prominence that each of them occupied within the intellectual life of Restoration Spain. The eventual acceptance of this imperial national identity was helped also, however, by the fact that it was the National-Catholic fascists who would emerge victorious from the Spanish Civil War of 1936–1939. Because the fascists did win that war, they were able to celebrate the Quixotists of Restoration Spain as forerunners of their own ideology and assign to them a place of eminence within the National-Catholic cultural pantheon. Yet, it is not as though this connection between Quixotism and National-Catholicism was constructed only with hindsight and only by the fascists. There are certain features of Quixotist thought, such as the idea of an essentially "tragic" and "messianic" Spanish national identity, and certain motifs, such as Don Quixote's self-sacrificing and cosmic love, that made Quixotism especially susceptible to the treatment that it received in National-Catholic Spain. Indeed, following the Civil War, the critical apparatus that Hispanists in Spain most commonly used in order to study the Quixotists—the notion of the *generación del '98,* was created and disseminated by some of the Quixotists themselves. Beginning with Azorín, then Ortega, and ending, ultimately, with Laín Entralgo, this notion served to perpetuate the same timeless heroic national and imperial identity that the Quixotists imagined for modern Spain.

As a form of cultural nationalism, Quixotism did generate new imaginary ways in which Spaniards could represent to themselves their real relationship to the modern world. Insofar as these imaginary representations served to nationalize the modern nation, Quixotism helped to lay the conceptual groundwork for the political nationalism that became a permanent feature of fascist Spain. None of this should be taken to mean, however, that the Quixotists were what Tierno Galván has called Spain's "protofascists."[1] With the exception of Maeztu, none of the other major Quixotists of Restoration Spain ever completely embraced either a prototype of fascism or the Falange's version of it. Thus, while it would be wrong to overlook the conceptual ties that bind the Quixotism of Restoration Spain to the National-Catholicism of fascist Spain, it would also be mistaken to objectify this apparent kinship without taking into account its differences.

In arguing for national and imperial regeneration, the Quixotists were not only imagining the possibility of a regenerating dictatorship, they were also formulating imaginative projects for Spanish cultural transformation and renewal. For the most part, these Quixotist projects did not require, as did the fascist project for national and imperial renewal, a strong economy, strong military, or strong state. Worldwide in scope, the projects that the Quixotists proposed for national and imperial regeneration were primarily intended as cultural replacements for the political and economic empires that Spain had lost. In this respect, the inward focus of Quixotism, its nearly exclusive regard for the spiritual and moral identity of the nation, is both what imaginatively ties Quixotism to National-Catholicism and realistically separates it from fascism.

Whereas the Quixotists were not, on the whole, fascists, their respective projects for national and imperial regeneration did resonate with the ideological precepts of National-Catholicism. These included, according to a sixteen-point program of 1931, the denunciation of both micronationalist separatism and class warfare; the approval of Spanish imperial expansion; the necessary "cleansing" to rid Spain of atheists, communists, and anarchists; and, finally, the notion that the Roman Catholic religion embodied the essential cultural and spiritual identity of Spaniards.[2] Underlying this program for the National-Catholic conquest of the Spanish state was a belief in the transformative power of ascetic discipline. In order to regenerate, argued the National-Catholics, the nation needed to submit itself to the discipline imposed on it by its Catholic tradition and imperial destiny.

As I have sought to stress throughout this book, belief in the regenerating power of ascetic idealism is one of the key factors that the four major Quixotists of Restoration Spain shared. It informed their construction of Don Quixote as a variously stoic, mystical, tragic, and messianic hero as well as their views of Sancho as a variously hedonistic, materialistic, comic, and skeptical antihero. Ascetic idealism, and the discipline and self-sacrifice that the Quixotists associated with it, was the key to understanding the nation's decadence and promoting its regeneration. It is, also, the key to understanding the links that tie Quixotism to National-Catholicism.

At issue in both the Quixotist celebration of ascetic idealism and that of the National-Catholics was the question of freedom. Freedom, for the Quixotists, was essentially a matter of positive liberty, or a liberty that is realized not at the individual level and within civil society but at the supra-individual level of the nation.[3] To be free in this positive sense meant, for the Quixotists, that individuals and their social associations could attain the status of freedom only insofar as they submitted their personal "negative freedom" to the regenerating nation and thus came to participate in its universal historical mission. The positive freedom of the Quixotists required, in other words, ascetic discipline: in order to regenerate, the nation's Sanchos had to submit their will to the self-sacrificial ideals of the nation's Quixotes.

It was in this sense, for instance, that Ganivet wrote of his Quixotist hero, Pío Cid, as if he were the decadent nation's regenerating and self-sacrificing stoic priest; for his part, Unamuno constructed a messianic Don Quixote whose agony was to satisfy the modern nation's need for a tragic transvaluation of life; likewise, Maeztu referred to the Holy Trinity of national values—love, power, and wisdom—which the nation's Quixotist elite was to embody; and, finally, Ortega wrote of the combative love by means of which his Quixotic elite would conquer and transform the nation's resentful Sanchos. What Ganivet, Unamuno, Maeztu, and Ortega espoused as freedom was tantamount to voluntary servitude. A similar conception of freedom pertained to Spain's National-Catholics: "Only he who forms part of a strong nation is truly free . . . No one shall be allowed to use his freedom to undermine the nation's unity, strength and liberty. Rigorous discipline shall prevent all attempts to poison and destroy the nation or to motivate Spaniards to resist the nation's destiny."[4] Freedom, according to this view, was a matter of the nation-state and had only a world-historical, not an individual, value.

For worldly evidence in support of this positive view of freedom, the Quixotists did little more than superficially contemplate the spectacle of Restoration Spain's crises. Everywhere, and ready at hand, there seemed to be proofs of the masses' incapacity for responsible moral self-government: colonial uprisings, class warfare, separatist movements, all of which the Quixotists put down to resentment. Keeping in mind these examples of negative freedom, the Quixotists feared that the nation, or rather Spanish national culture as such, would all but disappear into a vortex of chaotic anarchy. Accordingly, the Quixotists sought to persuade the masses to relinquish their claims to negative freedom and submit to the morally superior will and understanding of the nation's elite. In exchange, they promised that the masses would be reborn as members of a positively free and regenerating national community. Again, the National-Catholics would eventually affirm much the same thing: "We believe in the supreme reality of Spain. To strengthen it, elevate it and exalt it is the pressing collective duty of all Spaniards. The personal interests of individuals, groups and classes must inexorably yield to the realization of that duty."[5]

In part, the Quixotists of Restoration Spain resorted to flattery in their attempts to persuade the masses to enter this state of voluntary servitude. They promised the nation's masses that in return for relinquishing their self-governance they would, quite literally, inherit the earth. By submitting themselves to the Quixotist regime of ascetic discipline and self-sacrifice, the Sanchos of modern Spain were to be transformed into the spiritual leaders of a new age. Indeed, unlike the Don Quixote of Cervantes, who only promises to make Sancho the governor of an island, the Don Quixote that Ganivet, Unamuno, Maeztu, and Ortega imagined, promised to make Sancho the worldly emperor of a universal, spiritual, and as was the case with Maeztu, political empire. In keeping with this Quixotist promise of empire, the National-Catholics also would promise to the Spanish masses that, with the fascists in power, the nation would realize its imperial destiny: "Spain will again seek its glory and riches by sea . . . Spain asserts its condition as the spiritual axis of the Hispanic world as its right to preeminence in universal affairs."[6]

In the event that the Sanchos of Spain should refuse to voluntarily relinquish their negative freedom, the Quixotists reasoned that the nation's Quixotes would be justified in resorting to coercion. It was in this regard that Ganivet affirmed the need for a regenerating dictatorship; that Unamuno argued for a new and impossible Middle Age modeled after the nation's prototypical warring communities; that Maeztu asserted the regenerating ascetic discipline of both the military and the Catholic Church; and that, for his part, Ortega called for the regenerating submission of the resentful masses to the nation's charismatic elite. Similarly, the National-Catholics would affirm the need to impose on the nation a regenerating ascetic discipline: "Our state shall be a totalitarian instrument that will serve the integrity of the nation . . . We shall insure . . . that a military sense of life informs all of Spanish existence."[7]

At the beginning of Spain's first century without empire, it was the Quixotists of Restoration Spain who first sought to imaginatively deny the loss of Spain's colonies. They did so by formulating a program for cultural imperialism. In order for the Spanish nation to conquer that cultural empire, however, the Quixotists argued that it first would need to undergo a spiritual transformation or conversion. The nation, and in particular its masses, would need to abandon their desire for secular modernization and embrace the premodern spiritual idealism of the nation's heroic elite. Based in ascetic idealism and in the belief that the Spanish nation had a messianic role to play in the modern world, this imagined empire would serve to culturally regenerate, not only Spain, but also the entire Hispanic world and even Europe.

Spain's fascists took this view of Spain's messianic mission in the modern world to heart. Unlike the Quixotists, however, they did not seek to realize this mission culturally. They sought to achieve it politically. Sharing with the Quixotists a belief in the Spanish nation's messianic destiny, and sharing with them also the belief in the transformative power of ascetic idealism, the National-Catholics declared war on the Republic and seized control of the state. They did so in the belief that, with their formula for the totalitarian regeneration of Spanish society, they would actually provide the economic, military, and political strength needed to embark on a modern quest for Spanish national imperium.

Today, at the start of Spain's second century without empire, Spaniards enjoy a wealth of negative freedoms. Spain is now, to all intents and purposes, as healthy a democracy as any that has survived into the twenty-first century in Europe or the Americas. Yet, something akin to the imperial longings of the Quixotists and National-Catholics continues to inform Spanish national and political life. Throughout the decade of the 1990s, the economic and cultural policies of Aznar asserted the "transatlantic destiny" of Spain, striking a glaring resemblance to the national-imperial destiny imagined by the Quixotists and the National-Catholics.[8] Then, in 2003, Aznar again affirmed the Spanish nation's imagined imperial destiny and joined forces with the Anglo-led coalition that invaded Iraq.

Admittedly, Aznar justified that move by claiming that Spain had to secure the cooperation of its allies in Spain's own internal struggle against the terrorism of ETA. "Terrorism is the principal threat that we face and it is the principal threat faced by the world. A country like Spain cannot be insensitive to this. How are we going to ask for international cooperation in our own fight with terrorism and, when others need our help, say that we are not willing to help? This is not possible. When we need international cooperation, and we need it; when we are in need of our allies, and we need them; we will be able to say: we have also contributed; we have not remained faithful only in the best of times, but also in the worst of times, in difficult moments."[9] Fair enough. But when one keeps in mind Aznar's professed belief in the transatlantic destiny of the Spanish nation, it is reasonable to question whether, by joining the Anglo-led anti-terrorist coalition, Aznar also sought to secure for Spain an important role in the formation of a global empire dedicated to securing "freedom." The horrifying terrorist attacks on Madrid in March 2004 revealed, as perhaps no other events in recent Spanish history, the real insanity that has, since 1898 to today, informed modern Spain's Quixotist longings for empire.

SUPPLEMENT

Don Quixote in Exile and Spain's Ex-colonies

In Restoration Spain, the question of national identity made for an explosive conjunction of art and politics. The cultural nationalism that Ganivet, Unamuno, Maeztu, and Ortega proposed as a regenerating response to the events of 1898 helped spawn the political nationalism that Spain's fascists promoted as an alternative to the Second Republic. After the Civil War, Hispanists in Spain embraced the notion that their primary task should be to safeguard the imperial cultural patrimony of Spain. To that end, they took as their gospel the generational schemes for Spanish national regeneration devised, earlier in the century, by Azorín and Ortega. The work of Laín Entralgo apropos the so-called generation of '98 was paradigmatic in this regard.

Insofar as other Hispanists, who were neither working nor living in fascist Spain, also accepted these generational schemes, they too helped to reconfirm, either wittingly or unwittingly, the essential, timeless and fixed heroic national identity that the Quixotists and fascists had imagined and fashioned for Spain. There were, of course, many other Hispanists, particularly non-Spanish scholars, for whom the nationalist emphasis of fascist Hispanism was an irritant. Rather than take Quixotism as their gospel, these Hispanists sidelined it, preferring to focus, instead, on other aspects of the literature produced by Ganivet, Unamuno, Maeztu, and Ortega. It is to scholars such as these that we owe, for example, the view of Ganivet as a feminist, the view of Unamuno as an existentialist, the view of Maeztu as a socialist, and the view of Ortega as a phenomenologist. While it is certainly true that these approaches to the work of Ganivet, Unamuno, Maeztu, and Ortega have enriched the understanding that

Hispanists have of these authors and their work, they do not, either individually or as a whole, provide a far-reaching alternative to the approach most commonly taken to these same authors and works by the National-Catholic Hispanists of fascist Spain.

The emphasis that the Quixotists themselves placed on their own Quixotism ought neither to be blindly celebrated as an example of Spanish national genius nor summarily dismissed as one among several motifs that characterize their work. Quixotism should, rather, be acknowledged as the crucial contribution to modern Spanish national life that its authors believed it to be. The Quixotism of Restoration Spain should, in other words, be deemed as worthy of serious study. To that end, in this book I have underscored the negative historical consciousness that informs the Quixotist essays of Ganivet, Unamuno, Maeztu, and Ortega and shown how, on the basis of that ahistorical, mythopoeic consciousness, these thinkers sought to imaginatively deny their nation's loss of empire. Moreover, in opposing my critique of Quixotism to the tradition of the generation of '98 as well as to other approaches that tend to minimize the centrality of Quixotism to the thought of Ganivet, Unamuno, Maeztu, and Ortega, I have undertaken to demonstrate the extent to which Hispanism has served to further, rather than to question, the interests of modern Spanish cultural imperialism. In short, throughout this book, I have sought to interpret—in both the analytic and performative senses of that word—a meaningful and lasting alternative to the ways that Hispanists have studied the literature produced by Ganivet, Unamuno, Maeztu, and Ortega.

My attempt at providing such an alternative is not without its own historical antecedents. Thus, as a counternarrative, this book has its own would-be "forgotten" historical beginnings and political ends, which also require critical reconstruction. As I conceive it, this book belongs to an extranational and antinationalist tradition within the field of Hispanism. I am referring to the broken, often silenced and ignored tradition of exiled Spanish liberal thought, a tradition that was begun in the early nineteenth century by republican thinkers such as José María Blanco White, was picked up again during the mid-twentieth century by, among others, Américo Castro, and continues to this day in the works of such expatriates as Juan Goytisolo and Eduardo Subirats.[1] It would be misleading, however, to suggest that either the Quixotism of Restoration Spain or the critique of it that I have presented in this book can be adequately supplemented by appealing to this alternative Spanish intellectual tradition alone. A similar appeal must also be made to the views developed on Don Quixote from the varying perspectives of Spain's ex-colonies—the perspectives, in other words, of modern Spain's other "outsiders."

Accordingly, in this final section, I supplement my critique of the Quixotism of Restoration Spain in two ways. First, by grafting onto the Quixotist canon some of the representative views of Don Quixote that exiled Spanish and post-colonial Hispanic American intellectuals have held, I point to the nationalist limits of the Quixotism that Ganivet, Unamuno, Maeztu, and Ortega espoused. My aim here is to supplement Quixotism as a critical category by highlighting its relation to the critique of modern Spanish nationalism that was developed by thinkers who, like the Quixotists of Restoration Spain, had a vested interest in elaborating an Hispanicist Quixote myth. Second, by aligning the critical project of this book with these other counternarratives, I aim to make explicit the "alternative" character of the foundation on which my own critical project is grounded. These counternarratives, however, also contain their own blind spots: they are, in epistemological terms, often the same blind spots as those of the Quixotists. There is, in other words, a propensity among the writers who I study in this Supplement, to frame their discourse in mythological terms. Thus, if these counternarratives are to serve as a foundation for the renewal of Hispanism, their conceptual limits must also be reconstructed.

Don Quixote in Exile

Much like Ganivet, Unamuno, Maeztu, or Ortega, Américo Castro (1885–1972) was an intense and complicated Spanish thinker whose changing views on the significance of Don Quixote coincided with the evolution of his thought concerning the perceived decadence of modern Spain. Initially trained in Spain as a philologist, Castro made his first mark in the world of Spanish letters as a defender, not of the uniqueness of Spanish literary culture, but of this culture's decidedly European character. For Castro, at the beginning of his intellectual career, Spanish national decadence was a question of the nation's repeated attempts at separating itself from its European roots. He was, in short, what in Restoration Spain was often referred to as a Europeanizer.[2] In this regard, Castro advanced the view, in his 1925 *Pensamiento de Cervantes,* that Cervantes was an Erasmian humanist and, consequently, that the key to a proper understanding of his *Quixote* was not allegorical, as the Quixotists would have had it, but conceptual.[3]

Following the Spanish Civil War—a conflict that led Castro to seek sanctuary first in Buenos Aires, then in Madison, Wisconsin, and eventually in Princeton, New Jersey—Castro advanced quite a different view of Cervantes and the significance of the *Quixote* vis-à-vis the question of Spain's modern decadence. Impressed, as he had become, by the virulent character of modern Spain's militant Catholicism and the imperialist ideology of the fascists, Castro came to see in the Spanish nation's celebrated *casticismo* not the source of its *intrahistoric* regeneration but of its historic decadence.[4] Castro argued that the Spanish nation had always and already been in the throes of something akin to a civil war: an encounter, at once bellicose and creative, among Spain's three historical and religious castes—the Jews, the Muslims, and the Christians.

Spain, Castro now agreed with the Quixotists, was different from the rest of Europe by virtue of its *casticismo*. But he differed with them completely in regard both to what the defining characteristics of *casticismo* were and how to interpret those characteristics. With studied irony, Castro writes in this regard: "Unique among the nations of the West, the Spanish nation guides itself, with regard to its understanding of its past and of itself, by means of an historiography that is based in fabulous notions."[5] For Castro, the monoreligious *casticismo* of the Quixotists, the idea that being Spanish meant first and foremost being Catholic, was one of these "fabulous notions"; indeed, he perceived it to be the most pernicious of them all.

As he would come to understand it, the Spanish nation's exclusive and fanatical identification with Catholicism was the real source of Spain's modern decadence. Castro analyzed this decadence in terms of the nation's historic deficiencies: insufficient philosophical curiosity; the absence of scientific and technological innovation; a lack of economic industry and administrative know-how; the need, in the final analysis, for a truly modern, self-critical historical consciousness and awareness.[6] Castro explained this lack of intellectual, cultural, and economic vitality, in large part, by pointing to the expulsion from Spain of its Jews, of its Muslims, and during the modern era, of its liberals. By reason of its religious intolerance, reasoned Castro, Spain's Christian caste had forced many of the society's better minds to leave the peninsula.[7]

Castro, however, also explained modern Spanish national decadence by revealing the hatred that lay beneath the Christian caste's sense of honor. This honor, reasoned Castro, served to separate those who remained on the peninsula into two distinct, yet imaginably homogenous groups: an honorable caste of "Old Christians"—the descendants of Catholic Spain's crusading heroes, and a dubiously honorable caste of "New Christians"—the descendants of those Jews and Muslims who, instead of being forced into exile, were forced to convert to Christianity. According to Castro, Spain's Old Christians came to consider themselves, after eight centuries of militant reconquest, as being too pure and too much in tune with God's work, to have to trouble themselves either with the business of trade and finance or with manual labor. Spain's Old Christians viewed these tasks as menial and the proper domain of either the Jews who, Castro maintains, the Old Christians typically associated with usury, or of the Muslims who, Castro argues, the Old Christians believed were more adept than the Jews in the traditional arts and crafts. In keeping with Castro's views, then, the hatred that the Old Christians felt for the Jews and the Muslims turned in due course into an abhorrence of all those economically stimulating and culturally enlivening activities that the Old Christians associated with their religious enemies.[8]

Indeed, in his attempt to reason through the sources of modern Spain's perceived decadence, Castro drew quite a dreary picture: by reason of the military and political dominance of Spain's Christians, the Spanish nation had devolved into a near-homogenous whole where a complacent, arrogant, and self-righteous caste of Old Christians ruled over a caste of converts who had no recourse but to remake themselves in the vapid image of their rulers. Yet, it is not as though Castro altogether disavowed the possibility of Spanish national and cultural regeneration. To that end, he opposed to this depressing sketch of orthodox homogeneity the utopian and regenerative image of a multireligious *casticismo* and the vibrant, multicultural, conflictive life to which it had once given rise. Not unlike Unamuno and Maeztu, who had called for a regenerating recuperation of Spanish medievalism, Castro associated his regenerating utopia with the medieval life of Spain. Unlike Maeztu and Unamuno, however, Castro identified this medieval Spain with the religious tolerance, multicultural enrichment and cross-cultural dialogue of cities such as Toledo where, to this day, Christian Cathedrals, Jewish Synagogues, and Muslim Mosques mingle to form an architectural record of medieval Spain's multiform *casticismo*.[9]

The first systematic version of these views that Castro presented was in his 1948 *España en su historia*—a book that engendered a polemic that was both to haunt and to inspire Castro for the remainder of his career.[10] Thus, in his 1961 *De la edad conflictiva*, Castro elaborated his critique of Christian Spanish *casticismo* by linking it to a study of Spanish Golden Age honor plays. Then, in subsequent reworkings of *España en su historia*—published in 1962 and 1965 under the alternative title *De la realidad histórica de España*, Castro expanded the focus of his critique of *casticismo* to include not only the medieval and renaissance literatures of Spain but also the honor-bound, nationalist historiography that this literature had prompted over the centuries.

In an attempt both to argue against the decadent practices of such historiography and to provide a regenerating alternative, in 1966 Castro turned—or rather returned—to the study of the one book that had launched his career as a literary critic and historian: Cervantes' *Quixote*. It was in his 1966 *Cervantes y los casticismos* that Castro applied his critique of *casticismo* most forcefully to the reading of Cervantes' *Quixote*. In this work, Castro presented the *Quixote* as an ironic protest against the caste conflicts of Spain's conflictive nationality and as a solution to that conflict. He identified Cervantes as a New Christian descendant of Jewish converts and, consequently, as an author who in his personal life had had to develop the double consciousness and critical self-awareness of the convert. This critical self-awareness of Cervantes, reasoned Castro, was what marked his *Quixote* as truly modern and gave rise to the novel's ironic, self-referential style.

In this respect, Castro proposed that Cervantes' *Quixote* arose as "a dispute between one *self* and another *self*. . . Novelistic dialogue was preceded by the silent monologue of those who judged themselves to be conscious enough of who they were so that they could be who they were, exercise their right to speak in the first person of all that which occurred to them, and . . . seek out interlocutors. It became necessary to possess an interiority that could be exhibited publicly."[11] Here, Castro depicts the tensions that characterized relations between Old and New Christians in Cervantes' time as the principal motive behind the narrative confrontation of an exterior, official reality with an intimate, intellectual imagination in the *Quixote*. The result of this narrative dialectic of recognition is the constitution of identities, such as those of Don Quixote and Sancho Panza, which in themselves are problematic, not absolute and certainly not heroic—or at least not in the premodern terms that the Quixotists of Restoration Spain understood heroism.

As against the self-certain nobility and messianic self-righteousness of the Old Christians, Castro posits the Cervantine figure of Don Quixote as representative of a problematically split, New Christian consciousness. Castro's New Christian Don Quixote constitutes a bifurcated consciousness insofar as he must negate his historically bound and culturally significant difference—his non-Christian ancestry—in an attempt to outwardly prove himself identical to the Old Christian values of chivalry. In effect, Castro's Don Quixote is at war with himself: in part, he is eager to portray the role of an Old Christian knight-errant; in part, he is overwhelmed by the refusal of the Old Christians to recognize his imagined knight-errantry. This intimate war, pitting Don Quixote's desire for recognition against the world's failure to yield to his desire, leads Don Quixote to develop a critical self-awareness of himself as mad as well as a critical sense of the world's madness. This innovative awareness, in combination with Cervantes' ironic treatment of it, constitutes the "novelty" of the *Quixote* according to Castro.[12]

Clearly, Castro's reading of the *Quixote* complicates the idea that Don Quixote can be appropriated as the representative icon for a heroically self-sufficient and imperial Spanish national identity. In opposition to the heroic Quixotism of Ganivet, Unamuno, Maeztu, and Ortega, Castro posits a "cervantine-quixotist world that was born under the sign of liberty": Castro posits a reading of the *Quixote*, in other words, that celebrates the subjectivity of individuals and their freedom to make of themselves and their lives what they will.[13] By contrast, Ganivet, Unamuno, Maeztu, and Ortega associate the figure of Don Quixote, not with the negative freedoms of individuals, but with the positive freedom of an ascetically disciplined national totality.

Despite the fact that Castro's work focuses mostly on the literature of medieval and renaissance Spain, Castro did have something to say, also, about 1898 and the thinkers whose work has come to be associated with that date. Given the mythologizing spirit with which the Quixotists confronted the perceived decadence of Restoration Spain, Castro could not permit himself the luxury of ignoring them nor, much less, that of forgetting them. In effect, as Castro understood it, the critique of Spanish national decadence that Ganivet, Unamuno, Maeztu, and Ortega developed was mistaken in that it centered exclusively on the notion of anarchy. By extension, he also considered that the elitist formulas for regeneration espoused by the Quixotists were fundamentally flawed. For his part, Castro contended that anarchy and elitism were two extreme, yet complimentary, sides of the same decadent tendency—a decadence that he explained in terms of the caste identity of Spain's Old Christians.[14]

As Castro interpreted them, Ganivet, Unamuno, Maeztu, and Ortega did not, as their official commemorators have often held forth, represent the heroic origin of a modernizing and Europeanizing Spanish literary tradition but the false, would-be "modern" origin of a persistent continuation of the historic caste identity of Spain's Old Christians. It is for this reason that Castro renounces the intellectual legacy of the generation of '98 qualifying it, from the often-celebrated *intrahistory* of Unamuno to the no less applauded *resentment* of Ortega's masses, as historiographically inefficient and conceptually mystifying: "the generation of '98 and those of us who continue it, as a form of historic knowledge and understanding of what Spain is and could have been, have not contributed any decisive, fortifying or consoling truth."[15] In order for Spaniards to develop a truly critical sense of their literary and national history, reasons Castro, they must not deny their history but rather turn their backs on those historiographic schemes, such as Azorín's and Ortega's generations, that have wrongly encouraged them to forget it. "If a Spaniard does not decide to live with his own history," he asks, "how will he agree with his fellow Spaniards? How will he know to elude oppression, anarchy or chaos?" And then, striking a note that is very much in tune with the Quixotism of Restoration Spain, Castro adds: "Or perhaps something even worse: how will he avoid insignificance?"[16] His answer, in no uncertain terms, is that by embracing the multiform *casticismo* that he discovers in Spain's medieval and renaissance literatures and about which he theorizes in his works, the Spanish nation might, someday, recuperate the magnificence, not of an empire, but of a fecund, cross-cultural, cross-generational culture of learning.[17]

As a result of Castro's counter-Quixotist narrative and, especially, of his thesis concerning the conflictive character of Spanish *casticismo,* this incredibly tense and energetic thinker has been largely silenced by those who, together with the Quixotists, would defend the idea of a Spanish cultural empire. It is not difficult to understand the appreciable interest with which Hispanists who sympathize with the dual legacy of the Quixotists and Franco's regime have sought to silence the voice of Castro.[18] After all, his thesis concerning the conflictive yet creative encounter of Spain's three historic and religious castes does call into question the nationalist assumption of a uniform and monolithic Catholic Spanish national identity. It is less easy to understand the silence with which Castro's theses have continued to be received in Spain after the oftentimes-lauded transition of modern Spanish society toward democracy.[19] Still, if one considers how awkwardly Castro's notion of a multiform Spanish *casticismo* fits into the Europeanizing and culturally neo-imperialist project that has dominated official cultural policies in Spain since the transition, that silence becomes transparent. And so it is that, whether by reason of traditional intransigence or by reason of a Europeanizing triumphalism, Castro's cosmopolitan voice of dialogue and solidarity has been decisively censured and all but criminalized in Spain.[20]

Castro's theory on the conflictive life of Spain's *casticismo* represents one of the most compelling alternatives to the Quixotist tradition of heroic literary generations that has been proposed to date by a Spanish intellectual. Notwithstanding his contribution to the modernization of Hispanism as a field of genuine inquiry, Castro's thought also had its definite blind spots.[21] One of these, and certainly the most significant as concerns his critique of the thought of the Quixotists, was his pro-Hispanicism, or belief in a historically transcendent "Hispanicity." The latent Spanish cultural imperialism of Castro's Hispanicism is made evident in his 1940 study of the linguistic peculiarities of Argentina, *La peculiaridad lingüística rioplatense.*

Under the guise of a philological analysis of the Spanish spoken and written in Buenos Aires—the city to which Castro first fled as an exile—in this book Castro affirms the existence of an Hispanic family of peoples to which the Argentines, despite their concerted efforts to develop an independent national language and literature, invariably belong. "Hispanic countries," writes Castro in this regard, "find themselves inscribed within a Hispanic tradition and destiny, and they become more firmly grounded in them the more they seek to belie or elude them."[22] Not unlike Maeztu, whose time living abroad in Buenos Aires inspired him to write his *Defensa de la Hispanidad,* Castro's time in Buenos Aires also led him to entertain the possibility of a regenerating Hispanicism. In contrast to Maeztu, however, who imagined the regeneration of the Hispanic world in terms of a recuperation of Spain's Catholic empire, Castro viewed the regeneration of the Hispanic family of nations to be a question of Hispanic American ascendance: "As essential zones of Hispanic culture, the countries of the Rio de Plata region have a continental mission to fulfill, which one day shall be global."[23] Although this view of Argentina's future left some room for the nation to develop of its own accord, Castro stipulated that in order for Argentina to realize its continental mission, it would first have to abandon its isolating nationalism and submit its "anarchic" linguistic and literary tendencies to the normative rules of the Spanish language and its literary traditions elsewhere in the Hispanic world.[24]

Curiously, Castro formulated this defense of a common Hispanic destiny for all of the Spanish-speaking countries of the world from the perspective of a Spanish exile who was living and working at one of the leading intellectual centers of Anglo-America: Princeton University. Perhaps it was because he had, in effect, fled his native Spain and its modern culture of denial for a new life at the center of an ever-increasing and expanding Anglo-American empire that Castro felt compelled to reach out, in however shy and uncertain a fashion, to all those imperialist and Quixotist compatriots of his from whom he had otherwise become so utterly isolated. Whatever the reason he may have had for advancing these Hispanicist views, the fact remains that insofar as they posit a Hispanic essence and a Hispanic destiny, these views of Castro's also assert the existence of a monolithic Spanish cultural and linguistic imperialism that is clearly incompatible with the multiform *casticismo* that he elaborates elsewhere in his work.

Here, then, in Castro's Hispanicism is one instance of the kinds of shady beginnings that one must confront even within the tradition of exiled Spanish liberal thought. Clearly, the critique that I have put forth in this book with regard to the ascetic and messianic ideals of the Quixotists finds a precedent in Castro's critique of the *casticismo* of Spain's Old Christian caste. What is also clear, however, is that the critical project that I have undertaken in this book cannot be grounded securely in the example of Castro's work alone. Indeed, given the extent to which Castro held to a latently imperialist, Hispanicist view of Hispanic America, Castro also falls within the critical scope of this book. Thus, it is necessary to step beyond the confines of Spanish national intellectual culture—a culture that Castro shares with the Quixotists of Restoration Spain, and venture into the intellectual life of late nineteenth and early twentieth-century Hispanic America. Here, among Spain's ex-colonies, intellectuals such as Caro, Darío, and Rodó developed their own brand of Quixotism. Unlike Ganivet, Unamuno, Maeztu, and Ortega, who used both the *Quixote* and the figure of Don Quixote to espouse an imperialist Quixotism, and unlike Castro as well, who promoted a Spain-based Hispanicism, these thinkers elaborated a pan-national, Hispanicist Quixote myth that was squarely situated within the parameters of Hispanic-American republicanism.

Don Quixote in Colombia

Although the Colombian philologist, classicist, and politician Miguel Antonio Caro (1843–1909) occupies a place in Hispanic-American literary studies that is in no way comparable to that of Darío or Rodó, as a Hispanic-American thinker and politician whose writings supplement the Quixotism of

Restoration Spain his significance is incontrovertible. He is first among the Hispanic-American intellectuals to be considered here, then, because in several respects his work as a literary historian and a politician is the most complementary. Caro's views on Don Quixote are as colored by his faith in Catholic doctrine as are those of Maeztu; likewise, his political career grew out of Colombia's regenerationist movement much in the same way that the political career of Joaquín Costa had from the regenerationist movement of Restoration Spain. Yet, in spite of these evocative similarities with the Quixotists and regenerationists of Restoration Spain, Caro's messianism and regenerationism do not lead him to embrace dictatorial and imperial solutions to the perceived moral, political and cultural decadence of the Hispanic world. To the contrary, Caro elaborates his views on the spiritually regenerating value of Don Quixote within the scope of a pan-nationalist republican discourse.

In an essay of 1874 titled "El *Quixote*," Caro—who by this point had already achieved a degree of notoriety for his Spanish translation of the *Aeneid*—affirms that "the *Quixote* is the poem of Spaniards . . . it is to Spain . . . what great epics are to other nations."[25] Similarly, he maintains a bit further on that "insofar as the *Quixote* is the book of our race, it is also the book of our nations of America."[26] Caro makes these affirmations in an attempt to compensate for the lack that he perceives in the national literatures of Spain and Hispanic America of any true epic tradition capable of expressing the unity of the Hispanic world. Caro considers that the nations that make up the "Iberian family" should recognize Cervantes' *Quixote* as their unifying epic because it is written in an elevated style that is "beautifully executed," it contains "the peculiar attributes that encapsulate the Spanish nation" and presents "a way of thinking that interests humanity."[27] In sum, the *Quixote* qualifies as an epic for Caro in that it satisfies three of the basic criteria that he, as a translator of Virgil, associates with all great epics: its rhetorical structure and narrative style are appropriately elevated; it summarizes the Spanish nation's, and by extension the Hispanic world's, basic characteristics and it has a universal appeal. But none of these criteria explain why the *Quixote* is, according to Caro, precisely the sort of epic that the Hispanic world requires in order to reaffirm its cultural unity.

In an attempt to answer that question, Caro underscores the philosophical and theological background on which he believes the *Quixote* rests. For Caro, the *Quixote* is an example of what he calls "Christian art" and he sees its hero, Don Quixote, as being motivated by a religious vocation: Don Quixote's mission, Caro asserts, is to "distinguish weakness from guilt, pain from crime, poverty from dishonor" and make "pain, poverty and weakness beautiful."[28] His mission is, in short, to inspire in his fellow men a proper respect for the Christian values around which the nations of the Hispanic world are to unite. As such, Caro seeks to derive from the religious background that he discovers in the *Quixote* not merely a moral lesson, but a specifically political lesson appropriate to the modern world.

According to Caro, the modernizing nations of the Hispanic world have forgotten the epic acts of heroism that gave shape to their world. This common heroic cultural beginning, argues Caro, can be found in Spain's conquest of the Americas. In this respect, Caro celebrates the figures of conquistadors such as Hernán Cortés and Gonzalo Jiménez de Quesada as "our fathers," who he opposes to the "men of the conquered race"; moreover, in a vein similar to that of Aeneas's nation-building conquest of Rome, Caro sustains that the Spanish conquest of the Americas did not have as its sole object "the destruction" of the autochthonous civilizations of the Americas, the conquest also provided for "a fusion of races."[29] In this manner, Caro posits the violent, "epic" heroism of the conquistadors as the symbol of Hispanic America's racial unity. According to Caro, this racial unity finds its cultural equivalent, not in syncretism, but in the imperial language and the universal religion that the conquistadors imposed on those with whom they mixed their blood. As such, the Hispanic community that Caro imagines represents an imperially coerced ecumenical unity: "a beautiful Catholic unity," he calls it.[30] Moreover, Caro sustains that this unity is reflected in "all of the literary monuments of Spain's Golden Age."[31] As the most representative of these so-called literary monuments, the *Quixote* becomes, for Caro, the most effective symbol for an Hispanic world that he conceives as the virtual equivalent of the orbis christianus.

As one of the principal ideologues behind Colombia's turn-of-the-century regenerationist movement—a movement that sought to reaffirm the traditional ties between Colombian republicanism and the Catholic Church—Caro believed that the traditional spiritual unity of the Hispanic world had been placed under attack by the utilitarian values of modern paganism.[32] Caro identifies this paganism with the secularization of the state, which he sees in turn as "the crucial error of the present era . . . an error that everywhere is triumphant."[33] The modernizing nations of the Hispanic world, Caro sustains, are in decadence; they are "diseased nations" that have succumbed to "barbarism."[34] By depicting decadence as barbarism, Caro harkens back to the binary division of civilization and barbarism with which, in 1845, the Argentine politician and polemicist, Domingo Faustino Sarmiento, sought to argue against the debilitating effects of Quiroga's and Rosas's tyranny. Caro, however, frames this binary opposition in moral and religious, as opposed to strictly political, terms. For Caro, the barbaric decadence of modern Hispanic America, results from hedonism: "pleasure is now the measure of goodness and force, that of right."[35] As a result, the modern nations of Hispanic America are no longer able to fulfill their true Hispanic mission in the world, a mission that Caro defines, in keeping with Don Quixote's supposed spiritual mission, as "believing and praying . . . being the submissive sons of the universal Church."[36]

It is precisely in an attempt to argue in favor of the religious reconstitution of Hispanic America's modern nation-states that Caro appeals to the *Quixote* as the epic of the Hispanic world. Indeed, Caro presents the *Quixote* as a regenerating solution to the perceived moral and political decadence of his time. Echoing the Spanish obscurantist Nicolás Díaz de Benjumea, for whom the *Quixote* was "a profane Bible," Caro interprets the *Quixote* as a sacred book, as a book that imparts the "teachings of the highest Catholic philosophy" that are necessary to the regeneration of the Hispanic world.[37] He identifies the Christian theology that supposedly underscores the *Quixote* as stemming from "a love and cult of the religious unity of the nation."[38] Similarly, Caro considers that Cervantes was "a great Catholic as a man" and that, as a consequence of his Catholicism, "pagan egotism . . . could not have guided his pen."[39] Cervantes and his *Quixote* constitute, for Caro, the ideal expression of Spanish national and imperial unity.

The undercurrent of religious and national idealism that Caro claims to discover in the *Quixote* informs his understanding of Don Quixote as an agent of regenerating spiritual values and of Sancho as an expression of the materialistic tendencies of the modernizing world. Caro argues that in the first part of the *Quixote* Don Quixote's spirituality is expressed by means of his "religious words," and that, in the second part, it is expressed primarily by means of his "prudent acts." In this way, Caro discovers a progressive process of Christianization in the figure of Don Quixote by means of which Cervantes demonstrates what were his real intentions in writing the *Quixote:* "Cervantes wanted to prepare . . . the Christian death of his hero," writes Caro in this respect, adding that, by reason of his Christian progress, Don Quixote eventually comes to recognize that he must not only seek to serve his lady Dulcinea but also to serve, love, and fear God.[40] Not unlike the Don Quixote that Unamuno constructs in his *Vida de Don Quijote y Sancho*, Caro's Don Quixote is a lover of glory who, in the end, is transformed into an exemplary lover of Christ.

With regard to Sancho, Caro sustains that his faith in Christianity also progresses throughout the *Quixote.* Caro interprets Sancho's progress in terms of his changing attitudes toward the island that Don Quixote has promised him in exchange for his service. In this regard, he notes how before governing the island, Sancho maintains that "I would be as much the king of my State as each man is of his own estate, and being the king, I would do as I please, and doing as I please, I would satisfy my desires, and satisfying my desires, I would be happy, and being happy, I would have nothing more to desire"—an argument that Caro associates with "the modern sensualist professors . . . of the new paganism."[41] But after attempting to govern his island kingdom on his own and realizing that he requires the advice of his master Don Quixote, Caro suggests that Sancho learns to govern in agreement with the principles of "Christian political philosophy."[42] Caro reduces this Christianizing political philosophy to the following formula: "each man should contribute to the common work . . . with sacrifice . . . with effective virtues . . . with humility of understanding and purity of intention."[43] In this regard, Caro considers that Sancho's government "implies . . . a beneficial political lesson" that is more appropriate to "our time than to Cervantes' time."[44]

By following Sancho's example and attempting to implement Don Quixote's Christian political philosophy, the modernizing and secularized nation-states of the Hispanic world will be able to recuperate the unity and glory that was the Spanish empire under its Catholic kings.[45] This, at any rate, is the promise that Caro holds out to the Hispanic world in his Hispanicist essays. Consequently, in order to regenerate the modern nation-states of the Hispanic world, Caro reasons that they must be reconstituted and reorganized around "a center that assures order and guarantees peace."[46] Caro finds this center in the "permanent interest" that is represented by "patriotic institutions," institutions which, according to Caro, "should be grounded in a religious base, the foundation of all civilizations."[47] In the case of the nation-states that are members of what Caro denominates the "Iberian family," the religious reconstitution of these "patriotic institutions" should be modeled after the example of the institutions of the Catholic Church: "the Catholic, apostolic Church . . . universal teacher of all peoples."[48]

It is in this manner, then, that the religiously based moral and political regeneration that Caro sees outlined in the *Quixote* is to serve as a regenerating example to an entire imagined community of nations that Caro baptizes as Hispanic. The sensual, self-serving and materialistic Sanchos of the modern era are to obey and believe in the Christian ideals of their traditional, Don Quixote–like religious leaders. Such are, in sum, the duty, the mission, and the vocation of Christian politics, according to Caro. "Today," he writes in this regard, "the world seems to vacillate between true Christianity, which is to say Catholicism, and modern paganism, which is much worse than the paganism of the ancients."[49] Despite this perceived vacillation, Caro confesses to a degree of optimism: "compelled by experience, the Christian nations will reunite."[50] A unity similar to this is, of course, what the Quixotists of Restoration Spain would, at the turn of the century, espouse: a Hispanic and Catholic totus orbis.

In spite of the many suggestive similarities between Caro's Christianizing views of Hispanic unity and those of the Quixotists, there are some significant differences that cannot be ignored. Caro himself expressed his understanding of these differences in an essay of the turn of the century titled "El quijotismo español" where he sets himself the task of explaining Spain's defeat in 1898 by the United States. In this essay, Caro characterizes as depraved the Spanish nation's reaction to the United States' declaration of war. The Spanish nation responded, he affirms, with "collective vanity, conceit and arrogance."[51] "It is an extraordinary fact," observes Caro in this respect, "that the Spaniards believed that the principal cause of their victory over the United States would be the purity of their race and the cleanliness of their blood."[52] The vanity of the Spanish nation, its faith in its honorable purity, in a word its *casticismo,* is a phenomenon which, Caro assures his readers, is known throughout the Hispanic world "by the generic name of quixotism."[53]

In keeping with this observation, Caro understands the "quixotism" of the Spanish nation to be an expression of a chivalric illness—"an illness of knight-errantry"—which, moreover, represents the "degeneration" of the nation and the "falsification of national pride."[54] This "false quixotism," Caro reasons, ultimately leads to the breakdown of the nation into "local estates and tyranny"; in the final analysis, it represents "Spanish national pride divorced from Christian morality."[55] Clearly, this view of Spain's immediate reaction to the events of 1898 runs contrary to the romanticized Quixotism that Ganivet (in 1897), Unamuno (in 1905 and 1913), Ortega (in 1914), and Maeztu (in 1926) would eventually develop and extol. However, Caro's view is not far removed from that which Unamuno initially held with regard to the War of 1895–1898. Like Caro in Colombia, at the turn of the century in Spain, Unamuno argued that "We [Spaniards] must forget our previous life of adventure and how we went about the world imposing on others what we believed was best for them . . . instead, the mission of our nation must be to Christianize itself . . . Death to Don Quixote and may [the Christian] Alonso el Bueno be reborn!"[56] Indeed, like the Christianizing national rebirth that Unamuno initially imagined for Restoration Spain, Caro maintains that the regeneration of modern Spain is to come about in much the same manner as that of the Hispanic world at large: that is, by implementing the Christianizing political philosophy that Caro claims to discover in the *Quixote.* Accordingly, Caro suggests that the "greatest enemy" that the "false quixotism" of Spain can find "is Catholicism . . . the doctrine of regeneration by means of pain, self-abnegation, and sacrifice."[57]

Elsewhere, Caro formulates this enmity between the "false quixotism" of a vain and arrogant Spain and his own Catholicizing brand of regeneration by advancing a comparative theory of regenerative politics: "Whenever it becomes extreme, nations do not overcome disorder except by means of either a unifying dictatorship, which because it imposes itself on provincial dictators and town bosses teaches obedience to all those who would like to govern, or by means of collective and patriotic movements, of a totality of self-abnegating wills, guided by a superior intelligence."[58] The first of these two formulas for regeneration is based in vanity and would transform the nation by imposing on it the political will-to-power of a single and energetic "caudillo." This was, according to Caro's rendering of the "false quixotism" of Restoration Spain, the formula favored by Spain's political leaders at the outbreak of the war with the United States. Conversely, the second formula is based in humility and would transform the nation by submitting its political interests to a superior, transcendental will. According to Caro's interpretation of the *Quixote*, this is the formula that was sketched out by Cervantes; it is also the formula that Caro sought to implement as leader of Colombia's regenerationist movement; and it is, finally, also the formula that Caro favors for the regeneration of the "Iberian family."

Caro is right on the mark when he identifies the "false quixotism" of Restoration Spain with a regenerationist policy that is based in the fierce elitism of a national dictatorship. What he could not have realized at the turn of the century was that, during the first three decades of the twentieth century, certain thinkers in Restoration Spain, in particular Unamuno, Maeztu, and Ortega, would affirm as true Quixotism precisely what he viewed as false. In this respect, Unamuno espoused the virtues of a Medieval *caudillismo* of "militant Christianity," Maeztu celebrated the "guild-discipline" of a nation singularly dedicated to a religious crusade, while Ortega also clamored for an oligarchy composed of those he referred to, rather simply, as "the best." In comparison to this panorama of enthusiastic and adulatory celebrations of the spiritually transforming power of dictatorships and oligarchies, the national Catholic political philosophy that Caro professed seems relatively tame. In any case, despite his insistence on the need to reestablish the institutions of the modern nation-state on a firm religious grounding, Caro did not attempt to dismantle the republic.

Although the "false quixotism" that Caro associated with Restoration Spain's initial response to war was at odds with the Quixotism that Ganivet, Unamuno, Maeztu, and Ortega would ultimately develop, the same cannot be said about the interpretation that Caro put forth of the *Quixote* as a unifying Hispanic epic and of Don Quixote as a Christian leader. This is true, in particular, as concerns the Quixotism of Unamuno and Maeztu. Like these two Spanish Quixotists, Caro affirmed the Catholic faith as the basis for Hispanic unity. In the case of Unamuno, it should be noted, this affirmation can be made only with qualifications: by celebrating the "tragic" Catholic faith of the Spanish nation, Unamuno never advocated strict adherence to the dogma of the Catholic Church. As concerns both Maeztu and Caro, however, this affirmation of Catholic Hispanic unity is decidedly dogmatic. Moreover, and perhaps more important, Caro shared with all his Quixotist counterparts from Spain a belief in the regenerating power of ascetic discipline. Like the Quixotists, Caro proposed an interpretation of the *Quixote* that justified submitting the sensuous, licentious, and anarchic Sanchos of the Hispanic world to a life of regenerating spiritual and moral discipline. Neither Caro nor the Quixotists were willing, in the final analysis, to allow the Sanchos of their time to govern themselves independently and freely pursue their own interests.

Still, there is one crucial difference between Caro and the Quixotists that it would be misleading to not highlight. Whereas ascetic idealism led the Quixotists of Restoration Spain to propose authoritarian and imperial projects for regeneration, in Caro it led to regenerationist projects that always remained within the parameters of Spanish America's pan-nationalist republican tradition. For all its apparent ultraconservativism, the Quixote myth that Caro developed in his writings demonstrates how a Christianizing and nationalizing "quixotism" may be imagined without also imagining, as did the Quixotists of Spain, a need for the dictatorial seizure of the state and an expansionist, imperial project.

Don Quixote in Nicaragua

Of the various Hispanic American intellectuals who shared with the Quixotists of Restoration Spain an interest in elaborating the Quixote myth and aligning this myth to a regenerating project of Hispanicism, perhaps the most prominent was the Nicaraguan poet and journalist Rubén Darío (1867–1916). Widely regarded in Hispanic America and Spain as one of the preeminent founders of modernism, Darío exerted enormous influence on the literary and intellectual culture of his time. With his poetry—which combined a Parnassianist concern for form, the subdued emotional content of Symbolism, and the intricate imagery of Gongorism, Darío mounted a stylistic revolution in Hispanic America and Spain that was comparable to the innovations that the poets of Spain's so-called Golden Age had introduced in the sixteenth and seventeenth centuries. Among the nationalistically entrenched keepers of the Spanish nation's cultural patrimony, Darío's modernism was perceived as a threat to the literary "classicism" of Spain's Golden Age tradition and as nothing short of an attempt, by one of the premier artists and intellectuals of modern Hispanic America, to "conquer" Spain.[59] In order to counter that perceived threat, the Quixotists of Restoration Spain and their Hispanophilic cohorts sought to naturalize Darío and make him one of their own. In effect, they sought to honor Darío by including his name among the members of Spain's would-be heroic generation of '98.[60] Certainly, by crafting his views on Don Quixote in such a way that they might appeal to his Hispanic American and Spanish readers alike, Darío contributed to this process of naturalization.[61]

Yet, Darío's importance to the nationally entrenched Hispanophiles of Restoration Spain was not the product of his literary achievements alone. As a correspondent for the Argentine newspaper, *La nación,* Darío had come to Spain immediately following the demise of the Spanish empire in 1898 and was perceived by the Quixotists as their emissary to the rest of the Spanish-speaking world. Darío had first visited Spain in 1892, in connection with the festivities dedicated to the fourth centenary of Spain's discovery and conquest of the Americas. At that time, Darío was, to all intents and purposes, a Hispanophobe.[62] Yet, when Darío returned to Spain in 1898 and again in 1905, he established close ties with such Quixotists as Maeztu and Unamuno and enthusiastically embraced these Spanish thinkers' apologetic and celebratory views of Spain's undying spiritual and cultural values. He adopted these Quixotist views, however, with ambiguity, seeking to strike a balance between Hispanic America's Spanish cultural heritage and the political independence of Hispanic America's young republics. Irrespective of Darío's ambiguously formulated anti-imperialism, the Quixotists and their acolytes persisted in their attempt to appropriate and naturalize him while, for his part, Darío represented the cause of Hispanic America's cultural unity with Spain to his international reading public.

Darío's newfound Hispanophilia can be explained, in part, by the fact that 1905 was an important date for all writers who claimed the language of Cervantes as their own. If Darío wanted to earn his keep by literary and journalistic production in that year, he needed to find positive things to say about both the *Quixote* and Don Quixote, to say nothing of Spain itself. In part also, his decision to celebrate the common cultural patrimony of Spain and Hispanic America can be explained by the fact that between his first visit to Spain in 1892 and his visit of 1905 the threat of U.S. imperialism had come to seem much more formidable, in Hispanic America, than that of Spanish cultural imperialism. Be this all as it may, in one of the poems that Darío published in 1905 in connection with the third centenary of the *Quixote*'s publication, his "Letanía a Nuestro Señor Don Quijote," Darío's Hispanophilia does seem authentic.

The Don Quixote that Darío constructs in this poem is a reaffirming complement to the Quixotism envisioned by Ganivet, Unamuno, Maeztu, and Ortega. In his poem, Darío postulates a transcendent and saintly Don Quixote that represents the Spanish nation and its imperial spirit; in the name of a Quixotist-like faith, he articulates a critique of the theories on modern Spanish decadence that were then in vogue in Spain; and he presents a notion of Spanish national regeneration that is made to rely on Don Quixote's intervention as a transcendental agent of hope for the entire Spanish-speaking world.

The "Letanía a Nuestro Señor Don Quijote" has an elaborate structure that gives to this poem the elevated musicality, controlled rhythm, and familiar echoes of a medieval religious chant. Appropriately, in the title, Darío classifies his poem as a litany, presenting his prayer-like song as an apostrophe that is directed to an absent and saintly Don Quixote and in which the two voices of a poet-priest and his anonymous yet unified congregation take part alternately: the poet-priest reciting supplications, and the congregation responding in the fixed manner of a chorus. Structurally, then, the poem enacts a spiritual exercise that is based in a relationship between an elite and the masses that calls to mind Unamuno's regenerating confessional relationship between the *videntes* and the *intrahistoric* nation.

Appropriating this religious language, Darío's song opens and closes with a communal apostrophe. Consisting of two sestets, this chorus alludes to the saintly and regenerating powers of Don Quixote: "King of the hidalgos, lord of the melancholy / encouraged by strength and covered in daydreams / . . . Noble pilgrim of pilgrims, / you sanctified all the roads / with the august stride of your heroism."[63] As king of the hidalgos, Darío's Don Quixote wears a crown of illusion; as the pilgrim of pilgrims, he is depicted as a hero who fights against both traditional religious authority and the half-truths of positivist science. He represents, in short, the spiritually regenerating imaginative heroism by means of which the "melancholy" members of the Spanish congregation are to be rejuvenated.

In between this communal song, which serves at once as prelude and coda, Darío inserts eight stanzas, most all of them sestets, in which the isolated voice of the poet-priest is made to resound with supplicant angst. The first of these eight stanzas renames Don Quixote the "Knight-errant of the errant knights, / man of men, prince of the fierce, / equal among equals" and, finally, "master." This recital of the sacred names of Don Quixote ends with the poet-priest hailing him and wishing him the best of health: "Hail! / Health because today I judge you have little / among the applause or the disdain / . . . and the stupidities of the multitude." With this greeting, the poet-priest names the purpose of his supplication—Don Quixote's recuperation of health on the day that has been set aside to celebrate his birth. But in doing so, he also separates himself from the multitude, that is, those gathered to celebrate the centenary with their topical debates on the *Quixote* and Don Quixote. In this manner, the poet-priest affirms his place among the celebrators, not as their equal but as their mediating guide.

Accordingly, in the following stanzas, this priestly poet suggests to his beloved Don Quixote that the litany that he is singing is unlike all the other songs that have been dedicated to him in 1905. The poet-priest thus begs Don Quixote to listen attentively to his song and asks that he take pity on his Spanish flock who, as Darío depicts them, "Have lost their faith." Proceeding with his litany of supplications, the poet-priest then asks Don Quixote to intervene and help renew the gathered congregation's faith: "From so much gloominess, from so much pain, / from the Overmen of Nietzsche, from tuneless songs / from prescriptions that a doctor signs / from epidemics, from the Academies / Liberate us, Lord!" Here, the poet-priest lists a catalogue of the commemorations: some simply a source of grief, some trendily updating Don Quixote in Nietzschean terms, some tuneless hymns, and others, finally, formulaic pieces of would-be scientific scholarship. This catalog also reads, however, as a critique of the kinds of programs for national regeneration that Spain's intellectuals were busily debating at the time. Some, like Mallada's *Los males de la patria,* were pessimistic and gloomy; some, like Maeztu's *Hacia otra España,* were decidedly Nietzchean; some, like Manuel de Sandoval's sonnets were tuneless occasional prayers; while others, like Altamira's *Historia de España y de la civilización española* or Menéndez y Pelayo's *La historia de los ortodoxos españoles,* were formulaic works of erudition. Darío would have Don Quixote revive the faith, not only of those who have gathered in 1905 to commemorate him, but the whole of the decadent Spanish nation as such. Appropriately, Darío's litany closes with a celebration of Don Quixote's spiritually regenerating power: his power, in short, to inspire a truly regenerating imagination.

Darío takes up this Quixotist theme of regenerating imagination again in his "Salutación del Optimista," also published in 1905. In this hymn, Darío opposes the hopeful image of a resuscitating Hispanic world to the perception of that world's hopeless decadence: "Illustrious fertile races, blood of fecund Hispania, / fraternal spirits, luminous souls, Greetings! / Because the time nears when you shall sing new hymns / tongues of glory. A vast rumble fills the air; magic / waves of life soon to be reborn."[64] Significantly, this celebration of the reemerging life and vitality of the Hispanic world is based in a reversal of Spain's loss of empire: "Forgetfulness backs away, death retreats deceived; a new kingdom is announced . . . we find suddenly . . . the divine queen of light, celestial Hope!"[65] The melancholy of loss, gives way to the memory of past glory, announcing a new hope. Darío discovers the source of this hope in the unity of the Hispanic world: "One and another continent, renewing the lineage of old, / united in spirit, in spirit, in eagerness and language, / see how the time nears when they shall sing new hymns / . . . Thus might hope become our permanent vision."[66] With this postulated cultural unity, and the future-oriented hope that it inspires in the permanence of a Hispanic dominion, Darío again complements the imperial imagination of the Quixotists of Restoration Spain.

Aditionally, Darío's poetry involves a defense of the perceived decadence of the Hispanic world. Unlike the Quixotists, however, who sought to excuse modern Spanish decadence in spiritual terms and viewed the Hispanic world with imperialistic longing, Darío constructs his defense of the Hispanic world as an anti-imperialist protest. "If these songs contain politics," he writes in the preface to his 1905 *Cantos de vida y esperanza,* "it is because it seems to be universal . . . Tomorrow we may be Yankees (and this is our most probable future); at any rate, I have written my protest."[67] Explicitly, Darío objects to the specter of emerging U.S. imperialism in the Americas. Nevertheless, his protest also implies the cultural imperialism of Spain's Quixotists. In this regard, Darió's views on the regenerating power of Don Quixote's illusions and the power of these illusions to generate hope among the unified peoples of the Hispanic world are sufficiently ambiguous to unsettle the monolithic nature of the cultural imperialist identity espoused by Restoration Spain's Quixotists.

As Darío sees it, Hispanic America's cultural and spiritual unity with Spain is worth affirming only insofar as it serves to counter the threat posed to Hispanic America by the United States. In another poem of 1905 titled "Los cisnes" Darío considers the future cultural and political independence of Hispanic America vis-à-vis the United States of Anglo America precisely in the terms of a defense: "Spanish America just as all of Spain / has its eyes fixed on the horizon of its fatal destiny / . . . Will we be made to submit to the fierce barbarians? / So many millions of men will speak English? / Are there no longer any noble hidalgos or brave knights? / Will we remain silent now only to cry later?"[68] Here, Darío depicts the prospect of Hispanic America coming under the sway of U.S. imperialism as nothing short of an historical calamity. At stake is not the Spanish nation's claim to cultural imperialism, but the independence of Hispanic America's Spanish-speaking nations per se.

In his 1905 "A Roosevelt," which is more a song of war than a song of hope, the independentist and pan-nationalist scope of Darío's Hispanicism comes into fuller view. In this poem, Darío personifies the threat of U.S. imperialism in Hispanic America by appealing to the figure of a "rough-riding" Roosevelt—the same Roosevelt who had led a makeshift cavalry into battle during the United State's Caribbean campaigns of 1898 and 1903. In this song, where Roosevelt is presented as a tyrant, Darío addresses the emerging rift between the two Americas. To one side, there is the America of the Anglos, excessively materialistic, excessively democratic, excessively powerful, both economically and militarily: "Primitive and modern, simple and complicated, / with a certain something of Washington and four times more of Nimrod. / You are the United States, / you are the future invader / of the ingenuous America that has indigenous blood, / that still prays to Jesus Christ and still speaks Spanish / . . . You combine a cult of Hercules with a cult of Mammon."[69] To the other side, there is what Darío, echoing the hero of Cuban independence, José Martí, refers to as "our America," an America that counters the excesses of the Anglos with its own cultural and spiritual values.[70] "Yet our America . . . / the America of the great Montezuma, of the Inca, the fragrant America of Christopher Columbus, / the Catholic America, the Spanish America, / . . . that America which trembles with hurricanes and lives from Love, / men of Saxon eyes and barbaric souls, it lives. / And dreams. And loves, and pulsates; and she is the daughter of the Sun. / Beware. Spanish America lives! / The Spanish Lion has let loose one thousand cubs. / . . . And, although you have everything, you are missing one thing: God!"[71] As Darío here constructs it, Hispanicism is to act as a moral and spiritual counterweight to the overly materialistic and decadent values of Anglo America. In the end, suggests Darío, Hispanic America will survive the confrontation because it alone is spiritually anchored and favored by God.

In light of this poem's impassioned defense of the spiritual and cultural independence of Hispanic America, the faith that Darío expresses elsewhere in the unifying and regenerating culture of the Hispanic world is seen to differ from the faith in cultural empire espoused by the Quixotists of Restoration Spain. For Darío, Hispanicism is much more a question of "our America"—a spiritual, ingenuous, mixed, and sensual America that possesses itself—than it is a question of Spain's America. In this respect, the Hispanicism of Darío and the transcendental Don Quixote associated with it do not fit neatly within the nationally delimited, imperialistically motivated Quixotism of Restoration Spain's Quixotists. To the contrary, Darío's Quixote myth demonstrates how Hispanicism could be effectively interposed between U.S. imperialism and Hispanic America in order to defend a pan-national ideal of cultural and political autonomy.

Don Quixote in Uruguay

Significantly, when Darío published his *Cantos de vida y esperanza* in 1905, he did not dedicate it to any of his Quixotist counterparts from Spain. Instead, he dedicated it to the Uruguayan essayist and politician José Enrique Rodó (1872–1917) who, in his 1900 *Ariel*, argued for the solidarity of the Hispanic world as a necessary means to defending Hispanic America from the threat of impending Yankee imperialism. Unlike the imperial Hispanicism of the Quixotists, Rodó's Hispanicism is clearly and explicitly articulated within the framework of a republican and democratic project for Hispanic American independence. Accordingly, by dedicating his collection of Hispanicist poems to Rodó, Darío signaled to his readers, many of whom were Spaniards, the extent to which his views concerning the cultural unity of the Spanish-speaking world did not coincide with the imperialistic longings of Restoration Spain's Quixotists. Indeed, in aligning himself with Rodó, Darío surreptitiously suggested that what united his own Hispanicism to that of the Quixotists was not so much a matter of Spain's and Hispanic America's common cultural and historical heritage, but a question of their sharing a common enemy: the United States of America. Whereas Spain, after the War of 1895–1898 had lost its few remaining colonies in the Caribbean and the Pacific to the United States, in 1903 Hispanic America saw its hegemony over the continent challenged by the U.S.-backed revolution for "independence" in Panama.

It was the specter of U.S. imperialism in Hispanic America, and not some vague nostalgia for unity with Spain, that led Rodó to promote Hispanicism.

Like Darío and the Quixotists of Restoration Spain, Rodó seized on the figure of Don Quixote to give expression to his Hispanicism. He saw in the figure of Don Quixote an example of the regenerating spiritual idealism of the Hispanic world; and he opposed this ennobling spirituality to the secular values and self-serving utilitarian practices that he associated with U.S. imperialism. Moreover, Rodó saw in Cervantes' *Quixote* the quintessential expression of the linguistic and cultural unity of the Spanish-speaking world and a basis on which to affirm Hispanic America's difference vis-à-vis the United States. Still, in order to fully appreciate and understand Rodó's position in regard both to the regenerating idealism of Don Quixote and the unifying character of Cervantes' *Quixote,* his views concerning the historical trajectory of Hispanic American independence must first be taken into account.

As he makes explicitly clear in *Ariel*—an essay that is written in the manner of a loving teacher's farewell address to his youthful Hispanic American pupils—the future cultural and political independence of Hispanic America's republics rests entirely on the ability of that region's youths to ensure that their republics become the site for an aristocratically and spiritually edifying form of democracy. Rodó begins *Ariel,* which he dedicates to the youth of America, by invoking the Shakespearean figure of Ariel. As Rodó understands it, this figure represents "the empire of reason and of sentiment over the lowly stimulus of irrationality . . . the generous enthusiasm, the high and disinterested motive of action, the spirituality of culture . . . the ideal end toward which human selection ascends."[72] Thus would Rodó encourage his readers, the future leaders of Hispanic America, to develop and perfect in themselves an awareness of what is most human about them—that is, their rationality—and thereby assure that they will have a place among the natural aristocracy that is to renovate and regenerate the moral, political, and cultural life of Hispanic America's republics.

However much Rodó's *Ariel* reads like an apology for the virtues of a "noble democracy," Rodó nevertheless begins his discussion of democracy in the Americas by acknowledging the links that tie this form of government to the perceived cultural decadence of the modern world. As Rodó conceives it, decadence results whenever the spiritual, aesthetic, and moral ideals of high culture—a high culture that Rodó associates both with the playful rationality of classical Greece and with the ascetic, self-sacrificing values of Christianity—are weighed down by the individuating interests, vulgar tastes, and moral relativity of low culture. Democracy, reasons Rodó, by reason of its egalitarian tendencies, brings about such decadence. "In order to face the problem squarely," he writes, "we must begin by recognizing that, when democracy fails to combine a strong preoccupation for its ideals with a preoccupation for its material interests, it does not exalt its spirit. Instead, it leads fatally to mediocrity and, because more than any other regime, it lacks effective barriers to such mediocrity, it also fails to provide an adequate guarantee of the inviolability of high culture. Left to itself . . . democracy gradually extinguishes all notions of superiority."[73] Rodó conceives of decadence, then, in much the same elitist terms that the Quixotists of Restoration Spain do; that is, as a manifestation of what Ortega would, in years to come, refer to as the resentment of the masses.[74] It is precisely this tendency to morally empower the resentment of the masses, their "hatred of the extraordinary" as Rodó calls it, that constitutes, for this Uruguayan intellectual, the most troubling aspect of America's modern democracies.[75] Following Renan, Morice, Guyau, and Carlyle, Rodó argues that the excessive egalitarianism inherent in modern democracies leads inevitably either to the tyranny of Jocobinism, as in the case of France, or to the no-less decadent imposition of the masses' "tendency toward what is utilitarian and vulgar," as in the case of the United States.[76]

Meaning to correct this spirit of egalitarianism, Rodó posits the civilizing influence of a morally superior elite as necessary to the social and political vitality of Hispanic America's republics. Indeed, like the Quixotists, Rodó is a firm believer in heroism and, like Ganivet, he is convinced of the modern world's need for appropriately modern forms of heroic activity.[77] Unlike the Quixotists, however, Rodó does not consider that the solution to this decadence lies in the imposition of a traditional aristocracy or, much less, in that of a dictatorship.[78] Rather, he understands that the sorts of regenerating heroes that can best correct the decadent egalitarianism of the modern world will arise only out of democracies. Such is the case, for Rodó, because he considers that it is only in a democracy that the process of natural selection, by means of which Rodó's heroic aristocrats are to be selected, is permitted to occur freely. "Conceived rationally," writes Rodó in this respect, "democracy always allows for an incontrovertible aristocratic element, which consists in establishing the superiority of those who are best, and assures it on the basis of the free consent of the associated citizens . . . Recognizing, in this way, that the selection and predominance of those who are best qualified is a necessity of progress, democracy excludes . . . the effect of humiliation and pain that is . . . the harsh lot of the vanquished."[79]

In sum, Rodó conceives democracy as a space where, on the basis of each citizen's equal freedom to pursue his own perfection as an agent of rationality, the historically competing tendencies of egalitarianism and aristocracy are "naturally," "rationally," and "progressively" reconciled. Since Rodó's aristocrats are chosen by a process of natural selection—that is to say, by a process that is based in no tradition other than that of the laws of Nature itself, this "noble" form of democracy does away altogether with the resentment that the vanquished masses typically feel when an artificial, man-made aristocracy has been imposed on them. Thus, the "noble democracy" that Rodó constructs in *Ariel* is one that gives rise to a natural aristocracy, a meritocracy, that is theoretically able to counter the vulgarity and mediocrity of mass culture with the regenerating examples of its own culture of superior talent, artistry, and spirituality. There is, certainly, room for skepticism concerning this imagined, theoretical outcome of the process of "natural selection." Rodó does not, for instance, theorize the possibility of a rational and political challenge to this process. Nor does he explain what ought to happen within this "aristocratic democracy" should the masses withdraw their freely given consent to be ruled by Rodó's spiritualizing elite. Indeed, because Rodó does not theoretically provide for any rational, political challenge to the outcomes of this process of supposed "natural selection," his ideal version of democracy must be held to be as elusive and as readily perverted as Maeztu's ideal of "objective function" or Ortega's ideal of "combative love."

These irksome theoretical ambiguities find there way, as well, into the essays that Rodó dedicates to the figure of Don Quixote and to Cervantes' *Quixote*. In these works, Rodó makes clear that the rise of Hispanic America's heroic aristocrats, while theoretically guaranteed by democracy, relies for its cultural and spiritual content on the historical character of the region's national identities. These identities, argues Rodó, are inextricably linked to Spanish national identity and the modern heroic values that Rodó associates with it. In particular, he associates Spanish heroism with the Spanish nation's civilizing, imperial project in the Americas. Rodó first formulates this celebratory view of Hispanic America's Spanish heritage in his 1906 "El Cristo a la jineta" and he further elaborates on it in his 1915 "El centenario de Cervantes."

In "El Cristo a la jineta," which was published a year after Unamuno's *Vida de Don Quijote y Sancho,* Rodó constructs an image of Don Quixote that is not unlike that which Unamuno envisions. Following Unamuno's Christianizing interpretation of the *Quixote,* in this essay Rodó imagines a militantly Christian Don Quixote whose life mirrors that of the Christ.[80] He begins the essay by establishing a correspondence between Jesus, as the Christ of peace, and Don Quixote, as the Christ of war: "After the Christ of peace, human history required the warring Christ, and then you were born, Don Quixote."[81] From here, Rodó proceeds to sketch out the various ways in which Don Quixote's adventures and misadventures as a warring messiah parallel the life of the Christ. Like Jesus of Nazareth, Rodó's Don Quixote is born in a humble little town and takes on the name of his place of origin; he is then baptized; he does penitence; he purifies whores and frees slaves; he promises a new kingdom to his followers but is spurned by those who doubt his authenticity as a knight-errant; finally, he is persecuted, ridiculed, betrayed, and, ultimately, sent to his death by the illegitimate authority of the false and worldly justice of his enemies. Also like the Christ, Rodó's Don Quixote has two natures, one human and the other divine. As Rodó explains it, however, the divine aspect of Don Quixote is unlike that of the Christ in that the spirit of Don Quixote has not ascended to the heavens but has remained forever on earth, among its brethren peoples: "You resuscitated on the third day: not in order to rise to the heavens, but in order to continue and complete your glorious adventures; to this day you wander around the world, although invisible and ubiquitous, and you still right wrongs, still correct injustices, still wage wars against false enchanters, and you favor those who are weak, in need and humble. Oh sublime Don Quixote, executive Christ, Lion-Christ, Christ mounted on horseback!"[82]

With this Christianizing interpretation, Rodó links the figure of Don Quixote to the notion of divine justice and to a socially edifying, spiritually exemplary form of self-sacrifice. He celebrates Don Quixote as the defender of the weak. However, Rodó also ties Don Quixote to the long-standing Spanish national tradition of militant, crusading, empire-building Catholicism. In this regard, Rodó's Christianized Don Quixote is first and foremost a crusader and conqueror. It is precisely this warring aspect of Don Quixote that Rodó emphasizes as specifically Hispanic. Accordingly, Rodó opposes this militantly Christianized Don Quixote to the utilitarianism of that other representative of the Americas, the Robinson Crusoe of Anglo America: "Devoted followers of that cult of individual energy that makes of each man the creator of his destiny," he writes in characterizing the citizens of the Unites States, "they have modeled their society after the image of a group of exemplary Robinsons, and once they have crudely fortified their personality by seeking to satisfy their self interests, they will become the filament of a finely woven fabric."[83] In the end, Rodó's Christianized and crusading Don Quixote is to act as an inspiration to the naturally selected aristocrats of Hispanic America in their battle with the Robinsons of the North.

By 1915, the year in which "El centenario de Cervantes" first appeared in the Argentine paper *La Nota,* Rodó shifts the focus of his interpretation away from Don Quixote and onto Cervantes. Already in his 1906 "El Cristo a la jineta," Rodó suggests why this shift in focus might prove necessary: "Christ in arms," he writes, "implies contradiction, from which is born, in part, the comic aspect of your figure, and also what is sublime about it."[84] According to this reasoning, Don Quixote is not only a figure that provides an edifying example for heroic action, but also a comic figure, whose flights of imagination and evident lack of physical prowess, make him a poor example of regenerating heroic action. Consequently, in "El centenario de Cervantes" Rodó complements his Christianized Don Quixote of 1906 with an assessment of Cervantes' empire-building heroism.

Rodó sees Cervantes as Spain's highest spiritual representative and as the one author around whom the entire Hispanic world might be made to turn.

Whereas in his *Ariel* of 1900 Rodó had appealed to Shakespeare in an attempt to construct an icon for the unity of Hispanic America, in "El centenario de Cervantes" Rodó opposes the genius of Cervantes to that of Shakespeare.[85] Here, Rodó associates Cervantes' *Quixote* with the birth of the Spanish empire: "Between the genius of Cervantes and the appearance of America on the globe, there is a profound historical correlation. The discovery, the conquest of America, constitute the magnum opus of the Spanish Renaissance, and the word of this Renaissance is the novel of Cervantes."[86] By thus suggesting that the *Quixote* is no less than "The Word" by means of which the Spanish nation first gave expression to its imperial will, Rodó elevates Cervantes' *Quixote* to the status of an imperial and culturally unifying icon. Accordingly, Rodó considers, in much the same way that the Quixotists of Spain did, that "there is no other statue but that of Cervantes to symbolize in America the Spain of our common past, the Spain on which the sun never set."[87]

Unlike the Quixotists of Restoration Spain, however, who tied Don Quixote to Spanish imperialism by proffering a romantic and tragic reading of the *Quixote,* Rodó does so by highlighting the irony that informs Cervantes' narrative strategies in the *Quixote.* "The irony of this marvelous creation, by tearing down an old and worn out ideal, affirms and exalts a new and potent ideal. It is this new ideal . . . that opens in Europe the portico of the modern age. An objective of hallucinations and chimeras, such as the one that the worn out ideal of knight-errantry pursued, gives way to the firm objective of reality . . . vast and beautiful, America overpowers all the fictions. And with the incentive of possessing her, America provides the stage for deeds that are more outrageous and astonishing than the useless adventures of knights-errant. The philosophy of the *Quixote* is, therefore, the philosophy of the conquest of America."[88] The irony with which Cervantes treats the "worn out ideal" and the "useless adventures" of errant knights such as Amadís de Gaula announces, or so Rodó would have it, the inception of a new world, a new reality and its correspondingly new forms of heroism. Not unlike the ahistorical and mythopoeic conjectural histories that the Quixotists of Restoration Spain narrated in their Quixotists essays, Rodó's reconstruction of the "philosophical" relationship between the *Quixote* and the conquest of America is counterhistorical. The conquest, of course, began in 1492. Cervantes did not publish the first part of his *Quixote* until 1605.

Keeping to this ahistorical ordering of events, elsewhere in "El centenario de Cervantes" Rodó underscores the essential character of the relationship between the *Quixote* and the conquest: "America was born so that Don Quixote could die; or better yet, so that he might be reborn entirely with reason and strength, incorporating into his magnanimous courage and his heroic imagination a real objective, an aptitude for collective and solitary action and the control of means proportioned to their ends."[89] Not unlike the simultaneously love-inspired, powerful and wise Don Quixote that Maeztu would imagine in his 1926 *Don Quixote, Don Juan y la Celestina,* Rodó's Don Quixote of 1913 is reborn in America, not in the form of a knight-errant, but in that of the new heroes of the new world, the conquistadors: Cortés, Pizarro and Balboa.[90] "In this way," concludes Rodó, "the critical sense of the *Quixote* has as its affirmative complement the great enterprise of Spain, which is the conquest of America . . . Accordingly, the name of Miguel de Cervantes . . . can serve as an abiding link that will forever remind America and Spain of the unity of their history and the fraternity of their destinies."[91] Cervantes, argues Rodó, is best suited to represent the spiritual and cultural unity of the Hispanic world because in his *Quixote* he treats with irony the chivalric values of the old world and proclaims the need for newer, regenerating forms of heroism.

When the essays that Rodó dedicated to Don Quixote and to Cervantes' *Quixote* are considered together, they make clear what sorts of heroic values Rodó believed that the aristocratic youths of Hispanic America's republics could recuperate from their Spanish heritage. By reclaiming Don Quixote's warring idealism, reaffirming the cultural unity and heroic spirit of the *Quixote,* and emulating Cervantes' rejuvenating irony, Rodó suggests that the naturally selected aristocrats of Hispanic America will successfully put into effect their brand of noble democracy and resourcefully defend themselves from the encroachment of U.S. imperialism.

Ultimately, argues Rodó, these recuperated Hispanic values should serve as the basis for a renewed attempt to realize Simón Bolivar's image of a Hispanic American confederation of republican states: "Latin America will be great, strong and glorious," argues Rodó, "if, despite the cosmopolitanism that is a necessary condition for its growth, it manages to maintain the continuity of its history and the fundamental originality of its race, and if, over the conventional borders that divide it into nations, it raises its superior unity as a sublime and maximum fatherland, the spirit of which will come to fruition in the realization of the dream of the Liberator."[92] When it is considered against the background of both U.S. imperialism and the imperialist Quixotism of Restoration Spain, Rodó's evocation of Bolivar's confederation takes on the quality of an unconditional challenge to any and all imperial pretensions that might be imposed on Hispanic America from without. In the end, the Quixote myth that Rodó develops in his essays reveals this thinker's commitment to a new form of imperium for Hispanic America; Spanish in its cultural and so-called philosophical roots, it is, nevertheless, pan-national and republican in its form.

Don Quixote and Robinson Crusoe

With this Supplement, I have sought to inscribe my critique of Quixotism within an intellectual tradition that runs counter, first and foremost, to those interpretations of Ganivet, Unamuno, Maeztu, and Ortega that have tended to celebrate these thinkers as examples of modern Spanish national genius. I have also sought to counter those other interpretations of these thinkers that have tended to dismiss Quixotism as if it were merely one among several motifs that characterize the thought of the Quixotists. By aligning my own critical project with the alternative perspectives of Castro, Caro, Darío, and Rodó, I have wanted to highlight both the weaknesses and strengths of this countertradition of exiled Spanish and Hispanic American thinkers.

As concerns this tradition's strengths, I consider that these all share one common denominator: republicanism. Contrary to the Quixotism of Restoration Spain, the Quixote myths that these thinkers elaborate provide for a modern heroism that does not necessitate either dictatorship or imperialism. This is so even in the case of such ultraconservative thinkers as Caro and Rodó, whose Catholicism and elitism respectively challenge the idea that they are, indeed, committed to the freedoms associated with Hispanic-American republicanism. This holds true, as well, even in the case of Castro, who despite his national chauvinism and culturally normative Hispanicism, develops an interpretation that expresses the novelty of the *Quixote* and the modernity of Don Quixote.

As concerns the weaknesses of this alternative countertradition, they are primarily of an epistemological order. From Castro to Caro and from Darío to Rodó, the Quixote myths that this alternative tradition provides are just that: myths. Not unlike the conjectural national and imperial histories imagined by the Quixotists of Restoration Spain, the pan-national and Hispanicist myths imagined by these thinkers are based in a mythopoeic historiography. Castro envisions a medieval utopia; Caro imagines a regenerating Catholic pan-national unity; Darío visualizes a new age of Hispanicist revival; and Rodó predicts the realization of Bolivar's imperial dream for Hispanic America. In short, the pan-national Hispanicism that each of these thinkers professes is, not unlike the national imperialism imagined by the Quixotists, also an "imagined community." And like the Quixotists of Restoration Spain, these thinkers turn to the figure of Don Quixote in order to represent that community in its imagined moral and spiritual essence.

There is, however, an upside to this Hispanicism that is not found in Quixotism. Insofar as it is articulated within the parameters of a republican tradition, the Hispanicism that Castro, Caro, Darío, and Rodó develop asserts the values of that imagined pan-national community in a language that is common to both the Hispanic world and its perceived enemy: the Anglo-

Saxon world. This shared language is the language of enlightenment, of republicanism, and democracy. The Hispanicism of these thinkers suggests, in other words, that the relationship between Don Quixote and Robinson Crusoe need not always be bellicose. It can also be creative, mutually enlightening, and liberating. It is with this shared spirit of emancipation that I have undertaken, in this book, to critique the Quixotism of Restoration Spain.

Notes

INTRODUCTION

1. José María Aznar, "Primer Pleno de la Comisión Organizadora del 'Centenario de 1898'" (Salamanca, Spain, 1997), online, Moncloa, Internet. "En el transcurso de un siglo, desde 1898 al cercano 1998, España ha superado . . . la inevitable frustración inicial para encarar el presente y el futuro con optimismo." Unless otherwise noted, this and all other subsequent translations are my own.

2. Aznar, "Primer Pleno." "[Nosotros los Españoles] formamos, como nos corresponde, parte de las sociedades política, económica y científicamente desarrolladas de Europa. Somos hoy . . . aquel pueblo en alza, laborioso y culto, europeo y americano, que soñaron los pensadores y poetas del 98."

3. James Fernández, "Conmemoraciones para el olvido: España 1898–1998," *Quimera*, 188/189 (2000): 56–61.

4. Javier Figuero, *La España del Desastre* (Barcelona: Plaza & James Editores, S.A., 1997), 1. "En este año de 1898 . . . un nuevo sentimiento común de esperanza y modernidad se abría paso tímida pero indicativamente."

5. José Andrés Gallego, *Un 98 distinto: Restauración, desastre, regeneracionismo* (Madrid: Ediciones Encuentro, 1998), 11. "La política de hoy," he affirms, "está pasada . . . por ese tamiz regenerador, que ha venido siendo heredado, de generación en generación, por la mayoría de los gobernantes de España que se han planteado la posibilidad y la conveniencia de mejorar las cosas . . . se llamase Joaquín Costa o Maura, Canalejas o Primo de Rivera, Azaña o Franco, incluso Felipe Gonzalez o Aznar."

6. Javier Leralta, *Viajes y viajeros del 98: Andanzas literarias por España de la generación del 98* (Madrid: Editorial Viajes Ilustrados, S.L., 1998), 9.

7. *Casa de las Américas,* 211, 1998.

8. See for instance: Manuel Moreno Fraginals, "El 98 en Cuba," in *El 98 Iberoamericano* (Madrid: Editorial Pablo Iglesias, 1998), 35–45. Arcadio Diaz-Quiñones, "Repensar el 1898: raza, nacionalidad, fronteras culturales e imperio," *Revista de Critica Cultural* 16 (1998): 22–28.

9. Juan Goytisolo, "El 98 que se nos viene encima," in *Cogitus interruptus* (Barcelona: Editorial Seix Barral, 1999), 205–214. Luís Fernández Cifuentes, "Cartografías del 98: Fin de siglo, identidad nacional y diálogo con América," *Annals of Contemporary Spanish Literature* 23:1 (1998) 117–145. Eduardo Subirats, "Decadencia y Modernidad," España miradas fin de siglo (Madrid: Ediciones Akal, 1995), 67–70.

10. Azorín, *Obras Completas*, vol. 9 (Madrid: Aguilar, 1954), 901. "¿Qué entendemos por un hombre moral? Un hombre que obra de acuerdo con los preceptos . . . las costumbres, las instituciones del tiempo y del país en que vive. Y un hombre inmoral . . . [es] un hombre que obra en contradicción con estas leyes, prácticas, instituciones y costumbres."

11. Azorín, 902. "Esa espontaneidad [de los Clásicos] . . . a nosostros ahora—sentimentales y democráticos—se nos puede antojar inmoralidad."

12. Azorín, 902. "[Un hombre amoral es] . . . un hombre que . . . se crea él mismo sus prácticas, sus leyes y sus costumbres; o bien un hombre que . . . es bastante fuerte para colocarse 'por encima del bien y del mal' y proceder según su voluntad y sus instintos."

13. Azorín, 902. "Nuestros predecesores de los siglos XVI y XVII."

14. Azorín, 1149.

15. Azorín, 1142.

16. Pío Baroja, *Divagaciones apasionadas* (Madrid: Caro Raggio, 1924); Miguel de Unamuno, *Obras Completas*, vol. 8 (Madrid: Escelicer, 1968), 409; Ramiro de Maeztu, *Autobiografía* (Madrid: Editorial Nacional, 1962), 67.

17. In 1934, for instance, the literary historian and critic, Federico de Onís, likened the presumably generational and national issue of 1898 to the advent of Modernism in Latin American and European literatures: "El modernismo es la forma hispánica de la crisis universal de las letras y del espíritu que inicia hacia 1885 la disolución del siglo XIX y que se había de manifestar en el arte, la ciencia, la religión, la política y gradualmente en los demás aspectos de la vida entera, con todos los carácteres, por lo tanto, de un hondo cambio histórico cuyo proceso continúa hoy." Federico de Onís, *Antología de la poesía española e hispanoamericana: (1882–1923)* (Madrid: Casa Editorial Hernando, 1934), xv.

18. José Ortega y Gasset, *Obras Completas* (Madrid: Revista de Occidente, 1955), 147. ". . . un nuevo cuerpo social íntegro, con su minoría selecta y su muchedumbre."

19. Ortega, *Obras Completas*, 147. "[Cada generación] ha sido lanzada sobre el ámbito de la existencia con una trayectoria vital determinada."

20. Typically, the practitioners of modern Hispanism have been only too happy to distinguish between the "casticism" of the *generación del 98* and the "cosmopolitanism" of the Modernists, thereby perpetuating Azorín's own nationalist vision of his invented literary generation as uniquely "classical" and Spanish. In 1930, Ángel Valbuena Prat split the poets of Restoration Spain into two groups: *modernistas* and *noventayochistas*. In 1931, Dámaso Alonso reiterated the division. In 1934, Pedro Salinas fed the fire by publishing *El problema del modernismo en España o un conflicto entre dos espíritus*. In

1945, Laín Entralgo contributed his *Generación del Noventayocho.* By 1951, the supposed uniqueness of the *generación del 98* had been sufficiently well defended, so as to encourage Díaz-Plaja to publish a study of the debate under the clearly confrontational title, *Modernismo frente a 98.* By so doing, Diaz-Plaja, together with other critics who participated in the debate before him, managed to perpetuate Azorín's nationalist vision of the literary *generación del 98* as a singularly "Spanish" identity.

21. Laín Entralgo, *La generación del noventayocho* (Madrid: Diana, 1945), 444. "Sobre el alma de todos, sépanlo o no lo sepan, gravitará el peso, dulce y desazonante a la vez, del ensueño que inventó en el filo de los siglos XIX y XX una parva gavilla de españoles egregios."

22. Ricardo Gullón, *La invención del 98 y otros ensayos* (Madrid: Gredos, 1969), 7–18.

23. Inman Fox, "Hacia una nueva historia literaria para España," in *Dai Modernismi Alle Avanguardie: Atti del Convengo dell' Associazione degli Ispanisti Italiani* (Palermo: Flaccovio Editor, 1990), 12.

24. For instance, René Rapin concludes, in 1672, that Cervantes' novel is fundamentally an attack on the Duke of Lerma; also in 1688, an anonymous writer determines that Don Quixote is a caricature of Ignatius of Loyola, an interpretation adhered to by Voltaire in the following century. See Dana B. Drake and Dominick Finello. *Criticism on Don Quixote (1790–1893)* (Newark, Delaware: Juan de la Cuesta, 1987), 2.

25. Azcárate, for instance, considers Cervantes to be the initiator, in Spain, of a rational inductive method of inquiry similar to that which Descartes espoused in his "Meditations." Such a view is certainly questionable on grounds of the difference between the Humanist skepticism of Cervantes and the ontological skepticism of Descartes; nevertheless, Azcárate's analogy clearly suggests that Cervantes, like Descartes, is to be considered as a founder of modern self-consciousness. For his part, Campoamor affirms that Cervantes and Goméz de Pereira were the "verdaderos fundadores del psicologismo moderno, son los primeros que intentaron certificarse de su existencia, para partir en sus investigaciones de un principio cierto." See, for these references, Adolfo Bonilla y San Martín, "Don Quijote y el pensamiento español" in *El Ateneo de Madrid en el III Centenario de la Publicación de "El ingenioso hidalgo don Quijote de La Mancha* (Madrid: Imprenta de Bernardo Rodríguez, May 1905), 317–336.

26. The protagonist of *Fortunata y Jacinta,* Maximiliano, is Galdós's quixotic character *par excellence.*

27. Nicolas Díaz de Benjumea. *La estafeta de Urganda: o aviso de Cid Asam-Ouzad Benenjeli sobre el desencanto del Quijote* (London: J. Wertheimer & Co., 1861), 7. "Cervantes ha sido y es el ídolo de todas las Naciones, y como de la España de los Carlos y Felipes, me atrevo a decir que *'no se pone el sol para su fama.'* El *Quixote* es . . . la Biblia en lo profano."

28. Anthony J. Close. *The Romantic Approach to Don Quijote* (London: Cambridge University Press, 1978), 103.

29. Drake and Finello, 14.

30. Benedict Anderson. *Imagined Communities: Reflections on the Origin and Spread of Nationalism* (London: Verso, 1991), 1–46.

31. Drake and Finello, 7.

32. María Cruz Seoane, "La prensa en la época de La Restauración," in *Oratoria y periodismo en la España del Siglo XIX* (Madrid: Fundación Juan March y Editorial Castalia, 1977), 399–423.

33. Anderson 76.

34. Sebastian Balfour, *The End of the Spanish Empire: 1898–1923* (Oxford: Clarendon Press, 1997), 64–91.

35. In this distinction between the inner and outer domains of sovereignty fought over by nationalism I am following, somewhat loosely, the arguments advanced by Partha Chatterjee in his excellent account of anticolonial nationalisms in *The Nation and Its Fragments: Colonial and Postcolonial Histories* (Princeton: Princeton University Press), 1993.

36. For a detailed exposition of the premodern forms of Spanish heroism and their link to Spain's empire-building exploits in the Americas refer to Eduardo Subirats, *El continente vacío: La conquista del Nuevo Mundo y la conciencia moderna* (Mexico: Siglo Veintiuno Editores, 1994), 53–73, 300–320.

37. Manuel de Sandoval, "A Don Quijote," *República de las Letras,* 2 (May 13, 1905), 1.

A Don Quijote

Quebrantada del sepulcro que te encierra,
manchego ilustre, la pesada losa,
y vuelva tu locura generosa
a ser pasmo y asombro de la tierra.

Ya Rocinante, tu corcel de guerra,
te aguarda fiel al borde de la fosa;
monta, enristra la lanza poderosa,
y contra el mal y la injusticia cierra.

¡Sin miedo a que te ultrajen a mansalva
forzados viles y asquerosos cerdos,
sal, como antaño, al despuntar el alba!

¡Vuelve al campo que pueblan tus recuerdos,
a ver si un LOCO regenera y salva la nación
destrozada por los CUERDOS!

38. Francisco Navarro y Ledesma, "Discurso Resumen," in *El Ateneo de Madrid en el III centenario de la publicación de* El ingenioso hidalgo don Quijote de la Mancha, 473–481. "Existe entre nosotros, quizás como no existió nunca, un sentimiento quijotesco, que ha sobrepujado a los siglos, que ha vencido á la derrota . . ."

39. Navarro y Ledesma, 478. "Nuestro sentimiento amoroso hace revivir á Don Quijote . . . Dejemos el Hidalgo que levante la losa de su sepulcro; pero, ¡mucho cuidado!, no vayamos á dejarle que ascienda á los cielos, como el otro Redentor."

40. Navarro y Ledesma, 480. "Matemos á la muerte."

41. Navarro y Ledesma, 479. "Saquemos de la muerte la vida."

42. Eric Hobsbawm. *The Invention of Tradition* (Cambridge: Cambridge University Press, 1993), 281.

43. "América," editorial, *Vida Nueva,* April 16, 1899. "Han pasado los días del odio y deben comenzar los del amor. Ha llegado la hora de que España reconquiste a América, mejor dicho, el corazón de América. Emprendemos una obra de paz; sin ella sería inutil pensar en aquellos mercados para nuestra industria y nuestro comercio."

44. Cited in James D. Fernández, "The Bonds of Patrimony: Cervantes and the New World," *PMLA* 109 (1994): 971. "La fuente del idioma castellano: cuya taza irá orlada con los escudos de todas las naciones de habla castellana."

45. Fernández, "The Bonds of Patrimony," 971. "Los artistas han querido expresar el hecho histórico de la invasión del Nuevo Mundo por nuestro idioma. La relación entre la fuente y el monumento es la siguiente: como Cervantes es la cumbre de nuestra Literatura y el soberano del idioma castellano, sus obras deben aparecer como los principales diseminadores de ese idioma."

46. Delegación Nacional de Prensa y Propaganda, *La Falange y Cataluña* (Madrid, Spain: 1947), 12–13. "España es una unidad de destino en lo universal. Toda conspiración contra esa unidad es repulsiva"; "Tenemos voluntad de imperio . . . España alega su condición de eje espiritual del mundo Hispánico como título de preeminencia en las empresas universales"; "España volverá a buscar su gloria y su riqueza por las rutas del mar."

47. The film "Raza," begins with a dramatic scene in which the protagonist, who symbolizes Franco himself, dies. His death is blamed on the incompetence and lack of patriotism of Restoration Spain's "liberal" politicians.

48. José María Aznar, *La Segunda transición* (Madrid: Espasa Calpe, 1994), 170. "España no es únicamente un país mediterraneo. Su rostro atlántico, que mira a América, no ha tenido la suficiente nitidez a la hora de dibujar nuestra política exterior en los últimos años. Debemos recuperarlo, porque sería un suicidio histórico renunciar o postergar . . . el 'destino transatlántico' de España."

Chapter 1

1. The political career of Antonio Cánovas del Castillo (1828–1897) began with the revolution of 1854, during which time he worked as O'Donnell's undersecretary, helping to draft the *Manifiesto de Manzanares.* This document was designed to give ideological credibility to the so-called *bienio progresista* of 1854–1856. For a lucid study of Cánovas's career as an intellectual and conservative political ideologue, see Jose Luis

Abellán, *Historia crítica del pensamiento español, Tomo V: La crisis contemporánea (1875–1936)* (Madrid: Espasa Calpe 1989).

2. Carolyn Boyd, *Historia Patria: Politics, History, and National Identity in Spain, 1875–1975* (Princeton, NJ: Princeton University Press, 1997), 66.

3. Boyd, 99–100.

4. Boyd, 104.

5. Merry y Colón and Merry Villalba, *Compendio,* cited in Boyd, 109.

6. Boyd, 107.

7. Boyd, 108.

8. Boyd, 102 (the translation is Boyd's).

9. For an analysis of the development of the ILE, see Vicente Cacho Viu, *La Institución Libre de Enseñanza* (Madrid: Rialp, 1962).

10. Boyd, 32.

11. Boyd, 35.

12. Boyd, 143–145.

13. Boyd, 145.

14. Boyd, 145–147.

15. Benjamin Martin, *The Agony of Modernization: Labor and Industrialization in Spain* (Ithaca, NY: Cornell University Press, 1990), 9.

16. Martin, 6.

17. David Miller, *Anarchism* (London: Dent and Sons Ltd., 1984), 125.

18. José Luís Comellas, *Historia de España Contemporánea* (Madrid: Ediciones Rialp, 1988), 333–335.

19. Miller, 136.

20. Martin, 178–194.

21. Miller, 189.

22. Martin, 189–191.

23. See, in this regard, the study of Vicente Marrero *Maeztu* (Madrid: Rialp, 1955), as well as Gonzalo Sobejano's *Nietzsche en España* (Madrid: Gredos, 1967).

24. See, in this respect, Elías Díaz, *Revisión de Unamuno. Análysis crítico de su pensamiento político* (Madrid: Tecnos, 1968).

25. For an unforgiving analysis of the limits of Ortega's republican liberalism see Eduardo Subirats "Las selectas élites de Ortega" *Quimera* 150 (1996), 50–55.

26. Raymond Carr, *Modern Spain: 1875–1980* (Oxford: Oxford University Press, 1980), 65.

27. Martin, 232–234.

28. Shlomo Ben-Ami, *Fascism from Above* (Oxford: Oxford University Press, 1983).

29. Antonio Ramos Oliviera, *Politics, Economics and Men in Modern Spain: 1808–1946* (London: V. Gollancz, 1946), 197–210.

30. Josep Fontana and Jordi Nadal, "Spain, 1914–1970," in *Fontana Economic History of Europe* (London: Collins/Fontana Books, 1976), quoted in Martin, 266.

31. Among the more important titles of this period are: Valentín Almirall's 1886 *L'Espagne telle qu'elle est;* Pompeyo Gener's 1887 *Herejías;* Joaquín Sánchez de la Toca's 1887 *La crisis agraria europea y sus remedios en España;* Mallada's 1890 *Los males de la patria y la futura revolución española;* Picavea's 1891 *El problema nacional: Hechos, causas, remedios* and Joaquín Costa's pre-imperial demise 1898 *Colectivismo agrario en España.*

32. Unión Nacional was divided by contradictions. Some delegates represented agrarian sectors close to the oligarchy that were content to stir up pressure on the government to protect agrarian interests. Others preferred to create a new, more radical party that might do considerably more damage to the interests of the entrenched parties. See Balfour, 74.

33. Balfour, 75.

34. Comellas, 324.

35. Shlomo Ben-Ami, 237–255.

36. Joaquín Costa, *Oligarquía y Caciquismo; Colectivismo agrario y otros ensayos* (Madrid: Alianza Editorial, 1992), 22. "La libertad se había hecho papel, sí, pero no se había hecho carne."

37. Costa, 24. "Oligarquías de personajes sin ninguna raíz en la opinión ni más fuerza que la puramente material . . ."

38. Costa, 20–21. "La nación sigue viviendo sin leyes, sin garantías, sin tribunales, sujeta al mismo degradante yugo de aquel feudalismo inorgánico que mantiene a España separada de Europa por toda la distancia de una edad histórica."

39. Costa, 21. "Una revisión del movimiento revolucionario de 1868."

40. Costa, 25. "La aristocracia, entendida . . . a la manera aristotélica sería legítima en nuestro país; más aún, siéntese vivamente la necesidad de ella."

41. Joaquín Costa, *Oligaquía y caciquismo como la fórmula actual de gobierno en España: urgencia y modo de cambiarla. Información en el Ateneo Científico y Literario de Madrid sobre dicho tema* (Madrid: Imprenta de los Hijos de M. G. Hernández, 1902) 82. "Esa política quirúrgica . . . tiene que ser cargo personal de un cirujano de hierro, que conduzca bien la anatomía del pueblo español y sienta por él una compasión infinita."

42. Balfour, op. cit., 90.

43. Costa, *Oligarquía . . . y otros ensayos,* 219.

44. Azorín, "Generaciones de escritores," 1912. Miguel de Unamuno: "Sobre la tumba de Costa," 1911. Ortega: "La herencia viva de Costa," 1911. Giménez Caballero: "Interpretación de dos profetas: Joaquín Costa y Alfredo Oriani," 1931.

45. José Luís Abellán. *Historia crítica del pensamiento español,* vol. 5.1 (Madrid: Espasa Calpe, 1989), 467–482. See also, in regard to *costismo,* the seminal work of Enrique Tierno Galván, "Costa y el regeneracionismo," *Escritos* (Madrid: Editorial Tecnos) 1971.

46. Costa. *Oligarquía . . . y otros ensayos,* 171–172. "La humanidad terrestre necesita una raza española grande y poderosa, contrapuesta a la raza sajona, para sostener el equilibrio moral en el juego infinito de la historia: no correspondería a la grandeza de la habitación terráquea la grandeza del inquilino hombre, si al lado del Sancho británico [Robinson Crusoe] no se irguiese puro, luminoso, soñador, el Quijote español, llenando el mundo con sus locuras, afirmando a través de los siglos la utopía de la Edad de Oro, y manteniendo perenne aquí abajo esa caballería espiritual que cree en algo, que siente pasión por algo, que se sacrifica por algo, y que con esa pasión y con esa fe y con ese sacrificio hace que la tierra sea algo más que una factoría y que un mercado donde se compra y se vende."

47. Lucas Mallada, *Los males de la patria* (Madrid: Alianza, 1969), 42. "[Los males de la patria] . . . serán cuestión de latitud geográfica . . . influirán nuestras discordias civiles, tan largo tiempo sostenidas, e influirá . . . la pobreza de nuestro suelo; pero son de todo el mundo conocidas . . . nuestra insigne pereza, nuestra afrentosa indolencia, nuestra grande apatía."

48. Miguel de Unamuno, *En torno al casticimo* (1895; Madrid: Alianza, 1986), 48. "Si Castilla ha hecho la nación española, ésta ha ido españolizándose cada vez más."

49. Unamuno, *En torno,* 57. "Un paisaje uniforme y monótono . . . sobre que se extiende el azul intentísimo del cielo."

50. Unamuno, *En torno,* 58. "Es, si cabe decirlo, más que panteístico, un paisaje monoteístico este campo infinito en que, sin perderse, se achica el hombre, y en que siente en medio de las sequías de los campos sequedades del alma."

51. Unamuno, *En torno,* 66. "Un realismo vulgar y tosco y un idealismo seco y formulario, que caminan juntos, asociados, como don Quijote y Sancho."

52. Azorín. *La ruta de Don Quijote* (1905; Madrid: Biblioteca Renacimiento, 1915), 48. "¿No es este el medio en que han nacido y se han desarrollado las grandes voluntades, fuertes, poderosas, tremendas, pero solitarias, anárquicas, de aventureros, navegantes, conquistadores?"

53. Miguel de Unamuno, *Vida de Don Quijote y Sancho* (1905; Madrid: Espasa-Calpe, 1985), 53, 104–105. "Nuestros Sanchos de hoy buscan ante todo eso que llaman soluciones concretas . . . ¡Soluciones concretas! ¡Oh Sanchos prácticos, Sanchos positivos, Sanchos materiales! ¿Cuándo oiréis la silenciosa música de las esferas espirituales? . . . nuestra patria no tendrá agricultura, ni industria, ni comercio, ni habrá aquí caminos que lleven a parte adonde merezca irse mientras no descubramos nuestro cristianismo, el quijotesco."

54. Miguel de Unamuno, *Del sentimiento trágico* (Madrid: Alianza, 1993), 36. "[A]caso la enfermedad misma sea la condición esencial de lo que llamamos progreso, y el progreso mismo una enfermedad."

55. José Ortega y Gasset, *España invertebrada* (1922; Madrid: Revista de Occidente en Alianza Editorial, 1992), 112.

Chapter 2

1. Eric Hobsbawm, *Nations and Nationalism since 1780: Programme, Myth, Reality* (Cambridge: Cambridge University Press, 1990), 10.

2. "Decadencia," editorial, *Vida Nueva* October 30, 1898, 21. "Esa lepra cuyo nombre sólo mancha el papel en que se estampa."

3. José Ortega y Gasset, *Obras Completas,* vol. 1 (Madrid: Alianza Editorial, 1983), 551. "El decadentismo, el arte de decaer, es fatal para quien teme haber caído ya como nosostros."

4. Unamuno, *En torno,* 33.

5. Angel Ganivet, *Idearium Español con el porvenir de España* (1897; Madrid: Espasa Calpe, 1990), 46. "Fuerza madre, algo fuerte e indestructible, como un eje diamantino."

6. Ramiro de Maeztu, *Defensa de la Hispanidad* (Madrid: 1946), 20. "El ímpetu sagrado de que se han de nutrir los pueblos que ya tienen valor universal es su corriente histórica. Es el camino que Dios señala. Y fuera de la vía, no hay sino extravíos."

7. Ortega, *España invertebrada,* 113. "Radical perversión de los instintos sociales."

8. Miguel de Unamuno, *Obras Completas* (Madrid: Escelicer, 1968), 926–928. "Debo confesar que cuanto más en ello medito, más descubro la íntima repugnancia que mi espíritu siente hacia todo lo que pasa por principios directores del espíritu europeo moderno, hacia la ortodoxia científica de hoy, hacia sus métodos, hacia sus tendencias . . . [L]a ciencia . . . busca los medios de prolongar, acrecentar, facilitar, ensanchar y hacer llevadera y grata la vida . . . [busca] la felicidad."

9. Unamuno, *Obras,* 926. "[C]on el descubrimiento de América y nuestro entrometimiento en los negocios europeos, nos vimos arrastrados en la corriente de los demás pueblos. Y entró en España la poderosa corriente del Renacimiento, y nos fue borrando el alma medieval. Y el Renacimiento era en el fondo todo eso: ciencia . . . y vida. Y se pensó menos en la muerte, y se fue disipando la sabiduría mística."

10. Unamuno, *Obras,* 929. "La verdadera vida es una preparación para la muerte."

11. Unamuno, *Obras,* 927. "El objeto de la ciencia es la vida, y el objeto de la sabiduría es la muerte."

12. Refer, in this respect, to the survey of Nietzsche's reception in modern Spain that Gonzalo Sobejano presents in his book *Nietzsche en España* (Madrid: Editorial Gredos, S.A., 1967).

13. Maeztu, *Defensa* 48. "Vivir es . . . llenarse de angustia ante la contingencia de dejar de ser."

14. J. Francos Rodriguez, "La mendicidad," *La República de las Letras* 1. (6 May, 1905) 2. "la mendicidad [que] se ha generalizado como sistema en la vida española."

15. Enrique Lluria, "Pueblos vivos y pueblos moribundos," *Vida Nueva* (10 July, 1898).

16. Enrique Lluria, "La voluntad nacional enferma," *Vida Nueva* (August 14, 1898) "los muertos gobiernan a los vivos."

17. Ricardo Burguete, "Hombres resuletos," *La República de las Letras* (6 June, 1905), 3.

18. Maeztu, *Defensa,* 23. "[Una] empresa evangélica [que creó] la unidad física del mundo" and "la unidad moral del género humano."

19. Maeztu, *Defensa,* 21–22. "La necesidad urgente del mundo entero . . . es que resucite y se extienda por todo el haz de la tierra aquél espíritu español, que consideraba a todos hombres como hermanos . . . Así la obra de España, lejos de ser ruínas y polvo, es . . . una sinfonía interrumpida, que está pidiendo los músicos que sepan continuarla."

20. Ramiro de Maeztu, *Authority, Liberty and Function* (London: George Allen & Unwin, 1916).

21. Maeztu, *Authority,* 204–211.

22. Burguete, 3. "Si algo influye en nuestras vacilaciones es el exceso de cerebralidad. No necesitamos hombres vacilantes; necesitamos hombres resueltos."

23. Unamuno, *Del sentimiento trágico,* 276. "¡[Q]ue inventen ellos! Ellos a la ciencia de que nos aprovecharemos; nosotros, a lo nuestro."

24. Unamuno, *Del sentimiento trágico,* 295. "Cuál es, pues, la nueva misión de Don Quijote hoy en este mundo? Clamar, clamar en el desierto."

25. Unamuno, *Del sentimiento trágico,* 293. "Don Quijote . . . como no es pesimista, como cree en la vida eterna, tiene que pelear, arremetiendo contra la ortodoxia inquisitorial científica moderna por traer una nueva e imposible Edad Media, dualística, contradictoria, apasionada . . . El mundo tiene que ser como Don Quijote quiere."

CHAPTER 3

1. Ganivet and Unamuno exchanged a series of open letters, originally published under the title "El porvenir de España" in which they debated with one another not only their respective views concerning modern Spain's decadence and need for regeneration but the role that Don Quixote was to play in the nation's future regeneration.

2. Ganivet, *Idearium,* 169. "El origen de nuestra decadencia y actual postración, se halla en nuestro exceso de acción, en haber acometido empresas enormemente desproporcionadas con nuestro poder."

3. Ganivet, *Idearium,* 105. "Apenas constituida la nación, nuestro espíritu se sale del cauce que le estaba marcado y se derrama por todo el mundo en busca de glorias

exteriores y vanas, quedando la nación convertida en un cuartel de reserva, en un hospital de inválidos, en un semillero de mendigos."

4. Ganivet, *Idearium,* 170. "La sumisión de grandes masas de hombres a una inteligencia directriz."

5. Ganivet, *Idearium,* 45. "Muchas veces reflexionando sobre el apasionamiento con que en España ha sido defendido y proclamado el dogma de la Concepción Inmaculada, se me ha ocurrido pensar que en el fondo de ese dogma debía de haber algún misterio que por ocultos caminos se enlazara con el misterio de nuestra alma nacional; que acaso ese dogma era el símbolo, ¡símbolo admirable!, de nuestra propia vida, en la que tras larga y penosa labor de maternidad, venimos a hallarnos a la vejez con el espíritu virgen; como una mujer que, atraída por irresistible vocación a la vida monástica y ascética y casada contra su voluntad y convertida en madre por deber, llegara a cabo de sus días a descubrir que su espíritu era ajeno a su obra, que entre los hijos de la carne el alma continuaba sola, abierta como una rosa mística a los ideales de la virginidad."

6. Ganivet, *Idearium,* 46. "Algo fuerte e indestructible, como un eje diamantino . . . firme y erguido."

7. Ganivet, *Idearium,* 65. "En presencia de la ruina espiritual de España, hay que ponerse una piedra en el sitio donde está el corazón, y hay que arrojar aunque sea un millón de españoles a los lobos, si no queremos arrojarnos todos a los puercos."

8. Ganivet, *Idearium,* 49. "Hay que confundirlos a todos, conmoldearlos por medio de un fuego ardiente, que venga de muy alto y que destruyendo construya, y abrasando purifique."

9. Ganivet, *Idearium,* 104.

10. Ganivet, *Idearium,* 66–74.

11. Ganivet, *Idearium,* 77. "Una serie inacabable de invasiones y de expulsiones, una guerra permanente de independencia."

12. Ganivet, *Idearium,* 72, 77–79. "Guerrillero que trabajaba por cuenta propia."

13. Angel Ganivet, *Conquista del Reino de Maya* (1895; Madrid: Planeta, 1988), 229–237.

14. Ganivet, *Idearium,* 79. "No son conquistadores quienes sirven un breve tiempo en una colonia por obtener riquezas u honores, sino quienes conquistan por necesidad, espontáneamente, por impulso natural hacia la independencia."

15. Angel Ganivet, "¡Ñaññň!," *Vida Nueva* (October 16, 1898). "Para civilizar pueblos se imponen creencias en que no se puede creer, y se dan leyes que nadie podrá obedecer, y entre tantos civilizadores necios y filantrópicos de la rutina, no aparece jamás un verdadero hombre que, sin ideas vanas, mire con ojos de amor a un semejante suyo embrutecido o abyecto, y después de ver lo que dentro hay y lo que de allí puede sinceramente nacer a la vida espiritual, hunda sus dedos con fuerza y aún con crueldad, si fuese necesario, e infunda, por la virtud de la naturaleza, no por la de ideas convencionales, vida nueva en la arcilla humana."

16. Ganivet, *La conquista,* 230. "Quizá nuestra patria hubiera sido más dichosa si, reservándose la pura gloria de sus heroicas empresas, hubiera dejado a otras gentes más prácticas la misión de poblar las tierras descubiertas y conquistadas, y el cuidado de todos los bajos menesteres de la colonización."

17. Ganivet, *Idearium,* 147. "Colonizar no es ir al negocio, sino civilizar pueblos y dar expansión a las ideas."

18. Ganivet, *Idearium,* 156.

19. Ganivet, *Idearium,* 89. "Este español está autorizado para hacer lo que le dé la gana."

20. Ganivet, *Idearium,* 82. "La guerra civilizada . . . profundamente egoista y salvaje."

21. Ganivet, *Idearium,* 82.

22. Ganivet, *Idearium,* 89. "Obras magistrales creadas por los maestros y una rápida degradación provocada por la audacia y desenfado de los apréndices"

23. Ganivet, *Idearium,* 104.

24. Ganivet, *Idearium,* 162–164.

25. Ganivet, *Idearium,* 169.

26. Ganivet, *Idearium,* 177. "El individualismo indisciplinado que hoy nos debilita y nos impide levantar cabeza ha de ser algún día individualismo interno y creador, y ha de conducirnos a nuestro gran triunfo ideal."

27. The example of Santa Teresa is paradigmatic in this regard. As James Fernández points out "Santa Teresa's *Vida* is, in part, a document solicited by her personal confessors and, ultimately, by the Inquisition." In other words, as a piece of confessional writing, her autobiography is an "internal juridification of religious law" not unlike the purifying discipline that Ganivet would have every member of the Spanish nation fulfill in the name of national unity. James Fernández, *Apology to Apostrophe* (Durham: Duke University Press, 1992), 12.

28. Ganivet, *Idearium,* 98.

29. Ganivet, *Idearium,* 147.

30. Ganivet, *Idearium,* 155. "Hay que cerrar con cerrojos, llaves y candados todas las puertas por donde el espíritu español se escapó de España para derramarse por los cuatro puntos del horizonte . . . y en cada de esas puertas . . . pondremos un rótulo que diga . . . imitando a San Agustín: *Noli foras ire; in interiore Hispaniae habitat veritas.*"

31. Ganivet, *Idearium,* 158. "Una nación fundadora de numerosas nacionalidades logra, tras un largo período de decadencia, reconstituirse como fuerza política animada por nuevos sentimientos de expansión: ¿qué forma ha de tomar esta segunda evolución para enlazarse con la primera y no romper la unidad histórica a que una y otra deben de subordinarse?"

32. Ganivet, *Idearium,* 158–159. "El problema . . . que España ha de resolver no tiene precedentes claros y precisos en la historia . . . si por el sólo esfuerzo de nues-

tra inteligencia lográsemos reconstituir la unión familiar de todos los pueblos hispánicos, e infundir en ellos el culto de unos mismos ideales, de nuestros ideales, cumpliríamos una gran misión histórica y daríamos vida a una creación, grande, original, nueva en los fastos políticos; y al cumplir esa misión . . . trabajaríamos por nuestros intereses, por intereses más trascendentales que la conquista de unos cuantos pedazos de territorio."

33. Ganivet, *Idearium,* 177. "Tipo [que] encarna . . . [las] propias cualidades [de la nación] . . . Nuestro Ulises."

34. Ganivet, *Idearium,* 177. "Metamorfosis espiritual . . . acción es una inacabable creación."

35. Ganivet, *Idearium,* 177. "Preocupaciones materiales"; "descarg[ar] sobre un escudero."

36. Ganivet, *Idearium,* 178. "Ulises anglosajón, Robinson Crusoe."

37. Ganivet, *Idearium,* 178. "Ingenioso solamente para luchar con la naturaleza; es capaz de reconstruir una civilización material; . . . aspira al mando, al gobierno 'exterior' de otros hombres; pero su alma carece de expresión y no sabe entenderse con otras almas."

38. Ganivet, *Idearium,* 178. "Aptitudes naturales . . . para la creación ideal"; "al renacer hallaremos una inmensidad de pueblos hermanos a quienes marcar con el sello de nuestro espíritu."

39. Ganivet, *Idearium,* 178. "Sancho Panza . . . podría ser Robinson; y Robinson, en caso de apuro, aplacaría su aire de superioridad y se avendría a ser escudero de don Quijote."

40. Ganivet, *Idearium,* 178.

CHAPTER 4

1. Unamuno, *En torno,* 21. "Suele buscarse la verdad completa en el justo medio . . . por exclusión de los extremos . . . y asi solo se llega a una sombra de la verdad, fría y nebulosa. Es preferible, creo, seguir otro método: el de la afirmación alternativa de los contradictorios; es preferible hacer resaltar la fuerza de los extremos en el alma del lector para que el medio tome en ella vida, que es resultante de lucha."

2. Unamuno, *En torno,* 21.

3. For a thoughtful comparison of Unamuno and Kierkegaard see Alison Sinclair, "Concepts of Tragedy in Unamuno and Kierkegaard," in *Re-reading Unamuno,* ed. Nicholas G. Round (Glasgow: University of Glasgow Department of Hispanic Studies, 1989), 121–138.

4. Unamuno, *En torno,* 140.

5. A recent example of this long-standing tradition among Unamuno scholars is Inman Fox' *La invención de España* (Madrid: Ediciones Cátedra, 1997), 112–123.

6. Unamuno, *En torno,* 12. "En estas páginas están en gérmenes los más de mis trabajos posteriores . . . Escribí estas páginas antes del desastre de Cuba y Filipinas, antes del encontranazo entre Robinson y Don Quijote . . . Al releer lo que escribí entonces, para correjir las pruebas de imprenta, me encuentro con afirmaciones y juicios que no quiero pasen sin cierto correctivo."

7. Cited in Keith Hansen, *Tragic Lucidity* (New York: Peter Lang, 1993, 52).

8. Unamuno, *Del sentimiento trágico,* 278.

9. Unamuno, *Del sentimiento trágico,* 278. "Aquella hórrida literatura regeneracionista . . . que provocó la pérdida de nuestras últimas colonias americanas . . . En esa ridícula literatura . . . yo di un ¡muera Don Quijote!, y de esta blasfemia, que quería decir todo lo contrario que decía—así estábamos entonces—brotó mi *Vida de Don Quijote y Saancho* y mi culto al quijotismo como religión nacional."

10. See, in this regard, Carlos Blanco Aguinaga's *Unamuno, teórico de lenguaje* (Mexico: El Colegio México, 1954).

11. Martin Nozick, *Miguel de Unamuno* (New York: Twayne Publishers, 1971), 37.

12. The emphasis is my own.

13. Unamuno, loc. cit.

14. Unamuno, *En torno,* 33. "Gran anarquistas."

15. Unamuno, *En torno,* 21. "Elévanse a diario en España quejas porque la cultura extraña nos invade y arrastra o ahoga lo castizo, y va zapando poco a poco, según dicen los quejosos, nuestra personalidad nacional."

16. Unamuno, *En torno,* 22–23. "despreciadores sistemáticos de lo castizo y lo propio . . . en el seno de la confianza, revelan hiperbólicamente sus deseos . . . exclamando: *¡Que nos conquisten!.*"

17. Unamuno, *En torno,* 140, 142. "Europeizarnos y chapuzarnos en pueblo . . . teniendo fe en que no perderemos nuestra personalidad al hacerlo."

18. Unamuno, *En torno,* 23–24. "Lo mismo los que piden que cerremos o poco menos las fronteras y pongamos puertas al campo, que los que piden más o menos explícitamente que nos conquisten, se salen de la verdadera realidad de las cosas, de la eterna y honda realidad, arrastrados por el espíritu de anarquismo que llevamos todos en el meollo del alma."

19. Unamuno, *En torno,* 36. "Asi como es la vanidad individual tan estúpida que, con tal de originalizarse y distinguirse por algo, cifran muchos su orgullo en ser más brutos que los demás, del mismo modo hay pueblos que se vanaglorian de sus defectos . . . Los españoles caemos . . . en este pecado."

20. Unamuno, *Obras Completas,* 284. "¡La envidia! Ésta, ésta es la terrible plaga de nuestras sociedades [Hispánicas]; ésta es la íntima gangrena del alma española . . . Es la envidia, es la sangre de Caín más que otra cosa, lo que nos ha hecho descontentadizos, insurrectos y belicosos."

21. José Luis Abellán, introduction, *Able Sánchez*, by Miguel de Unamuno (Madrid: Editorial Castalia, 1990), 9–42.

22. Unamuno, *Abel Sánchez*, 35, 33. "Consciente . . . [de] lo que en el pueblo es inconsciente."

23. Unamuno, *Abel Sánchez*, 35. "Guiarle así mejor [al pueblo]."

24. In a 1910 essay titled "Educación por la Historia," Unamuno writes: "no acierto a explicarme un sólido patriotismo sin una cierta base religiosa. Claro que no quiero decir precisamente base dogmática de una Iglesia determinada, sino que no me explico una patria que sea tal, un pueblo que tenga un cierto vislumbre de su misión y papel en el mundo no siendo que su conciencia colectiva responda, aunque sea por manera oscura, a los grandes y eternos problemas humanos de nuestra finalidad última y nuestro destino. Lo que da más fuerza al ardiente y místico patriotismo . . . es su fuerte base religiosa." Here, as in his definition of the intrahistorical as the source for spiritual national transformation and redemption from anarchistic sin, Unamuno stresses the religious and reductive character of what he calls the nation's mystical philosophy. Unamuno, *Obras Completas*, 541.

25. Unamuno, *En torno*, 40–41. "Mientras no sea la historia una confesión de un examen de conciencia . . . no habrá salvación para nosotros . . . Por el examen de su conciencia histórica penetran [los hombres] en su intra-historia y se hallan de veras."

26. Unamuno, *En torno*, 41.

27. Unamuno, *En torno*, 24.

28. Unamuno, *En torno*, 88. "Bajo la previsión de invasores."

29. Unamuno, *En torno*, 88.

30. Unamuno, *En torno*, 88. "Norma y dique de anarquía."

31. Unamuno, *En torno*, 94. "Método para ganar el cielo."

32. Unamuno, *En torno*, 51. "Siguiendo el espíritu de conquista . . . la idea del unitarismo conquistador, de la *catolización* del mundo . . . Castilla . . . llevó a cabo la expulsión de los moros . . . y clavó la cruz castellana en Granada, poco después descubrieron un Nuevo Mundo . . . y se siguió todo lo que el lector conoce."

33. Unamuno, *En torno*, 102. "Asenta[ndo] la individualidad sobre la renuncia de ella misma."

34. Unamuno, *En torno*, 53.

35. Unamuno, *En torno*, 54. "Nuestra literatura clásica castiza brotó cuando se había iniciado la decadencia."

36. Unamuno, *En torno*, 54. "Este Alonso Quijano, que por sus virtudes y a pesar de sus locuras mereció el dictado de el Bueno, es el fondo eterno y permanente de los héroes de [España]."

37. Unamuno, *Del sentimiento trágico*, 270.

38. Unamuno, *Del sentimiento trágico*, 270.

39. In a vividly descriptive passage, Unamuno bids his reader to imagine death as follows: "Recójete, lector, en ti mismo, y figúrate un lento deshacerte de ti mismo, en que la luz se te apague, se te enmudezcan las cosas y no te den sonido, envolviéndote en silencio, se te derritan de entre las manos los objetos asideros, se te escurra de bajo los pies el piso, se te desvanezcan como en desmayo los recuerdos, se te vaya disipando todo en nada, y disipándote también tú, y ni aun la conciencia de la nada te quede siquiera como fantástico agarradero de una sombra." Unamuno, *Del sentimiento trágico,* 56.

40. Unamuno, *Del sentimiento trágico,* 63. "Ante este terrible misterio de la mortalidad el hombre adopta distintas actitudes y busca por varios modos consolarse de haber nacido."

41. In this respect, Unamuno writes: "El ansia de no morir, el hambre de inmortalidad personal . . . es la base afectiva de todo conocer"; elsewhere he adds "El dolor es el camino de la conciencia, y es por él cómo los seres vivos llegan a tener conciencia de sí [a la cual] . . . se llega . . . por el dolor . . . del propio límite." Unamuno, *Del sentimiento trágico,* 51, 141.

42. Unamuno, *Del sentimiento trágico,* 72. "El descubrimiento de la muerte es el que nos revela a Dios, y la muerte del hombre perfecto, del Cristo, fué la suprema revelación de la muerte, la del hombre que no debía morir y murió."

43. Unamuno, *Del sentimiento trágico,* 73.

44. Unamuno, *Del sentimiento trágico,* 86. "La solución católica a nuestro problema, de nuestro único problema vital, del problema de la inmortalidad y la salvación eterna del alma individual, satisface a la voluntad y, por tanto, a la vida; pero . . . no satisface a la razón."

45. Unamuno, *Del sentimiento trágico,* 81. "Es lo vital que [el catolicismo] afirma, y para afirmarse crea, sirviéndose de lo racional, su enemigo, toda una construcción dogmática, y la Iglesia la defiende contra racionalismo, contra protestantismo y contra modernismo. Defiende la vida."

46. Unamuno, *Del sentimiento trágico,* 83. "La tradición y la revelación de la palabra de Dios."

47. Unamuno, *Del sentimiento trágico,* 83–84. "La fe no se siente segura ni con el consentimiento de los demás, ni con la tradición, ni bajo la autoridad . . . el apoyo de su enemiga la razón."

48. Unamuno, *Del sentimiento trágico,* 86. "Así se hizo la dogmática católica un sistema de contradicciones, mejor o peor concordadas . . . [que] no satisface la razón. Y ésta tiene sus exigencias, tan imperiosas como las de la vida."

49. Unamuno, *Del sentimiento trágico,* 84. "Teología . . . no es sino cristianismo despotencializado."

50. Unamuno, *Del sentimiento trágico,* 270. "A *desenciar* . . . esto es, a descatolizar a Europa, han contribuído el Renacimiento, la Reforma y la Revolución, sustituyendo aquel ideal de una vida eterna ultraterrena por el ideal del progreso, de la razón, de la ciencia."

51. Unamuno, *Del sentimiento trágico*, 271. "La famosa *maladie du siècle* . . . no . . . es otra cosa que la pérdida de la fe en la inmortalidad del alma, en la finalidad humana del Universo."

52. Unamuno, *Del sentimiento trágico*, 52.

53. Unamuno, *Del sentimiento trágico*, 36. "Acaso la enfermedad misma sea la condición esencial de lo que llamamos progreso, y el progreso mismo una enfermedad."

54. Unamuno, *Del sentimiento trágico*, 40. "Primariamente al servicio del instinto de conservación personal"

55. Unamuno, *Del sentimiento trágico*, 292.

56. Unamuno, *Del sentimiento trágico*, 112. "Ni . . . el anhelo vital de inmortalidad humana halla confirmación racional, ni tampoco la razón nos da aliciente y consuelo de vida y verdadera finalidad a ésta. Mas he aquí que en el fondo del abismo se encuentran la desesperación sentimental y volitiva y el escepticismo racional frente a frente, y se abrazan como hermanos. Y va a ser de este abrazo, un abrazo trágico . . . de donde va a brotar manantial de vida, de una vida seria y terrible."

57. Unamuno, *Del sentimiento trágico*, 283. "Tragedia de Cristo, la tragedia divina."

58. Unamuno, *Del sentimiento trágico*, 283. "La tragedia humana, intrahumana . . . de Don Quijote."

59. Unamuno's "tragic sense" is agonic, as Ferrater Mora has noted, in that it justifies life in terms of the painful struggle, or battle, against death, and not in terms of an affirmation of the grandeur and dignity, joy and pleasure that are possible in human life: life conceived as an agonic struggle is life as a "lucha . . . entre dos series de contendientes: la voluntad de ser, y la sospecha de que se puede dejar de ser; el sentimiento y el pensamiento; la duda y la fe; la certidumbre y la incertidumbre; la esperanza y la desesperación; la cabeza y el corazón o . . . la razón . . . y la vida." Ferrater Mora *Unamuno: Bosquejo de una filosofía* (Madrid: Alianza Editorial, 1985), 41.

60. Paul Ilie, for instance, considers that Unamuno "anticipates the more systematic—and less vital—analyses of Heidegger, Buber, Jaspers, and Sartre. Although the latter have been recognized as the leaders of modern existentialism, Unamuno wrote well in advance of [their developing] their philosophies, and specifically enough to be considered more than just a precursor." Paul Ilie, *An Existential View of Self and Society* (Madison: The University of Wisconsin Press, 1967), 4. For other, more recent studies of Unamuno's purported "existentialism" refer to: Frances Wyers, *Miguel de Unamuno: The Contrary Self* (London: Tamesis, 1977) and Keith W. Hansen, *Tragic Lucidity*.

61. Friedrich Nietzsche. *The Birth of Tragedy* (New York: Vintage Books, 1967), 141–143.

62. Nietzsche, 140.

63. Unamuno, *Del sentimiento trágico*, 253. "Imitar a Cristo es tomar cada uno su cruz . . . como Cristo tomó la suya."

64. Unamuno, *Del sentimiento trágico*, 268.

65. Unamuno, *Del sentimiento trágico,* 288.

66. Unamuno, *Del sentimiento trágico,* 267. "Lo que llamo el sentimiento trágico de la vida en los hombres y en los pueblos es . . . nuestro sentimiento trágico de la vida, la de los españoles y el pueblo español."

67. Unamuno, *Del sentimiento trágico,* 272: "¡Europa! . . . cuando me pongo a escudriñar lo que llaman Europa nuestros europeizantes, paréceme a veces que queda fuera de ella mucho de lo periférico—España, desde luego, Inglaterra, Italia, Escandinavia, Rusia—y que se reduce a lo central, a Franco-Alemania, con sus anejos y dependencias."

68. In this regard, Keith Hansen has noted how "the unacknowledged goal behind the elaboration of a tragic human condition [in *Del sentimiento trágico de la vida*] is the attempt to transcend some historically engendered loss [the loss of empire] through a metaphysical abstraction of this loss, thereby recuperating it within a hypostatized 'tragic.'" Hansen, *Tragic Lucidity,* 49–50.

69. Unamuno, *Del sentimiento trágico,* 283. "La tragedia de Cristo, la tragedia divina, es la de la cruz. Pilato, el escéptico . . . quiso convertirla por la burla en sainete, e ideó aquella farsa del . . . '¡He aquí el hombre!'; pero el pueblo, más humano que él, el pueblo que busca tragedia, gritó: '¡Crucifícale! ¡Crucifícale!.' Y la otra tragedia, la tragedia humana . . . es la de Don Quijote."

Chapter 5

1. Although originally published in English, this book reappeared in Spanish in 1919 under the title *La crisis del humanismo.*

2. Ramiro de Maeztu, *Hacia otra España* (1899; Madrid: Ediciones Rialp, 1956), 39–41. "Parálisis, no de otra suerte puede calificarse ese amortiguamiento continuado de la vida colectiva nacional . . . Parálisis . . . Así se explica la espantosa indiferencia del país hacia los negocios públicos . . . Parálisis intelectual . . . Parálisis moral . . . Parálisis imaginativa . . . España prefiere su carrito de paralítica, llevado atrás y adelante por el vaivén de los sucesos ciegos, al rudo trabajo de rehacer su voluntad y enderezarse."

3. Maeztu, *Hacia otra España,* 253.

4. As Maeztu sees it, this notion derives from classical deductive reasoning: "Sucede que al abstraernos para pensar sobre las cosas las vemos en estado de reposo y lo primero que de ellas se destaca es su aparente coexistencia armónica. Si nos imaginamos . . . una ciudad . . . notamos que cada cosa ocupa su lugar, sin que se estorben las unas a las otras . . . De ello inferimos que la armonía y el orden es una ley anterior a las cosas. Y de ahí la noción de la justicia, ¿pues qué otra cosa es la justicia sino la armonía de las cosas aplicada a los hechos humanos, la coexistencia armónica de los hombres?" Maeztu, *Hacia otra España,* 231.

5. "No pensamos en que ese reposo de las cosas es puramente imaginario y aparente. No advertimos que se están moviendo y que en ellas y dentro de ellas los áto-

mos se juntan y disgregan con velocidad inaudita. No pensamos en que esa coexistencia armónica es una pura fantasía, un resultado de la imperfección de nuestros sentidos, incapaces . . . de seguir el movimiento . . . y condenados a representárnoslo . . . en reposo." Maeztu, *Hacia otra España,* 232.

6. Maeztu, *Hacia otra España,* 232. "Las cosas no se armonizan . . . cada minuto devora al precedente, cada vida es el resultado de infinitas muertes, y si de esa brutalidad suprema . . . pudiera inferirse alguna ley fundamental ¡sería la del asesinato!"

7. Maeztu, *Hacia otra España,* 231. "De ahí nuestro desencanto al comprobarnos la experiencia que esa armonía no se realiza, de ahí nuestro ajetreo en busca de una fórmula que la realice . . ."

8. Maeztu, *Hacia otra España,* 229. "Lo que se llama justicia para con los débiles es y será siempre, siempre, caridad—yo diría abdicación—del poderoso."

9. Maeztu, *Hacia otra España,* 233. "Instinto de . . . asociación y defensa mutuas," "entes de razón, fantasmas librescos."

10. Maeztu, *Hacia otra España,* 121. "España tenía que decir 'sí' a la guerra, porque nuestra razón de ser siempre ha sido la lucha y no íbamos a desmentirnos en la hora suprema."

11. Maeztu, *Hacia otra España,* 121. "Quiero . . . que nuestra caída sea bella; quiero . . . que si no hemos sabido decir 'sí' a la vida, sepamos decírselo a la muerte, haciéndola gloriosa, digna de España."

12. Maeztu, *Hacia otra España,* 121–122. "Agonía repugnante del condenado que . . . desmintiendo la leyenda de su valor . . . deshonra . . . el prestigio de la muerte."

13. Maeztu, *Hacia otra España,* 138. "Después del dolor, es necesario un heroísmo más tenaz y más intenso para decirle 'sí' a la vida, que para decírselo a la muerte."

14. Ramiro de Maeztu, *El sentido reverencial del dinero* (Madrid: Editorial Nacional, 1957), 302. "Hombres poderosos y tenaces, de voluntad inquebrantable"; "En las raíces de la vida económica se encuentra siempre la moral. La economía es espíritu. El dinero es espíritu."

15. The problem with Spain's economy, as Maeztu sees it, is that it lacks unity. While the economy of the northern coastal regions of Catalonia and the Basque Countries is capitalist and industrial, the remainder of the country, particularly the interior region of Castille, is still a backward agricultural economy in need of modernization. Maeztu's vision, not unlike that of Joaquín Costa per his "política hidráulica," is to unite the two economies into a single national economy by means of a modernizing, capitalistic reconquest of Castille's agriculture: "La industrialización del patrio suelo es, ante todo, un gran negocio. ¿Quien duda que . . . la nueva España, [está] en esas llanadas hoy estepas, en esos montes preñados de minerales, en esos ríos que se pierden miserablemente? . . . La explotación de esas riquezas corresponde a los hombres de negocio . . . ¡Ellos han de explotarlas. . . !" Economic national unity is thus made to depend on the economic activity of Maeztu's willful, visionary "hombres de negocios." Maeztu, *Hacia otra España,* 249.

16. Maeztu, *Hacia otra España,* 253–254. "Cantemos al oro, el oro *vil* transformará la amarillenta y seca faz de nuestro suelo en juvenil semblante: ¡el oro *vil* irá haciendo la otra España!"

17. Maeztu, *Hacia otra España,* 232. "La noción de la justicia sólo intoxica la inteligencia."

18. Maeztu, *Hacia otra España,* 232. "La vida no es justa ni injusta . . . es . . . movimiento."

19. Maeztu, *Authority,* 282.

20. Maeztu, *Authority,* 225.

21. Maeztu, *Authority,* 13–14.

22. Ramiro de Maeztu, *El nuevo tradicionalismo y la revolución social* (Madrid: Editora Nacional, 1959) 83, 209.

23. Maeztu, *Authority,* 26.

24. Maeztu, *Authority,* 272.

25. Maeztu, *Authority,* 15.

26. Maeztu, *Authority,* 107–194.

27. Maeztu, *Authority,* 52.

28. The ethicopolitical consequences of Maeztu's notion of original sin are perhaps best borne out by his critique of democracy. "The real cause of the failure of democracy is that it cares much more for happiness than for justice. And democracy will continue to fail until it is cured of its hedonism or ideal of pleasure. Not that a perfect cure is possible, for hedonism—its real name is lust—is one of the aspects of original sin, and, therefore, ineradicable in human nature. What can be done . . . is to refute its arguments, and, by continually refuting them, keep up a state of eternal vigilance against it." A democratic society, argues Maeztu, is incapable of performing this act of vigilant self-mastery because it lacks a "normative right, a right of rights, or a right to right," which can undo the injustices created by the subjective principles of Liberal democratic theory. What is amiss in democracy is the "legitimacy" with which power and wealth are used. Maeztu, *Authority,* 169–170; 273–274.

29. Maeztu, *Authority,* 17, 272.

30. Maeztu, *Authority,* 256. The notion that man is, at heart, a sinner who is in need of constant vigilance, discipline, punishment, and redemption is, for Maeztu, an "eternal and inevitable fact" which, when the lives of so-called good men are studied with "impartial eyes" cannot but be acknowledged. The lives of saints, Maeztu claims, are paradigmatic in this regard: "The saints, who, overcoming their nature, lived, on the whole, saintly lives, were only sinners. What makes a saint a saint is that he hardly ever loses the consciousness of being a sinner. And the sin of the devil"—continues Maeztu—"is pride. The devil is the devil because he believes himself to be good." By way of this reasoning, Maeztu argues that, first, man is always and already a criminal—even saints are only sinners; and, second, that it is the failure to recognize or acknowledge this "eternal and inevitable" fact that leads to a life of unbridled sin. Maeztu, *Authority,* 232.

31. Maeztu, *Authority,* 208.

32. Maeztu, *Authority,* 208.

33. Maeztu, *Authority,* 208–209.

34. "Social rules—writes Maeztu—exist because without them society itself could not exist, and these social rules are disciplinary because every society is in itself a discipline. The social rule is based upon solidarity, and solidarity on the fact of men's interdependence." Maeztu, *Authority,* 216.

35. Maeztu, *Authority,* 204.

36. Maeztu, *Authority,* 202.

37. Maeztu, *Authority,* 202.

38. Maeztu, *Authority,* 202.

39. Maeztu, *Authority,* 205.

40. Maeztu, *Authority,* 211.

41. Maeztu, *Authority,* 269.

42. Maeztu, *Authority,* 251.

43. Maeztu, *Authority,* 251.

44. Maeztu, *Authority,* 251.

45. Maeztu, *Authority,* 266.

46. Maeztu, *Authority,* 266.

47. Maeztu, *Authority,* 266.

48. Maeztu, *Authority,* 266.

49. Maeztu, *Defensa,* 287.

50. Maeztu, *Defensa,* 185. "Por primera vez desde hace dos siglos se encuentran los pueblos hispánicos con que no pueden ya venerar a esos grandes países extranjeros . . . como los reverenciaban cuando pensaban o parecía que pensaban por todas las naciones de la tierra . . . Alemania . . . Francia . . . los Estados Unidos."

51. Maeztu, *Defensa,* 181. "Los pueblos que hemos tenido por modelos se hallan en la hora actual en situación tan crítica y penosa que ya no pueden mostrar a ningún otro los caminos de la prosperidad . . . ¿A qué pueblo extranjero volveremos ahora los ojos donde no hallemos la estampa del fracaso."

52. Maeztu, *Defensa,* 180. "Los dioses se van."

53. Maeztu, *Defensa,* 70. "Si cada hombre obedece solamente sus propios mandatos, desarrollará sus facultades hasta el máximo de sus posibilidades."

54. Maeztu, *Defensa,* 71. "La bandera individualista . . . ha acabado por convertirse en la divisa de los pueblos que se creen superiores."

55. Maeztu, *Defensa,* 73. "Igualdad esencial de los cuerpos . . . una sociedad en que las diferencias sociales sean suprimidas inexorablemente . . . [y] trabajen todos para todos y cada uno reciba su ración de la comunidad."

56. Maeztu, *Defensa,* 74. "La razón del fracaso comunista es obvia, la economía no es una actividad animal o fisiológica, sino espiritual."

57. Maeztu, *Defensa,* 65. "no hay pecador que no pueda redimirse, ni justo que no esté al borde del abismo."

58. Maeztu, *Defensa,* 65.

59. Maeztu, *Defensa,* 21.

60. Maeztu, *Defensa,* 23. "Aquellos españoles . . . crea[ron] la unidad física del mundo . . . constitu[yeron] la unidad moral del género humano, al emplazar una misma posibilidad de salvación ante todos los hombres . . . [hicieron] posible la Historia Universal, que hasta nuestro siglo XVI no pudo ser sino una pluralidad de historias inconexas."

61. Maeztu, *Defensa,* 191. "Nuestro destino en el porvenir es el mismo que en el pasado: atraer a las razas distintas a nuestros territorios y moldearlas en el crisol de nuestro espíritu universalista."

62. Maeztu, *Defensa,* 262. "Don Quiote es el amor . . . es el término de la epopeya nacional del siglo XVI, el desencanto que sigue al sobreesfuerzo y al exceso de ideal, pero también la iniciación de un mandamiento nuevo: '¡No seas Quijote!,' a veces prudente, a veces matador de entusiasmos . . . Con lo que indico que . . . el *Quijote* está por rehacer."

63. Maeztu, *Defensa,* 20.

Chapter 6

1. José Ortega y Gasset, "De la crítica personal," *Obras Completas* (1983), 16. "Los hombres de criterio delicado, al formar parte de un público, pierden sus bellas cualidades. De suerte que una multitud de cien individuos formando un público es inferior a la suma de esas cien intelectualidades separadas."

2. Ortega, *Obras Completas* (1983), 38. "El literato no es otra cosa que el encargado en la república de despertar la atención de los desatentos, hostigar la modorra de la conciencia popular con palabras agudas e imágenes tomadas a ese mismo pueblo para que ninguna simiente queda vana."

3. "Vieja y Nueva Política," *Obras Completas* (Madrid: Espasa Calpe, 1932), 115. "Es forzoso aspirar a introducir la actuación política en los hábitos de las masas españolas. ¿Cómo sería posible lograr esto sin la existencia de una minoría entusiasta que opere sobre ellas con tenacidad, con energía, con eficacia? No cabe empujar España hacia ninguna mejora apreciable mientras el obrero en la urbe, el labriego en el campo, la clase media en la villa y en las capitales no hayan aprendido . . . a desear un porvenir claro, concreto y serio."

4. Ortega, *España invertebrada,* 87. "He aquí el mecanismo elemental creador de toda sociedad: la ejemplaridad de unos pocos se articula en la docilidad de otros muchos. El resultado es que el ejemplo cunde y que los inferiores se perfeccionan en el sentido de los mejores."

5. José Ortega y Gasset, *La rebellion de las masas* (1937; Madrid: Espasa Calpe, 1966), 44. "La sociedad humana *es* aristocrática siempre, quiera o no, por su esencia misma, hasta el punto de que es sociedad en la medida en que sea aristocrática, y deja de serlo en la medida en que se desaristocratice."

6. The works of one of Ortega's disciples, Julián Marías Aguilera, of Spanish intellectual historians such as Tuñon de Lara and Ferrater Mora and of other Hispanists such as Philip Silver and Andrew Dobson tend to associate Ortega's political philosophy with the so-called Europeanization of modern Spanish intellectuals.

7. Inman Fox's treatment of Ortega is one of the more recent examples of this long-standing tradition of "Europeanizing" interpretation. See, in this regard, Fox *La invención de España*, 138–142.

8. Ortega, *España invertebrada*, 75. "Concluyo, pues, estos estudios sobre la hora presente de España con tres sencillas observaciones: Primera. Un pueblo vive de lo mismo que le dio la vida: la aspiración . . . Segunda. Esas grandes empresas no pueden hoy, por lo pronto, consistir más que en una gigantesca, dinámica reforma de la vida interior de España orientada hacia un destino internacional: *la unificación espiritual de los pueblos de habla española* . . . Tercera. Culto al hombre selecto."

9. José Ortega y Gasset, *Meditaciones del Quixote* (Madrid: Alianza, 1987), 15. "El rencor es una emanación de la conciencia de inferioridad."

10. Ortega, *Meditaciones*, 112–113. "Pocas cosas odia tanto nuestro plebeyo interior como al ambicioso. Y el héroe, claro está que empieza por ser ambicioso . . . El instinto de inercia y de conservación [de las masas] no lo puede tolerar y se venga."

11. Ortega, *Obras* (1955), 226. "Parece una cosa óptima."

12. Ortega, *Obras* (1955), 228. "La nivelación de privilegios, no propiamente de derechos."

13. Ortega, *Obras* (1955), 229. "La época en que la democracia era un sentimiento saludable y de impulso ascendente pasó. Lo que hoy se llama democracia es una degeneración de los corazones."

14. Ortega, *Obras* (1955), 226. "La democracia exasperada y fuera de sí, la democracia en religión o en arte, la democracia en el pensamiento y en el gesto, la democracia en el corazón y en la costumbre es el más peligroso morbo que puede padecer una sociedad."

15. Ortega, *Obras* (1955), 226. "El plebeyismo . . . el más insufrible de los tiranos . . . [que] tiraniza en España."

16. Ortega, *España invertebrada*, 92, 108. "*Aristofobia* u odio a los mejores . . . ganglio nervioso y centro cerebral."

17. Ortega, *España invertebrada*, 76. "[C]uando en una nación la masa se niega a ser masa—esto es, a seguir a la minoría directora—, la nación se deshace, la sociedad se desmembra, y sobreviene el caos social, la invertebración histórica."

18. Ortega, *España invertebrada*, 80.

19. Ortega, *España invertebrada,* 80. "Confundiendo las cosas, generaliza las objeciones que aquella determinada aristocracia [decadente] inspira, y . . . tiende a eliminar todo intento aristocrático."

20. Ortega, *España invertebrada,* 80. "Es posible la existencia social sin minoría excelente . . . [esto es] positivamente imposible . . . [y la sociedad] prosigue acceleradamente su trayectoria de decadencia."

21. Ortega, *España invertebrada,* 113. "Radical perversión de los instintos sociales."

22. Ortega, *España invertebrada,* 107–108. "Lo único verdadero, substantivamente grande que ha hecho España . . . En la [colonización] española, es el 'pueblo' quien directamente, sin propósitos conscientes, sin directores, sin táctica deliberada, engendra otros pueblos. Grandeza y miseria de nuestra colonización vienen ambas de aquí. Nuestro 'pueblo' hizo todo lo que tenía que hacer: pobló, cultivó, cantó, gimió, amó. Pero no podía dar a las naciones que engendraba lo que no tenía: disciplina superior, cultura vivaz, civilización progresiva."

23. Ortega, *España invertebrada,* 104. "La historia de España entera . . . ha sido la historia de una decadencia."

24. Ortega, *España invertebrada,* 108. "[E]n España, lo ha hecho todo el 'pueblo,' y lo que no ha hecho el 'pueblo' se ha quedado sin hacer."

25. Ortega, *España invertebrada,* 104. "Si España no ha tenido nunca salud—ya vemos que su hora mejor tampoco fue saludable—, no cabe decir que ha decaído."

26. Ortega, "La pedagogía social como programa político," *Obras* (1983), 503–521.

27. Ortega, *España invertebrada,* 32.

28. Ortega, *España invertebrada,* 32.

29. Ortega, *España invertebrada,* 113.

30. Ortega, *La rebelión,* 40. "Son individuos o grupos de individuos especialmente calificados."

31. Ortega, *La rebelión,* 40. "Por razones *especiales,* relativamente individuales."

32. Ortega, *La rebelión,* 40. "El hombre selecto no es el petulante que se cree superior a los demás, sino el que se exige más que los demás, aunque no logre cumplir en su persona esas exigencias superiores."

33. Ortega, *La rebelión,* 40. "Masa es todo aquel que no se valora a sí mismo . . . por razones especiales, sino que se siente como 'todo el mundo' y, sin embargo, no se angustia, se siente a sabor al sentirse idéntico a los demás."

34. Ortega, *La rebelión,* 67.

35. Ortega, *La rebelión,* 63. "El hombre-masa es el hombre cuya vida carece de proyectos y va a la deriva."

36. Ortega, *La rebelión,* 73. "Contra lo que suele creerse, es la criatura de selección, y no la masa, quien vive en esencial servidumbre. No le sabe su vida si no la hace con-

sistir en servicio a algo trascendente. Por eso no estima la necesidad de servir como una opresión. Cuando ésta, por azar, le falta, siente desasosiego e inventa nuevas normas más difíciles, más exigentes, que le opriman. Esto es la vida como disciplina—la vida noble."

37. Ortega, *España invertebrada,* 32. "Mandar . . . no es simplemente convencer ni simplemente obligar, sino una exquisita mixtura de ambas cosas."

38. Ortega, *España invertebrada,* 89.

39. Ortega, *España invertebrada,* 87. "En la imitación actuamos . . . fuera de nuestra auténtica personalidad, nos creamos una máscara exterior. Por el contrario, en la asimilación al hombre ejemplar . . . toda nuestra persona se polariza y orienta hacia su modo de ser, nos disponemos a reformar verídicamente nuestra esencia, según la pauta admirada."

40. Ortega, *España invertebrada,* 89. "Se obedece a un mandato, se es dócil a un ejemplo, y el derecho a mandar no es sino un anejo de la ejemplaridad."

41. Ortega, *España invertebrada,* 14. "El reconocimiento de que la misión de las masas no es otra que seguir a los mejores, en vez de pretender suplantarlos."

42. Ortega, *España invertebrada,* 80–81. "Al fin, el fracaso alumbra en sus cabezas, como un descubrimiento, la sospecha de que las cosas son más complicadas de lo que ellas suponían . . . Cuando la sensibilidad colectiva llega a esta sazón, suele iniciarse una nueva época histórica. El dolor y el fracaso crean en las masas una nueva actitud de sincera humildad, que les hace volver la espalda a todas aquellas ilusiones y teorías antiaristocráticas. Cesa el rencor contra la minoría eminente."

43. Ortega, *España invertebrada,* 113.

44. Ortega, *España invertebrada,* 80. "[La] enfermedad [de la masa] consiste precisamente en que no quiere dejarse influir, en que no está dispuesta a la humilde actitud de escuchar. Cuanto más se le quiera adoctrinar, más herméticamente cerrará sus oídos y con mayor violencia pisoteará a los predicadores. Para sanar será preciso que sufra en su propia carne las consecuencias de su desviación moral."

45. Ortega, *Obras* (1955), 195.

46. Ortega, *España invertebrada,* 40. "Ser emperador de sí mismo es la primera condición para imperar los demás."

47. Ortega, *Obras* (1932), 638. "La guerra suscita un jefe y requiere una disciplina . . . unidad de jefe y disciplina trae consigo y, a la vez, fomenta unidad de espíritu, la preocupación en común por todos los grandes problemas."

48. Ortega, *España invertebrada,* 35.

49. Ortega, *España invertebrada,* 35. "Dirige el espíritu industrial un cauteloso afán de evitar el riesgo, mientras el guerrero brota de un genial apetito de peligro."

50. Ortega, *Obras* (1932), 561. "La realidad histórica es la lucha, y que en ella, quienes luchan, más que los hombres, son los instrumentos."

51. Ortega, *Obras* (1932), 561. "La vida en cada época sería, no lo que fuesen los instrumentos de producción, sino, al revés, los instrumentos de destrucción. El poder social parece repartido en cada época según la calidad y cantidad de medios de destrucción que cada hombre posea."

CHAPTER 7

1. Ganivet, *Idearium*, 164, 169, 177, 178.

2. As Francisco García Lorca has noted, Ganivet's parody of the Spanish chroniclers of the conquest and colonization of the Americas is without precedence in the history of peninsular Spanish literature. Yet, insofar as Ganivet's parody of such works evokes an imaginary world in which the civilized and the savage are satirically contrasted, Gracián's *Criticón* may be supposed to be a distant, Spanish influence on Ganivet. Indeed, just as in Gracián, satire, in the case of Ganivet, serves to show up the false pretenses of civilization. Thus, Ganivet's parody of the Spanish chronicles of the conquest serve to highlight the way in which these chronicles were often constructed rhetorically, so as to justify conquest as well as legitimize colonial rule.

Moreover, although this satirical parody of the chroniclers of the Spanish conquest of the Americas was, until Ganivet, relatively unknown in Spain, Ganivet's work nevertheless does form a part of a long European tradition of works in which civilization and savagery are not only in opposition to each other, but also often located, vaguely, in an American context: Moor's *Utopia;* Bacon's *New Atlantic;* Montaigne's essays on the savage; Shakespeare's *The Tempest;* and Swift's *Gulliver's Travels.* See, in this regard the intelligent study of Francisco García Lorca: *Angel Ganivet: Su idea del hombre* (Buenos Aires, Editorial Losada, 1952), 26–29.

3. Angel Ganivet. *La conquista del reino de Maya; Los trabajos del infatigable creador Pío Cid* (1895, 1897; Barcelona: Planeta, 1988), 551. "Desde que el mundo es mundo ha habido hombres que han influido sobre el espíritu de otros hombres."

4. Ganivet, *Pío Cid,* 543. "Los héroes del porvenir triunfarán en secreto, dominando invisiblemente el espíritu y suscitando en cada espíritu un mundo ideal."

5. Judith Ginsberg, *Angel Ganivet* (London: Tamesis Books, 1985), 85.

6. Ganivet, *Idearium,* 277. "Un nuevo Hércules . . . que volviera de arriba abajo la nación."

7. Ganivet, *Idearium,* 277–278. "Yo creo que . . . si Hércules resucitara no querría cuentas con nosotros . . . aquí tendría que . . . limpiar los establos por doce veces . . . y esta operación me parece más propia de un basurero que de un héroe semidivino."

8. Michael K. Goldberg, introduction. *On Heroes, Hero-Worship, and the Heroic in History* by Thomas Carlyle (Berkeley, California: University of California Press, 1993), lvii.

9. Miguel Olmedo Moreno, "Carlyle," in *El pensamiento de Ganivet* (Madrid: Revista de Occidente, 1965), 303–304. "La característica fundamental que Carlyle

asigna a los tiempos nuevos, la falta de fe en la virtud del esfuerzo individual y la esperanza puesta en los medios, [es] justamente el punto en que la nueva época result[a] inadmisible para Ganivet y nos explica su repugnancia por ella."

10. Ganivet, *Pío Cid,* 375. "Nuestro gobierno natural es un gobierno fuerte y duro, como nuestro temperamento; la filantropía democrática nos parece una degeneración de nuestro carácter, puesto que nosotros . . . todos somos reyes en nuestra casa . . . nos gusta que el rey o gobernador . . . lo sea de verdad."

11. Ganivet, *Pío Cid,* 602. "Nosotros . . . necesitamos para andar derechos un dictador y una batería en cada bocacalle."

12. George Lukács, *The Theory of the Novel* (Cambridge, Massachusettes: MIT Press, 1990), 56.

13. Oswald Spengler, *The Decline of the West* (New York: Knopf, 1926), 506.

14. Ganivet, *La conquista,* 18. "El más original caballero andante que se haya visto en el mundo."

15. Ganivet, *La conquista.* The primitive Kingdom of Maya and nineteenth-century Spain have a good deal in common: both possess democratic juristic practices and principles (22); parliamentary governments (37, 56); bureaucratically entrenched educational systems (24); and monotheistic national religions (46). Satiric as Ganivet's portrayal of primitive Mayan society is, the main thrust of his criticism is directed at the progressive reforms initiated in Maya by Pío Cid. When Pío Cid first arrives in Maya, he finds the Mayans to be bucolic and "as happy as beasts"; later, as a result of his reforms, innovations and progress on the European model, they become—in the words of the ghost of Hernán Cortes—"as unhappy as men" (232).

16. Ganivet, *La conquista,* 27. "Contra lo que creen algunos pesimistas, es más difícil gobernar a los animales que al hombre, porque los animales no se someten más que a la fuerza o la razón, interpretada por sus instintos, en tanto que el hombre se contenta con algunas mentiras agradables e inocentes, cuya invención está al alcance de hombres de mediano entendimiento . . . el gobierno de las naciones no exige hombres de Estado, ni legistas, ni soldados, sino poetas, comediantes, músicos y sacerdotes."

17. Ganivet, *La conquista,* 164–176.

18. Ganivet, *La conquista,* 170. "La sumisión de grandes masas de hombres a una inteligencia directriz."

19. Ganivet, *La conquista,* 230. "¿Qué significa—se pregunta Cortés—ni qué vale un siglo, dos o cuatro de dominación real, si al cabo todo se desvanece, y el más poderoso y el más noble viene a quedar el más abatido y el más calumniado? Quizá nuestra patria hubiera sido más dichosa si, reservándose la pura gloria de sus heroicas empresas, hubiera dejado a otras gentes más prácticas la misión de poblar las tierras descubiertas y conquistadas, y el cuidado de todos los bajos menesteres de la colonización."

20. Ganivet, *La conquista,* 230. "Las empresas más grandiosas son aquellas en que no interviene el dinero, en que los gastos recaen exclusivamente sobre el cerebro y el corazón."

21. Ganivet, *La conquista,* 231. "Su *Don Quijote* para señalarnos a qué altura podemos llegar cuando huimos de las groseras y vulgares aspiraciones que contrarían nuestra naturaleza y nos apartan de nuestra congénita austeridad."

22. Ganivet, *La conquista,* 231. "Heroes inmortales . . . que lo mismo escriben una epopeya con la pluma que con la espada."

23. Ganivet, *La conquista,* 229. "De la que nuestra pobre patria está en gran manera necesitada."

24. Ganivet, *La conquista,* 232. "Los Mayas eran felices como bestias, y tú les has hecho desgraciados como hombres. Ésta es la verdad. El salvaje ama la vida fácil, en contacto directo con la naturaleza, y rechaza todo esfuerzo que no tiene utilidad perentoria."

25. Ganivet, *La conquista,* 232. "El hombre civilizado detesta esa vida natural, y halla su dicha en el esfuerzo doloroso que le exige su propia liberación."

26. Ganivet, *La conquista,* 232. "Conquistar, colonizar, civilizar, no es, pues, otra cosa que infundir el amor al esfuerzo que dignifica al hombre sacándole del estado de ignorante quietud en que viviría eternamente."

27. Ganivet, *La conquista,* 230. "Los medios necesarios para que ellos entre sí se destruyeran, para que el placer que de ello recibieran les llevara de la mano a la cumbre de la civilización."

28. Ganivet, *La conquista,* 233. "La muerte ennoblece mucho más que [el] desmesurado apego a la vida y [la] cobarde aspiración a terminarla en un lecho . . . Amable es la vida; pero ¿cuánto más amable no es el ideal a que podemos elevarnos sacrificándola?"

29. Ganivet, *La conquista,* 233.

30. Ganivet, *La conquista,* 234. "Lo que hoy llamamos civilización bien pudiera ser la barbarie precursora de otra civilización más perfecta; así como en Maya la aparente civilización de hoy es sólo el anuncio de un esplenderoso porvenir."

31. Ganivet, *La conquista,* 265. "A ratos pienso que quien está a mi cabecera no es una pobre sirvienta, sino España, toda España."

32. The play, here, on Nietzsche's *Ecce Homo* is obvious. Ganivet's ideal, total man is in this regard a man characterized by an overhuman will-to-power. See, in this regard, Sobejano, *Nietzsche en España,* 259–276.

33. Ganivet, *Pío Cid,* 545–546. "No es facil hallar un hombre verdadero . . . la calidad del hombre se ha de conocer no por simples palabras, sino en hechos, en la comprensión total de la vida. He aquí un hecho usual, que puede servirnos de medio de prueba: ¿qué hombre no ha hallado alguna vez a una mujer caída en el vicio? Este hallazgo vulgar inspira varios pensamientos, en los cuales cada hombre da la medida de su humanidad. La mayor parte no piensa más que en aprovecharse de la desgracia para satisfacer su sensualidad . . . En otros más intelectuales, la sensualidad queda dominada por la curiosidad . . . ¿Cuánto más noble no es el que siente piedad y ama a la mujer caída, y por el amor la regenera y la redime?"

34. Ganivet, *Pío Cid,* 379. "El ideal humano . . . una condición generosa: la de no pensar nunca en utilizar en nuestro provecho a nuestros semejantes."

35. Ganivet, *Pío Cid,* 601.

36. Ganivet, *Pío Cid,* 546. "El que mira con amor al desválido es más humano que el que le estudia sin amarle. Pero se puede hacer por esa mujer caída algo más que redimirla por el amor: se puede subir aún más alto . . . Se puede hacer más . . . pero esto no está en mi mano declararlo, porque, si lo declarara . . . descub[riría] la ley primitiva y perenne de la creación."

37. Ganivet, *La conquista,* 246. "Rara sabiduría."

38. Ganivet, *Pío Cid,* 539. "Los grandes místicos se forman en la soledad, y los grandes filósofos en el silencio." Also, Carlyle, in his sixth lecture on heroism "The Hero as King" formulates silence as the sign of a divine, prophetic nobility.

39. Ganivet, *Idearium,* 178.

40. Ganivet, *Pío Cid,* 539. "La sombra es el ambiente propio de la creación; pero si la creación es noble y espiritual, busca luego la luz."

41. Ganivet, *Pío Cid,* 390. "La muerte es fecunda y crea la vida . . . un hombre que llevase la muerte absolutamente dentro de su espíritu, y que se viera obligado a trabajar, sería un creador portentoso, porque ya no teniendo ideas de vida, que siempre son pequeñas y miserables, crearía con ideas de muerte, que son más amplias y nobles."

42. Ganivet, *Pío Cid,* 601. "La Divinidad tiene dos principales atributos: el de crear y el de destruir."

43. Ganivet, *Pío Cid,* 244. "Notábase en él un menosprecio profundo por sus semejantes . . . que era expresión de un poder misterioso, semejante al que los dioses paganos mostraban en sus tratos con las criaturas: mezcla de energía y de abandono, de bondad y de perversión, de seriedad y de burla."

44. Ganivet, *Pío Cid,* 547. "Aplazo la revelación para después de mi muerte . . . que poco ha de tardar . . . la dejaré en una tragedia que tengo ya escrita . . . la tragedia invariable de la vida."

45. Ganivet, *Pío Cid,* 544. "El único testamento que debe dejar un hombre honrado . . . es . . . el ejemplo de [s]u vida."

Chapter 8

1. Miguel de Unamuno, "Muera Don Quijote," *Vida Nueva* (June 26, 1898). "Hay que olvidar la vida de aventuras, aquél ir a imponer a los demás lo que creíamos les convenía y aquél buscar fuera un engañoso imperio . . . la misión [del] pueblo [es] cristianizarse . . . puede el hidalgo Alonso el Bueno realizar la justicia callada, sin ruido de armas y sin buscar sitio en la condenada historia . . . ¡Muera Don Quijote para que renazca Alonso el Bueno!"

2. Unamuno, *En torno,* 40. "Es menester que pueda decirse que 'verdaderamente *se muere* [Don Quijote] y verdaderamente está cuerdo Alonso Quijano el Bueno'; que

esos 'cuentos' viejos que desentierran de nuestro pasado de aventuras, y que 'han sido verdaderos en nuestro daño, los vuelva nuestra *muerte* con ayuda del cielo en provecho nuestro.'" Here Unamuno professes the view that, in order to regenerate itself and overcome its cultural "backwardness," the Spanish nation must confess to its error of wanting to cling to heroic discourses, like that of Don Quixote, that celebrate the nation's warring identity or "casticismo," and seek instead to affirm its common links to other, European nations.

3. Eric Ziolkowski, *The Sanctification of Don Quijote: From Hidalgo to Priest* (University Park, Pennsylvania: The Pennsylvania State University Press, 1991), 170. As Eric Ziolkowski has noted, from this point onward, Unamuno's sympathy for the knight takes on the aspect of religious reverence and his idealization of the Quixote figure definitively turns toward deification.

4. Unamuno, *Obras* (1958), 842. "En pocas cosas se muestra más de relieve que en lo que con el *Quijote* ocurre en España la tristísima decadencia de nuestro espíritu nacional."

5. Unamuno, *Obras* (1958), 850. "La Biblia nacional de la religión patriótica de España."

6. Unamuno, *Obras* (1958), 852, 855. "Un caso típico de un escritor enormemente inferior a su obra, a su *Quijote* [quien] volvió a ser el pobre escritor andariego, presa de todas las preocupaciones literarias de su tiempo."

7. Unamuno, *Obras* (1958), 853–854. "Cervantes no fue más que un mero instrumento para que la España del siglo XVI pariese a Don Quijote."

8. Unamuno, *Obras* (1958), 854. "En caso de volver Cervantes al mundo, se haría cervantista y no quijotista."

9. Unamuno, *Obras* (1958), 854. "Basta leer atentamente el *Quijote* para observar que el bueno de Cervantes . . . no alcanzaba a la robusta fe del hidalgo manchego."

10. Unamuno, *Obras* (1958), 847. "Lo que a los demás se nos ocurra ver en él."

11. Ziolkowski, 173.

12. Unamuno, *Obras* (1958), 847. "Desde que el *Quijote* apareció impreso y a la disposición de quien lo tomara en mano y lo leyese, el *Quijote* no es de Cervantes, sino de todos los que lo lean y lo sientan. Cervantes sacó a Don Quijote del alma de su pueblo y del alma de la humanidad toda, y en su inmortal libro se lo devolvió a su pueblo y a toda la humanidad. Y desde entonces Don Quijote y Sancho han seguido viviendo en las almas de los lectores del libro de Cervantes y aun en la de aquella de aquellos que nunca lo han leído."

13. Unamuno, *Obras* (1958), 847. "[L]o que se ha hecho con las Sagradas Escrituras del Cristianismo, ¿por qué no se ha de hacer con el *Quijote*?"

14. Unamuno, *Obras* (1958), 851–852. "Todo consiste en separar a Cervantes del *Quijote* y hacer que a la plaga de los cervantófilos o cervantistas sustituya la legión sagrada de los quijotistas. Nos falta quijotismo tanto cuanto nos sobra cervantismo."

15. Unamuno, *Obras* (1958), 843. "Hay . . . quienes lo leen [the *Quijote*] como por obligación o movidos por lo que de él se dice, mas sin maldito entusiasmo."

16. Unamuno, *Obras* (1967), 1244. "Una campaña para que se canonice a Don Quijote, haciéndole San Quijote"

17. Unamuno, *Obras* (1967), 1252–1253. "De la literatura nacional—y la historia no es ni más ni menos que literatura—surge una mitología, y de ésta una religión . . . que Dulcinea, la del Toboso nos acorra y nos dé verdad . . . la de la idealidad."

18. As is the case with the Christian drama of history, Unamuno links this self-perpetuating loss to a modern reinterpretation of the myth of Cain and Able which, of itself, is a favored theme in Unamuno's work, traversing the political, religious, and ontological aspects of his thought.

19. Unamuno, *Vida*, 57.

20. Unamuno, *Vida*, 35.

21. Unamuno, *Vida*, 207. "Cobardía [ante] los eternos problemas . . . pereza espiritual."

22. Unamuno, *Vida*, 53.

23. Unamuno, *Vida*, 104. "Todo nuestro mal es la cobardía moral, la falta de arranque para afirmar cada uno su verdad, su fe, y defenderla."

24. Unamuno, *Vida*, 11, 104–105. "Todos estos estúpidos bachilleres, curas y barberos de hoy . . . [que buscan] soluciones prácticas."

25. Unamuno, *Vida*, 105. "Toda vida heroica o santa corrió siempre en pos de la gloria, temporal o eterna, terrena o celestial."

26. Unamuno, *Vida*, 105. "Don Quijote amó a Dulcinea con amor acabado, sin exigir ser correspondido; dándose todo él y por entero a ella."

27. Unamuno, *Vida*, 205–206. "Es Aldonza [i.e., Dulcinea] . . . la fuente de sabiduría . . . Es la Virgen Madre . . . es donde se manifiesta, donde encarna la eterna e infinita Conciencia del Universo."

28. Unamuno, *Vida*, 29. "Dos mozas del partido hechas por Don Quijote doncellas, ¡oh poder de su locura redentora!, fueron las primeras en servirle con desinteresado cariño . . . Recordad a María de Magdala."

29. Unamuno, *Vida*, 26. "Siempre . . . un fiel discípulo."

30. Unamuno, *Vida*, 73.

31. Unamuno, *Vida*, 55. "Ministro de Dios en la tierra y brazo por quien se ejecuta en ella la justicia."

32. Unamuno, *Vida*, 203. "Reino de Dios . . . bajar a la tierra."

33. Unamuno, *Vida*, 33–37.

34. Unamuno, *Vida*, 55. "Es acaso, desgraciado Caballero . . . esto de creerte ministro de Dios en la tierra y brazo por quien se ejecuta en ella la justicia . . . tu pecado original."

35. Unamuno, *Vida,* 55. "Tu pueblo también, arrogante Caballero, se creyó ministro de Dios en la tierra . . . y pagó muy cara su presunción y sigue pagándola. Creyóse escojido de Dios y esto lo ensoberbeció."

36. Unamuno, *Vida,* 55.

37. Unamuno, *Vida,* 55. "Persuádete de que en todo cuanto hagas, bueno o malo a tu parecer, eres ministro de Dios en la tierra y brazo por quien se ejecuta en ella su justicia, y sucederá que tus actos acabarán por ser buenos."

38. Unamuno, *Vida,* 55. "Vale más daño infligido con santa intención que no beneficio rendido con intención perversa." In his 1913 *Del sentimiento trágico de la vida,* Unamuno argues in similar terms in defense of the Spanish Inquisition whose underlying "good intentions" he seeks to contrast with the base intentions of the "merchants" of the "modern inquisition." See, *Del sentimiento trágico,* 273.

39. Unamuno, *Vida,* 35. "Una de las más quijotescas aventuras de Don Quijote . . . una de las que más levantan el corazón de los redimidos por su locura."

40. Unamuno, *Vida,* 35. "Fué también tizona en la diestra y en la siniestra el Cristo, a hacer confesar a remotas gentes un credo que no conocían."

41. Unamuno, *Vida,* 38.

42. Unamuno, *Vida,* 36. "Tu triunfo fué siempre el de osar y no el de cobrar suceso, tú, sin par Caballero, molido y casi deshecho, tiéneste por dichoso, pareciéndote ser ésa 'propia desgracia de caballeros andantes,' y con este tu parecer, encumbras tu derrota, transmudándola en victoria."

43. Unamuno, *Vida,* 30, 64. "Nada hay imposible para el creyente . . . quien hace pasajeros los dolores los ha vencido ya con hacerlos tales."

44. Unamuno, *Vida,* 166, 197. "Don Quijote fué . . . fiel discípulo del Cristo . . . [que] n[o] subió a más ciudad que a Jerusalén, ni Don Quijote a otra que a Barcelona, la Jerusalén de nuestro Caballero" . . . "Porque si es en esa Barcelona, faro y como centro de la nueva vida industrial de España, si es en esa ciudad donde más se grita contra el quijotismo, es el espíritu bachilleresco, espíritu de socarronería y de envidia, el que lo anima."

45. Unamuno, *Vida,* 108. "Que no pueden sufrir locura heroica."

46. Unamuno, *Vida,* 130. "Voluntad loca de malas pasiones, de rencor, de soberbia, de envidia."

47. Unamuno, *Vida,* 87–88. "Ya tenemos al héroe siendo, en cuanto héroe, juguete de los hombres y motivo de risa . . . Sus más hermosas y más espontáneas aventuras quedan ya cumplidas; en adelante . . . serán . . . armadas por hombres maliciosos . . . ahora el mundo le conoce y le acepta . . . para burlarse de él."

48. Unamuno, *Vida,* 88. "Empieza tu pasión y la más amarga: la pasión de la burla. Más por esto mismo ganan tus aventuras en profundidad lo que en arrojo pierden . . . Te desquijotizas algo, pero es quijotizando a cuantos de ti se burlan."

49. Unamuno, *Vida,* 124. "Su vida toda fué una lenta entrega de sí mismo a ese poder de la fe quijotesca y quijotizante."

50. Unamuno, *Vida,* 42. "Arrastr[an] tras de sí a Sancho, convirtiéndole la codicia en ambición y la sed de oro en sed de gloria."

51. Unamuno, *Vida,* 42. "Prueba más quijotismo seguir a un loco un cuerdo que seguir el loco sus propias locuras. La fe se pega, y es tan robusta y arduosa la de Don Quijote, que rebasa a los que le quieren . . . crece vertiéndose y repartiéndose se aumenta."

52. Unamuno, *Vida,* 217–218. "¡Vuelva en sí! ¡Vuelva en sí y déjese de cuentos!"

53. Unamuno, *Vida,* 88, 218. "'He aquí el hombre,' dijeron en burla a Cristo Nuestro Señor; 'he aquí el loco,' di[cen] de ti, mi señor Don Quijote. [. . .] Tu muerte fué aún más heroica que tu vida, porque al llegar a ella cumpliste la más grande renuncia, la renuncia de tu gloria, la renuncia de tu obra. Fué tu muerte encumbrado sacrificio. En la cumbre de tu pasión, cargado de burlas, renuncias . . . a tu obra."

54. Unamuno, *Vida,* 218–219. "¡Pobre Sancho, que te quedas solo con tu fe, con la fe que te dió tu amo! . . . Don Quijote perdió su fe y murióse; tú [Sancho] la cobraste y vives; era preciso que él muriera en desengaño para que en engaño vivificante vivas tú."

55. Unamuno, *Vida,* 215. "La coronación de la vida de Don Quijote . . . En la muerte de Don Quijote se reveló el misterio de su vida quijotesca."

56. Unamuno, *Vida,* 225. "Hay quien cree que resucitó [Don Quijote] al tercer día, y que volverá a la tierra en carne mortal y a hacer de las suyas."

57. Unamuno, *Vida,* 220. "Mira . . . mira a tu pueblo [Don Quijote] y ve si no sanará de su locura para morirse luego. Molido y maltrecho y después de que allá, en las Américas, acabaron de vencerle, retorna a su aldea. ¿A curar de su locura? ¡Quién sabe! . . . Tal vez a morir. Tal vez a morir, si no quedara Sancho . . . Porque tu fe, Caballero, se atesora en Sancho."

58. Unamuno, *Vida,* 225. "Mira, Señor . . . Fundaste este tu pueblo, el pueblo de tus siervos Don Quixote y Sancho, sobre la fe en la inmortalidad personal; mira, Señor, que es esa nuestra razón de vida y esa nuestro destino entre los pueblos el de hacer que esa nuestra verdad del corazón alumbre las mentes contra todas tinieblas de la lógica y del raciocinio y consuele los corazones de los condenados al sueño de la vida."

59. Miguel de Unamuno, *Dos artículos y dos Discursos* (Madrid: Editorial Historia Nueva, 1931), 31. "Es la hora sagrada de sacar a la luz del sol todo el corazón, y ruín sea el que ruínmente juzgue—, y, tanto como el que más, yo. ¡Yo, sí, el despechado, e[l] loco, el ambicioso, el energúmeno, yo! Yo, que estoy llevando lo más íntimo del alma de nuestro pueblo, su esencia eterna, su divina sobre-razón de ser, el jugo de su cristiandad quijotesca, al conocimiento de los pueblos de lenguas latinas, anglosajónicas, germánicas, eslavas . . . a la humaniad civilizada. Imperialismo . . . sí, pero el del espíritu y la conciencia y la justicia."

60. Unamuno, *Del sentimiento trágico,* 268. "El papél que le está reservado a Don Quijote en la tragicomedia europea moderna."

61. Unamuno, *Vida,* 173. "En una obra de burlas se condensó el fruto de nuestro heroísmo, en una obra de burlas se eternizó la pasajera grandeza de nuestra España; en

una obra de burlas se cifra y se compendia nuestra filosofía española, la única verdadera y hondamente tal; con una obra de burlas llegó el alma de nuestro pueblo, encarnada en hombre, a los abismos del misterio de la vida. Y esa obra de burlas es la más triste historia que jamás se ha escrito; la más triste, sí, pero también la más consoladora para cuantos saben gustar en las lágrimas de la risa la redención de la miserable cordura a que la esclavitud de vida presente nos condena."

62. Unamuno, *Vida,* 36. "Encumbra[r] tu derrota, transmudándola en victoria."

63. Unamuno, *Vida,* 225. "Don Quijote . . . volverá cuando Sancho, agobiado hoy por los recuerdos, sienta hervir la sangre que acopió en sus andanzas escuderiles, y monte . . . en Rocinante, y revestido de las armas de su amo, embrace el lanzón y se lance a hacer de Don Quijote. Y su amo vendrá entonces y encarnará en él. ¡Ánimo, Sancho heroico, y aviva esa fe que encendió en ti tu amo. . . !"

64. Unamuno, *Vida,* 220. "Es Sancho el que ha de asentar para siempre el quijotismo sobre la tierra de los hombres."

65. Unamuno, *Vida,* 222. "Se ahoga todo heroísmo."

66. Unamuno, *Vida,* 141–144. "¡Muera la farándula! Hay que acabar con los retablos todos, con las ficciones sancionadas . . . Un retablo hay en la capital de mi patria y la de Don Quijote, donde se representa la libertad de Melisendra o la regeneración de España o la revolución desde arriba, y se mueven allí, en el Parlamento, las figurillas de pasta según les tira de los hilos maese Pedro. Y hace falta que entre en él un loco caballero andante, y sin hacer caso de voces derribe, descabece y estropee a cuantos allí manotean, y destruya y eche a perder la hacienda de maese Pedro."

67. Unamuno, *Vida,* 104–105. "Para establecer el reinado de . . . la sinceridad y de la verdad y del amor . . . tiene que haber guerra . . . necesitamos . . . una guerra civil."

68. Unamuno, *Vida,* 104–105. "Dijo que Él no venía a traer paz, sino guerra . . . cobardía moral."

69. Unamuno, *Vida,* 54. "No nos queda sino ir a hablar a los sencillos, y hablarles sin intentar siquiera ponernos a su alcance; hablarles en el tono más elevado, seguros de que sin entenderos os entienden."

70. Unamuno, *Vida,* 168. "Tu ambición [Sancho] debe cifrarse en buscar a Don Quijote: la ambición del que nació para ser mandado debe ser buscar quien bien le mande."

71. Unamuno, *Vida,* 221. "Cuando tu fiel Sancho, noble Caballero, monte en tu Rocinante . . . entonces resucitarás en él, y entonces se realizará tu ensueño. Dulcinea os cojerá a los dos, y estrechándoos con sus brazos contra su pecho, os hará uno solo."

72. Unamuno, *Obras* (1967), 1239. "Don Quijote apoyó su cabeza sobre el hombro . . . del Cristo y rompió a llorar. Lloraba, lloraba, lloraba. Sus lágrimas . . . mezclábanse a lágrimas del Redentor mismo . . . Y pensando su vida pública lloraba el Caballero . . . y oyó . . . estas palabras: '¡Bienaventurados los locos porque ellos se hartarán de razón!' Y el Caballero se sintió en la gloria eterna."

CHAPTER 9

1. Ramiro de Maeztu, "Paradojas del Doctor Whitney: El libro de los viejos," *Cuadernos Hispanoamericanos: Homenaje a Don Ramiro de Maeztu,* 33–34 (1952): 177–179.

2. Maeztu, "Paradojas del Doctor Whitney," 179.

3. Maeztu, *Authority,* 142.

4. Maeztu, "Paradojas del Doctor Whitney," 178.

5. Maeztu, "Paradojas del Doctor Whitney," 177. "La decadencia empieza . . . cuando se quieren cosas que no se pueden realizar, cuando tenemos que declararnos vencidos ante el ensueño imposible . . . Y si no me equivoco en ese juicio, ¿cabe mejor ejemplo de libro decadentista que el *Quijote?*"

6. Maeztu, "Paradojas del Doctor Whitney," 178. "El *Quijote* . . . [es] el espejo más acabado y la apología más genial de la decadencia, del cansancio de un pueblo."

7. Maeztu, "Paradojas del Doctor Whitney," 178. "Cervantes al escribir el *Quijote* se encontraba cansado, añoraba el descanso, con él soñaba y en esta necesidad de descansar hemos de ver el sentido íntimo de su obra."

8. Maeztu, "Paradojas del Doctor Whitney," 179. "El estado de Cervantes era el de toda la España de su tiempo. Aquel pueblo había expulsado a los moros y a los judíos, conquistado América, paseado sus banderas victoriosas por Flandes, por Italia, por Alemania, por Grecia, por Berberia, por Francia, por todo el mundo . . . Añádanse a estas luchas exteriores los combates de conciencia sostenidos para mantenerse inmune de la Reforma y del Renacimiento . . . De cada casa había salido un monje o un soldado, cuando no un soldado y un monje. ¿Cuál era el íntimo anhelo de aquella España pobre y despoblada, sino el de reposo?"

9. Maeztu, "Paradojas del Doctor Whitney," 179. "Don Quijote despertó de su locura para morirse de melancolía."

10. Maeztu, *Authority,* 142.

11. Maeztu, *Authority,* 143–144.

12. Maeztu, *Authority,* 148.

13. Maeztu, *Authority,* 148.

14. Ramiro de Maeztu, *Don Quixote, Don Juan y la Celestina* (Madrid: Espasa-Calpe, 1981), 64. "Al consumarse en 1898 la pérdida de los restos del imperio colonial español en América y en el Extremo Oriente, se irguió la figura de don Joaquín Costa para decirnos: 'Doble llave al sepulcro del Cid para que no vuelva a cabalgar.' Don Miguel de Unamuno . . . formuló también su sentencia: 'Robinsón ha vencido a Don Quijote' . . . Lo que se puede decir en contra nuestra es que si . . . en Cuba y Filipinas en 1895 . . . hubiéramos otorgado a tiempo a las colonias un régimen de autonomía, o si hubiéramos sabido avivar el amor o la admiración, o siquiera el temor, de nuestras posesiones ultramarinas, acaso las habríamos conservado. Pero lo primero que se les ocurrió a nuestros pensadores independientes fué atribuir a una quijotada, a una

imprudencia, a una aventura injustificada . . . la iniciativa de las guerras . . . Se pedía a los españoles que no volviesen a ser ni Cides ni Quijotes, y los que en aquellas horas de humillación y de derrota sentíamos la necesidad de rehacer la patria, de 'regenerarla' . . . no tardamos en ver que no se lograría sin que los regeneradores se infundiesen un poco, cuando menos, del espíritu esforzado del Cid y del idealismo generoso de Don Quijote."

15. For a discussion of Maeztu's exposition in "El Libro de los viejos" refer to: *Don Quijote, Don Juan y la Celestina,* 19–69, especially 24–26. With regard to his incorporation of earlier works into "Don Quijote o el amor" refer to his 1905 "Ante las fiestas del Quijote" which reappears under the new subtitle "Fiestas y Decadencia" as well as to his 1916 *Authority,* 140–148 where he advances an interesting thesis concerning the "cathartic" qualities of the *Quixote.*

16. Ricardo Landeira, *Ramiro de Maeztu* (Boston: Twayne Publishers, 1978), 97.

17. Maeztu, *Don Quijote* . . . , 11. In Maeztu's view, the so-called myths of Don Quixote, Don Juan, and La Celestina occupy a dominant position within the human "Olimpo de la imaginación."

18. Landeira, 98.

19. Maeztu, *Don Quijote* . . . , 22. "¿Qué hay en el *Quijote?* No busquemos interpretaciones esotéricas; leámoslo con humildad y sencillez." Also, in his 1905 article titled "Ante las fiestas del Quijote," Maeztu attacks the cervantists and their penchant for discovering esoteric meanings in Cervantes' text. To that end, he accuses the "cervantófilos . . . el elemento erudito del país," of standing in the way of the popular reception of the *Quixote* in modern Spain: "Nuestro actual pueblo no siente el *Quijote.* Buena parte de culpa corresponde a los cervantófilos. Han hecho cuanto estaba de su parte por esconderle a las miradas populares, suponiéndole significados esotéricos de dificil o imposible inteligencia . . . Se le han consagrado grandes volúmenes de intrincados conceptos y pocas páginas humanas, sinceras, humildes, sencillas . . . yace el *Quijote* sepultado por sus teólogos, augures, intérpretes, zelotes, exegetas, escoliastas, ergotistas, sacerdotes y profetas." See *Homenaje,* 182.

20. Maeztu, *Don Quijote* . . . , 23. "Se ejecuta en ella su justicia."

21. Maeztu, *Don Quijote* . . . , 23. "No se trata únicamente . . . de los libros de caballería sino del ideal caballeresco, del impulso que empuja a los espíritus nobles a intentar la realización de empresas grandes, sin reparar en los peligros ni detenerse a calcular las propias fuerzas."

22. Maeztu, *Don Quijote* . . . , 69. "Don Quijote es el prototipo del amor, en su expresión más elevada de amor cósmico . . . Todo gran enamorado se propondrá siempre realizar el bien de la tierra y resucitar la edad de oro en la de hierro."

23. Maeztu, *Don Quijote* . . . , 27. "Suprema bondad de Don Quijote . . . que se oculta detrás de su locura, de su ingenio, de su valor y de sus aventuras."

24. Close, 103.

25. Maeztu, *Don Quijote* . . . , 23.

26. Maeztu, *Don Quijote* . . . , 24. "Demasiado viejo para sus empresas. Quiere, pero no puede. Pues eso es decadencia."

27. Maeztu, *Don Quijote* . . . , 69. "El amor sin la fuerza no puede mover nada, y para medir bien la propia fuerza nos hará falta ver las cosas como son. La veracidad es deber inexcusable. Tomar los molinos por gigantes no es meramente una alucinación, sino un pecado."

28. Maeztu, *Don Quijote* . . . , 62. "Aunque el *Quijote* sea un libro de decadencia no deja de ser un libro sano . . . porque lo mejor que puede hacer un hombre cuando se halla cansado es descansar."

29. Maeztu, *Don Quijote* . . . , 66–67. "Comprenderemos que había que desengañar, por su propio bien, a los españoles de aquel tiempo. Y advertimos, a la vez, que lo que el nuestro necesita no es desencantarse y desilusionarse, sino, al contrario, volver a sentir un ideal."

30. Maeztu, *Don Quijote* . . . , 22. "En los individuos la decadencia es anuncio de muerte. En los pueblos no necesita serlo, sino de una situación nueva, de un período de reposo, de una pérdida de la iniciativa histórica, en la que, a cambio de padecer por algún tiempo el rango, se vuelve a crear otro ideal y la energía con que mantenerlo . . . Cuando los . . . pueblos se dan a un ideal, sienten que se les multiplican las energías con esta unificación de los afectos."

31. Maeztu was not the first Quixotist to consider the potentially regenerative implications of Don Juan's virulent will-to-power. Ortega, in his 1923 *El Tema de nuestro tiempo,* justifies Don Juan's "revolt" against morality as necessary, given that "la moral se había antes sublevado contra la vida"; thus, for Ortega, the figure of Don Juan comes to represent the promise of a new culture for a new, vitalistic age: "Sólo cuando exista una ética que cuente, como su norma primera, con la plenitud vital, podrá Don Juan someterse. Pero eso significa una nueva cultura: la cultura biológica. *La razón pura tiene que ceder su imperio a la razón vital.*" Ortega, *Obras* (1955), 178.

32. Maeztu, *Don Quijote* . . . , 72. "Don Juan de los pueblos del Norte, y aun Italia, que es el Don Juan enamorado," es "el Burlador . . . de Tirso y . . . Zorrilla."

33. Maeztu, *Don Quijote* . . . , 83, 88, 94. "Un alma brava y cargada de amor, que recorre el mundo en la vana busca de una mujer ideal . . . ante todo, una energía bruta, instintiva, petulante, pero inagotable, triunfal y arrolladora."

34. Maeztu, *Don Quijote* . . . , 74, 91. "El hombre de apetitos, pero sin ideales"; "la encarnación del capricho"; "imponer nuestra voluntad a otros hombres."

35. Maeztu, *Don Quijote* . . . , 94. "Don Juan es la libertad . . . la irresponsabilidad, la energía infinita . . . Sólo soñarlo es el paraíso para el que se siente con el agua al cuello."

36. Maeztu, *Don Quijote* . . . , 94. "Don Juan es la fuerza, y la fuerza es un bien."

37. Maeztu, *Don Quijote* . . . , 100–103. "Estamos sumidos en problemas enloquecedores e insolubles. Y entonces aparece la alternativa del capricho absoluto . . . porque . . . no sabemos, en horas de crisis de ideales, emplear mejor la vida, es [el ejemplo de Don Juan] nuestra tentación."

38. Maeztu, *Don Quijote . . .*, 106. "Es deber elemental conservar la energía; deber superior emplearla para fortalecer entre los hombres el saber y el amor."

39. Maeztu, *Don Quijote . . .*, 97–98. "Don Juan descubre . . . la posibilidad de un universo en que hombres e instituciones colaboran al servicio de Dios, en el que los individuos encuentran una felicidad superior a la que alcanzan considerándose a sí mismos como fines últimos."

40. Maeztu, *Don Quijote . . .*, 98. "Tenemos que elegir entre la intuición que nos dice que nos dice que Don Juan es el mal porque su vida es una ofensa contra el espíritu de servicio social, de castidad, de veracidad, de lealtad; y el impulso que nos lleva al donjuanismo, por las pasiones que hay en cada uno de nosotros, fauces abiertas que necesitan hacer presa."

41. Maeztu, *Don Quijote . . .*, 98. "Si nos decidimos por el deber, la historia seguirá en apoyo nuestro."

42. Maeztu, *Don Quijote . . .*, 98. "Esta confianza de andar con las estrellas infundirá a nuestro brazo el mismo brío que a Don Juan le presta la conformidad con sus instintos."

43. Maeztu, *Don Quijote . . .*, 106. "Para fortalecer entre los hombres el saber y el amor."

44. Maeztu, *Don Quijote . . .*, 130. "La santa del hedonismo."

45. Maeztu, *Don Quijote . . .*, 133. "Para Celestina no hay más bien, es decir, no hay más Dios que el placer. A ministrarlo se dedica."

46. Maeztu, *Don Quijote . . .*, 127–129. "Antes que la 'ciencia del mal por el mal,' es Celestina la ciencia a secas, el saber sin calificativos . . . todo su aparato de símbolos e hipótesis no se propone sino buscar el modo de explotar el universo."

47. Maeztu, *Don Quijote . . .*, 130.

48. Maeztu, *Don Quijote . . .*, 119. "El amor-pasión es una desgracia, porque un sentimiento tan excelso como es el del amor no nos fué dado para contentarse con lo particular, ni puede satisfacerse una esencia perdurable, cósmica, divina, con la forma pasajera de la criatura amada."

49. Maeztu, *Don Quijote . . .*, 117. "De la fuente misma de la voluptuosidad surge la amargura de malgastar la vida en la ociosidad o en los placeres."

50. Maeztu, *Don Quijote . . .*, 136. "Celestina representa la bandera del individuo contra la sociedad; el placer del instante frente al deber que el porvenir impone."

51. Maeztu, *Don Quijote . . .*, 153.

52. Maeztu, *Don Quijote . . .*, 153. "El espectáculo de su fin desastrado nos ofrece la purificación que el alma del hombre alcanza en la tragedia, porque el dolor moral, lo mismo que el físico, nos señala las cosas que nos pondrían en peligro y que debemos evitar."

53. Maeztu, *Don Quijote . . .*, 137. "Honor . . . fe en el bien, esperanza en su triunfo y ardiente caridad en su ejercicio."

54. Maeztu, *Don Quijote . . .*, 137.

CHAPTER 10

1. Ortega, *Meditaciones,* 11. "La catedra, el periódico o la política."

2. Ortega's choice in title invites speculation. Certainly, it is a title that creates many expectations. First, as a "meditation" it calls to mind the philosophical *Meditations* of Descartes. Indeed, insofar as Ortega refers to his own *Meditaciones del Quijote* as "ensayos de amor intellectual" it is within reason to assume that Ortega intended his work to be perceived as philosophical. Second, insofar as the title announces that the object of Ortega's "intellectual love" is to be the *Quixote,* it is also legitimate to expect that this little book will contain an analysis of the *Quixote.* Ortega, in fact, does more. He develops a theory of the novel based on his reading of the *Quixote.* Finally, the title—*Meditaciones del Quijote*—inspires a certain play on words. Does the book contain meditations on the book *Quijote* or does it contain the meditations of Don Quixote himself, or, at the very least of a Quixotist Ortega? To a greater or lesser degree, Ortega's book satisfies every one of these expectations.

3. Ortega, *Meditaciones,* 11. Apart from a study of Cervantes and his *Quijote,* Ortega's history was to include an analysis of the Spanish national epic poem "Mío Cid," an approximation to he comedies of Lope de Vega and, finally, an investigation into the contemporary novels of Baroja dn Azorín.

4. Ortega, *Meditaciones,* 30. "Intento [de] hacer un estudio del quijotismo."

5. Ortega, *Meditaciones,* 30. "Mi quijotismo no tiene nada que ver con la mercancía bajo tal nombre ostentada en el mercado . . . Generalmente, lo que . . . se entiende por 'quijotismo,' es el quijotismo del personaje. Estos ensayos [the *Meditaciones*], en cambio, investigan el quijotismo del libro."

6. Ortega, *Meditaciones,* 31. "Los errores a que ha llevado considerar aisladamente a Don Quijote son verdaderamente grotescos."

7. Ortega, *Meditaciones,* 31. "Unos, . . . nos proponen que no seamos Quijotes."

8. Ortega, *Meditaciones,* 31. "Otros, según la moda más reciente, nos invitan a una existencia absurda, llena de ademanes congestionados."

9. Ortega, *Meditaciones,* 79. "[E]s siempre el hombre el tema esencial del arte . . . los géneros . . . son amplias vistas que se toman sobre las vertientes cardinales de lo humano. Cada época trae consigo una interpretación radical del hombre . . . por esto, cada época prefiere un determinado género."

10. Ortega, *Meditaciones,* 83. "El tema de la épica es el pasado como tal pasado . . . [la épica] huye de todo presente . . . no es . . . el recuerdo, sino un pasado ideal."

11. Ortega, *Meditaciones,* 91–92. "Se permite la aventura."

12. Ortega, *Meditaciones,* 90–91. "Literatura de la imaginación."

13. Ortega, *Meditaciones,* 104. "El germen del realismo se halla en un cierto impulso que lleva al hombre a imitar."

14. Ortega, *Meditaciones,* 104–105. "El que imita, imita para burlarse . . . Sólo, pues, con motivo de una intención cómica parece adquirir la realidad un interés estético."

15. Ortega, *Meditaciones,* 20. "[En mis *Meditaciones*] yo sólo ofrezco *modi res considerandi,* posibles maneras nuevas de mirar las cosas."

16. Ortega, *Meditaciones,* 28. "General constitución reaccionaria de nuestro espíritu."

17. This negative view of Spanish national history would become the centerpiece of Ortega's 1922 *España invertebrada.*

18. Ortega, *Meditaciones,* 28. "¡Tierra de los antepasados!, no nuestra, no libre propiedad de los españoles actuales. Los que antes pasaron siguen gobernándonos y forman una oligarquía de la muerte, que nos oprime."

19. Ortega, *Meditaciones,* 74. "La realidad tradicional en España ha consistido precisamente en el aniquilamiento progresivo de la posibilidad España . . . No, no podemos seguir la tradición; todo lo contrario: tenemos que ir contra la tradición, más allá de la tradición. De entre los escombros tradicionales, nos urge salvar la primera sustancia de la raza, el módulo hispánico."

20. Ortega's notion of a regenerating elite presupposes the construction of a new, national, and historical subject that is to reform, modernize, and make the Spanish nation "European." Yet, his requirement that this elite abide by the aristocratic ideals of a master morality exposes his notion of "modernization" as being dependent on the premodern authority of a charismatic subjectivity. See, in this regard, Eduardo Subirats, "Cuarteto español," *Después de la lluvia* (Madrid: Ediciones Temas de Hoy, 1993), 182–184.

21. Ortega, *Meditaciones,* 119. "Nuestras acciones no pasan de reacciones."

22. Ortega, *Meditaciones,* 119.

23. Ortega, *Meditaciones,* 28. "La muerte de lo muerto es la vida."

24. Ortega, *Meditaciones,* 75. "Los que amen hoy las posibilidades españolas tienen que cantar a la inversa la leyenda de la historia de España, a fin de llegar a su través hasta aquella media docena de lugares donde la pobre víscera cordial de nuestra raza da sus puros e intensos latidos."

25. Ortega, *Meditaciones,* 63.

26. Ortega, *Meditaciones,* 75. Jaime de Salas has studied Ortega's *Meditaciones* in terms of its orientation within a genre of "tales of conversion." He explains that while the *Meditaciones* does not follow exactly the arrangement of a "quest for identity" it does, nevertheless, "describe the revelation of truth which not only concerns the form in which reality is interpreted, but also conditions the narrator's entire life." See Jaime de Salas, "Ethics and the Problem of Modernity in the *Meditaciones del Quijote,*" *Hispanic Issues Vol 5: Ortega y Gasset: The Question of Modernity* (Minneapolis, MN: The Prisma Institute, 1989), 325.

27. Ortega, *Meditaciones,* 13. "Estos ensayos son unos ensayos de amor intelectual . . . son 'salvaciones.' Se busca en ellos lo siguiente: dado un hecho—un hombre . . . un error, un dolor—llevarlo por el camino más corto a la plenitud de su significado . . . Esto es amor—el amor a la perfección de lo amado."

28. Ortega, *Meditaciones,* 13.

29. Ortega, *Meditaciones,* 14. "Es un divino arquitecto que bajó al mundo . . . a fin de que todo en el universo viva en conexión."

30. Ortega, *Meditaciones,* 20. "Pretexto y llamamiento a una amplia colaboración ideológica sobre los temas nacionales."

31. Ortega, *Meditaciones,* 14–15. "Yo quisiera proponer en estos ensayos a los lectores . . . que expulsen de sus ánimos todo hábito de odiosidad y aspiren fuertemente a que el amor vuelva a administrar el universo."

32. Ortega, *Meditaciones,* 16. "El amor combate, esta lucha con un enemigo a quien se comprende, es la verdadera tolerancia."

33. Ortega, *Meditaciones,* 17. "Reforma, corrección y aumento del ideal ético."

34. Ortega, *Meditaciones,* 73.

35. Ortega, *Meditaciones,* 73. "La mecánica psicológica del reaccionarismo español."

36. Ortega, *Meditaciones,* 77. Ortega writes, in this regard, that the *Quijote* is "la primera novela en el orden del tiempo y del valor." The novel, moreover, is for Ortega, the "género . . . predilecto de nuestro tiempo."

37. Ortega, *Meditaciones,* 58. "Los meditadores y los sensuales." In contrast to a "meditative" elite that is capable of possessing the world, the "sensual" masses are not at all capable of doing so. This is the case because, according to Ortega, the masses view the world "impressionistically" and, consequently, are locked in "a perpetual struggle with what is elemental." In this sense, the masses are, for Ortega, tantamount to mere things governed by the absolute laws of the physical and sensual world. As such, as things, they are devoid of spirituality; they lack will, except, of course, the negative will of resentment. Unmistakably, Ortega views the masses as slaves to necessity. Conversely, he views the elite, the heroes, as capable of willing and, by reason of their conceptual knowledge of the world, capable also of mastering necessity. Like the mythological figures that populate Ortega's notion of the epic, the heroic elites are capable of adventure. Hence, they are able to step beyond the laws of physics and into a world governed by the spiritual laws of the will. By mastering the "outside" and negating it, they are able, like the mystical virgin of Ganivet's *Idearium español,* to go "inside."

38. Ortega's theory of the novel is typically studied outside the immediate nationalist context of its conception and without taking properly into account the elitist ideals suggested by Ortega's aristocratic sociology. This helps to explain why Ortega's theory of the novel has often been compared to Lukács's 1914–1915 *The Theory of the Novel.* See, for example, Anthony J. Cascardi's "Between Philosophy and Literature," in *Hispanic Issues, Volume 5,* 337–368.

39. Ortega, *Meditaciones,* 109. "El sujeto trágico . . . es trágico . . . sólo en cuanto que quiere. La voluntad . . . es el tema trágico."

40. Ortega, *Meditaciones,* 110. "Dejemos . . . todas las teorías que, basando la tragedia en no sé qué fatalidad, creen que es la derrota, la muerte del héroe quien le presta la calidad trágica."

41. Ortega, *Meditaciones,* 111.

42. Ortega, *Meditaciones,* 111. "Es esencial al héroe querer su trágico destino."

43. Ortega, *Meditaciones,* 110. "Un poco inverosímil . . . [E]l villano piensa muy juiciosamente que todas las cosas malas sobrevienen al héroe porque se obstina en tal o cual propósito. Desentendiéndose de él, todo llegaría a buen arreglo."

44. Ortega, *Meditaciones,* "Asentarse y tener muchos hijos."

45. Ortega, *Meditaciones,* 106–107. "Es un hecho que existen hombres decididos a no contentarse con la realidad. Aspiran los tales a que las cosas lleven un curso distinto: se niegan a repetir los gestos que la costumbre, la tradición, y . . . los instintos biológicos les fuerzan a hacer. Estos hombres llamamos héroes . . . Cuando el héroe quiere, no son los antepasados en él o los usos presentes quienes quieren, sino él mismo. Y este querer él ser él mismo es la heroicidad."

46. Ortega, *Meditaciones,* 106. "Un hombre que quiere reformar la realidad."

47. Ortega, *Meditaciones,* 97. "Cervantes destaca a Sancho contra toda aventura, a fin de que al pasar por ella la haga imposible. Esta es su misión."

48. Ortega, *Meditaciones,* 113. "Instinto de inercia y de conservación"; "se venga . . . Envía contra . . . [Don Quijote] al realismo y lo envuelve en una comedia."

49. Ortega, *Meditaciones,* 100.

50. Ortega, *Meditaciones,* 115. "La caída violenta del cuerpo trágico, vencido por la fuerza de inercia, por la realidad."

51. Ortega, *Meditaciones,* 117. "Si la novela contemporánea pone menos al descubierto su mecanismo cómico, débese a que los ideales por ella atacados apenas se distancian de la realidad con que se los combate . . . el ideal *cae* desde poquísima altura . . . la novela del siglo XIX . . . contiene la menor cantidad posible de dinamismo poético."

52. Ortega, *Meditaciones,* 117. With regard to the decadence of the nineteenth century, Ortega writes: "este siglo, nuestro padre, ha sentido una perversa fruición en el pesimismo: se ha revolcado en él, ha apurado su vaso y ha comprimido el mundo de manera que nada levantado pudo quedar en pie. Sale de toda esta centuria hacia nosotros como una bocanada de rencor."

53. Ortega, *Meditaciones,* 117. "La novela del siglo XIX será ilegible muy pronto."

54. Ortega, *Meditaciones,* 119. "El hombre no es sujeto de sus actos sino que es movido por el medio en que vive . . . El medio es el único protagonista."

55. Ortega, *Meditaciones,* 30. "[E]s Don Quijote la parodia triste de un cristo más divino y sereno: es él un cristo gótico, macerado en angustias modernas; un cristo ridículo de nuestro barrio, creado por una imaginación dolorida que perdió su inocencia y su voluntad y anda buscando otras nuevas. Cuando se reúnen unos cuantos españoles sensibilizados por la miseria de su pasado, la sordidez de su presente y la acre hostilidad de su porvenir, desciende entre ellos Don Quijote . . . [que] como un hilo espiritual, los nacionaliza, poniendo tras sus amarguras personales un comunal dolor étnico."

56. Ortega, *Meditaciones,* 75. "¡Ah! Si supiéramos con evidencia en qué consiste el estilo de Cervantes, la manera cervantina de acercarse a las cosas, lo tendríamos todo logrado. Porque en estas cimas espirituales reina inquebrantable solidaridad y un estilo poético lleva consigo una filosofía y una moral, una ciencia y una política. Si algún día viniera alguien y nos descubriera el perfil del estilo de Cervantes, bastaría con que prolongáramos sus líneas sobre los demás problemas colectivos para que despertáramos a nueva vida. Entonces, si hay entre nosotros coraje y genio, cabría hacer con toda pureza el nuevo ensayo español."

57. Ortega, *Meditaciones,* 71. "No existe libro alguno cuyo poder de alusiones simbólicas al sentido universal de la vida sea tan grande y, sin embargo, no existe libro alguno en que hallemos menos indicaciones, menos indicios para su propia interpretación."

58. Ortega, *Meditaciones,* 12.

59. Ortega, *Meditaciones,* 29. "Fervoroso esfuerzo para potenciar la obra elegida."

60. Ortega, *Meditaciones,* 73. "Es, en definitiva, cada raza un ensayo de una nueva manera de vivir, de una nueva sensibilidad."

61. Ortega, *Meditaciones,* 20. "Posibles maneras nuevas de mirar las cosas."

62. Ortega, *Meditaciones,* 63. "Un órgano o aparato *para* la posesión de las cosas."

63. Ortega, *Meditaciones,* 63. "Sólo la visión mediante el concepto es una visión completa."

64. Ortega, *Meditaciones,* 25. "Yo soy yo y mi circunstancia, y si no la salvo a ella no me salvo yo."

65. Ortega, *Meditaciones,* 20. "Despertar en almas hermanas otros pensamientos hermanos, aun cuando fueren hermanos enemigos."

66. Ortega, *Meditaciones,* 23. "El acto específicamente cultural es el creador . . . La cultura adquirida sólo tiene valor como instrumento y arma de nuevas conquistas."

Conclusion

1. Enrique Tierno Galván, *Escritos* (Madrid: Editorial Tecnos, 1971).

2. Hugh Thomas, *The Spanish Civil War* (New York: Harper and Row, 1961), 69.

3. Isaiah Berlin, *Four Essays on Liberty* (Oxford: Oxford University Press, 1971).

4. Delegación Nacional de Prensa y Propaganda, 14. "Sólo es de veras libre quien forma parte de una nación fuerte . . . A nadie le será lícito usar su libertad contra la unión, la fortaleza y la libertad de la nación. Una disciplina rigurosa impedirá todo intento dirigido a envenenar, a desunir a los españoles o a moverlos contra el destino de la patria."

5. Delegación Nacional de Prensa y Propaganda, 12. "Creemos en la suprema realidad de España. Fortalecerla, elevarla y engrandecerla es la apremiante tarea colec-

tiva de todos los españoles. A la realización de esa tarea habrán de plegarse inexorablemente los intereses de los individuos, de los grupos y de las clases."

6. Delegación Nacional de Prensa y Propaganda, 13. "España volverá a buscar su gloria y su riqueza por las rutas del mar . . . España alega su condición de eje espiritual del mundo hispánico como título de preeminencia en las empresas universales."

7. Delegación Nacional de Prensa y Propaganda, 13. "Nuestro estado será un instrumento totalitario al servicio de la integridad patria . . . Haremos . . . que un sentido militar de la vida informe toda la existencia española."

8. Aznar, *La Segunda transición,* 170. "España no es únicamente un país mediterraneo. Su rostro atlántico, que mira a América, no ha tenido la suficiente nitidez a la hora de dibujar nuestra política exterior en los últimos años. Debemos recuperarlo, porque sería un suicidio histórico renunciar o postergar . . . el 'destino transatlántico' de España."

9. Interview of the President of the Government, Don José María Aznar, on Spanish Television, April 21, 2003. "El terrorismo es nuestra principal amenaza y es la principal amenaza del mundo. Un país como España no puede ser insensible a eso. ¿Cómo vamos a pedir nosotros cooperación internacional en la lucha contra el terrorismo y, cuando otros necesitan nuestra ayuda, decir que nosotros no estamos dispuestos a ayudar? Eso no es posible. Cuando nosotros necesitemos, que necesitamos, cooperación internacional; cuando necesitemos de nuestros aliados, que necesitamos de nuestros aliados, podremos decir: también hemos contribuido; no solamente hemos estado a las maduras, hemos estado también a las duras en los momentos difíciles."

Supplement

1. The modern origins of this tradition were first reconstructed by Vicente Lloréns, *Literatura, Historia, Política* (Madrid: Ediciones de la *Revista de Occidente,* 1967).

2. The pejorative use of the term *europeizante* has a definite tie to the also pejorative label *afrancesado* that became popular among Spain's patriots during the War of Independence. The *afrancesado,* not unlike his or her offspring the *europeizante,* is defined as a collaborator and traitor to Catholic and Monarchic Spain's traditional sense of its *casticismo.* See in this regard, Raymond Carr, *Spain: 1808–1975* (Oxford: Clarendon Press, 1982), 112–113.

3. For a compelling summary of Castro's views on Cervantes' *Quixote,* a summary based in personal correspondence, see: Stephen Gilman "The Last 'Don Quijote' of Don Américo," in Ronald E. Surtz, Jaime Ferrán, Daniel P. Testa, eds., *Américo Castro: The Impact of His Thought* (Madison, Wisconsin: Hispanic Seminary of Medieval Studies, 1988), 63–70.

4. In this respect, Castro followed in the footsteps of Blanco-White. Having fled Spain on the heels of that country's War of Independence from Napoleon, Blanco White formulated a critique of the nation's patriotism that explained this sentiment's

blind spots as the result of Christian Spain's *casticismo*. According to Blanco White this *casticismo* is "una extraña mezcla de odio, temor y desprecio que transform[a] la diferencia de credos en una fuente imaginaria de polución [y hace] de la ortodoxia el fundamento de una presunta superioridad de naturaleza que disting[ue] la casta superior de las inferiores y decadentes." This mixture is fused, argues Blanco White, with "un espíritu de fanatismo e intolerancia religiosa," which seeks to associate "toda idea de honor con ortodoxia y cuanto es odioso e indigno con heterodoxia y disconformidad." *Casticismo,* for Blanco White, becomes not only an obsession of the ruling Christian caste with the purity of its blood but also the principal motive that inspires the Spanish masses to submit themselves to the commands of Spain's double tyranny: that of its absolute monarchs and its no-less-absolute ecclesiastics. See José María Blanco White *Obra Inglesa* (Barcelona: Seix Barral, 1972), 173.

5. Américo Castro, *La realidad histórica de España* (Mexico: Editorial Porrúa, 1987), 1. "Unico entre los pueblos de Occidente, el español se rige, en cuanto al conocimiento de su pasado y de sí mismo, por una historiografía fundada en nociones fabulosas."

6. Castro, *La realidad histórica,* 40–46.

7. Castro, *La realidad histórica,* 246.

8. Castro, *La realidad histórica,* 234–241.

9. Castro, *La realidad histórica,* 21.

10. The uncompromising dispute between Américo Castro and Sánchez Albornoz is perhaps the most famous, to say nothing of infamous, form that such attacks took.

11. Américo Castro, *Cervantes y los casticismos españoles* (Madrid: Alianza Editorial, 1974), 73. "Una contienda entre un *yo* y otro *yo* . . . El diálogo novelístico estuvo precedido del callado monólogo de quienes se juzgaban con suficiente conciencia de ser quienes eran, con derecho a hablar en primera persona de lo que a uno le acontecía y . . . para buscarse interlocutores. Hacía falta poseer una interioridad capaz de exhibirse en público."

12. Castro, *Cervantes y los casticismos,* 106–129.

13. Castro, *Cervantes y los casticismos,* 118. "Mundo cervantino-quijotil [que] nació bajo el signo de la libertad."

14. Castro, *La realidad histórica,* 202–211.

15. Castro, *La realidad histórica,* vi. "La generación del '98 y quienes la continuamos, en cuanto saber histórico, e intelección de qué y cómo hubiese sido España, no aportamos ninguna verdad decisiva, fortificante y consoladora."

16. Castro, *La realidad histórica,* xi. "Si el español no se decide a convivir con su propia historia, ¿cómo se pondrá de acuerdo con sus prójimos españoles? ¿Cómo sabrá eludir la opresión, la anarquía o el caos? O quizá algo todavía peor: la insignificancia."

17. Castro, *La realidad histórica,* xii.

18. Joseph Silverman, "Américo Castro and the Secret Spanish Civil War," Surtz, Ferrán, Testa, *Américo Castro,* 83–95. As Joseph Silverman notes even the work of a

supposedly enlightened thinker such as José Antonio Maravall can be understood to be motivated by the "determination to undermine Castro's efforts to perceive and elucidate differences."

19. Ironically, the democracy that Castro so much wanted to see realized in his native Spain only yesterday, with the occasion of commemorating 1898, completely forgot him and his modernizing critique of the mono-religious *casticismo* espoused by Unamuno and other major figures associated with the *generación del 98*. This silence, indeed, was part and parcel of the official strategy of forgetfulness that informed Spain's acritical commemoration of 1898 and its Quixotists.

20. A noteworthy exception to this systematic censorship and nationally willed forgetting of Castro's work is the international congress "Américo Castro: Revisiones de la Memoria" that was organized in 1999 by Eduardo Subirats and held, first at NYU in April of that year, and in May at the Círculo de Bellas Artes in Madrid. For a review of the congress and its reception in Spain see "Américo Castro, azote de nacionalismos" *El Mundo* May 5, 1999: 62.

21. As concerns his anti-Semitism, Castro held that the violence and intolerance of the Spanish Inquisition could best be explained by the need that Spain's Jewish converts to Christianity felt to outwardly prove their Christianity: "De ahí que bastantes conversos . . . se hicieran perversos, y que de entre ellos salieran los más atroces enemigos de los israelitas y de los mismos conversos." By means of this anti-Semitism, Castro managed to minimize the role of Spain's Christians in persecuting the Jews. See: Castro, *La realidad histórica*, 45.

22. Américo Castro, *La peculiaridad linguística rioplatense* (Buenos Aires: Editorial Losada, 1941), 40. "Los países hispánicos se hallan inscritos en una tradición y destino hispánicos, y se ahincan más en ellos cuanto más pretenden desmentirlos o eludirlos."

23. Castro, *La peculiaridad linguística*, 108. "A los países rioplatenses les incumbe, les está incumbiendo, una misión continental, que un día será mundial, como zonas esenciales de la cultura hispánica."

24. Castro, *La peculiaridad linguística*, 108–109.

25. Miguel Antonio Caro, "El *Quijote*," Manuel Alcalá and Carlos Montemayor, eds., *Apuntes cervantinos hispanoamericanos*, vol. 2 (Mexico: Festival Internacional Cervantino, 1990), 100. "El *Quijote* es el poema de los españoles . . . es a España . . . lo que son a otros pueblos sus grandes epopeyas."

26. Caro, "El *Quijote*," 100. "Por cuanto es [el *Quijote*] el libro de nuestra raza, es también el libro de nuestros pueblos de América."

27. Caro, "El *Quijote*," 101, 93. "Familia Ibérica" . . . "hermoso en la ejecución" . . . "los atributos peculiares en que se abrevia [la] nación [española]" . . . "un pensamiento que interesa a la humanidad."

28. Miguel Antonio Caro, *Obras de Virgilio* (Bogotá: Voluntad, 1943), 29. "Distinguir la debilidad de la culpa, el dolor del crimen, la pobreza del deshonor [y dar] tanta belleza al dolor, a la pobreza y a la debilidad."

29. Caro, *Obras de Virgilio,* 24–25. "Nuestros padres" . . . "hombres de la raza conquistada" . . . "la destruccion . . . sino la fusión de las razas."

30. Miguel Antonio Caro, *Escritos políticos* (Bogotá: Caro y Cuervo, 1990), 101. "La hermosa unidad católica."

31. Caro, *Escritos políticos,* 101. "Todos los monumentos literarios del siglo de oro de España."

32. The Regenerationist movement in Colombia arises, above all, as a reaction against the ostracism that the Catholic Church experienced in that country during the period that its radical republican governments reigned under the Constitution of 1863. Under Caro's leadership, this movement gave rise to a new constitution in 1886 which led in due course to the signing of a new Concordant between the republic and the Holy Sede in 1887.

33. Caro, *Escritos políticos,* 88, 262. "El error capital de la época presente . . . error que por todas partes triunfa y se corona."

34. Caro, *Escritos políticos,* 101–102. "Naciones enfermas" . . . "la barabarie."

35. Caro, *Escritos políticos,* 104. "No hay más bien que el placer ni más derecho que la fuerza."

36. Caro, *Escritos políticos,* 88–89. "Creer y orar . . . ser hijos sumisos de la Iglesia universal."

37. Caro, "El *Quijote,*" 104. "Enseñanzas de alta filosofía católica."

38. Caro, "El *Quijot,*" 104. "Un afecto y culto a la unidad religiosa de la nación."

39. Caro, "El *Quijote,*" 103. "Un gran católico como hombre" . . . "el egoismo pagano . . . no pudo haber dirigido su pluma."

40. Caro, "El *Quijote,*" 100–102. "Quiso Cervantes preparar . . . la muerte cristiana de su héroe."

41. Caro, "El *Quijote,*" 94. "Tan rey sería yo de mi Estado como cada uno del suyo, y siéndolo, haría lo que quisiese, y haciendo lo que quisiese, haría mi gusto, y haciendo mi gusto, estaría contento, y estando contento, no tiene más que desear" . . . "los modernos catedráticos sensualistas . . . [del] nuevo paganismo."

42. Caro, "El *Quijote,*" 94. "La filosofía política cristiana."

43. Caro, *Escritos políticos,* 289. "Que cada cual concurra a la obra común . . . con sacrificios . . . con virtudes efectivas . . . con humildad de entendimiento y pureza de intención."

44. Caro, "El *Quijote,*" 103, 96. "Envuelve . . . una provechosa lección política" . . . "estos nuestros tiempos que a los de Cervantes."

45. Caro, "El *Quijote,*" 103–104.

46. Caro, *Escritos políticos,* 277. "Un centro que asegura el orden y afianza la paz"

47. Caro, *Escritos políticos,* 278. "[Han de] descansa[r] sobre la base religiosa, fundamento de todas las civilizaciones."

48. Caro, *Escritos políticos,* 92. "La Iglesia católica, apostólica . . . universal maestra de las gentes."

49. Caro, *Escritos políticos,* 107. "Hoy el mundo parece vacilar entre cristianismo verdadero, o sea el catolicismo, y el paganismo moderno, mucho peor que el antiguo."

50. Caro, *Escritos políticos,* "Compelidas por la experiencia, volverán las naciones cristianas . . . a la unidad."

51. Miguel Antonio Caro, "El Quijotismo español," *Ideario Hispánico* (Bogotá: Instituto Colombiano de Cultura Hispánica, 1952), 201. "Vanidad, fatuidad y jactancias colectivas."

52. Caro, "El Quijotismo español," 201. "Es un hecho extraordinario que los españoles tenían una fe implícita en la pureza de su raza y de su sangre como la principal causa que había de darles triunfo sobre los Estados Unidos."

53. Caro, "El Quijotismo español," 202. "Bajo el nombre genérico de quijotismo."

54. Caro, "El Quijotismo español," 202. "Falsificación del orgullo nacional."

55. Caro, "El Quijotismo español," 202. "Cacicazgos y caudillaje" . . . "el orgullo nacional divorciado de la moral cristiana."

56. Unamuno, "Muera Don Quijote."

57. Caro, "El Quijotismo español," 203.

58. Caro, *Escritos políticos,* 292. "Del desorden, cuando llega a los extremos, nunca han salido los pueblos sino por medio de una dictadura única, que sobreponiéndose a los dictadores de provincia y aldea, enseñe a obedecer a todos los que quieren mandar; o bien, por medio de movimientos colectivos y patrióticos, de la concurrencia de voluntades abnegadas, bajo la dirección de una inteligencia superior."

59. Fernández Cifuentes, "Cartografías del 98," 122. In a study of the truncated dialogues between the writers of Spain's *generación del 98* and their Hispanic American contemporaries Luis Fernández Cifuentes calls attention to the competing rhetorical strategies of "parentesco" and "posesión" that characterized those dialogues.

60. Azorín, *Obras Completas,* 1142–1149. It was Azorín himself who initially included Rubén Darío among the members of his fancied literary generation.

61. See, in this regard, my discussion in the Introduction of the debates in Restoration Spain pitting Hispanic American modernism against the Spanish *generación del 98* and, especially, notes 16 and 19 to the Introduction.

62. Frederick B. Pike, *Hispanismo: 1898–1936: Spanish Conservatives and Liberals and Their Relations with Spanish America* (London: University of Notre Dame Press, 1971), 66.

63. Rubén Darío, *Azul . . . , El salmo de la pluma, Cantos de vida y esperanza, Otros poemas* (Mexico: Editorial Porrua, 1990), 165–167. "Rey de los hidalgos, señor de los tristes / que de fuerza alientas y de ensueños vistes / . . . Noble peregrino de los peregrinos, / que santificaste todos los caminos / con el paso augusto de tu heroicidad."

64. Darío, *Azul . . . ,* 116. "Ínclitas razas ubérrimas, sangre de Hispania fecunda, / espíritus fraternos, luminosas almas, ¡salve! / Porque llega el momento en que habrán

de cantar nuevos himnos / lenguas de gloria. Un vasto rumor llena los ámbitos; mágicas / ondas de vida van renaciendo pronto."

65. Darío, *Azul* . . . , 116. "Retrocede el olvido, retrocede engañada la muerte; se anuncia un reino nuevo . . . encontramos de súbito . . . la divina reina de luz, ¡la celeste Esperanza!"

66. Darío, *Azul* . . . , 117. "Un continente y otro renovando las viejas prosapias, / en espíritu unidos, en espíritu y ansias y lengua, / ven llegar el momento en que habrán de cantar nuevos himnos / . . . Y así sea esperanza la visión permanente en nosotros."

67. Darío, *Azul* . . . , 110. "Si en estos cantos hay política, es porque aparece universal . . . Mañana podremos ser yanquis (y es lo más probable); de todas maneras, mi protesta queda escrita."

68. Darío, *Azul* . . . , 131. "La América Española como la España entera / fija está en el Oriente de su fatal destino / . . . ¿Seremos entregados a los bárbaros fieros? / ¿Tantos millones de hombres hablaremos inglés? / ¿Ya no hay nobles hidalgos ni bravos caballeros? / ¿Callaremos ahora para llorar después?"

69. Darío, *Azul* . . . , 123–124. "Primitivo y moderno, sencillo y complicado, / con un algo de Washington y cuatro de Nemrod. / Eres los Estados Unidos, / eres el futuro invasor / de la América ingenua que tiene sangre indígena, / que aún reza a Jesucristo y aún habla en español / . . . Juntáis al culto de Hércules el culto de Mammón."

70. José Martí, *Política de nuestra América* (Mexico: Siglo Veintiuno Editores, 1989).

71. Darío, *Azul* . . . , 124. "Más la América nuestra . . . / la América del gran Moctezuma, del Inca, la América fragrante de Cristóbal Colón, / la América católica, la América española, / . . . esa América que tiembla de huracanes y que vive de Amor, / hombres de ojos sajones y alma bárbara, vive. / Y sueña. Y ama, y vibra; y es la hija del Sol. / Tened cuidado. ¡Vive la América española! / Hay mil cachorros sueltos del León Español. / . . . Y, pues contáis con todo, falta una cosa: ¡Dios!"

72. José Enrique Rodó, *Ariel* (Mexico: Editorial Porrua, 1989) 1. "el imperio de la razón y el sentimiento sobre los bajos estímulos de la irracionalidad . . . el entusiasmo generoso, el móvil alto y desinteresado dé la acción, la espiritualidad de la cultura . . . el término ideal a que asciende la selección humana."

73. Rodó, *Ariel,* 24–25. "Para afrontar el problema es necesario empezar por reconocer que cuando la democracia no enaltece su espíritu por la influencia de una fuerte preocupación ideal que comparta su imperio con la preocupación de los intereses materiales, ella conduce fatalmente a la privanza de la mediocridad y carece, más que ningún otro régimen, de eficaces barreras con las cuales asegurar dentro de un ambiente adecuado la inviolabilidad de la alta cultura. Abandonada a si misma . . . la democracia extinguirá gradualmente toda idea de superioridad."

74. Rodó, *Ariel,* 27. In this regard, Rodó asserts that "[t]odo lo que en la civilización es algo más que un elemento de superioridad material y de prosperidad económica, constituye un relieve que no tarda en ser allanado cuando la autoridad moral pertenece al espíritu de medianía."

75. Rodó, *Ariel,* 27–28. Interestingly, Rodó links this "moral problem" of the masses' resentment to the "social problem" presented to Hispanic America's young republics by European immigration.

76. Rodó, *Ariel,* 28. "Tendencia a lo utilitario y lo vulgar."

77. Rodó, *Ariel,* 30. As Diego Alonso has noted, the modern heroic type that Rodó constructs throughout his essays and political writings is attuned to an aesthetically informed yet pragmatic spirituality. The hero, for Rodó, is the genius: at once adept in the finer points of the contemplative life and suited to action. See, in this regard: Diego Alonso, "Una estátua de Ceryanes para América: El *Quijote* y la cuestión de la conquista según José E. Rodó," *Siglo diecinueve* 5 (1999), 149–163.

78. Rodó, *Ariel,* 32. As regards the defunct and anti-heroic tendencies of traditional aristocracies, oligarchies, and dictatorships, Rodó reasons as follows: "El carácter odioso de las aristocracias tradicionales se originaba de que ellas eran injustas, por su fundamento, y opresoras, por cuanto su autoridad era una imposición. Hoy sabemos que no existe otro límite legítimo para la igualdad humana que el que consiste en el dominio de la inteligencia y la virtud, consentido por la libertad de todos." Rodó argues, in short, that because they are coercive, these forms of political authority are in essence unjust. Only a moral, and therefore political, authority grounded in liberty is, Rodó holds, truly just.

79. Rodó, *Ariel,* 32. "Racionalmente concebida, la democracia admite siempre un imprescriptible elemento aristocrático, que consiste en establecer la superioridad de los mejores, asegurándola sobre el consentimiento libre de los asociados . . . Reconociendo, de tal manera, en la selección y la predominancia de los mejor dotados una necesidad de todo progreso, [la democracia] excluye . . . el efecto de humillación y de dolor que es . . . el duro lote del vencido."

80. José Enrique Rodó, *Obras Completas* (Madrid: Aguilar, 1957), 1300–1322. Rodó and Unamuno maintained an active epistolary exchange between 1900 and 1916. Although in none of these letters do these two thinkers engage in a discussion concerning Don Quixote, they do exchanage their views in regard to various literary themes, beginning with Rodó's own *Ariel* and its, according to Unamuno "afrancesamiento," the virtues of English essayists and the decadent influence of the decadentist and modernist movements.

81. Rodó, *Obras Completas,* 521. "Después del Cristo de paz, hubo menester la humana historia del Cristo guerrero, y entonces naciste tú, Don Quijote."

82. Rodó, *Obras Completas,* 522. "Resucitaste al tercer día: no para subir al cielo, sino para proseguir y consumar tus aventuras gloriosas; y aún andas por el mundo, aunque invisible y ubicuo, y aún deshaces agravios, y enderezas entruertos, y tienes guerras con encantadores, y favoreces a los débiles, los necesitados y los humildes, ¡oh sublime Don Quijote, Cristo ejecutivo, Cristo-León, Cristo a la jineta!"

83. Rodó, *Ariel,* 39. "Perseverantes devotos de ese culto de la energía individual que hace de cada hombre el artífice de su destino, ellos han modelado su sociabilidad en un conjunto imaginario de ejemplares de Robinson, que después de haber fortificado rudamente su personalidad en la práctica de la ayuda propia, entrarán a componer los filamentos de una urdimbre firmísima."

84. Rodó, *Obras Completas,* 521. "Cristo con armas implica contradicción, de donde nace, en parte lo cómico de tu figura, y también lo que de sublime hay en ella."

85. Rodó, *Obras Completas,* 1146.

86. Rodó, *Obras Completas,* 1147. "Hay . . . entre el genio de Cervantes y la aparición de América en el orbe, profunda correlación histórica. El descubrimiento, la conquista de América, son la obra magna del Renacimiento español, y el verbo de este Renacimiento es la novela de Cervantes."

87. Rodó, *Obras Completas,* 1147. "No hay otra estatua que la de Cervantes para simbolizar en América la España del pasado común, la España del sol sin poniente."

88. Rodó, *Obras Completas,* 1147. "La ironía de esta maravillosa creación, abatiendo un ideal caduco, afirma y exalta de rechazo un ideal nuevo y potente, que es el que . . . abre en Europa el pórtico de la edad moderna. A un objetivo de alucinaciones y quimeras, como el que perseguía el agotado ideal caballeresco, sucede el firme objetivo de la realidad . . . la América vasta y hermosa sobre todas las ficciones, que con . . . el incentivo de su posesión ofrece el escenario de proezas más inauditas y asombrosas que las aventuras baldías de los caballeros andantes. La filosofía del *Quijote* es, pues, la filosofía de la conquista de América."

89. Rodó, *Obras Completas,* 1148. "América nació para que muriese Don Quijote; o mejor, para hacerle renacer entero de razón y de fuerzas, incorporando a su valor magnánimo y a su imaginación heroica el objetivo real, la aptitud de la acción conjunta y solitaria y el dominio de los medios proporcionados a sus fines."

90. Rodó, *Obras Completas,* 1148.

91. Rodó, *Obras Completas,* 1148. "Así, el sentido crítico del *Quixote* tiene por complemento afirmativo la grande empresa de España, que es la conquista de América . . . Y así el nombre de Miguel de Cervantes . . . puede servir de vínculo imperecedero que recuerde a América y España la unidad de su historia y la fraternidad de sus destinos."

92. Rodó, *Obras Completas,* 1128. "La América Latina será grande, fuerte y gloriosa si, a pesar del cosmopolitismo que es condición necesaria de su crecimiento, logra mantener la continuidad de su historia y la originalidad fundamental de la raza, y si, por encima de las fronteras convencionales que la dividen en naciones, levanta su unidad superior de excelsa y máxima patria, cuyo espíritu haya de fructificar un día en la realidad del sueño del Libertador."

Index